SCOTT FORESMAN · ADDISON WESLEY
Mathematics

Authors

Randall I. Charles
Janet H. Caldwell
Mary Cavanagh
Dinah Chancellor
Alma B. Ramirez

Warren Crown
Jeanne F. Ramos
Kay Sammons
Jane F. Schielack

Francis (Skip) Fennell
William Tate
Mary Thompson
John A. Van de Walle

Consulting Mathematicians

Edward J. Barbeau
Professor of Mathematics
University of Toronto
Toronto, Ontario, Canada

David M. Bressoud
DeWitt Wallace Professor of
Mathematics
Macalester College
Saint Paul, Minnesota

Gary Lippman
Professor of Mathematics and
Computer Science
California State University
Hayward
Hayward, California

PEARSON
Scott
Foresman

Editorial Offices: Glenview, Illinois • Parsippany, New Jersey • New York, New York

Sales Offices: Needham, Massachusetts • Duluth, Georgia • Glenview, Illinois
Coppell, Texas • Ontario, California • Mesa, Arizona

Reading Consultants

Peter Afflerbach
Professor and Director of
   The Reading Center
University of Maryland
College Park, Maryland

Donald J. Leu
John and Maria Neag
   Endowed Chair in Literacy and Technology
University of Connecticut
Storrs, Connecticut

Reviewers

Donna McCollum Derby
Teacher
Kernersville Elementary School
Kernersville, North Carolina

Terri Geaudreau
Title I Math Facilitator
Bemiss Elementary
Spokane, Washington

Sister Helen Lucille Habig, RSM
Assistant Superintendent of
   Catholic Schools
Archdiocese of Cincinnati
Cincinnati, Ohio

Kim Hill
Teacher
Hayes Grade Center
Ada, Oklahoma

Martha Knight
Teacher
Oak Mountain Elementary
Birmingham, Alabama

Catherine Kuhns
Teacher
Country Hills Elementary
Coral Springs, Florida

Susan Mayberger
Supervisor of English as a Second
   Language/Director of Migrant Education
Omaha Public Schools
Omaha, Nebraska

Judy Peede
Elementary Lead Math Teacher
Wake County Schools
Raleigh, North Carolina

Lynda M. Penry
Teacher
Wright Elementary
Ft. Walton Beach, Florida

Jolyn D. Raleigh
District Math Curriculum Specialist K-2
Granite School District
Salt Lake City, Utah

Vickie H. Smith
Assistant Principal
Phoenix Academic Magnet
   Elementary School
Alexandria, Louisiana

Ann Watts
Mathematics Specialist
East Baton Rouge Parish School System
Baton Rouge, Louisiana

ISBN: 0-328-11705-6

8 9 10 V064 09 08 07

Patterns and Readiness for Addition and Subtraction

CHAPTER 2 Understanding Addition and Subtraction

© Pearson Education, Inc.

Strategies for Addition Facts to 12

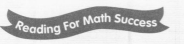

Strategies for Subtraction Facts to 12

 Instant Check System
- Check, daily
- Think About It, daily
- Diagnostic Checkpoint, 135, 147

 Test Prep
- Test Talk, 151
- Cumulative Review and Test Prep, 136, 148, 154A

Reading For Math Success
- Math Story, 4A
- Reading for Math Success, 131

Writing in Math
- Writing in Math exercises, 138, 146, 149

Problem-Solving Applications, 145

Discovery Discover Math in **SCHOOL** Your World, 152

Additional Resources
- Home-School Connection, 123
- Practice Game, 124
- Enrichment, 149
- Learning with Technology, 150
- Chapter 4 Test, 153

CHAPTER 5

Geometry and Fractions

Instant Check System
- Check, daily
- Think About It, daily
- Diagnostic Checkpoint, 163, 179, 195

Test Prep
- Test Talk, 199
- Cumulative Review and Test Prep, 164, 180, 196

Reading For Math Success
- Math Story, 5A
- Reading for Math Success, 175

Writing in Math
- Writing in Math exercises, 178, 188, 194

 Problem-Solving Applications, 193

Discovery CHANNEL SCHOOL Discover Math in Your World, 200

Additional Resources
- Home-School Connection, 155
- Practice Game, 156
- Enrichment, 197
- Learning with Technology, 198
- Chapter 5 Test, 201

CHAPTER 6

Time

Instant Check System
- Check, daily
- Think About It, daily
- Diagnostic Checkpoint, 217, 231

Test Prep
- Test Talk, 235
- Cumulative Review and Test Prep, 218, 232, 238A

Reading For Math Success
- Math Story, 6A
- Reading for Math Success, 213

Writing in Math
- Writing in Math exercises, 220, 230

 Problem-Solving Applications, 229

Discovery CHANNEL SCHOOL Discover Math in Your World, 236

Additional Resources
- Home-School Connection, 203
- Practice Game, 204
- Enrichment, 233
- Learning with Technology, 234
- Chapter 6 Test, 237

Counting to 100

CHAPTER 8
Place Value, Data, and Graphs

 Instant Check System
- Check, daily
- Think About It, daily
- Diagnostic Checkpoint, 293, 305, 321

 Test Prep
- Test Talk, 325
- Cumulative Review and Test Prep, 294, 306, 322, 328A

Reading For Math Success
- Math Story, 8A
- Reading for Math Success, 289

Writing in Math
- Writing in Math exercises, 294, 310, 314, 320, 323, 328B

 Problem-Solving Applications, 319

 Discover Math in Your World, 326

Additional Resources
- Home-School Connection, 279
- Practice Game, 280
- Enrichment, 323
- Learning with Technology, 324
- Chapter 8 Test, 327

© Pearson Education, Inc.

CHAPTER 9 Money

CHAPTER 10 Measurement and Probability

 Instant Check System
- Check, daily
- Think About It, daily
- Diagnostic Checkpoint, 381, 399, 407

 Test Prep
- Test Talk, 411
- Cumulative Review and Test Prep, 382, 400, 408, 414A

Reading For Math Success
- Math Story, 10A
- Reading for Math Success, 367

Writing in Math
- Writing in Math exercises, 368, 382, 406, 409, 414B

 Problem-Solving Applications, 405

Discovery CHANNEL SCHOOL Discover Math in Your World, 412

Additional Resources
- Home-School Connection, 363
- Practice Game, 364
- Enrichment, 409
- Learning with Technology, 410
- Chapter 10 Test, 413

CHAPTER 12
Two-Digit Addition and Subtraction

© Pearson Education, Inc.

Numbers 1, 2, 3

Write the number that tells how many.

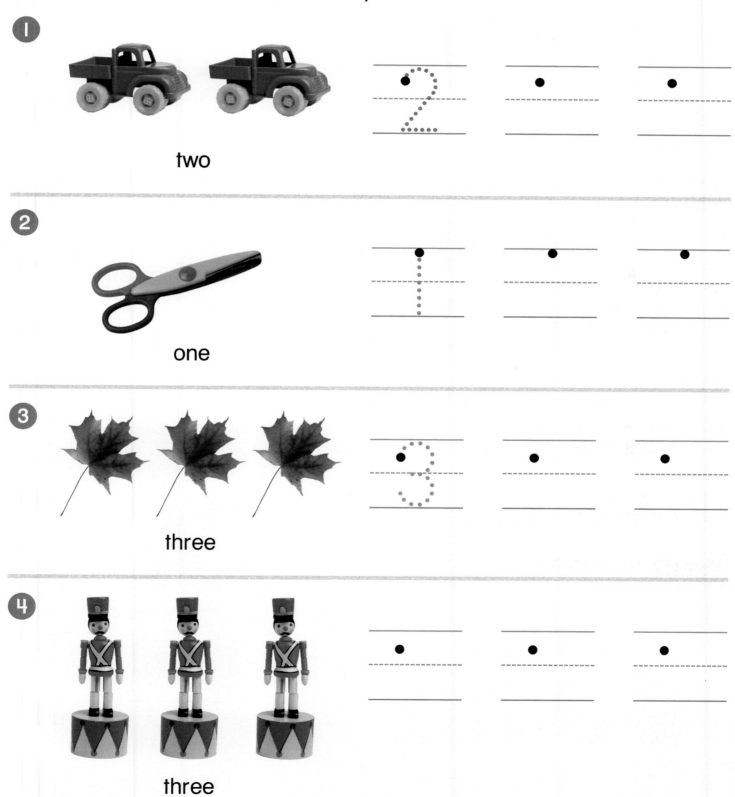

1 two

2 one

3 three

4 three

Name _____

Numbers 4, 5, 6

Write the number that tells how many.

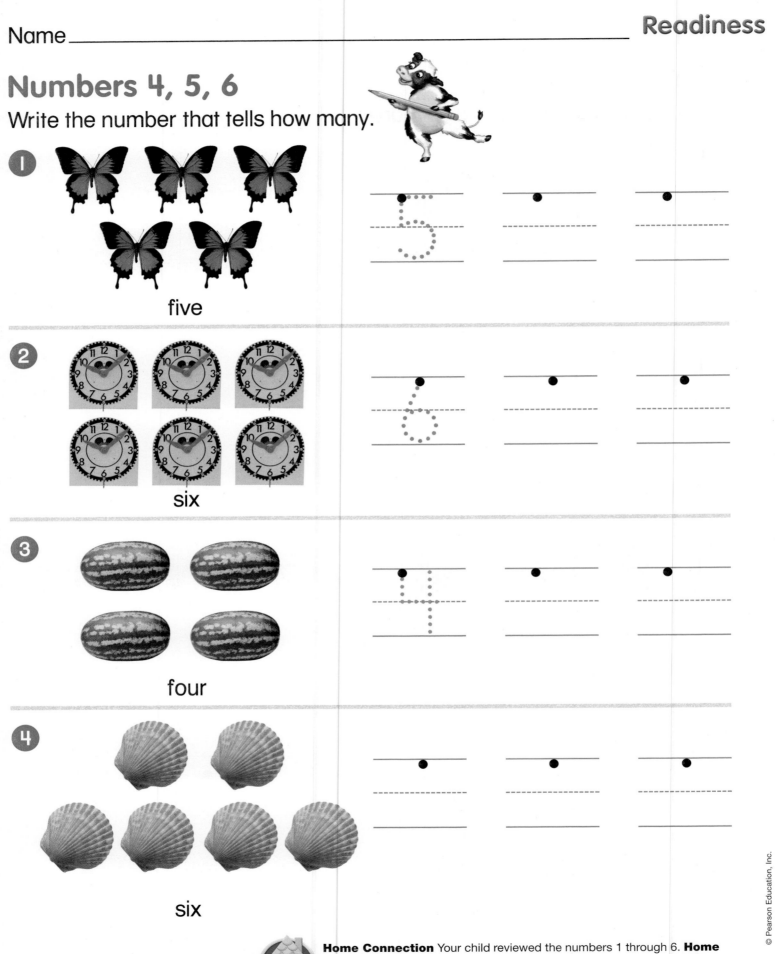

1 five

2 six

3 four

4 six

© Pearson Education, Inc.

Home Connection Your child reviewed the numbers 1 through 6. **Home Activity** Show your child from 1 to 6 small objects, such as pennies. Ask him or her to count how many there are and write the number.

Numbers 7, 8, 9

Write the number that tells how many.

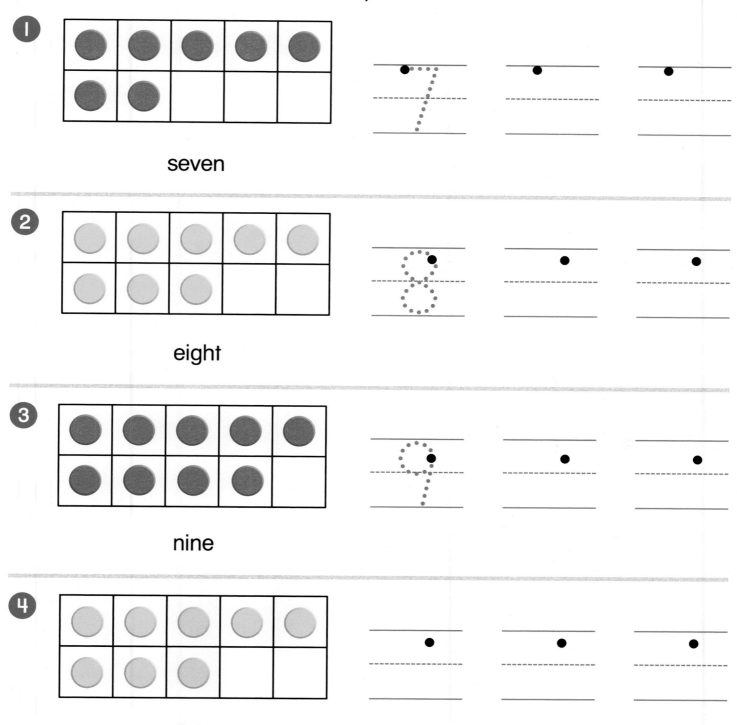

seven

eight

nine

eight

Zero

Write the number that tells how many.
If there are none, write 0.

1

⓪

zero

2

_____

3

_____

4

_____

5

_____

6

_____

© Pearson Education, Inc.

Home Connection Your child reviewed the numbers 0 through 9.
Home Activity Say a number from 0 through 9 and ask your child to hold up that many fingers. Switch roles with your child and repeat the activity.

Ten

Write the number that tells how many.
Then circle the groups that show 10.

1

10

ten

2

9

3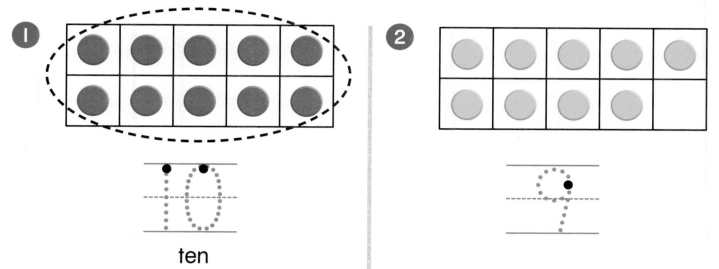

_____

4

_____

5

_____

6

_____

Number Writing Practice

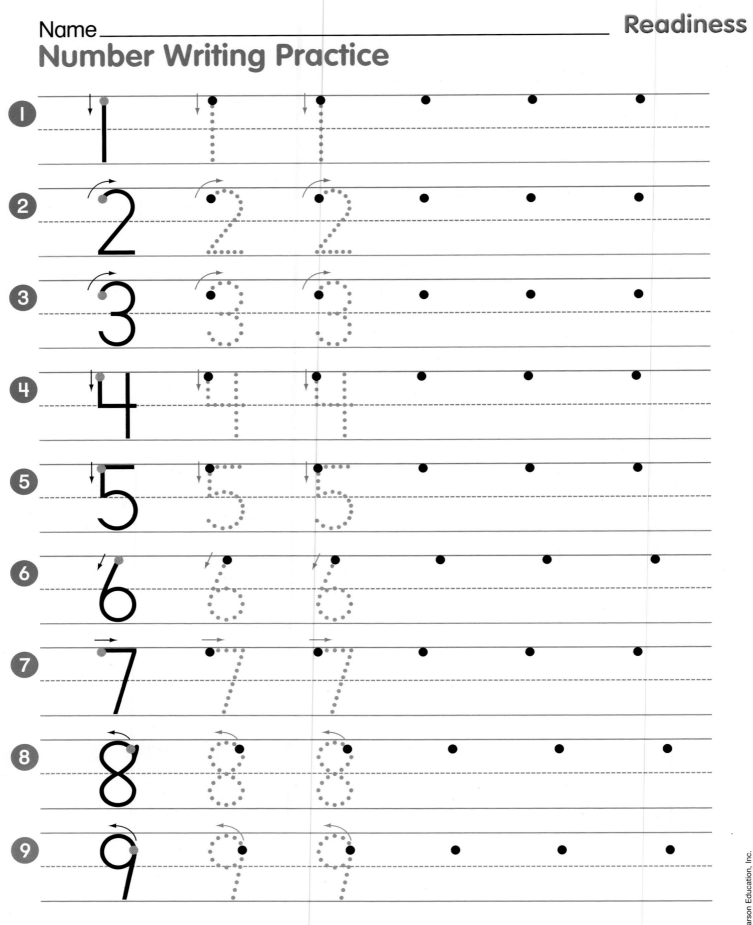

1   1

2   2   2

3   3   3

4   4   4

5   5   5

6   6   6

7   7   7

8   8   8

9   9   9

Home Connection Your child reviewed numbers through 10. **Home Activity** Practice writing numbers with your child.

Comparing Numbers

Write the number that tells how many.
Then circle the number that is more.

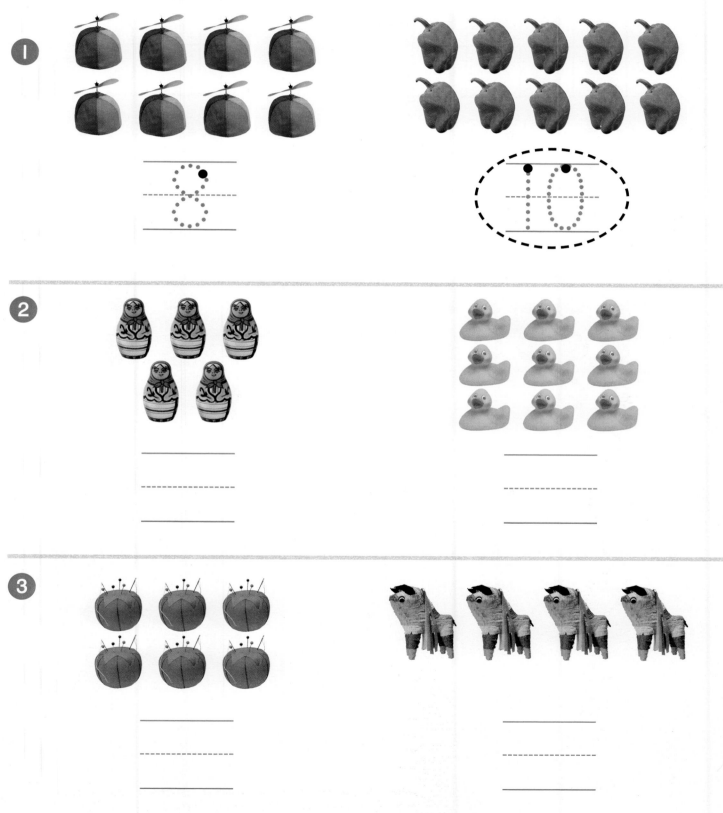

Numbers 11 and 12

Write the number that tells how many.

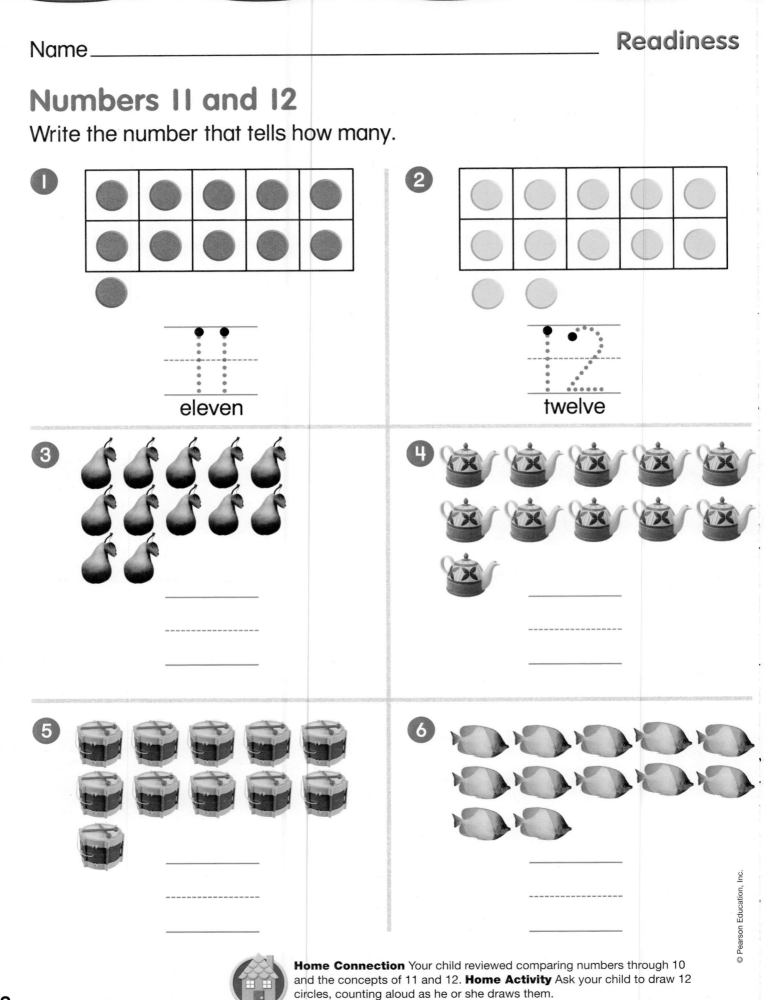

1

eleven

2

twelve

3 _____

4 _____

5 _____

6 _____

© Pearson Education, Inc.

Home Connection Your child reviewed comparing numbers through 10 and the concepts of 11 and 12. **Home Activity** Ask your child to draw 12 circles, counting aloud as he or she draws them.

Shapes

Color each shape below.

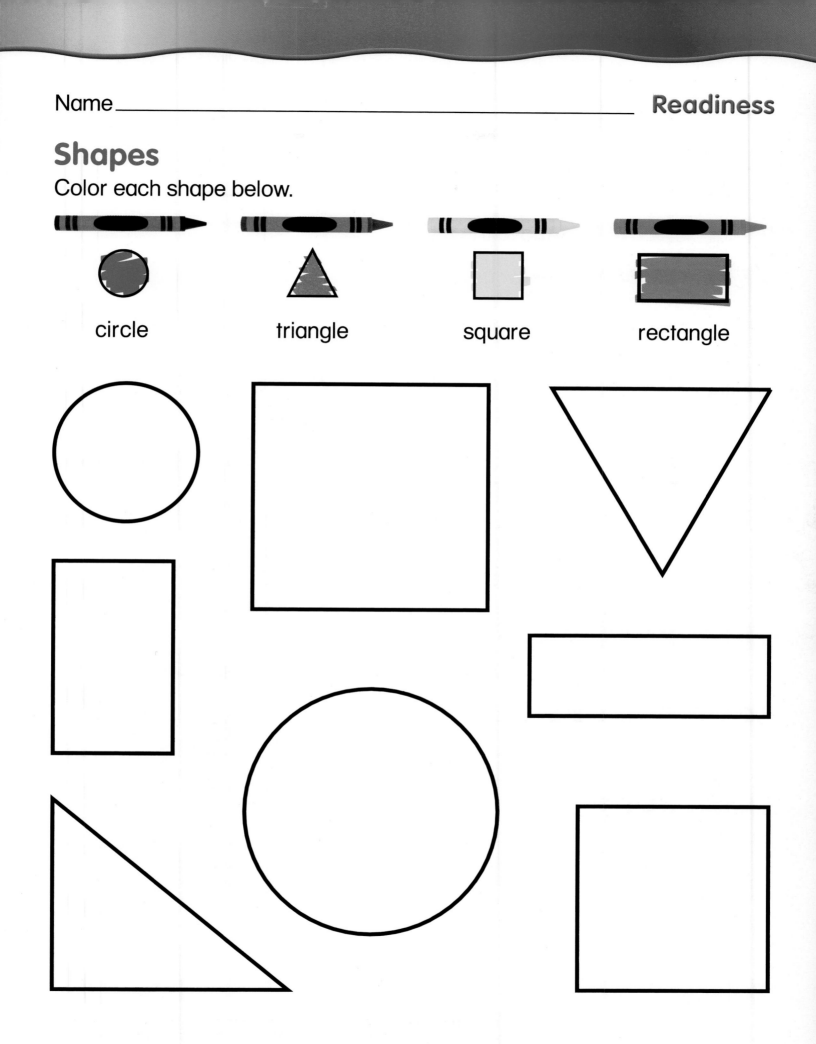

circle   triangle   square   rectangle

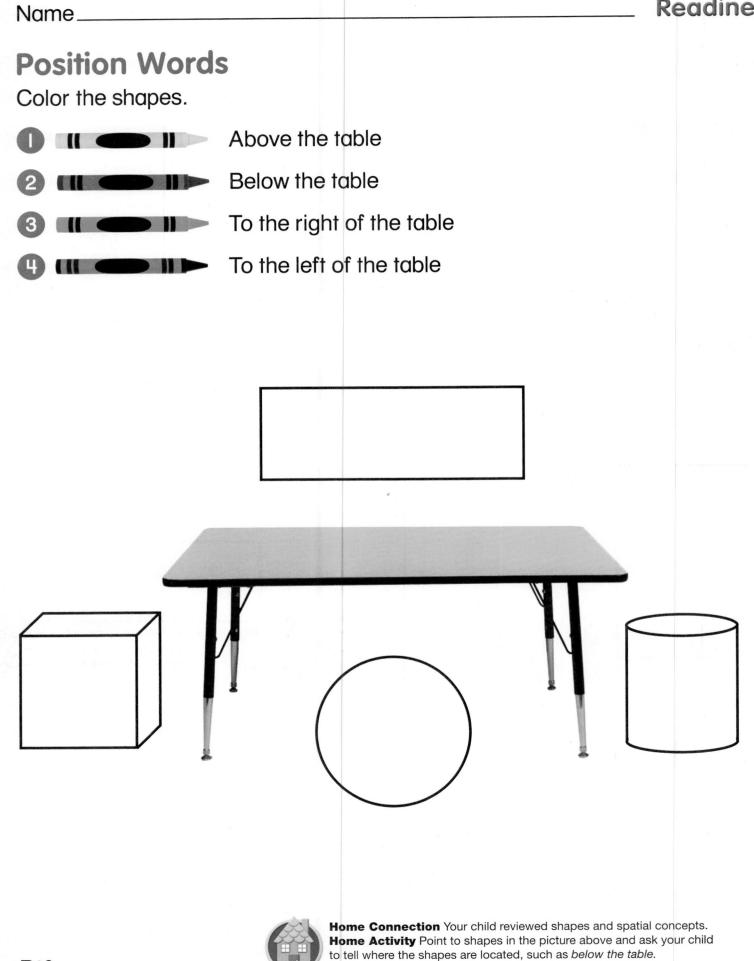

Name _____

Position Words

Color the shapes.

1. Above the table
2. Below the table
3. To the right of the table
4. To the left of the table

© Pearson Education, Inc.

Home Connection Your child reviewed shapes and spatial concepts.
Home Activity Point to shapes in the picture above and ask your child to tell where the shapes are located, such as *below the table*.

Extending Patterns
Circle what comes next in the pattern.

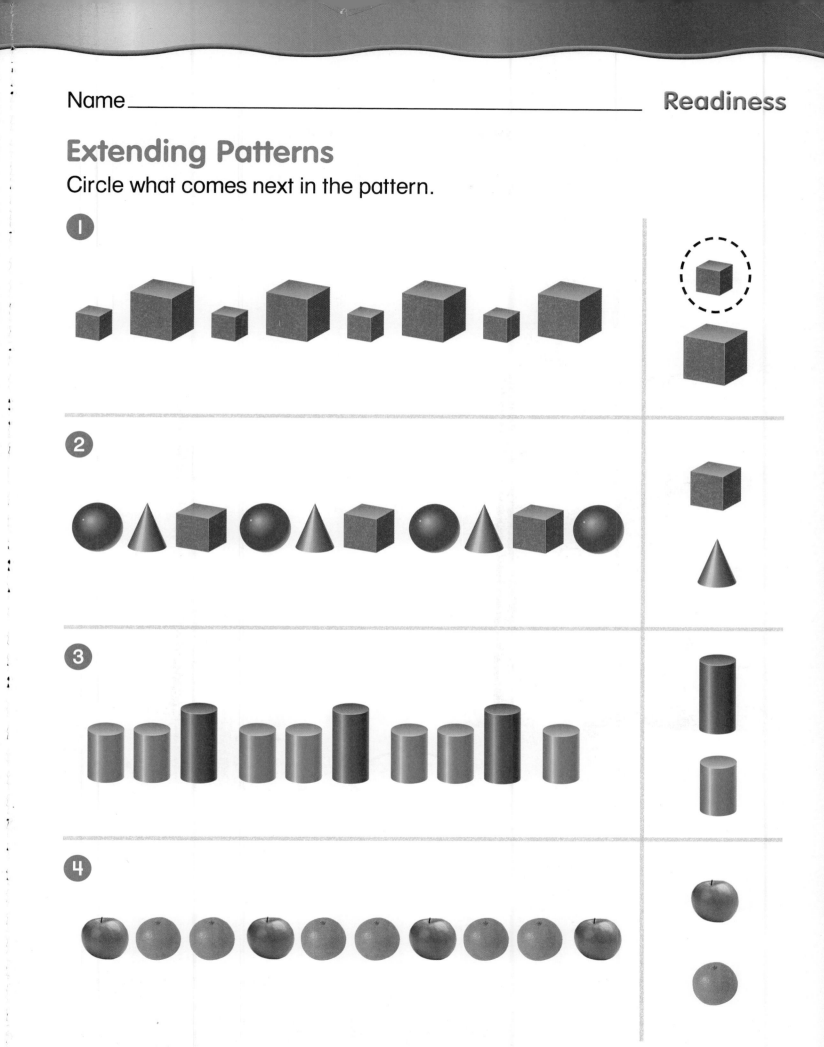

Number Patterns

Circle what comes next in the pattern.

1 1 2 1 2 1 2 1 2 1   1 (2)

2 2 1 2 1 2 1 2 1   1 2

3 1 2 3 1 2 3 1 2   3 1

4 4 5 5 4 5 5 4 5   5 4

Home Connection Your child reviewed extending shape, color, size, and number patterns. **Home Activity** Use small objects to make a pattern. Ask your child to extend the pattern by telling which object comes next.

Letter Patterns

Circle what comes next in the pattern.

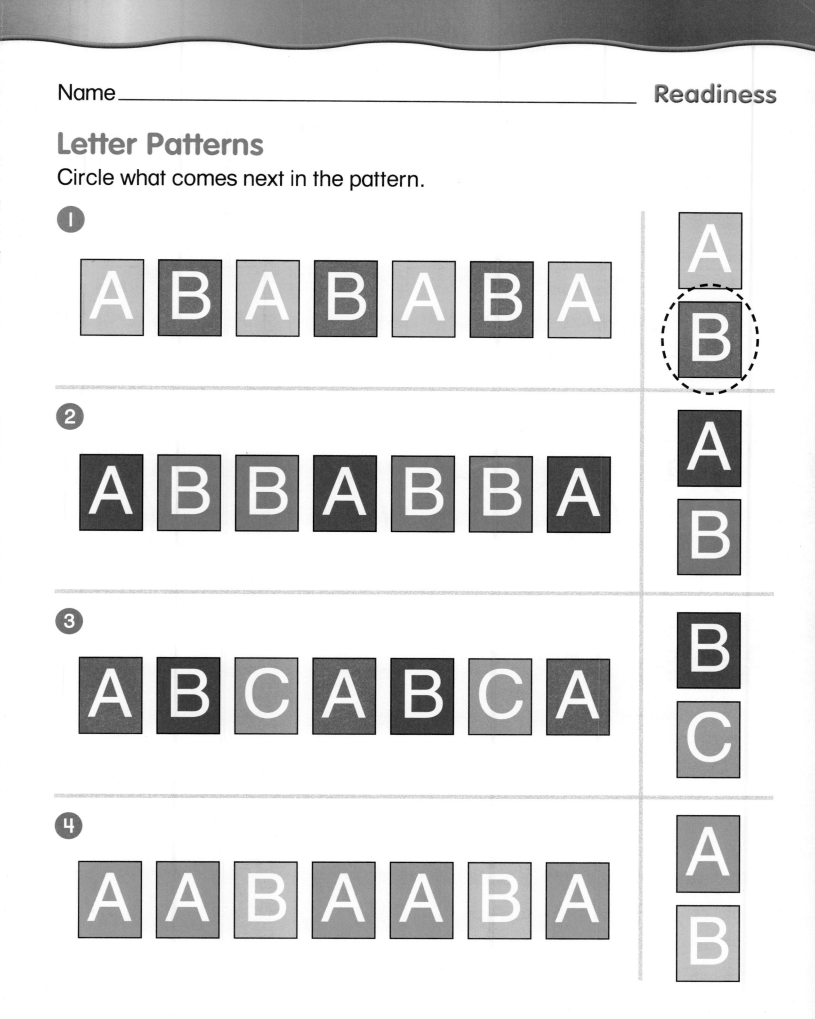

1   A B A B A B A | A **B**

2   A B B A B B A | A B

3   A B C A B C A | B C

4   A A B A A B A | A B

Create Patterns

Use 2 crayons.

Color the shapes to make a pattern.

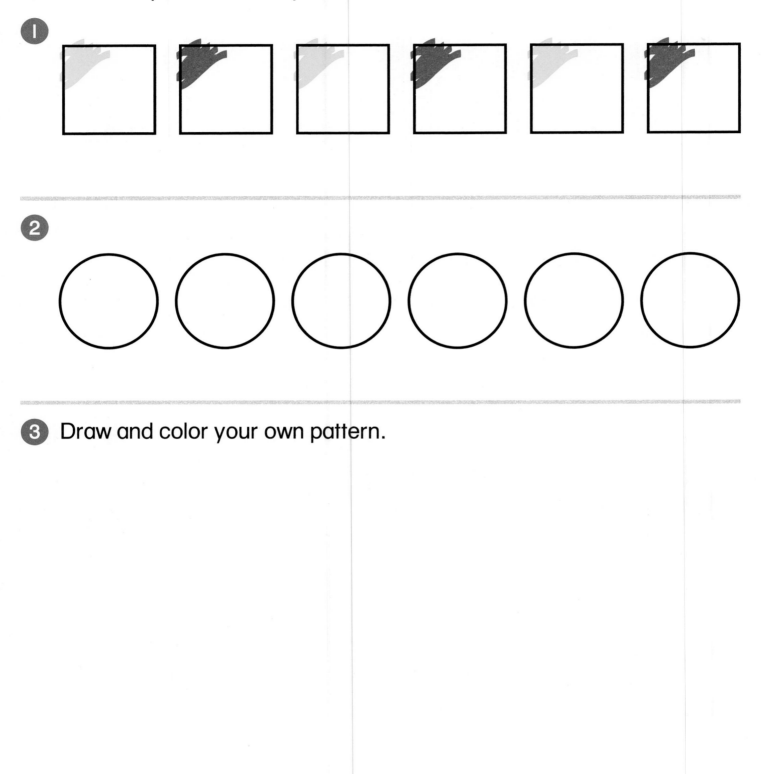

1

2

3 Draw and color your own pattern.

Home Connection Your child reviewed letter patterns and creating patterns.
Home Activity Help your child create a pattern using small objects.

Picture Graphs

1 Color a picture on the graph for each flower.

---

2 Are there more 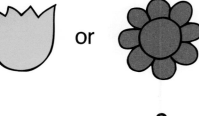 or ___ ?

Circle your answer.

3 How many more? **I more** or **2 more** ?

Circle your answer.

Name ____________________

Bar Graphs

1 Color a box on the graph for each bird.

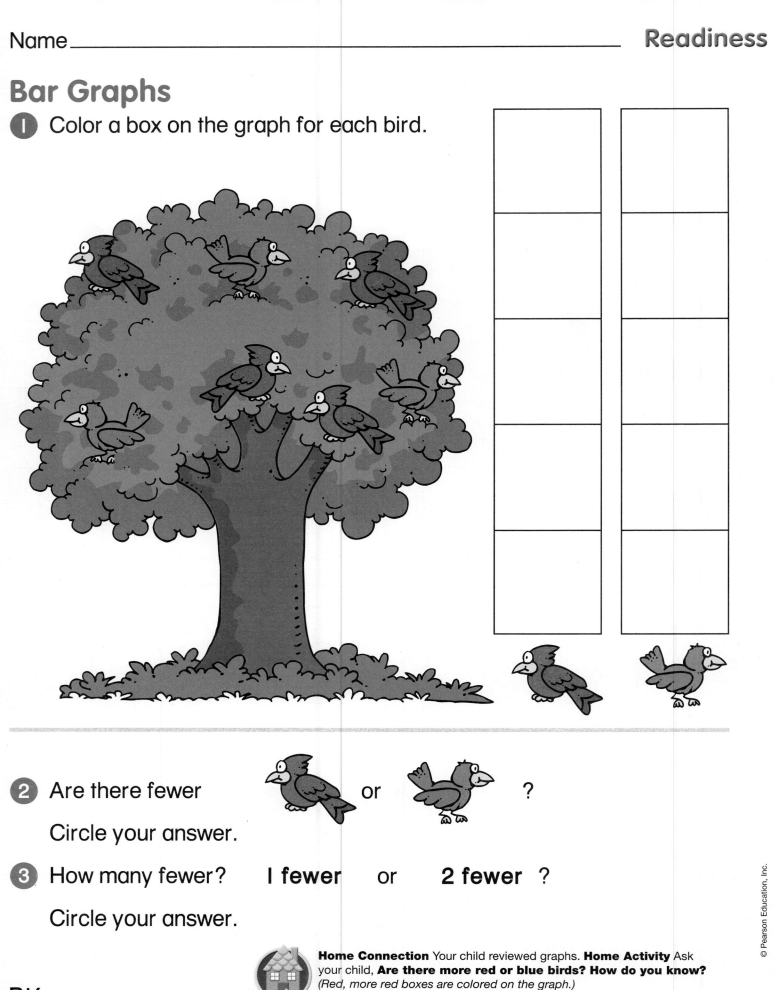

2 Are there fewer  or  ?

Circle your answer.

3 How many fewer? **1 fewer** or **2 fewer** ?

Circle your answer.

Home Connection Your child reviewed graphs. **Home Activity** Ask your child, **Are there more red or blue birds? How do you know?** *(Red, more red boxes are colored on the graph.)*

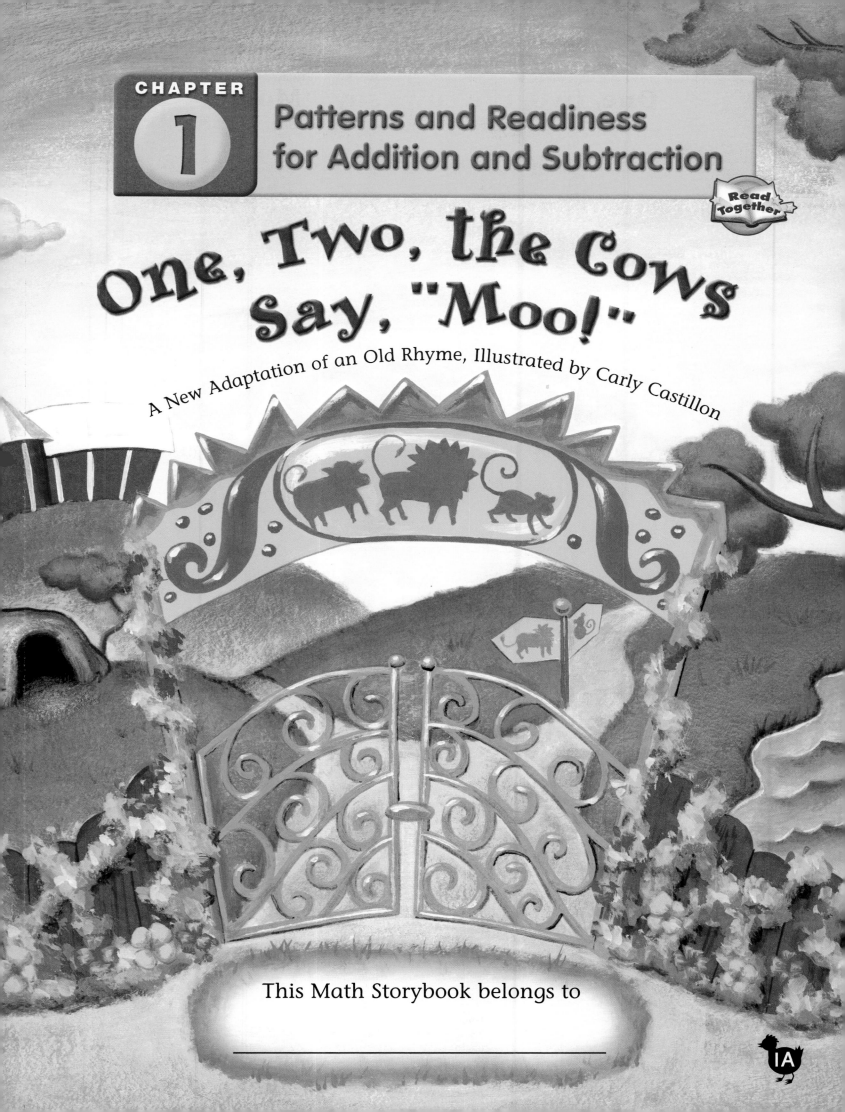

One, Two, the Cows Say, "Moo!"

A New Adaptation of an Old Rhyme, Illustrated by Carly Castillon

This Math Storybook belongs to

_____

Three, four, the lions roar.

Five, six, the monkeys do tricks.

Seven, eight, who's sitting on the gate?

Nine, ten, a big fat hen.
Now go back and count again!

Home-School Connection

Dear Family,

Today my class started Chapter 1, **Patterns and Readiness for Addition and Subtraction.** I will work with the numbers 6 through 12 and compare pairs of numbers. I will also learn about patterns. Here are some of the math words I will be learning and some things we can do to help me with my math.

Love,

_____

Math Activity to Do at Home

Help your child recognize and create simple patterns like this:

Give your child small objects with which to create patterns.

Books to Read Together

Reading math stories reinforces concepts. Look for these titles in your local library:

A Pair of Socks
By Stuart J. Murphy
(HarperCollins, 1996)

Fun with Patterns
By Peter Patilla
(The Millbrook Press, 1998)

My New Math Words

pattern unit A pattern unit is the part of a pattern that repeats over and over.

more than 6 is 2 more than 4.

fewer than 2 fewer than 6 is 4.

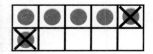

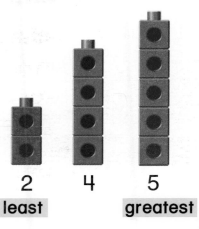

2
least

4

5
greatest

Name_____

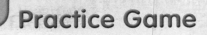

9, 10 Find the Hen!

How to Play

1. Take turns. Toss the cube. Count the dots.
2. Move your marker. If you land on a yellow space, follow the directions.
3. Keep playing until both of you find the big fat hen!

© Pearson Education, Inc.

Name_____

Learn!

We can show 6 in different ways.

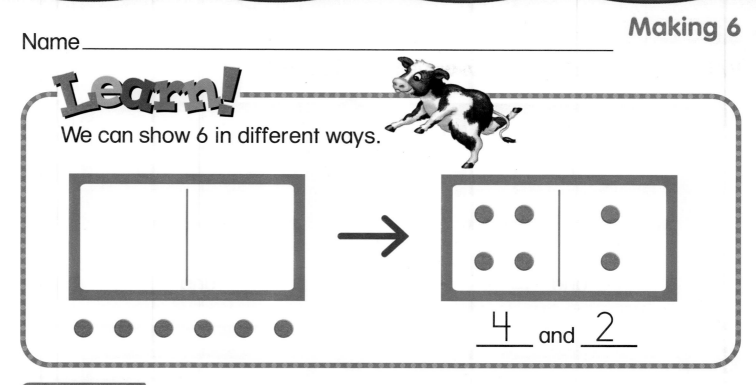

_4_ and _2_

Check ✓

Write the numbers that show ways to make 6.

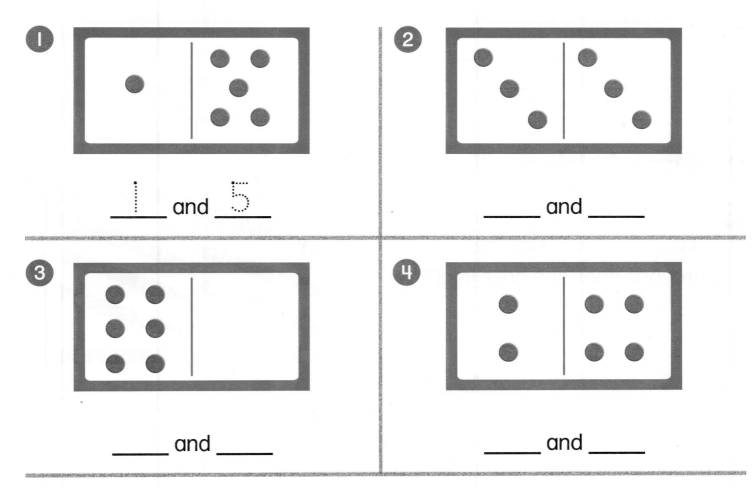

1. _1_ and _5_

2. ____ and ____

3. ____ and ____

4. ____ and ____

Think About It Reasoning

Is 3 and 3 the same as 2 and 4? Explain.

Write the numbers that show ways to make 7.

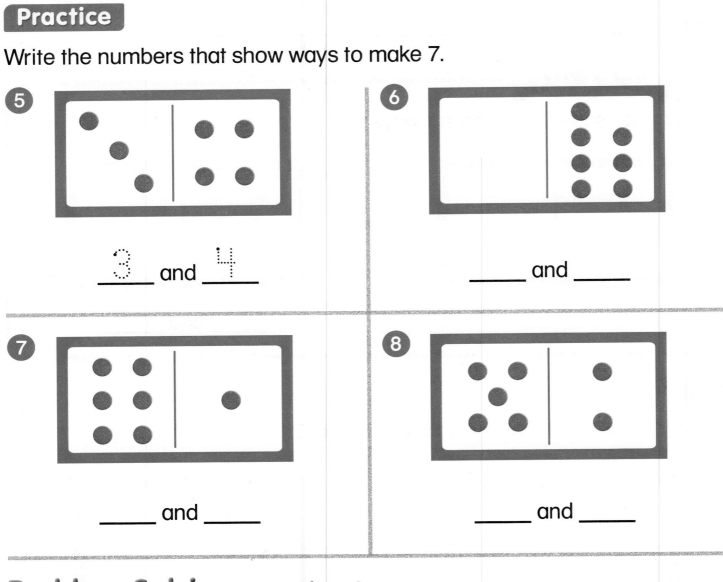

5

___3___ and ___4___

6

_____ and _____

7

_____ and _____

8

_____ and _____

Problem Solving   Number Sense

Circle **yes** or **no**

9 Jesse has 7 pennies. Can he put the same number in each bank? Explain.

yes   or   **no**

Home Connection Your child found different ways to show the number 7 in two parts. **Home Activity** Draw fewer than 7 circles. Have your child draw more circles to make 7.

Name_____

Learn!

We can show 8 in different ways.

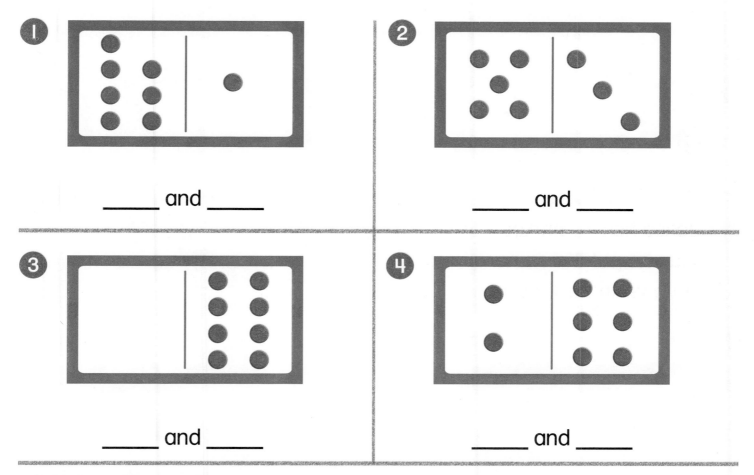

____4____ and ____4____

Check ✓

Write the numbers that show ways to make 8.

1

____ and ____

2

____ and ____

3

____ and ____

4

____ and ____

Think About It   Number Sense

Is 4 and 4 the same as 3 and 5? Explain.

We can show 9 in different ways.

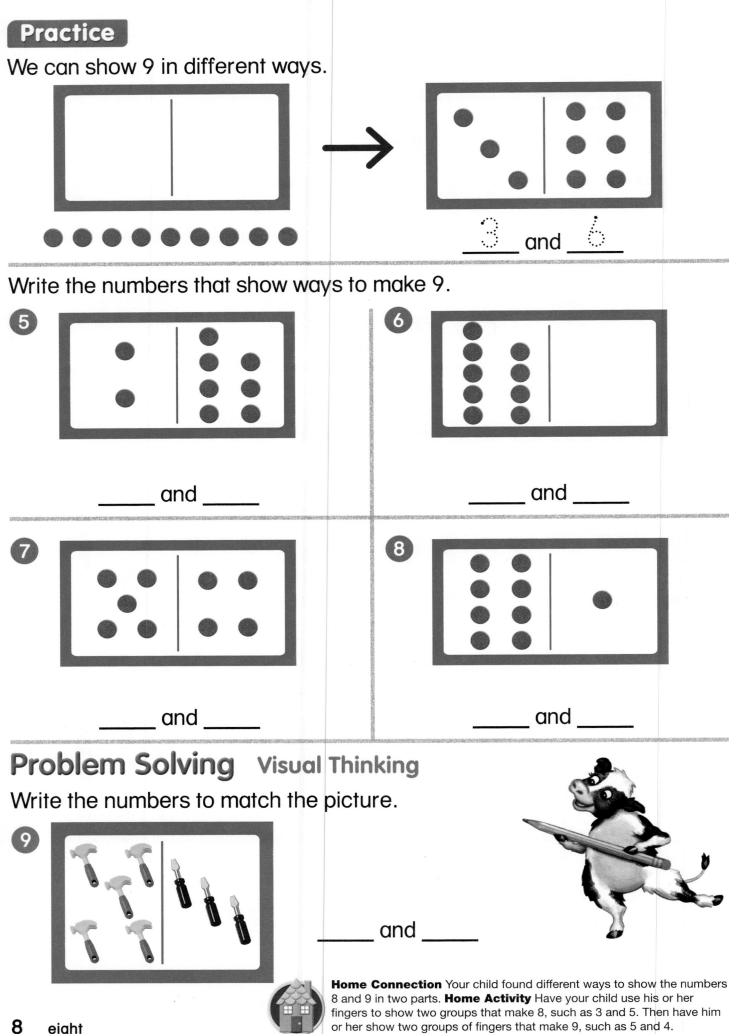

__3__ and __6__

Write the numbers that show ways to make 9.

5

_____ and _____

6

_____ and _____

7

_____ and _____

8

_____ and _____

Problem Solving   Visual Thinking

Write the numbers to match the picture.

9

_____ and _____

Home Connection Your child found different ways to show the numbers 8 and 9 in two parts. **Home Activity** Have your child use his or her fingers to show two groups that make 8, such as 3 and 5. Then have him or her show two groups of fingers that make 9, such as 5 and 4.

8   eight

Visualize

Listen as your teacher reads the story.
Picture in your mind what is happening.

 Sarah had **6** apples.
She put **1** apple in the green bowl.
She put **5** apples in the yellow bowl.
Draw the apples in the bowls.

2 Then Sara put **2** apples in the red bowl.
She put **4** apples in the blue bowl.
Draw the apples in the bowls.

Think About It   Reasoning

What is another way that Sara could
put the apples in the bowls?

Listen as your teacher reads the story.
Picture in your mind what is happening.

3 David had **7** balls.
He put some balls in a circle.
He put some balls in another circle.

Draw some balls in each circle.
Draw **7** balls in all.

4 Show a different way.
Draw balls in each circle.
Draw **7** balls in all.

Home Connection Your child listened to a story and drew pictures to solve a problem **Home Activity** Ask your child to draw pictures to show a different way of putting 7 books on two shelves.

Name_____

Learn!

What different ways can you put counters on Workmat 1?

Read and Understand

There are 7 counters in all.

Plan and Solve

Put **1** counter on the left part and **6** counters on the right part.

Move **1** counter from the right side to the left side.

Write the numbers.

Look Back and Check

How can you check that your answer is correct?

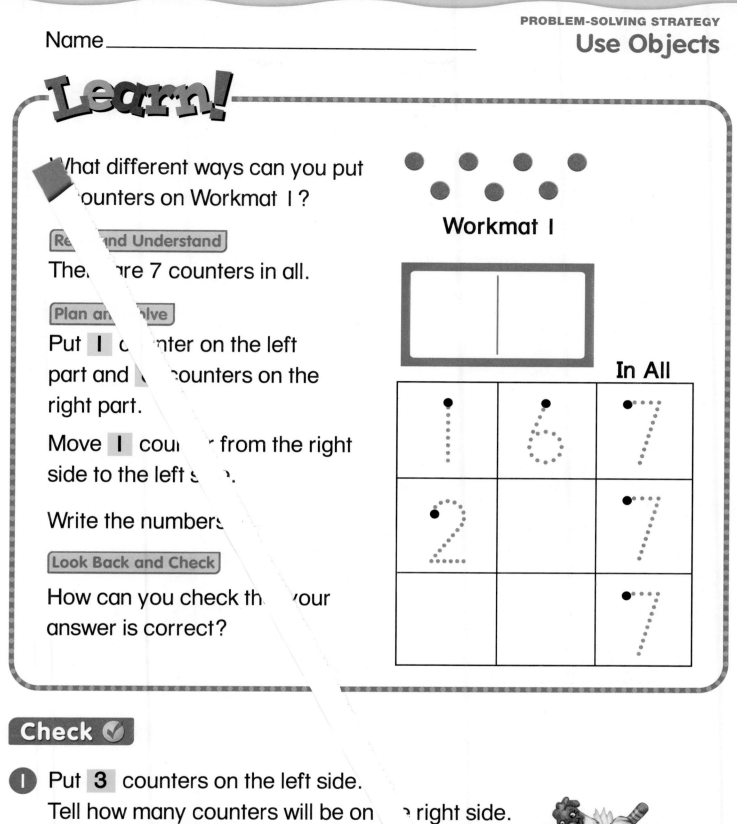

Workmat 1

In All

1	6	7
2		7
		7

Check ✓

1 Put **3** counters on the left side.
Tell how many counters will be on the right side.
Write the numbers in the chart.

Think About It   Number Sense

If you put all **7** counters on one part, how many are on the other part?

Complete the chart.

2 What different ways can you put 5 strawberries in two baskets?

		In All
1		5
2		5
3		5

Writing in Math

3 There are 3 strawberries in one basket and 2 in the other basket.

Write a complete sentence to tell how many strawberries there are in all.

_____

_____

_____

Home Connection Your child used objects to solve problems involving ways to show numbers in two parts. **Home Activity** Give your child 9 small objects, such as pennies. Ask him or her to show ways they can be put in two groups. *(1 and 8, 2 and 7, and so on)*

Write the numbers to show ways to make 7 and 8.

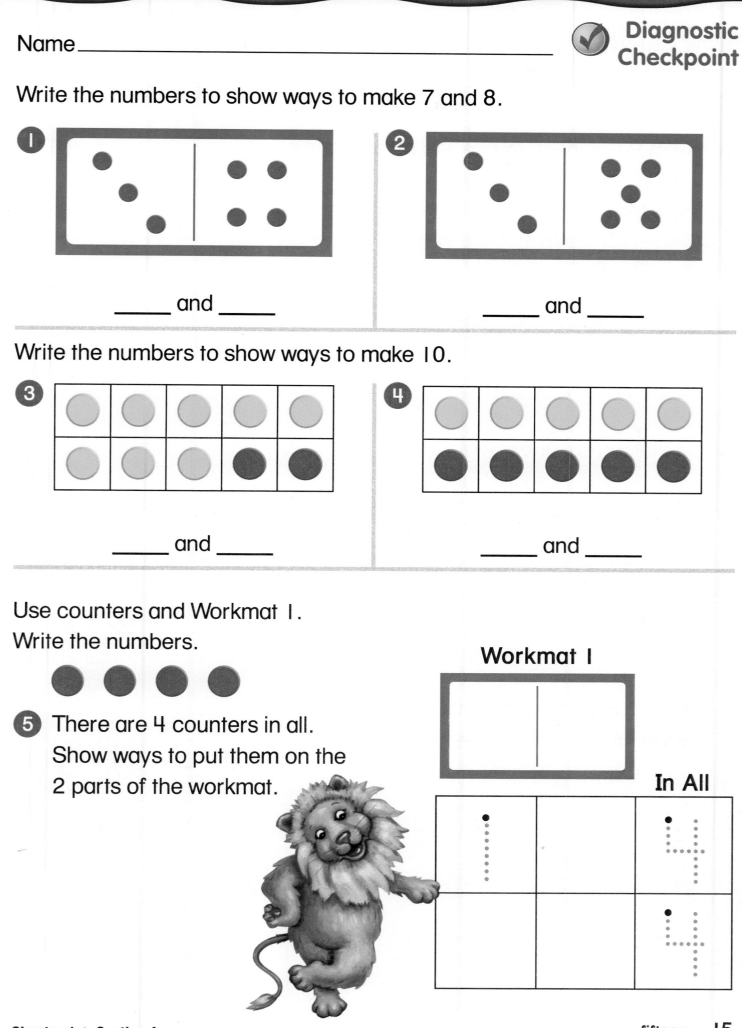

1 _____ and _____

2 _____ and _____

Write the numbers to show ways to make 10.

3 _____ and _____

4 _____ and _____

Use counters and Workmat 1.
Write the numbers.

5 There are 4 counters in all.
Show ways to put them on the
2 parts of the workmat.

Workmat 1

In All

4

4

Choosing the Answer

Sometimes you need to pick the correct answer.

1 How many counters are there in all?

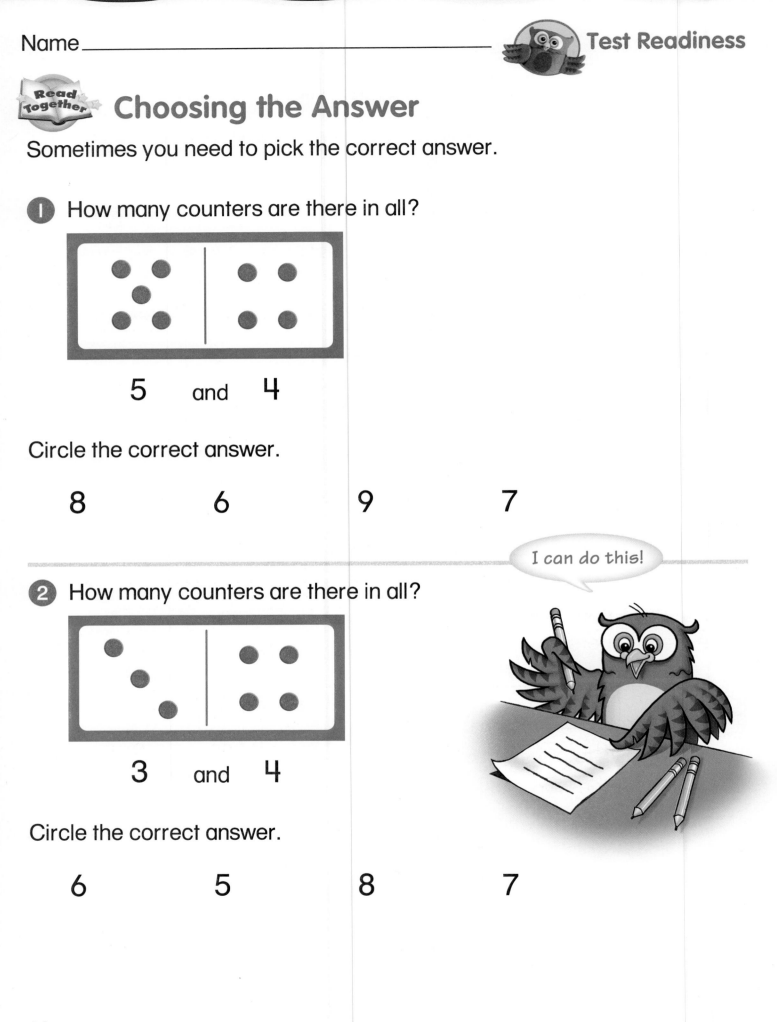

5   and   4

Circle the correct answer.

8   6   9   7

I can do this!

2 How many counters are there in all?

3   and   4

Circle the correct answer.

6   5   8   7

Name_____

Learn!

We can find 1 and 2 more than a number.

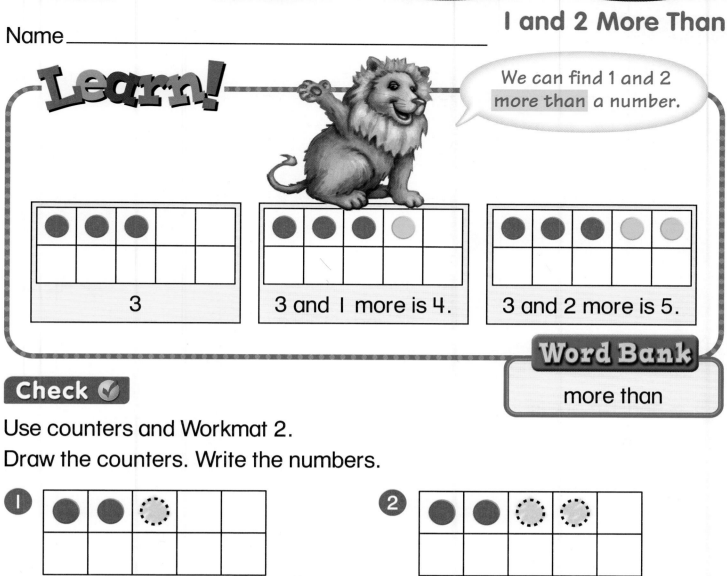

3

3 and 1 more is 4.

3 and 2 more is 5.

Word Bank

more than

Check ✓

Use counters and Workmat 2.

Draw the counters. Write the numbers.

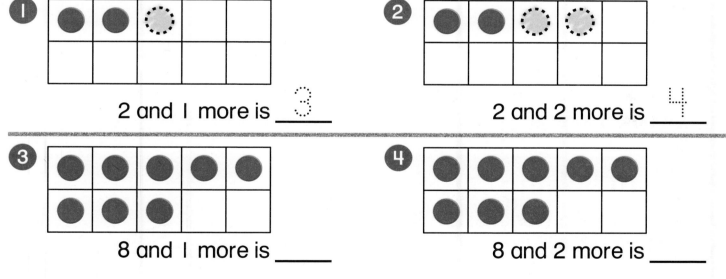

① 2 and 1 more is __3__

② 2 and 2 more is __4__

③ 8 and 1 more is _____

④ 8 and 2 more is _____

Think About It   Number Sense

What number is 1 more than 10?

What number is 2 more than 10?

Practice

Use counters and Workmat 2. Write the numbers.

7 and I more is __8__.

7 and 2 more is __9__.

---

5 5 and I more is _____.

5 and 2 more is _____.

6 6 and I more is _____.

6 and 2 more is _____.

7 9 and I more is _____.

9 and 2 more is _____.

8 0 and I more is _____.

0 and 2 more is _____.

Problem Solving   Algebra

Use counters and Workmat 2.
Write the numbers.

9 2 and _____ more is 3.

2 and _____ more is 4.

Name_____

Learn!

We can find 1 and 2 **fewer than** a number.

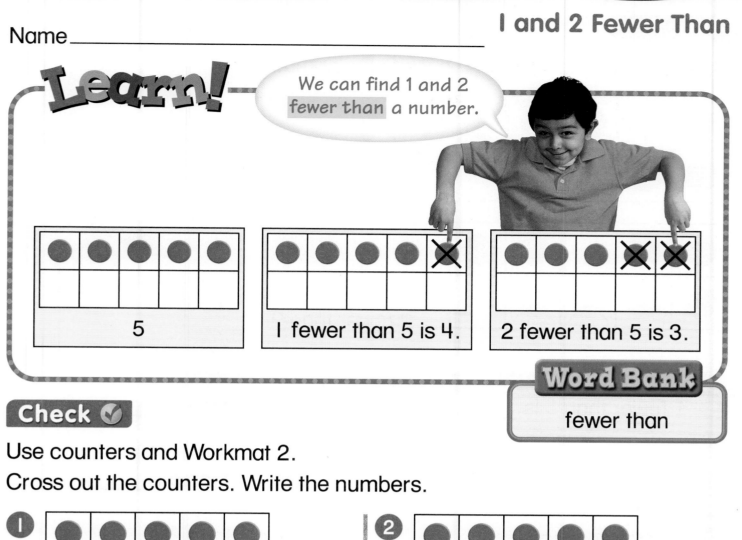

5

1 fewer than 5 is 4.

2 fewer than 5 is 3.

Word Bank

fewer than

Check ✓

Use counters and Workmat 2.

Cross out the counters. Write the numbers.

1

1 fewer than 8 is __7__.

2

2 fewer than 8 is __6__.

3

1 fewer than 2 is _____.

4

2 fewer than 2 is _____.

Think About It Number Sense

How can you find the number that is 2 fewer
than 9 without using counters and Workmat 2?

Use counters and Workmat 2. Write the numbers.

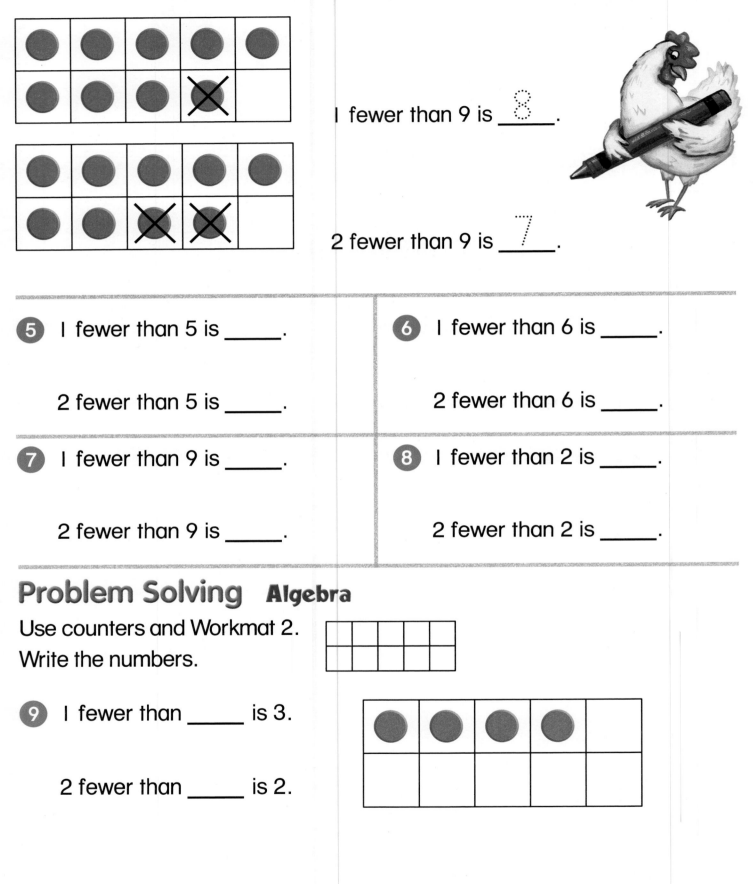

I fewer than 9 is __8__.

2 fewer than 9 is __7__.

5 I fewer than 5 is _____.

2 fewer than 5 is _____.

6 I fewer than 6 is _____.

2 fewer than 6 is _____.

7 I fewer than 9 is _____.

2 fewer than 9 is _____.

8 I fewer than 2 is _____.

2 fewer than 2 is _____.

Problem Solving Algebra

Use counters and Workmat 2.
Write the numbers.

9 I fewer than _____ is 3.

2 fewer than _____ is 2.

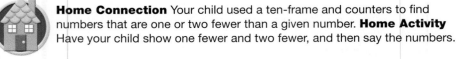

Home Connection Your child used a ten-frame and counters to find
numbers that are one or two fewer than a given number. **Home Activity**
Have your child show one fewer and two fewer, and then say the numbers.

Name_____

Learn!

5

7

10

> 7 is more than 5.
> 7 is fewer than 10.

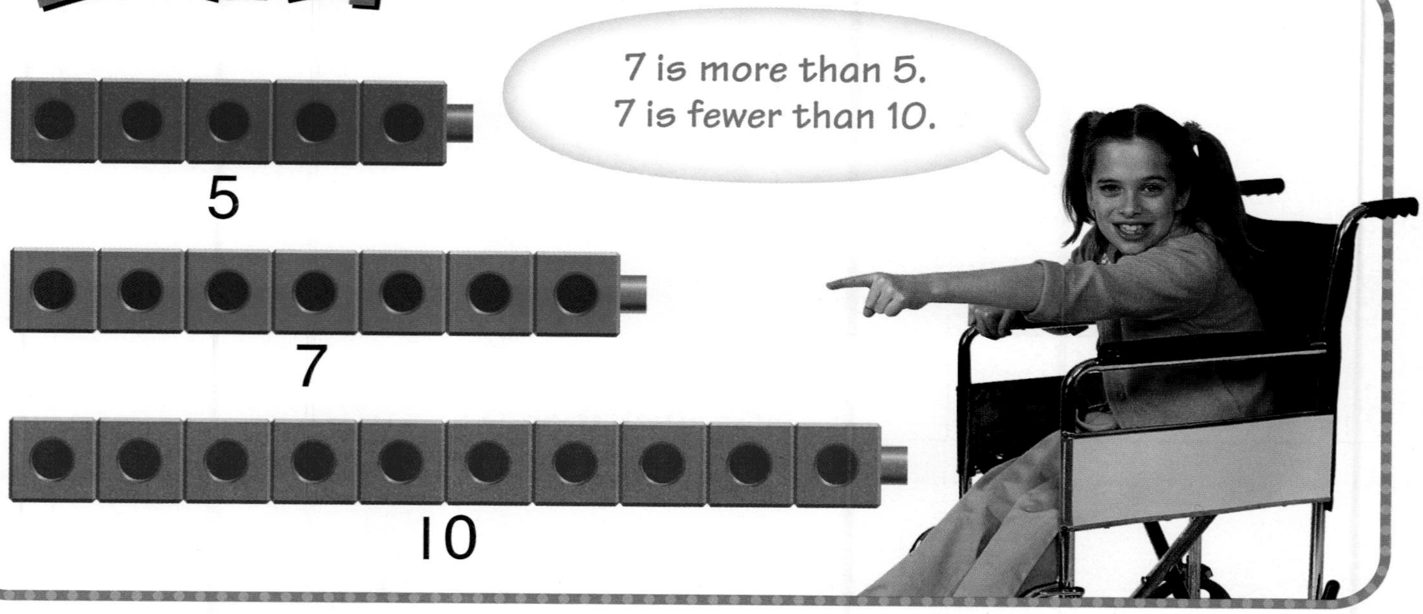

Check ✓

Use cubes. Circle **more** or **fewer**.

①

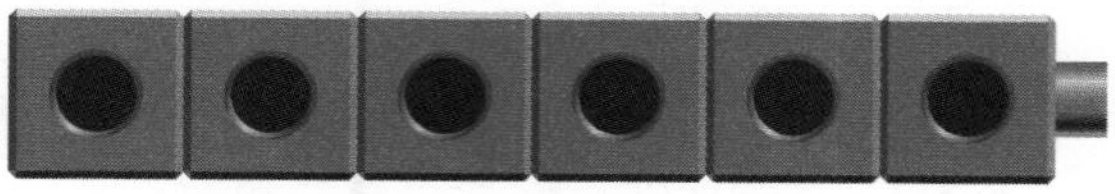

6 is _____ than 10.   **more**   **fewer**

②

6 is _____ than 5.   **more**   **fewer**

③

3 is _____ than 5.   **more**   **fewer**

Think About It Reasoning

There are four numbers that are more than 5 and
fewer than 10. What are they?

Use cubes. Circle **more** or **fewer**.

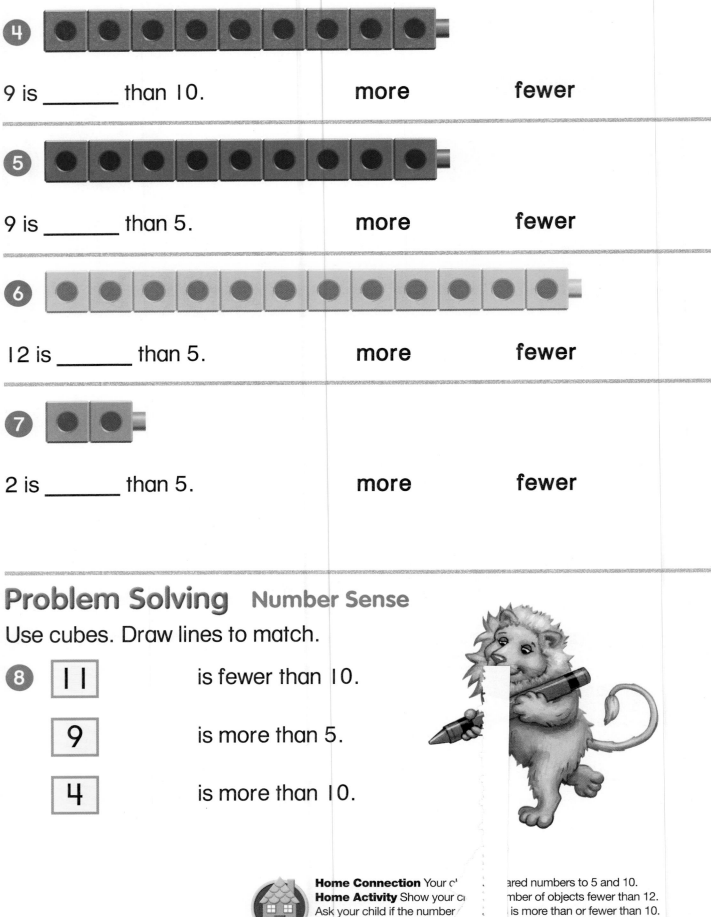

4

9 is _____ than 10.   **more**   **fewer**

5

9 is _____ than 5.   **more**   **fewer**

6

12 is _____ than 5.   **more**   **fewer**

7

2 is _____ than 5.   **more**   **fewer**

Problem Solving   Number Sense

Use cubes. Draw lines to match.

8

| 11 | is fewer than 10.

| 9 | is more than 5.

| 4 | is more than 10.

Home Connection Your c'......ared numbers to 5 and 10.
Home Activity Show your c.......mber of objects fewer than 12.
Ask your child if the number......is more than or fewer than 10.
Then ask your child if the r.......bjects is more than or fewer than 5.

Use counters and Workmat 2.
Draw the counters. Write the numbers.

1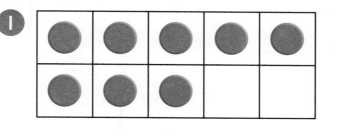

8 and 1 more is _____.

2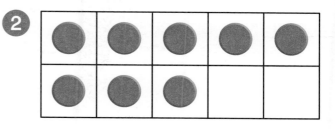

8 and 2 more is _____.

Use counters and Workmat 2.
Cross out the counters. Write the numbers.

3

1 fewer than 7 is _____.

4

2 fewer than 7 is _____.

Use cubes. Circle **more** or **fewer**.

5 7 is _____ than 10.   **more**   **fewer**

6 8 is _____ than 5.   **more**   **fewer**

Use cubes. Write the numbers in order from least to greatest.

7

| 10 | 3 | 7 |

_____, _____, _____
least   greatest

Name_____

Coloring an Answer Circle

Read Together

Sometimes there are letters next to the answer choices.

1 2 more than 3 is _____.

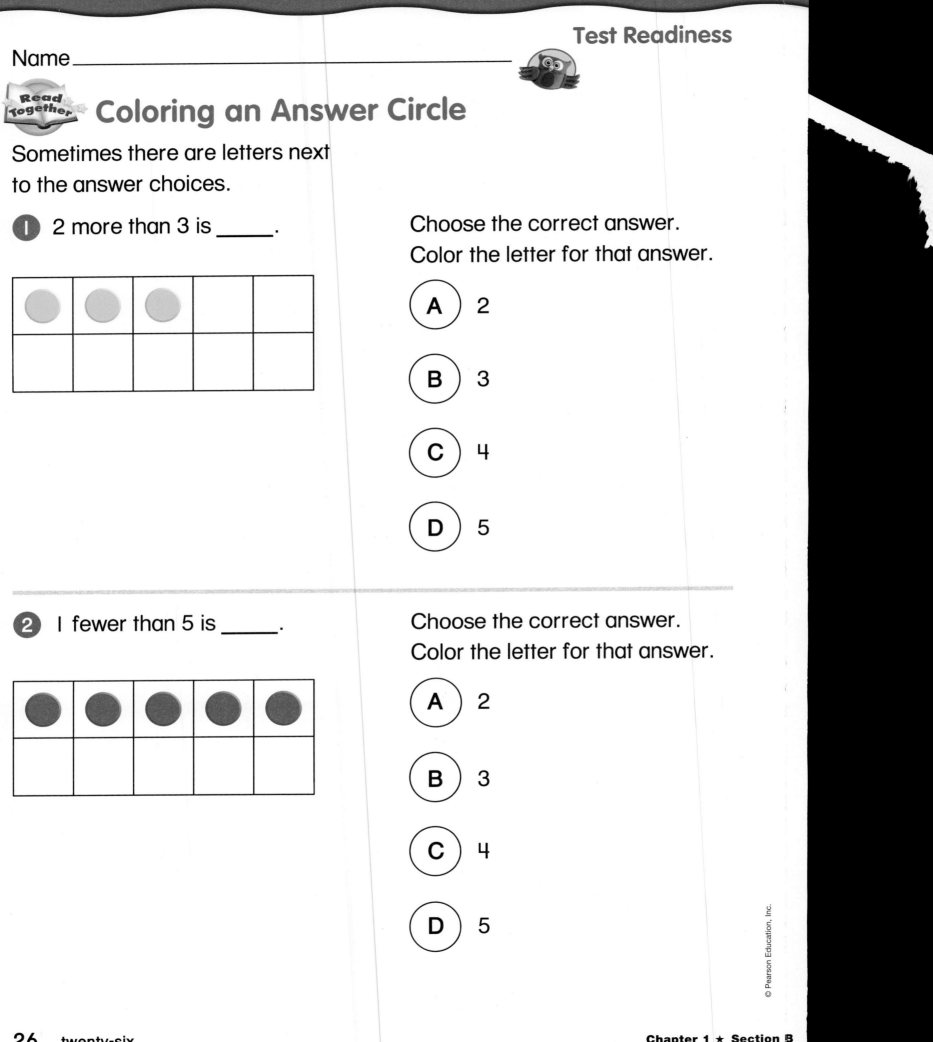

Choose the correct answer.
Color the letter for that answer.

(A) 2

(B) 3

(C) 4

(D) 5

2 1 fewer than 5 is _____.

Choose the correct answer.
Color the letter for that answer.

(A) 2

(B) 3

(C) 4

(D) 5

Name_____

Learn! Algebra

The **pattern unit** repeats over and over in a pattern.

Star, heart, flower is the part that repeats.

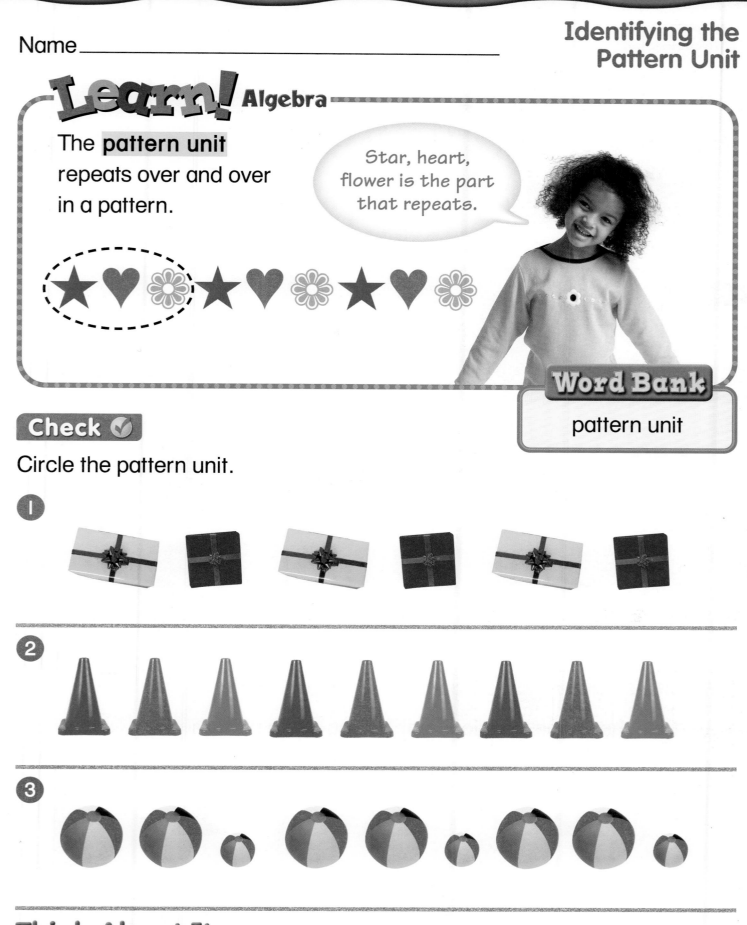

Word Bank

pattern unit

Check ✓

Circle the pattern unit.

1

2

3

Think About It   Reasoning

How did you find the pattern unit?

Circle the pattern unit.

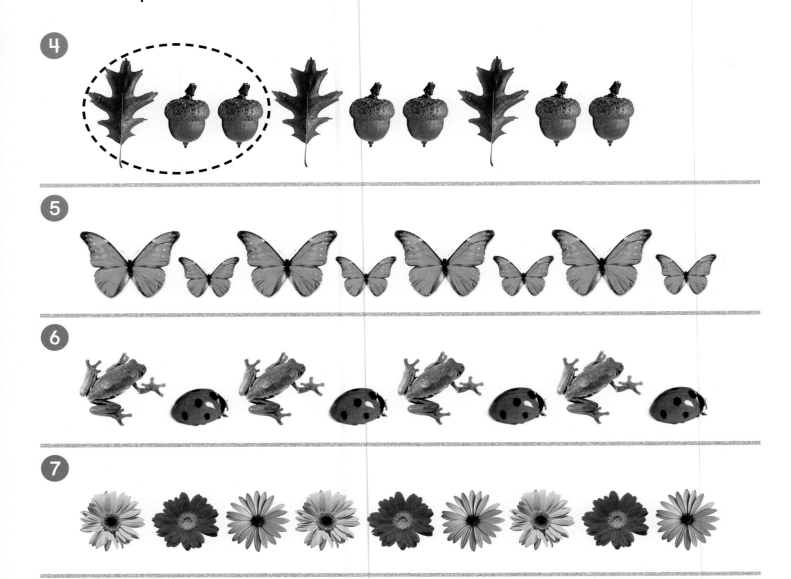

4

5

6

7

Problem Solving Algebra

8 Circle the shape that does **not** belong in the pattern.

© Pearson Education, Inc.

Home Connection Your child identified the pattern unit, the part that repeats in a pattern. **Home Activity** Make a sound pattern for your child, such as *clap hands, stomp feet, clap hands, stomp feet, clap hands, stomp feet,* and so on. Ask your child to tell what part you are repeating to make the pattern.

Name _____

Learn! Algebra

The shapes and the letters make the same pattern.

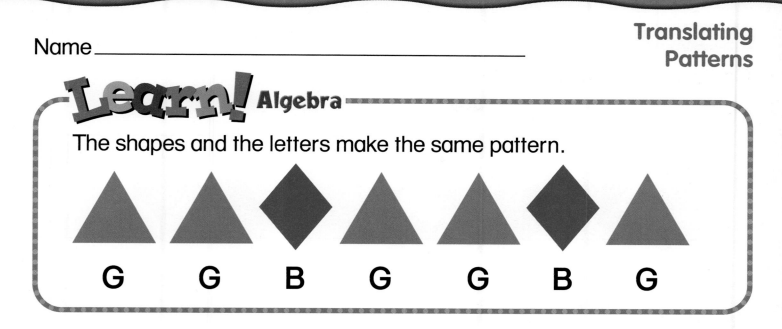

G   G   B   G   G   B   G

Check ✓

Make the same pattern using letters.

1

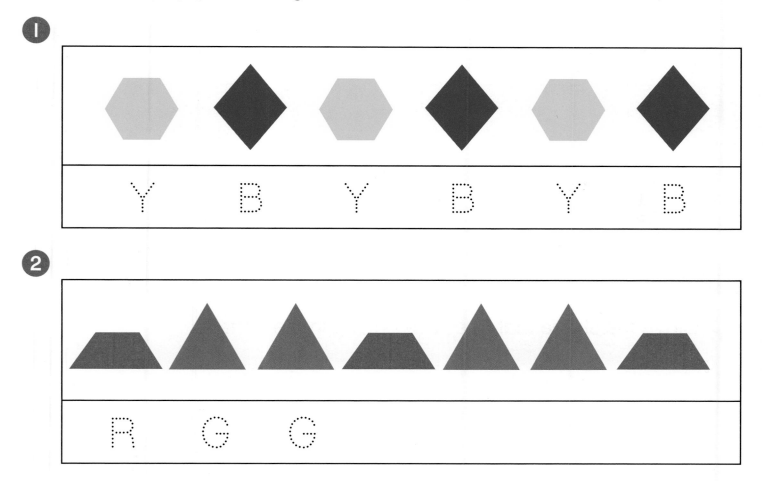

Y   B   Y   B   Y   B

2

R   G   G

Think About It   Reasoning

How did you decide which letters to use?

Make the same pattern using letters.

3

G B Y

4

B B R

5

Y R R

Problem Solving   Number Sense

6   Make the same pattern using letters.

1	2	3	1	2	3	1	2	3

Home Connection Your child translated a shape pattern into letters.
Home Activity Draw a shape pattern, and ask your child to make the same pattern using letters.

Name _____

Learn!

The stripes make a pattern.
What color should the white stripe be?

Check ✓

Find the pattern. Color what is missing.

1

Think About It   Reasoning

What is the pattern unit for the stripes
on the horse's blanket?

Find the pattern. Color what is missing.

2

3

Problem Solving Visual Thinking

Find the pattern. Color the white flowers
to complete the pattern.

4

© Pearson Education, Inc.

Home Connection Your child found out what was missing from the middle
of a pattern. **Home Activity** Without your child watching, draw a pattern,
such as square, circle, square, circle, square, circle, square, circle. Cover
one of the shapes and have your child tell what shape you covered.

Name_____

Flip-Flap
A lift-the-flap book of colors, numbers, shapes, opposites, sizes, and more!
Sandra Jenkins

Do You Know...
that people from all over the world have been decorating with patterns for thousands of years?

1 Josef is holding the first balloon in a pattern. If another balloon is added at the end of the pattern, what color should it be?

red   green

Fun Fact!
Zebras have stripes to confuse their enemies.

2 There will be 6 children at Josef's party. How many more balloons does Josef need?

_____ more balloons

Draw the present that should come next in the pattern.

3

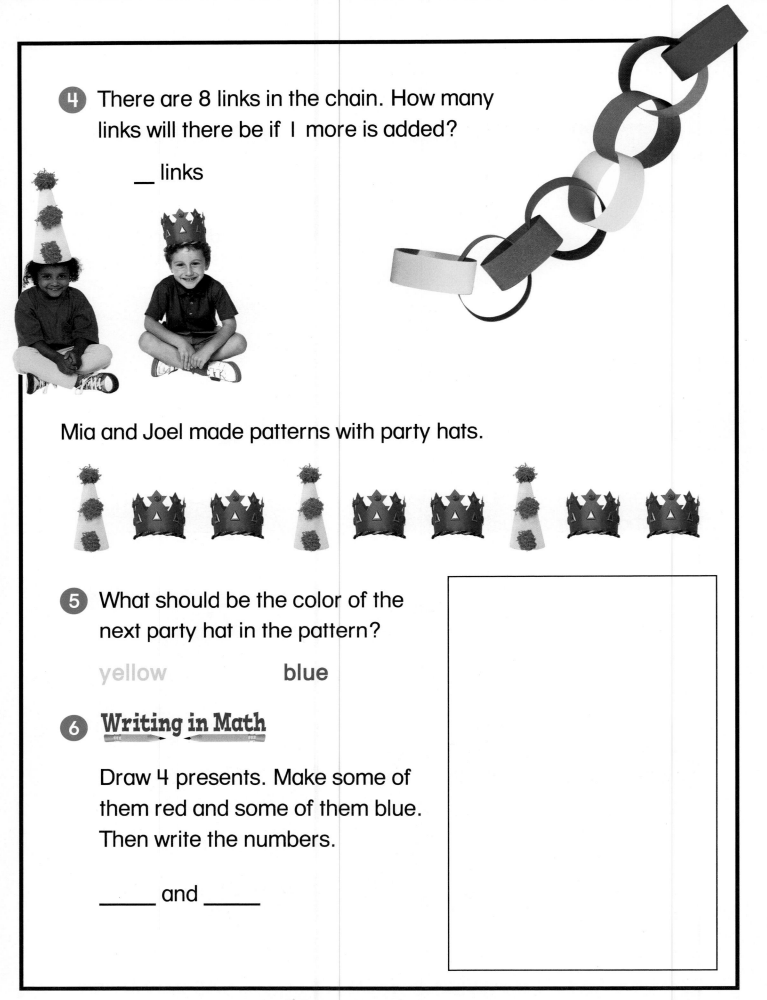

4 There are 8 links in the chain. How many links will there be if 1 more is added?

___ links

Mia and Joel made patterns with party hats.

5 What should be the color of the next party hat in the pattern?

yellow   blue

6 Writing in Math

Draw 4 presents. Make some of them red and some of them blue. Then write the numbers.

_____ and _____

Name _____

1 Circle the pattern unit.

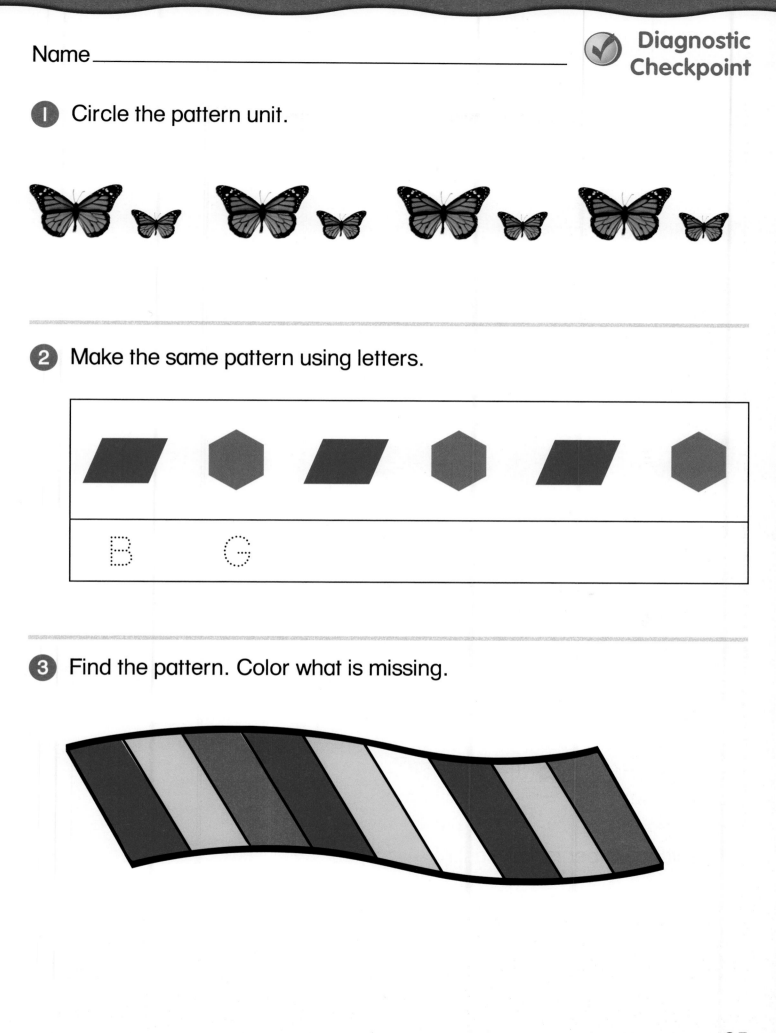

2 Make the same pattern using letters.

B G

3 Find the pattern. Color what is missing.

Name _____

Read Together · Filling in an Answer Bubble

Sometimes there are letters below the answer choices.

1 Which hat comes next in the pattern?

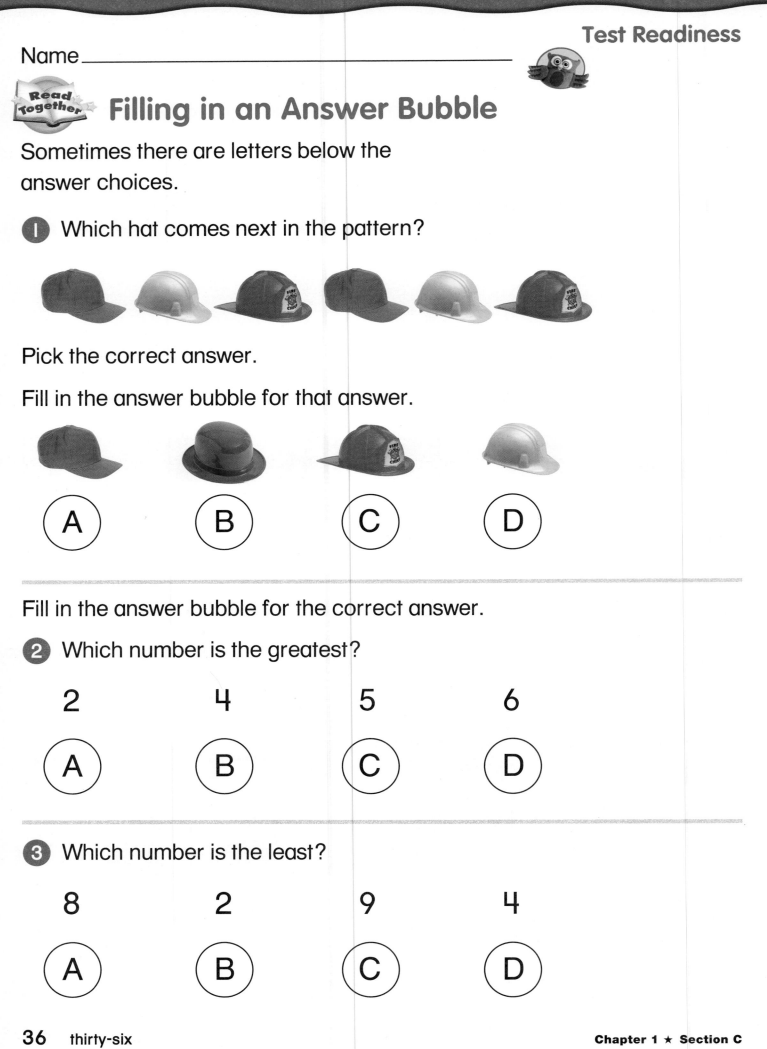

Pick the correct answer.

Fill in the answer bubble for that answer.

A	B	C	D

Fill in the answer bubble for the correct answer.

2 Which number is the greatest?

2	4	5	6
A	B	C	D

---

3 Which number is the least?

8	2	9	4
A	B	C	D

★ **Enrichment**

Growing Patterns

How do we make the next one?

Add one more square to the one before it.

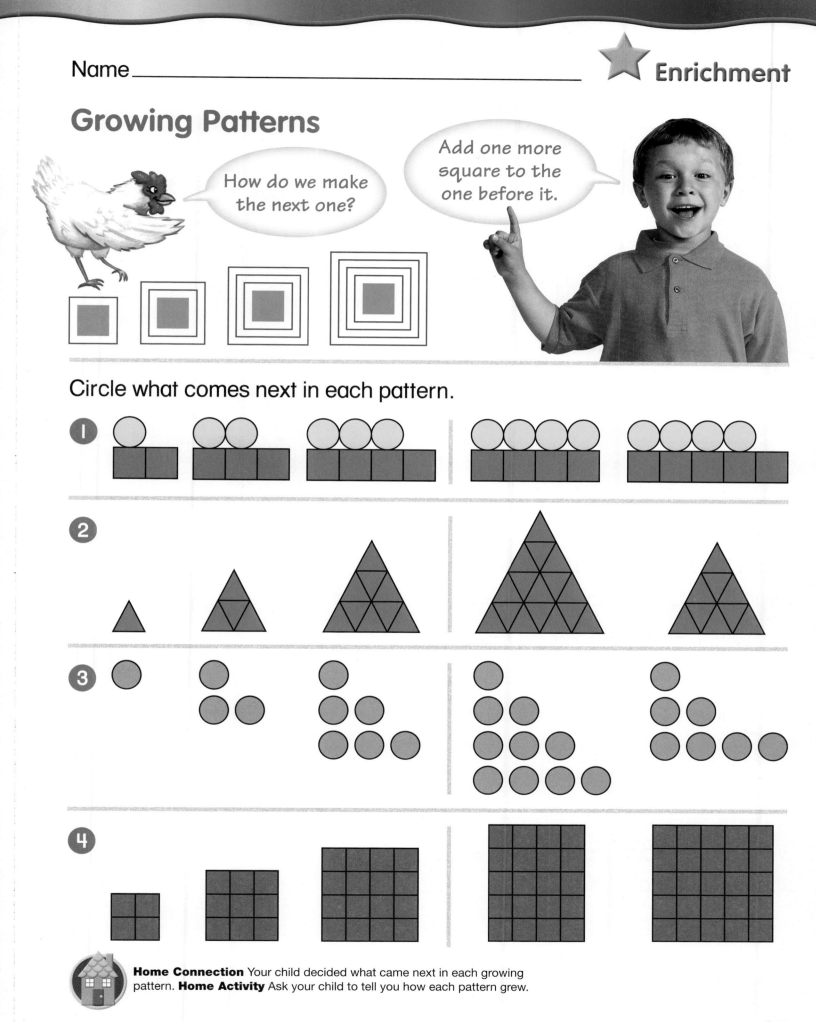

Circle what comes next in each pattern.

1

2

3

4

Home Connection Your child decided what came next in each growing pattern. **Home Activity** Ask your child to tell you how each pattern grew.

Name_____

Use the Keys of a Calculator

You can use a calculator to show numbers.
Press the keys. Write the numbers you see.

1 | ON/C | 6

_____6_____

2 | ON/C | 4

_____

3 | ON/C | 1 | 2

_____

4 | ON/C | 8

_____

Use your calculator. Press ON/C.

Show more numbers.
Write the numbers you press.

5 Show 10.

[1] [0]

6 Show 11.

[ ] [ ]

7 Show 12.

[ ] [ ]

8 Show 13.

[ ] [ ]

9 Show 14.

[ ] [ ]

10 Show 15.

[ ] [ ]

Think About It   Number Sense

Which keys would you press to show
the number that is after 15?

Home Connection Your child practiced using a calculator to show
numbers. **Home Activity** Ask your child to explain how he or she could
show any number from 1 to 12 on a calculator.

Name _____

 Read Together

Understand the Question

Important words help you understand
what a question is asking.

1. Which number of ducks is more
   than 5?

   Ⓐ 0 ducks

   Ⓑ 5 ducks

   Ⓒ 2 ducks

   Ⓓ 9 ducks

The most important words are **more than.**
Fill in the answer bubble.

Your Turn

What are the most important words?
Fill in the answer bubble.

I can do this!

2. Which number of cats is fewer than 10?

   Ⓐ 8 cats

   Ⓑ 11 cats

   Ⓒ 10 cats

   Ⓓ 12 cats

3. Which number of cows is more than 4?

   Ⓐ 3 cows

   Ⓑ 6 cows

   Ⓒ 4 cows

   Ⓓ 1 cow

 Home Connection Your child prepared for standardized tests by
identifying the most important words in math problems. **Home Activity** Ask
your child which words he or she identified as being the most important
words in Exercises 2 and 3. *(Fewer than, more than)*

Name _____

Discover Math in Your World

 ## Speaking of Math ...

Can you count from 1 to 10? Children around the world count in many different languages. This chart shows you how to count to 10 in English and in Spanish.

one	two	three	four	five	six	seven	eight	nine	ten
1	2	3	4	5	6	7	8	9	10
uno	dos	tres	cuatro	cinco	seis	siete	ocho	nueve	diez

Counting Around the Classroom

Use the chart. Solve each problem.

1 What is the English word for 1 more than 5? _____

2 What is the Spanish word for 1 fewer than 4? _____

3 What number is 1 more than **nueve**? _____

4 Write the numbers for these words in order
from least to greatest: **siete**   **diez**   **two**

_____

Take It to the NET
Video and Activities
www.scottforesman.com

Home Connection Your child learned the English and Spanish words for the numbers from 1 to 10. **Home Activity** Say any number, from 1 to 10, in English or in Spanish. Then ask your child to use the chart to find the number that is 1 more than, 1 fewer than, 2 more than, and 2 fewer than the number you said.

© Pearson Education, Inc.

Chapter 1

Write the numbers.

1

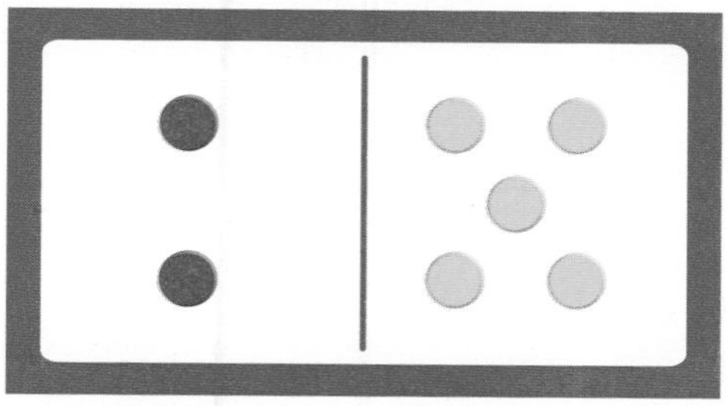

_____ and _____

2

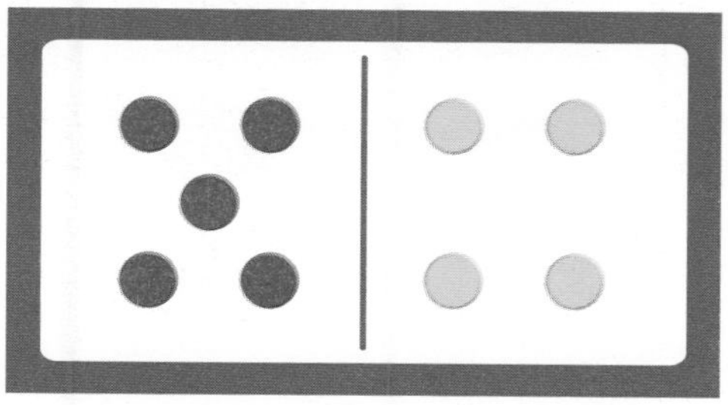

_____ and _____

3

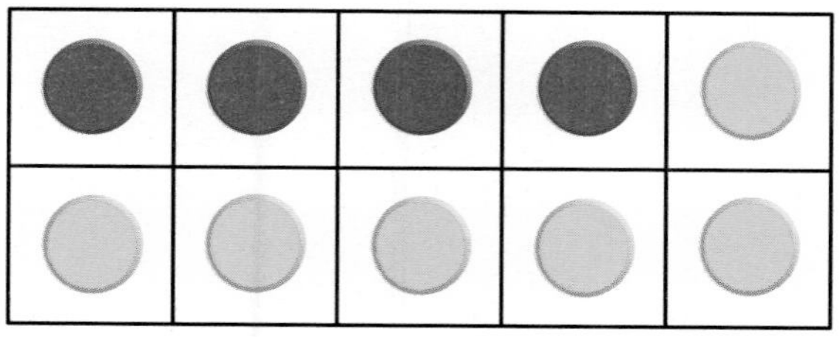

_____ and _____

4

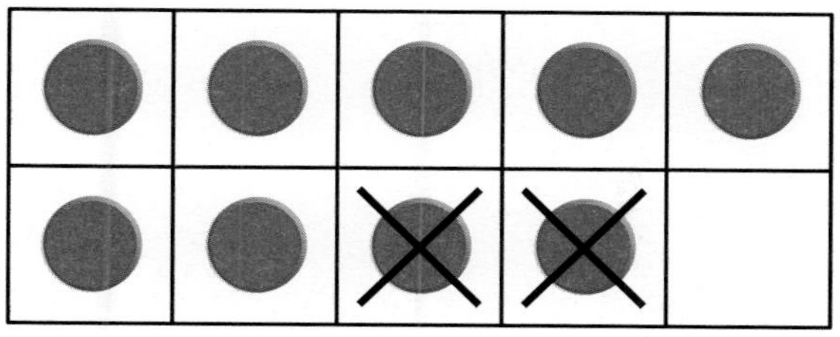

2 fewer than 9 is _____.

Use counters and Workmat 2. Write the numbers.

5 6 and 1 more is _____.

6 6 and 2 more is _____.

Use cubes.

7 Write the numbers in order from least to greatest.

| 10 | 3 | 7 |

_____, _____, _____

Use cubes. Circle **more** or **fewer**.

8

7 is _____ than 10.

more   **fewer**

9 Write one way to put
5 apples in 2 bowls.

In All

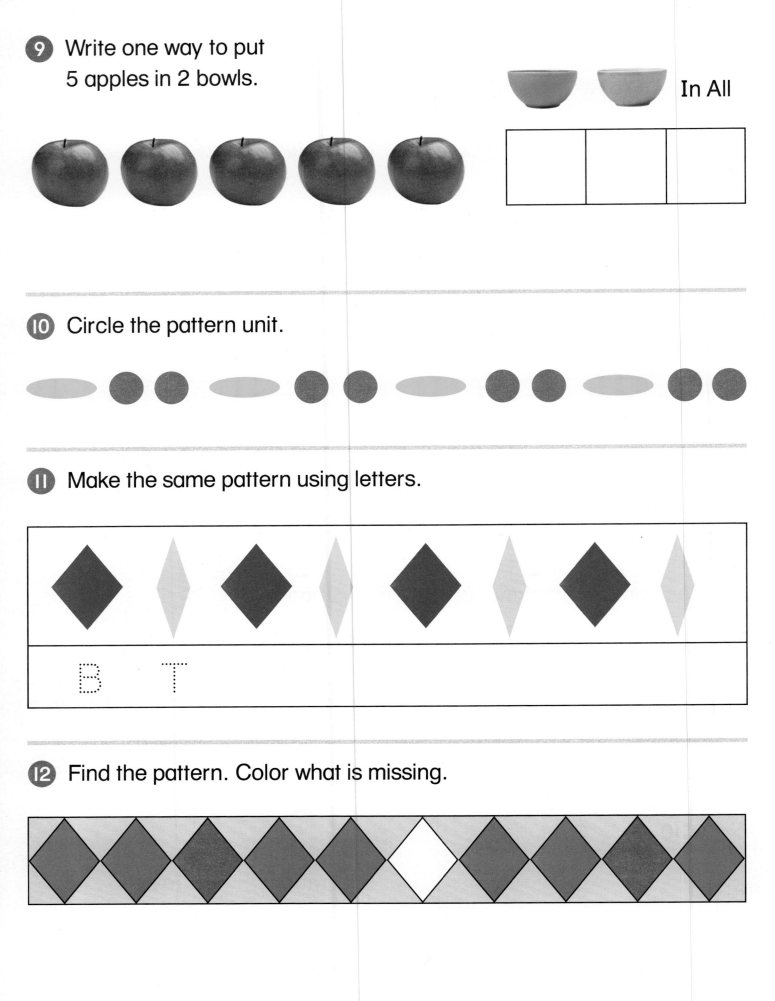

10 Circle the pattern unit.

11 Make the same pattern using letters.

B   T

12 Find the pattern. Color what is missing.

Read Together

Five Little Monkeys

A New Adaptation of a Childhood Classic
Illustrated by Kathi Ember

This Math Storybook belongs to

_____

2A

Five little monkeys jumping on the bed.
One fell off and bumped his head.
We called the doctor and the doctor said,
"No more monkeys jumping on the bed!"

Four little monkeys jumping on the bed.
One fell off and bumped her head.
We called the doctor and the doctor said,
"No more monkeys jumping on the bed!"

Stop it! Stop it right now!

Three little monkeys jumping on the bed.
One fell off and bumped his head.
We called the doctor and the doctor said,
"No more monkeys jumping on the bed!"

2D

Two little monkeys jumping on the bed.
One fell off and bumped her head.
We called the doctor and the doctor said,
"No more monkeys jumping on the bed!"

I told them to stop jumping!

One little monkey jumping on the bed.
He fell off and bumped his head.
We called the doctor and the doctor said,
"NO MORE MONKEYS JUMPING ON THE BED!"

Learn!

Join the groups to find how many fish there are in all.

There are 3 fish in all.

$\boxed{3}$ fish

Word Bank

join

Check ✓

Tell a joining story for each picture.
Use counters to tell how many in all.

❶

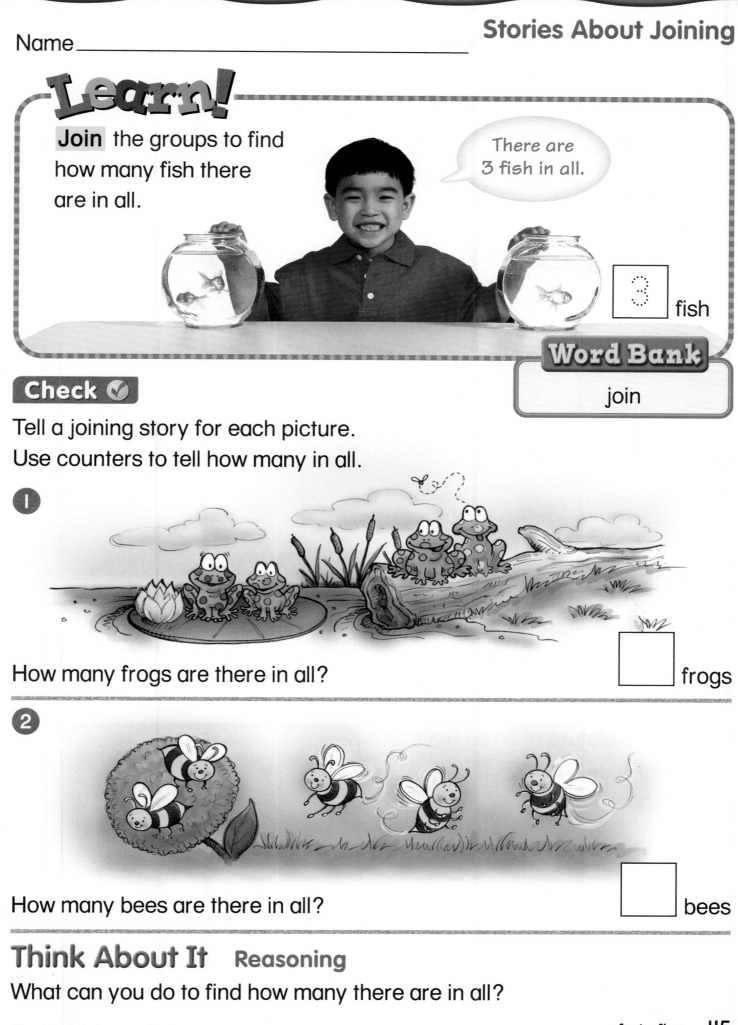

How many frogs are there in all? $\boxed{}$ frogs

❷

How many bees are there in all? $\boxed{}$ bees

Think About It   Reasoning

What can you do to find how many there are in all?

Use counters to answer each question.

3

4 rabbits are in the grass.
2 rabbits join them.
How many rabbits are there in all?

☐ rabbits

4

There are 3 ducks in the pond.
4 more ducks join them.
How many ducks are there altogether?

☐ ducks

Problem Solving   Writing in Math

5 Draw a picture of 5 red buttons
and 1 blue button.
Tell how many buttons there are
in all.

☐ buttons

Home Connection Your child joined two groups to find how many ̶ ill.
Home Activity Have your child show you two groups of paper pla̶ ̶nd
explain how to join the groups. Take turns showing and joining grou̶ each
time explaining what is happening.

Name _____

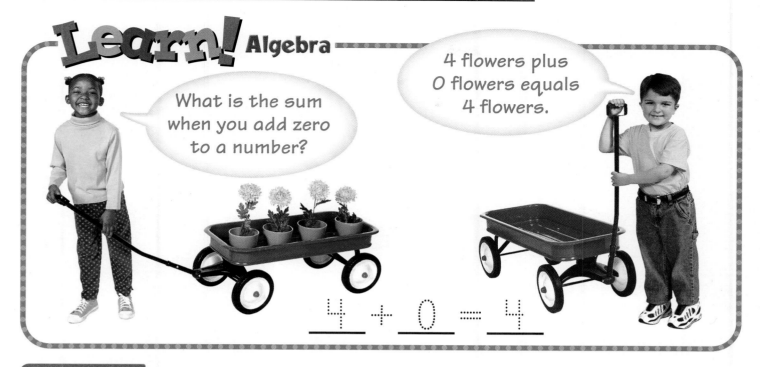

Learn! Algebra

What is the sum when you add zero to a number?

4 flowers plus 0 flowers equals 4 flowers.

$4 + 0 = 4$

Check ✓

Write an addition sentence.

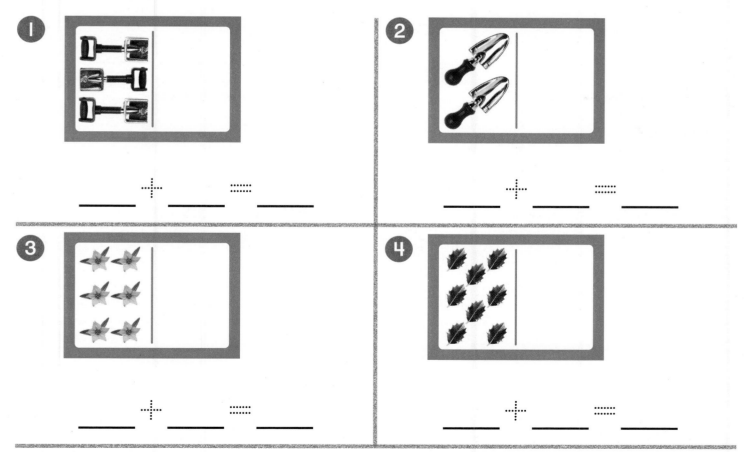

1. ___ + ___ = ___

2. ___ + ___ = ___

3. ___ + ___ = ___

4. ___ + ___ = ___

Think About It   Number Sense

What is the sum of $0 + 0$? Explain.

Write an addition sentence for each workmat.

5

You can also add a number to zero.

$0 + 3 = 3$

6

___ $+$ ___ $=$ ___

7

___ $+$ ___ $=$ ___

8

___ $+$ ___ $=$ ___

9

___ $+$ ___ $=$ ___

Problem Solving   Mental Math

10 You have 3 dimes in one pocket.
You have none in the other pocket.
How many dimes do you have in all?   ____ dimes

Home Connection Your child used the number zero in addition sentences.
Home Activity Use buttons and two paper cups turned upside-down. Take
turns hiding buttons under one cup and guessing which cup has zero
buttons. Then tell the total number of buttons under both cups.

Name_____

Identify the Main Idea

The main idea tells what a story problem is all about.
Knowing the main idea can help you solve story problems.

1 Read this story problem.

Luis has 2 puppets.
Alma has 2 puppets.
How many puppets do they have in all?

2 Circle what the story problem is all about.

3 Circle a good title for this story problem.

How Many Snacks?   **How Many Puppets?**   **My Friends**

4 Write the numbers in this story problem.

_____   _____

5 Solve this story problem.
Write a number sentence about the main idea.

____ + ____ = ____ puppets

Think About It   Reasoning

Why did you add to solve this story problem?

6 Read another story problem.

Skipper had 3 dog treats.
Then he got 2 more treats.
How many treats does Skipper have now?

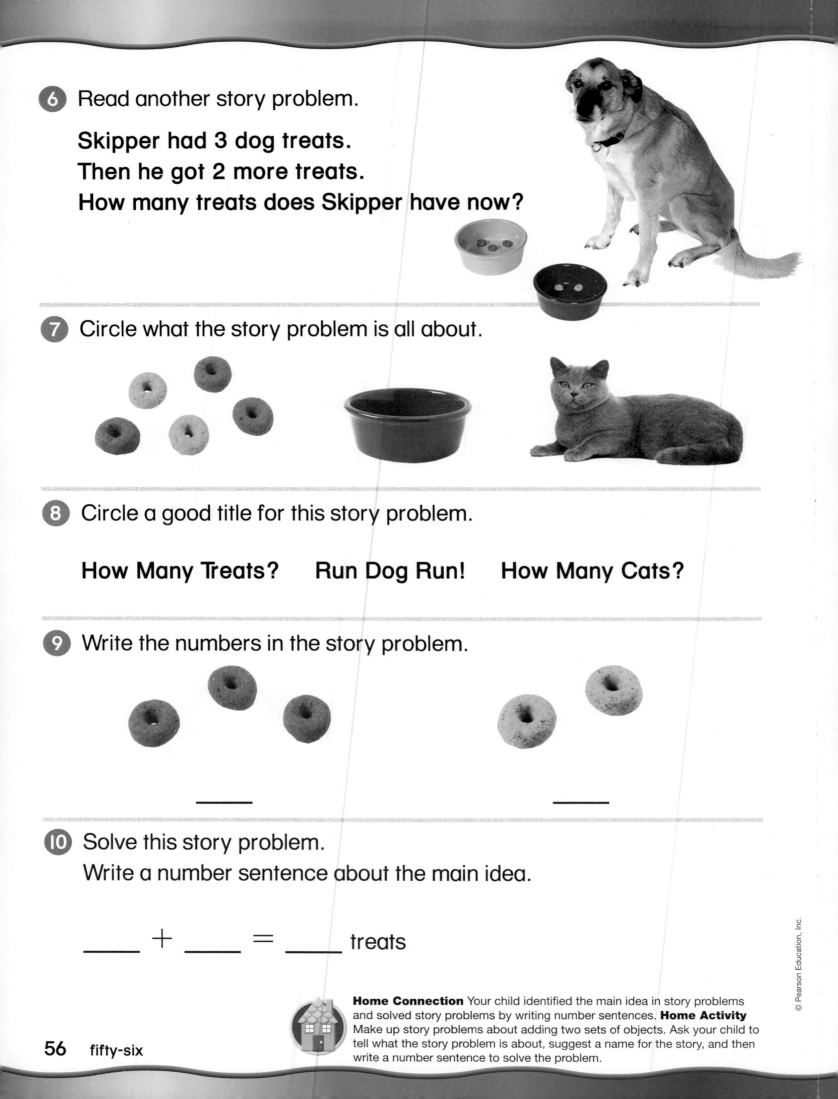

7 Circle what the story problem is all about.

8 Circle a good title for this story problem.

How Many Treats? **Run Dog Run!** **How Many Cats?**

9 Write the numbers in the story problem.

_____   _____

10 Solve this story problem.
Write a number sentence about the main idea.

_____ + _____ = _____ treats

Home Connection Your child identified the main idea in story problems and solved story problems by writing number sentences. **Home Activity** Make up story problems about adding two sets of objects. Ask your child to tell what the story problem is about, suggest a name for the story, and then write a number sentence to solve the problem.

Name_____

Add to find the sum.
Use counters if you like.

1

3 and 7 is _____.

2

5 and 5 is _____.

Write each addition sentence.

3

____ ╬ ____ ░ ____

4

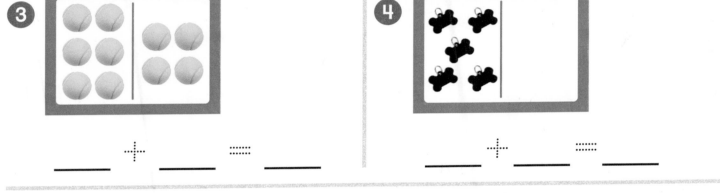

____ ╬ ____ ░ ____

Add to find the sum.

5

$\begin{array}{r} 6 \\ + 3 \\ \hline \end{array}$

6 + 3 = ___

6

$\begin{array}{r} 1 \\ + 8 \\ \hline \end{array}$

1 + 8 = ___

Write an addition sentence to answer the question.

7 There are 8 dogs in the park.
2 more dogs join them.
How many dogs are there in all?

_____ ╬ _____ ░ _____ dogs

Name_____

What is the missing number?

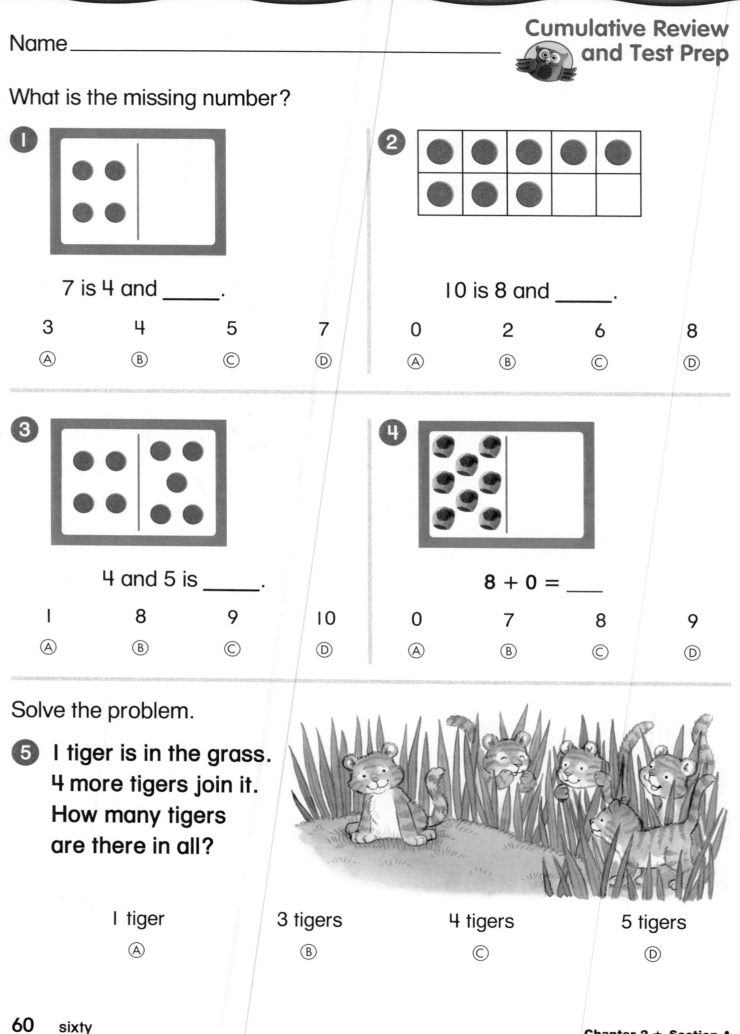

1

7 is 4 and _____.

3	4	5	7
Ⓐ	Ⓑ	Ⓒ	Ⓓ

2

10 is 8 and _____.

0	2	6	8
Ⓐ	Ⓑ	Ⓒ	Ⓓ

3

4 and 5 is _____.

1	8	9	10
Ⓐ	Ⓑ	Ⓒ	Ⓓ

4

8 + 0 = ___

0	7	8	9
Ⓐ	Ⓑ	Ⓒ	Ⓓ

Solve the problem.

5 I tiger is in the grass.
4 more tigers join it.
How many tigers
are there in all?

I tiger	3 tigers	4 tigers	5 tigers
Ⓐ	Ⓑ	Ⓒ	Ⓓ

Learn!

You can **subtract** to find the **difference**.

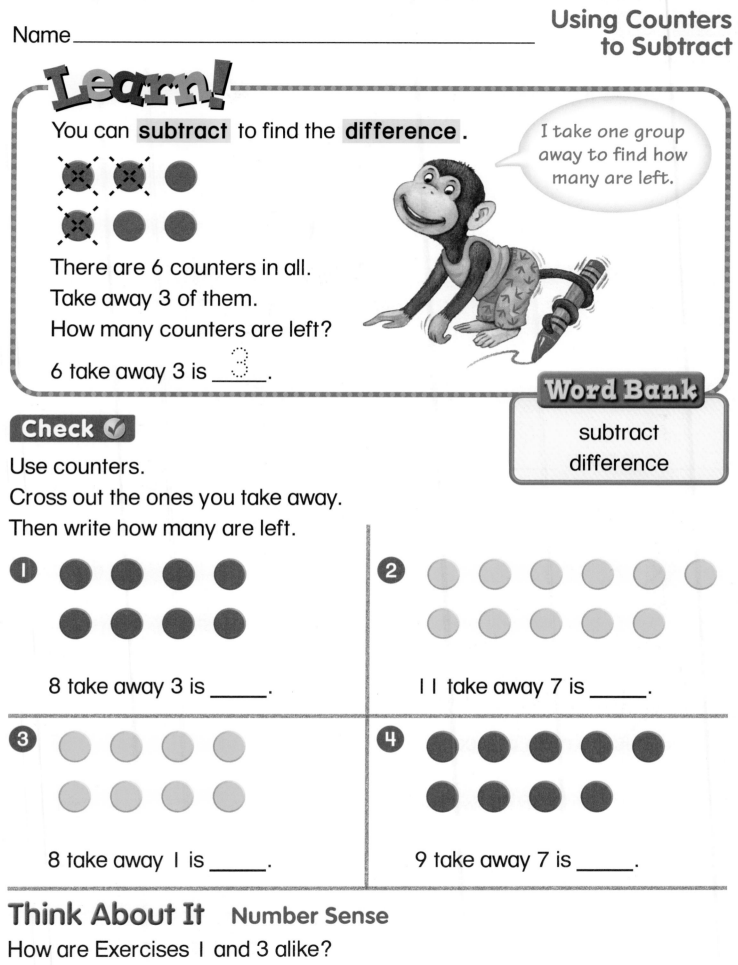

I take one group away to find how many are left.

There are 6 counters in all.

Take away 3 of them.

How many counters are left?

6 take away 3 is _3_.

Word Bank

subtract

difference

Check ✓

Use counters.

Cross out the ones you take away.

Then write how many are left.

❶ 8 take away 3 is _____.

❷ 11 take away 7 is _____.

❸ 8 take away 1 is _____.

❹ 9 take away 7 is _____.

Think About It   Number Sense

How are Exercises 1 and 3 alike?

How are they different?

Subtract to find the difference.
Use counters if you like.

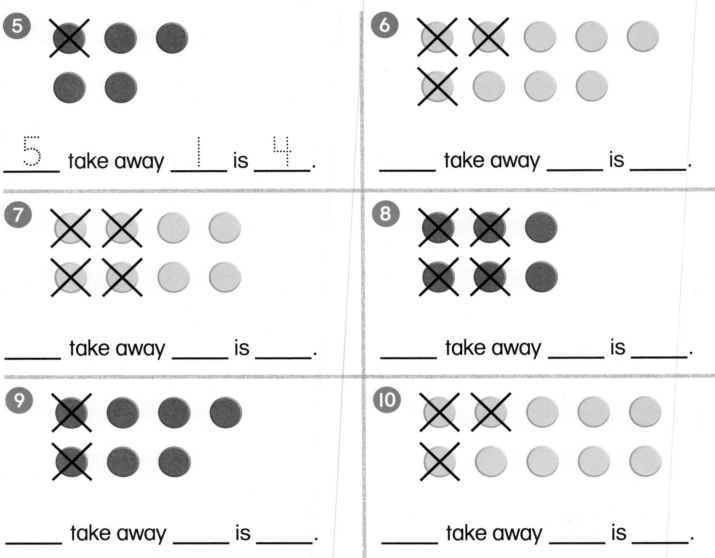

5 _5_ take away _1_ is _4_ .

6 ____ take away ____ is ____ .

7 ____ take away ____ is ____ .

8 ____ take away ____ is ____ .

9 ____ take away ____ is ____ .

10 ____ take away ____ is ____ .

Problem Solving   Number Sense

11 What is the most you can
take away from 8 counters?
Draw a picture to show
that number.

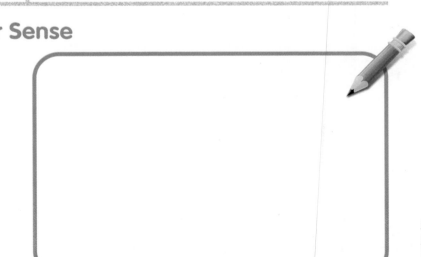

Home Connection Your child used counters to subtract and show how many are left. **Home Activity** Have your child show you how to use cereal pieces, coins, buttons, or other counters to act out "take away" stories. Take turns using counters to show subtraction stories you both make up.

Name_____

Learn! Algebra

If you take away all, zero are left.

If you take away zero, all are left.

6 — 6 = 0

6 — 0 = 6

Check ✓

Write a subtraction sentence.

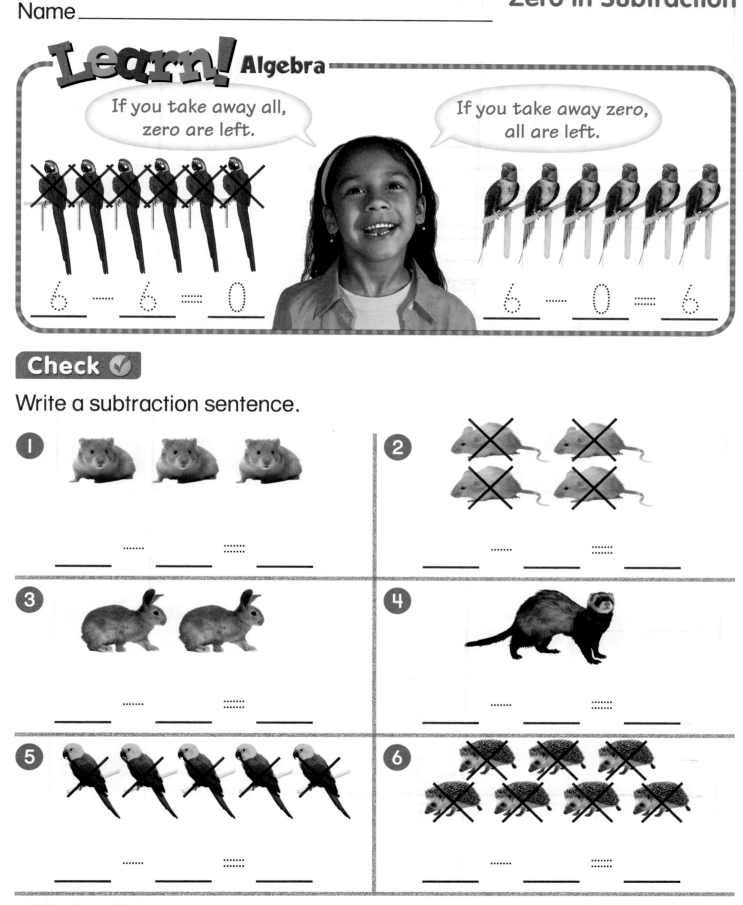

1.   ..... ::::: ____ ____ ____

2.   ...... ::::: ____ ____ ____

3.   ...... ::::: ____ ____ ____

4.   .... ____ ____ ____

5.   ..... ::: ____ ____ ____

6.   ..... ::: ____ ____ ____

Think About It   Reasoning

What do you always have left when you take away zero?

Subtract to find the difference.
Cross out the dots if you like.

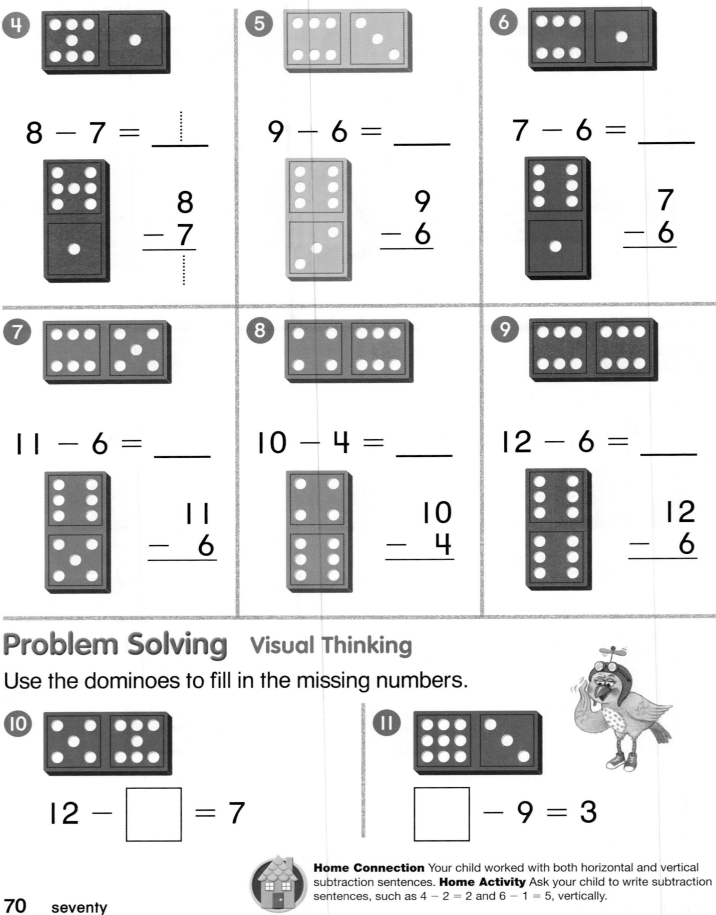

4

$8 - 7 = \underline{1}$

$\begin{array}{r} 8 \\ -\ 7 \\ \hline \end{array}$

5

$9 - 6 = \underline{}$

$\begin{array}{r} 9 \\ -\ 6 \\ \hline \end{array}$

6

$7 - 6 = \underline{}$

$\begin{array}{r} 7 \\ -\ 6 \\ \hline \end{array}$

7

$11 - 6 = \underline{}$

$\begin{array}{r} 11 \\ -\ 6 \\ \hline \end{array}$

8

$10 - 4 = \underline{}$

$\begin{array}{r} 10 \\ -\ 4 \\ \hline \end{array}$

9

$12 - 6 = \underline{}$

$\begin{array}{r} 12 \\ -\ 6 \\ \hline \end{array}$

Problem Solving   Visual Thinking

Use the dominoes to fill in the missing numbers.

10

$12 - \boxed{} = 7$

11

$\boxed{} - 9 = 3$

Home Connection Your child worked with both horizontal and vertical subtraction sentences. **Home Activity** Ask your child to write subtraction sentences, such as 4 − 2 = 2 and 6 − 1 = 5, vertically.

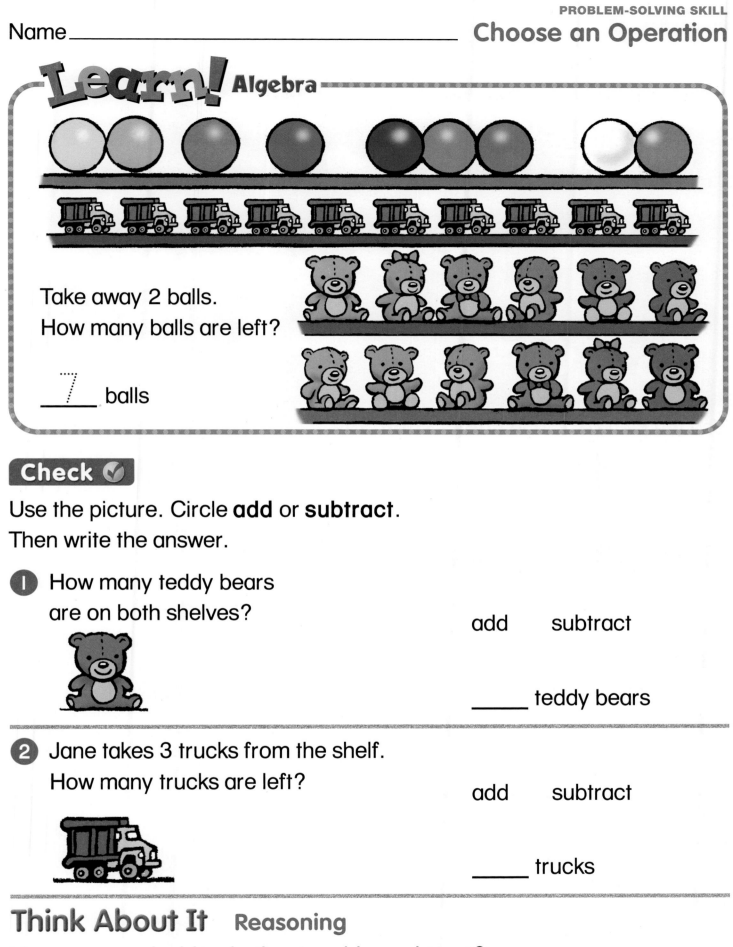

Learn! Algebra

Take away 2 balls.
How many balls are left?

____7____ balls

Check ✓

Use the picture. Circle **add** or **subtract**.
Then write the answer.

1 How many teddy bears
are on both shelves?

add   subtract

_____ teddy bears

2 Jane takes 3 trucks from the shelf.
How many trucks are left?

add   subtract

_____ trucks

Think About It   Reasoning

How can you decide whether to add or subtract?

Use the picture. Circle **add** or **subtract**.
Then write the answer.

---

3 There are 3 yellow chicks
and 5 white chicks.   add   subtract
How many chicks are there in all?

_____ chicks

---

4 7 cows live on the farm.
5 of the cows are eating.   add   subtract
How many cows are not eating?

_____ cows

---

5 There are 5 pigs on the farm.
4 pigs are in the mud.   add   subtract
How many pigs are not in the mud?

_____ pig

Home Connection Your child chose an operation to solve each problem.
Home Activity Point to a problem on the page. Ask your child to tell you
how he or she knew whether to add or subtract.

Name_____

Cross out the ones you take away.
Then write how many are left.

1

7 take away 6 is _____.

2

9 take away 4 is _____.

Write each subtraction sentence.

3

_____ _____ _____

4

_____ _____ _____

Subtract to find the difference.

5

9
− 3

9 − 3 = _____

6

6
− 3

6 − 3 = _____

Circle **add** or **subtract**.
Then write the answer.

7 There are 6 goats eating grass.
5 more goats are sleeping.
How many goats are there altogether?

add   subtract

_____ goats

1 What color block do you need to finish the wall?

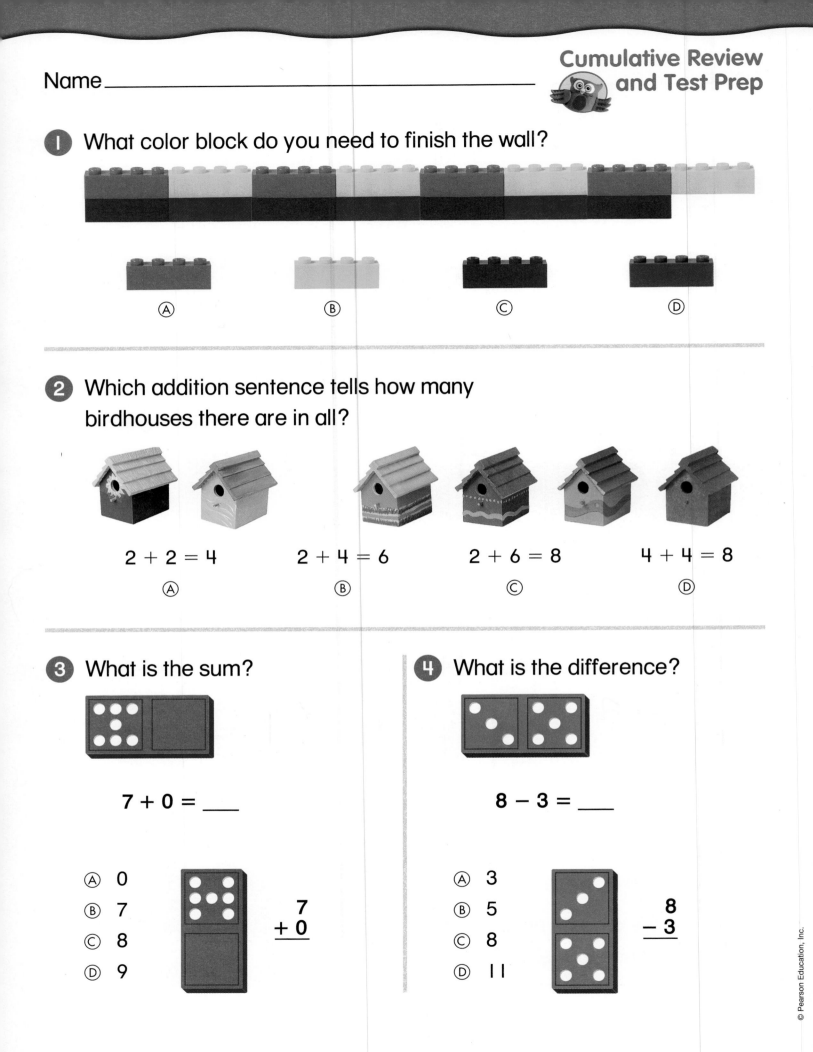

Ⓐ   Ⓑ   Ⓒ   Ⓓ

2 Which addition sentence tells how many
birdhouses there are in all?

$2 + 2 = 4$ $2 + 4 = 6$ $2 + 6 = 8$ $4 + 4 = 8$

Ⓐ   Ⓑ   Ⓒ   Ⓓ

3 What is the sum?

$7 + 0 = $ _____

Ⓐ 0
Ⓑ 7
Ⓒ 8
Ⓓ 9

$$\begin{array}{r} 7 \\ + 0 \\ \hline \end{array}$$

4 What is the difference?

$8 - 3 = $ _____

Ⓐ 3
Ⓑ 5
Ⓒ 8
Ⓓ 11

$$\begin{array}{r} 8 \\ - 3 \\ \hline \end{array}$$

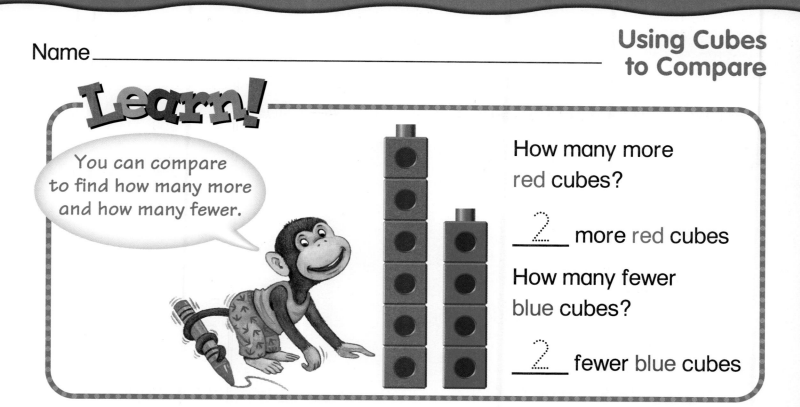

You can compare to find how many more and how many fewer.

How many more
red cubes?

_2_ more red cubes

How many fewer
blue cubes?

_2_ fewer blue cubes

Check ✓

Use cubes. Color to show the cubes.
Then write how many more and how many fewer.

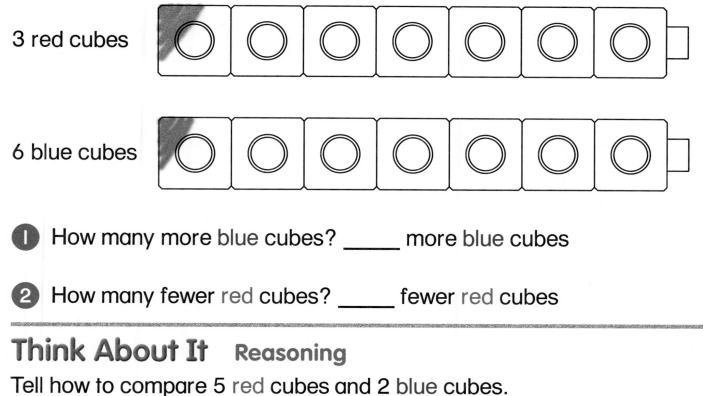

3 red cubes

6 blue cubes

1 How many more blue cubes? _____ more blue cubes

2 How many fewer red cubes? _____ fewer red cubes

Think About It   Reasoning

Tell how to compare 5 red cubes and 2 blue cubes.

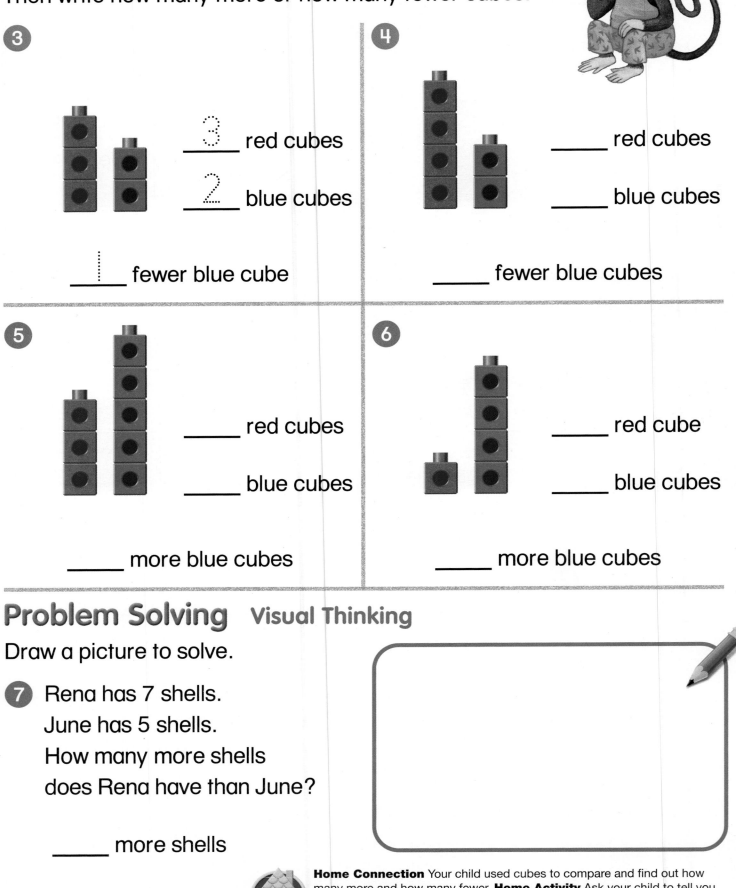

Write how many red cubes and how many blue cubes.
Then write how many more or how many fewer cubes.

3

_3_ red cubes

_2_ blue cubes

_1_ fewer blue cube

4

_____ red cubes

_____ blue cubes

_____ fewer blue cubes

5

_____ red cubes

_____ blue cubes

_____ more blue cubes

6

_____ red cube

_____ blue cubes

_____ more blue cubes

Problem Solving   Visual Thinking

Draw a picture to solve.

7 Rena has 7 shells.
June has 5 shells.
How many more shells
does Rena have than June?

_____ more shells

Home Connection Your child used cubes to compare and find out how many more and how many fewer. **Home Activity** Ask your child to tell you how many windows and doors there are in your home. Then talk about how many more windows there are than doors.

76 seventy-six

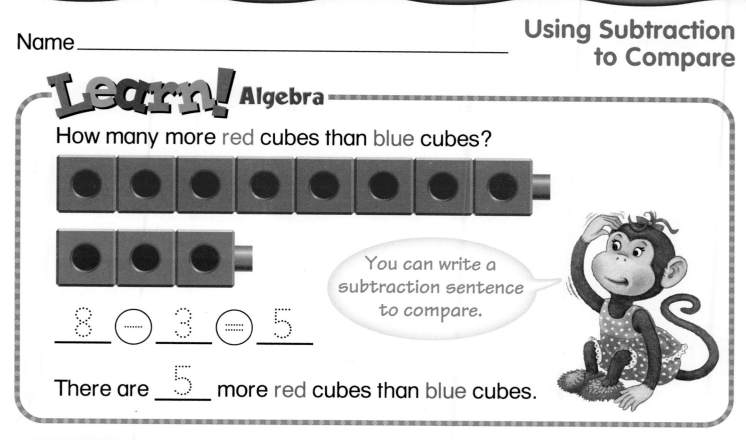

Learn! Algebra

How many more red cubes than blue cubes?

__8__ ⊖ __3__ ⊜ __5__

You can write a subtraction sentence to compare.

There are __5__ more red cubes than blue cubes.

Check ✓

Write a subtraction sentence.
Then write how many fewer.

1 How many fewer yellow cubes than green cubes?

__7__ ⊖ __2__ ⊜ __5__

There are _____ fewer yellow cubes than green cubes.

Think About It   Number Sense

There are 4 more red cubes than blue cubes.
How many fewer blue cubes are there?

Write each subtraction sentence.

Then write how many more or how many fewer.

2 How many fewer pots than lids?

8 ⊖ 6 ⊜ 2   2 fewer pots

3 How many more cups than plates?

8 ⊖ 5 ⊜ 3   3 more cups

4 How many more forks than spoons?

6 ⊖ 1 ⊜ 5   5 more forks

Problem Solving Estimation

Answer each question.

5 Does your classroom have more crayons or more children?

_____

6 Does your classroom have fewer children or fewer teachers?

_____

Home Connection Your child used subtraction to compare.
Home Activity Ask your child to write a subtraction sentence to compare a number of plates to a different number of cups.

Name_____

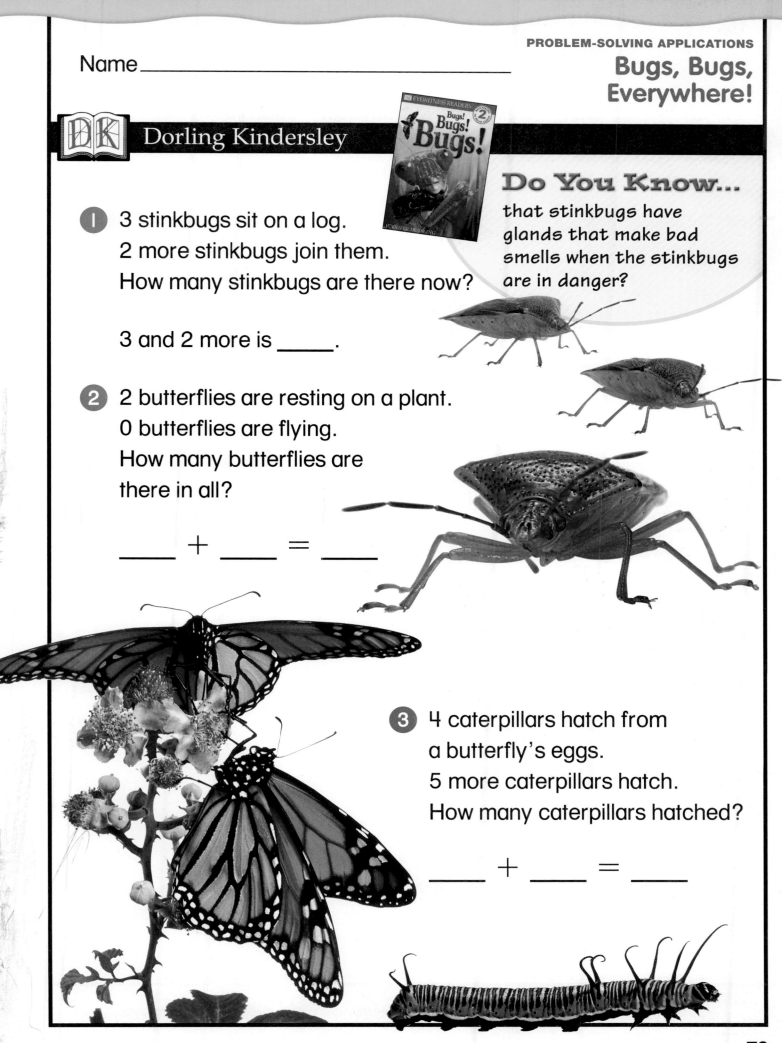

Dorling Kindersley

Bugs! Bugs! Bugs!

Do You Know...
that stinkbugs have glands that make bad smells when the stinkbugs are in danger?

1 3 stinkbugs sit on a log.
2 more stinkbugs join them.
How many stinkbugs are there now?

3 and 2 more is _____.

2 2 butterflies are resting on a plant.
0 butterflies are flying.
How many butterflies are there in all?

___ + ___ = ___

3 4 caterpillars hatch from a butterfly's eggs.
5 more caterpillars hatch.
How many caterpillars hatched?

___ + ___ = ___

4 There are 11 stinkbugs and 9 thorn bugs.
How many fewer thorn bugs are there?

_____ fewer thorn bugs

5 9 thorn bugs are on a stick.
A bird eats 0 thorn bugs.
How many thorn bugs are left on the stick?

____ – ____ = ____ thorn bugs

6 There are 3 stinkbugs and
9 thorn bugs in the tree.
How many more thorn bugs are there?

There are _____ more thorn bugs
than stinkbugs.

Fun Fact!
This bug is called a thorn bug because it looks like a thorn on a twig.

7 **Writing in Math**

Write an addition sentence or
a subtraction sentence.

____ ◯ ____ ◯ ____

Write a story about your number sentence.
Then draw a picture.

© Pearson Education, Inc.

 Home Connection Your child learned to solve problems by applying his or her math skills. **Home Activity** Talk to your child about how he or she solved the problems on these two pages.

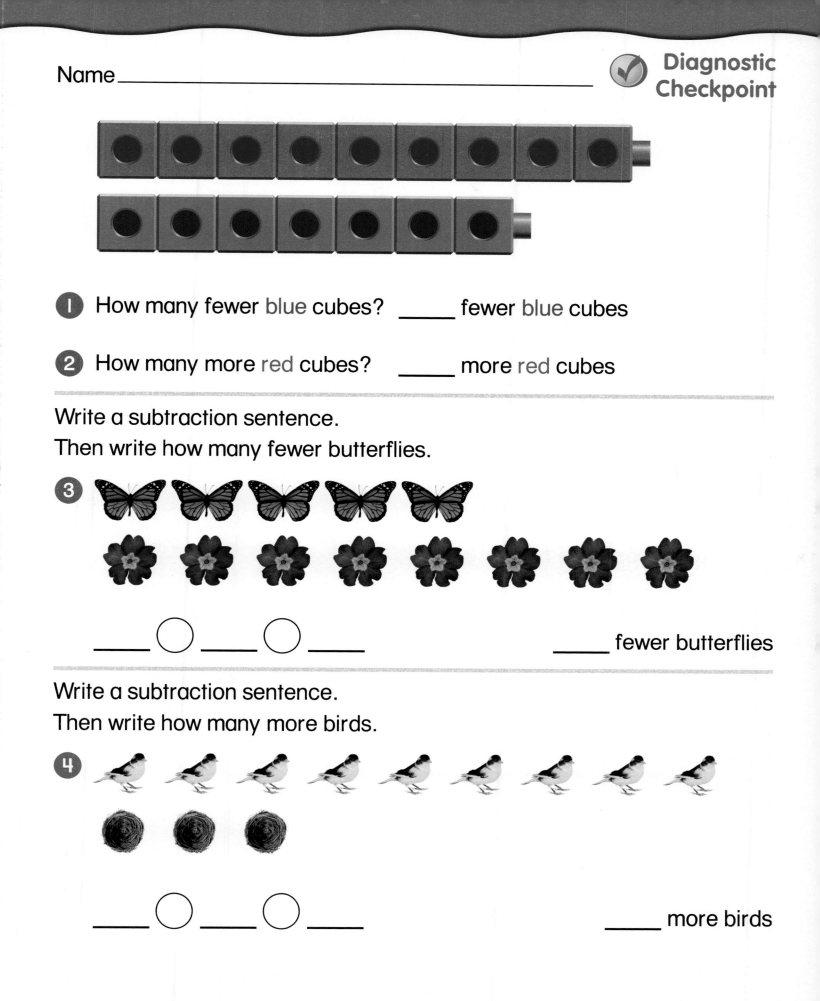

1 How many fewer blue cubes?   _____ fewer blue cubes

2 How many more red cubes?   _____ more red cubes

Write a subtraction sentence.
Then write how many fewer butterflies.

3

_____ ◯ _____ ◯ _____   _____ fewer butterflies

Write a subtraction sentence.
Then write how many more birds.

4

_____ ◯ _____ ◯ _____   _____ more birds

Name_____

1 What is one way you can put 12 eggs into 2 cartons?

12 is _____ and _____.

6 and 3
Ⓐ

5 and 7
Ⓑ

5 and 4
Ⓒ

7 and 7
Ⓓ

2 Which shows the numbers in order from **least** to **greatest**?

11, 8, 5
Ⓐ

8, 5, 11
Ⓑ

5, 8, 11
Ⓒ

8, 11, 5
Ⓓ

3 Which addition sentence answers the question?

5 kangaroos are resting.
5 kangaroos are hopping.
How many kangaroos are
there altogether?

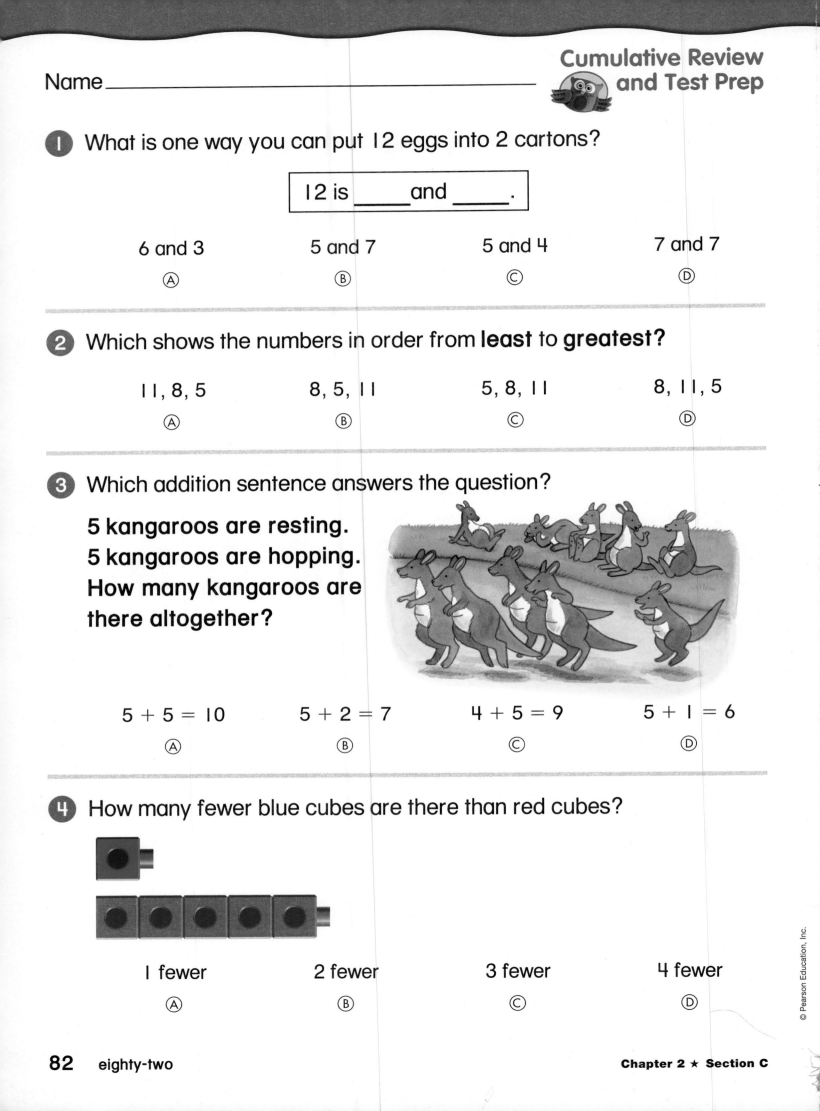

5 + 5 = 10
Ⓐ

5 + 2 = 7
Ⓑ

4 + 5 = 9
Ⓒ

5 + 1 = 6
Ⓓ

4 How many fewer blue cubes are there than red cubes?

1 fewer
Ⓐ

2 fewer
Ⓑ

3 fewer
Ⓒ

4 fewer
Ⓓ

Name _____

Read Together

Get Information for the Answer

Pictures may help you solve math problems.

1 Which number sentence tells how many fewer red cubes there are?

Test-Taking Strategies
Understand the Question
Get Information for the Answer
Plan How to Find the Answer
Make Smart Choices
Use Writing in Math

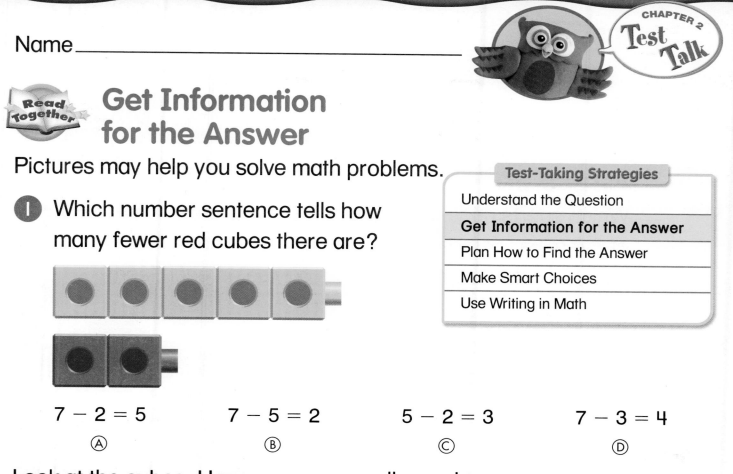

$7 - 2 = 5$ $7 - 5 = 2$ $5 - 2 = 3$ $7 - 3 = 4$

  Ⓐ   Ⓑ   Ⓒ   Ⓓ

Look at the cubes. How many more yellow cubes are there? Use this information to answer the question. Then fill in the answer bubble.

Your Turn

Look at the picture to get information.
Then fill in the answer bubble.

2 Which number sentence tells how many more blue cubes there are?

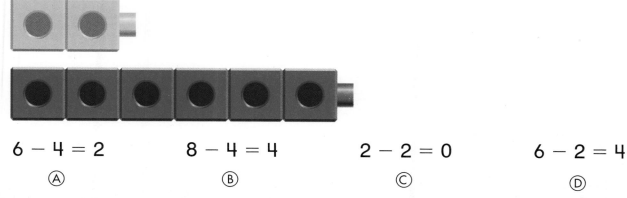

$6 - 4 = 2$ $8 - 4 = 4$ $2 - 2 = 0$ $6 - 2 = 4$

  Ⓐ   Ⓑ   Ⓒ   Ⓓ

Home Connection Your child prepared for standardized tests by using pictures to solve math problems. **Home Activity** Ask your child to describe how he or she used the picture to answer the question in Exercise 2.

Name _____

Who's on First?

Which sports do you like to play? Do you know some of the rules for those sports? Every sport has rules. One rule tells how many players can be on each team.

Teams by the Numbers

Use counters to show the players. Then solve.

1 Each soccer team has 1 goalie. How many goalies are on the field during a game?

_____ goalies

2 Doubles tennis has 2 players on each side of the court. How many players are on the court during a match?

_____ players

3 Both basketball teams have 5 players on the court at a time. How many players are on the floor at a time?

_____ players

4 There are 12 players ready for a game. How many of these players are on each team?

_____ players

 **Take It to the NET**
Video and Activities
www.scottforesman.com

Home Connection Your child solved problems about the number of players on sports teams. **Home Activity** Ask your child to solve similar kinds of problems. For example, ask your child how many players are on the field during a football game at any given time. *(11 players from each team; 22 players in all)*

Name_____

Write each addition sentence.

1

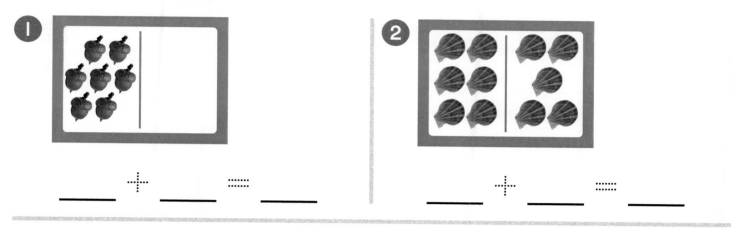

____ + ____ = ____

2

____ + ____ = ____

Write each subtraction sentence.

3

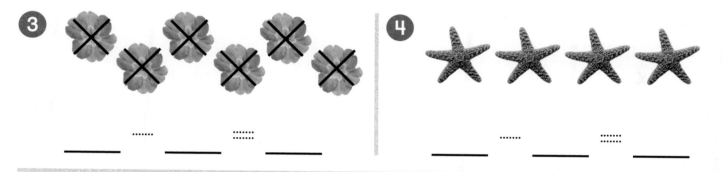

____ − ____ = ____

4

____ − ____ = ____

Add to find the sum.

5

$$\begin{array}{r} 5 \\ + 7 \\ \hline \end{array}$$

5 + 7 = ____

6

$$\begin{array}{r} 4 \\ + 6 \\ \hline \end{array}$$

4 + 6 = ____

Subtract to find the difference.

7

$$\begin{array}{r} 9 \\ - 7 \\ \hline \end{array}$$

9 − 7 = ____

8

$$\begin{array}{r} 8 \\ - 5 \\ \hline \end{array}$$

8 − 5 = ____

Write an addition sentence to answer the question.

9 Meg had 7 toy cars.
Pat gave her 4 more toy cars.
How many toy cars does Meg have now?

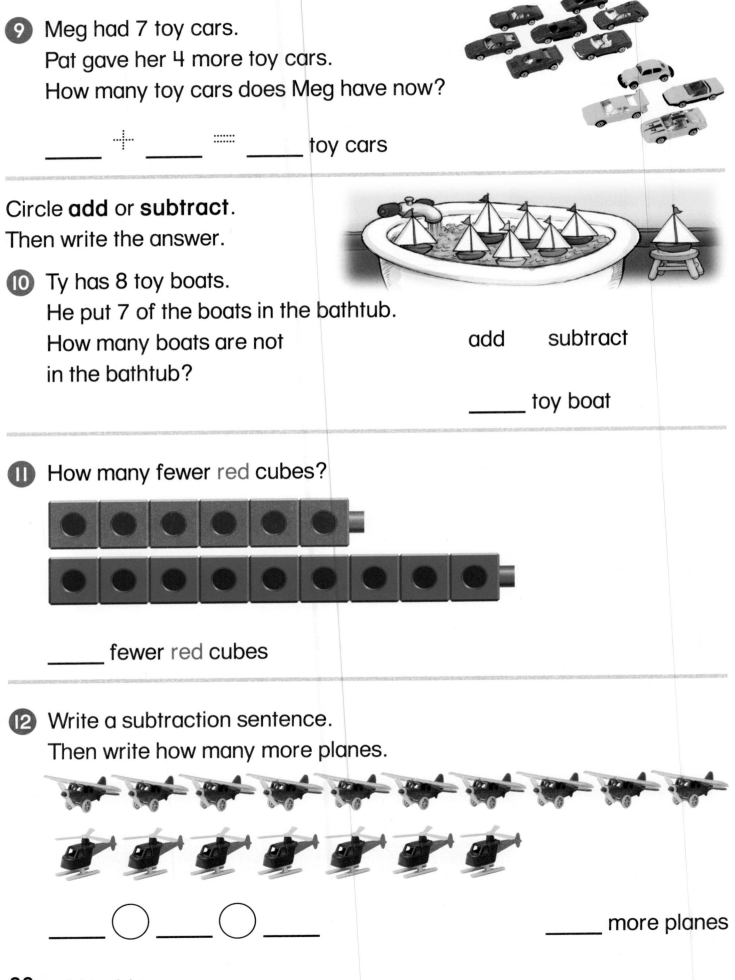

_____ + _____ = _____ toy cars

Circle **add** or **subtract**.
Then write the answer.

10 Ty has 8 toy boats.
He put 7 of the boats in the bathtub.
How many boats are not
in the bathtub?

add   subtract

_____ toy boat

11 How many fewer red cubes?

_____ fewer red cubes

12 Write a subtraction sentence.
Then write how many more planes.

_____ ◯ _____ ◯ _____   _____ more planes

Name_____

What is the missing number?

1
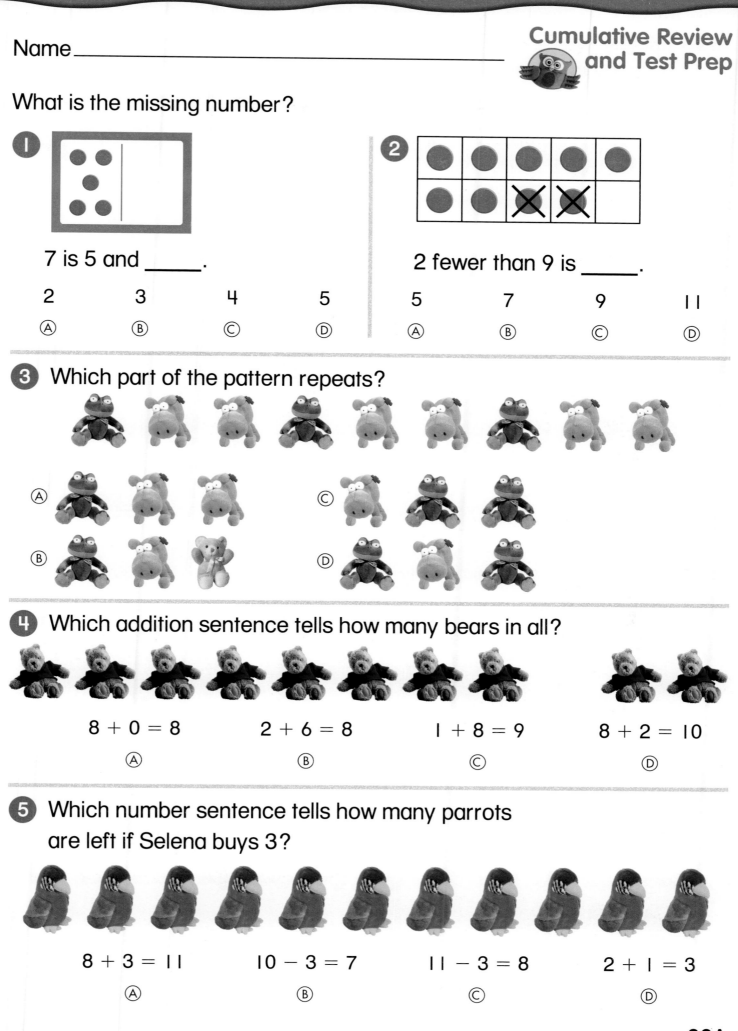

7 is 5 and _____.

2	3	4	5
Ⓐ	Ⓑ	Ⓒ	Ⓓ

2

2 fewer than 9 is _____.

5	7	9	11
Ⓐ	Ⓑ	Ⓒ	Ⓓ

3 Which part of the pattern repeats?

Ⓐ   Ⓒ

Ⓑ   Ⓓ

4 Which addition sentence tells how many bears in all?

8 + 0 = 8	2 + 6 = 8	1 + 8 = 9	8 + 2 = 10
Ⓐ	Ⓑ	Ⓒ	Ⓓ

5 Which number sentence tells how many parrots are left if Selena buys 3?

8 + 3 = 11	10 − 3 = 7	11 − 3 = 8	2 + 1 = 3
Ⓐ	Ⓑ	Ⓒ	Ⓓ

Draw the missing counters.
Then write the numbers.

6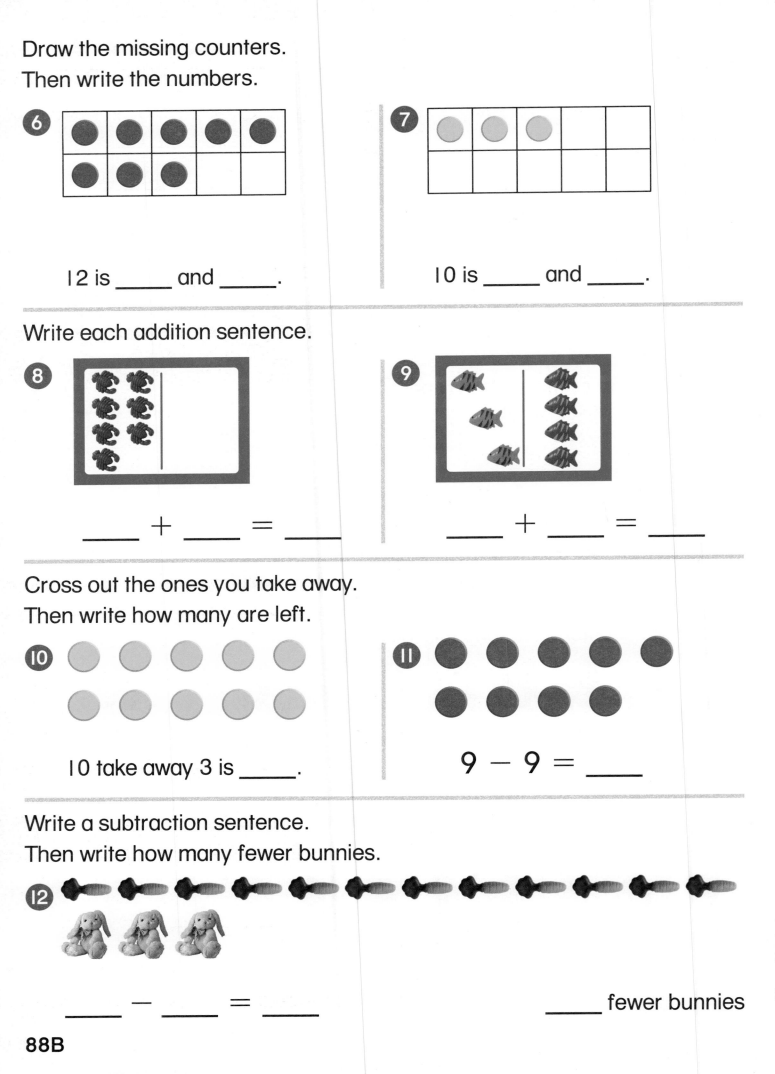

12 is _____ and _____.

7

10 is _____ and _____.

Write each addition sentence.

8

___ + ___ = ___

9

___ + ___ = ___

Cross out the ones you take away.
Then write how many are left.

10

10 take away 3 is _____.

11

9 − 9 = _____

Write a subtraction sentence.
Then write how many fewer bunnies.

12

____ − ____ = ____

_____ fewer bunnies

88B

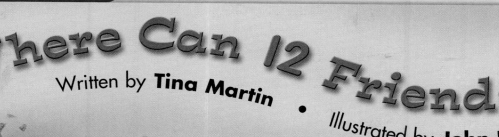

Where Can 12 Friends Play?

Written by **Tina Martin**　·　Illustrated by **John Patience**

Read Together

This Math Storybook belongs to

_____

3A

Can **2** birds play in this tree?
Yes, they can, as you can see.
2 birds can play in this tree.

Can **2** squirrels also play in this tree?
Yes, they can, as you can see.
2 birds and **2** squirrels
can play in this tree.

3C

Can **3** bears also play in this tree?
Yes, they can, as you can see.
2 birds and **2** squirrels and
3 bears can play in this tree.

Can **5** elephants also play in this tree?
There is no room, as you can see!
They need a place where
12 friends can be.

3E

Can **12** friends play around this tree?
Yes, they can, as you can see.
12 friends can play around this tree.

Name_____

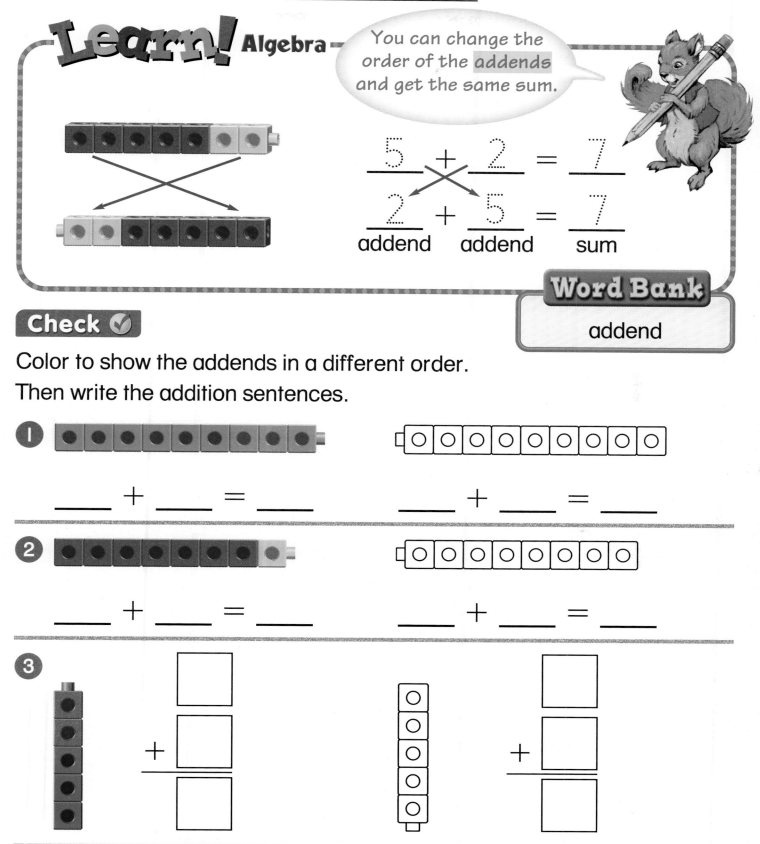

Learn! Algebra

You can change the order of the **addends** and get the same sum.

$$\frac{5}{\text{addend}} + \frac{2}{\text{addend}} = \frac{7}{\text{sum}}$$

$$\frac{2}{} + \frac{5}{} = \frac{7}{}$$

Word Bank

addend

Check ✓

Color to show the addends in a different order.
Then write the addition sentences.

1

___ + ___ = ___   ___ + ___ = ___

2

___ + ___ = ___   ___ + ___ = ___

3

☐ + ☐ = ☐   ☐ + ☐ = ☐

Think About It   Reasoning

How can you use cubes to show that
2 + 7 is the same as 7 + 2?

Chapter 3 ★ Lesson 2   ninety-three   **93**

Add. Then write an addition sentence with
the addends in a different order.

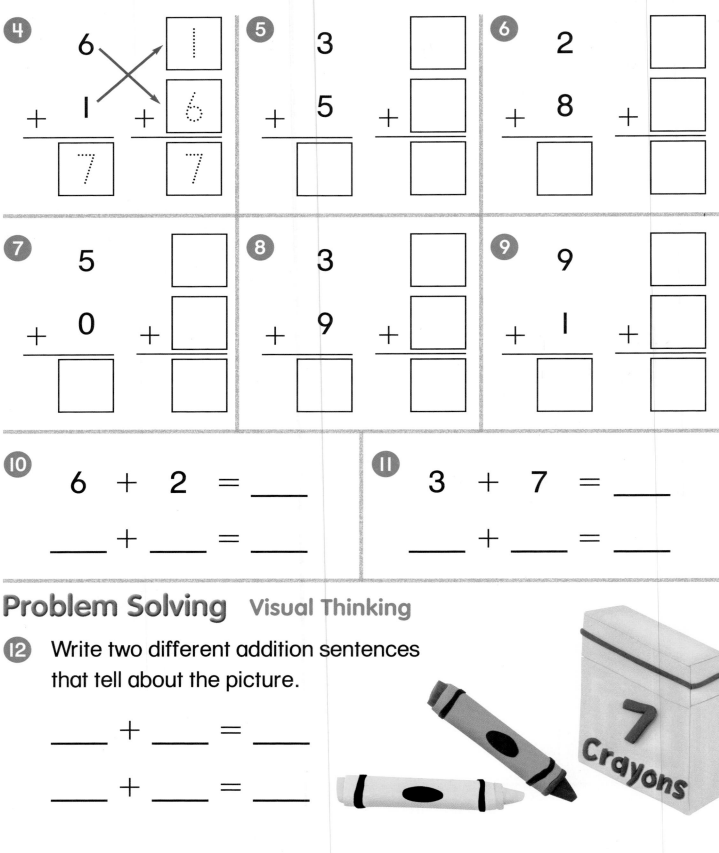

④
```
  6        1
+ 1      + 6
-----    -----
  7        7
```

⑤
```
  3        
+ 5      + 5
-----    -----
```

⑥
```
  2        
+ 8      + 8
-----    -----
```

⑦
```
  5        
+ 0      + 
-----    -----
```

⑧
```
  3        
+ 9      + 9
-----    -----
```

⑨
```
  9        
+ 1      + 1
-----    -----
```

⑩ 6 + 2 = ___

___ + ___ = ___

⑪ 3 + 7 = ___

___ + ___ = ___

Problem Solving Visual Thinking

⑫ Write two different addition sentences
that tell about the picture.

___ + ___ = ___

___ + ___ = ___

7
Crayons

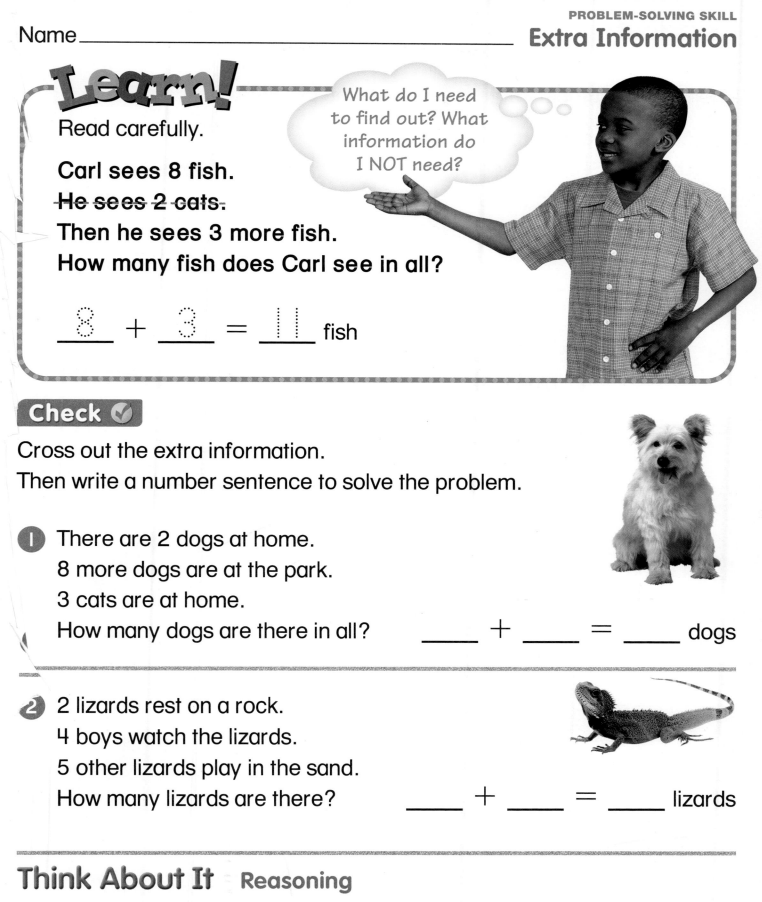

Learn!

Read carefully.

What do I need to find out? What information do I NOT need?

Carl sees 8 fish.

~~He sees 2 cats.~~

Then he sees 3 more fish.

How many fish does Carl see in all?

__8__ + __3__ = __11__ fish

Check ✓

Cross out the extra information.

Then write a number sentence to solve the problem.

1. There are 2 dogs at home.

   8 more dogs are at the park.

   3 cats are at home.

   How many dogs are there in all?   ____ + ____ = ____ dogs

2. 2 lizards rest on a rock.

   4 boys watch the lizards.

   5 other lizards play in the sand.

   How many lizards are there?   ____ + ____ = ____ lizards

Think About It   Reasoning

How do you know which sentence to cross out?

Cross out the extra information.
Then write a number sentence to solve the problem.

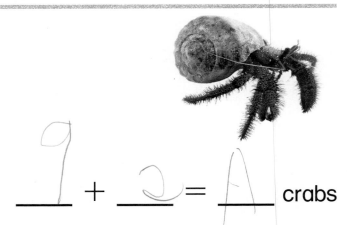

3 ~~Ali visits the pet store 2 times.~~
There are 4 orange cats.
There are 3 black cats.
How many cats are there in all?

__4__ + __3__ = __7__ cats

---

4 The dog has 6 red toys.
He also has 1 blue toy.
~~The boy has 5 toy cars.~~
How many toys does the dog have?

__6__ + __1__ = __7__ toys

---

5 3 birds are singing.
~~4 girls are singing.~~
7 more birds are asleep.
How many birds are there in all?

__3__ + __7__ = __10__ birds

---

6 9 crabs are eating.
2 more crabs are digging.
~~Sal wants to buy 2 pets.~~
How many crabs are there?

__9__ + __2__ = __11__ crabs

Home Connection Your child identified and excluded unnecessary information when solving a problem. **Home Activity** Create a word problem that contains extra information. Ask your child to identify the information that is not needed to solve the problem.

100 one hundred

Name_____

Count on to find the sum.

1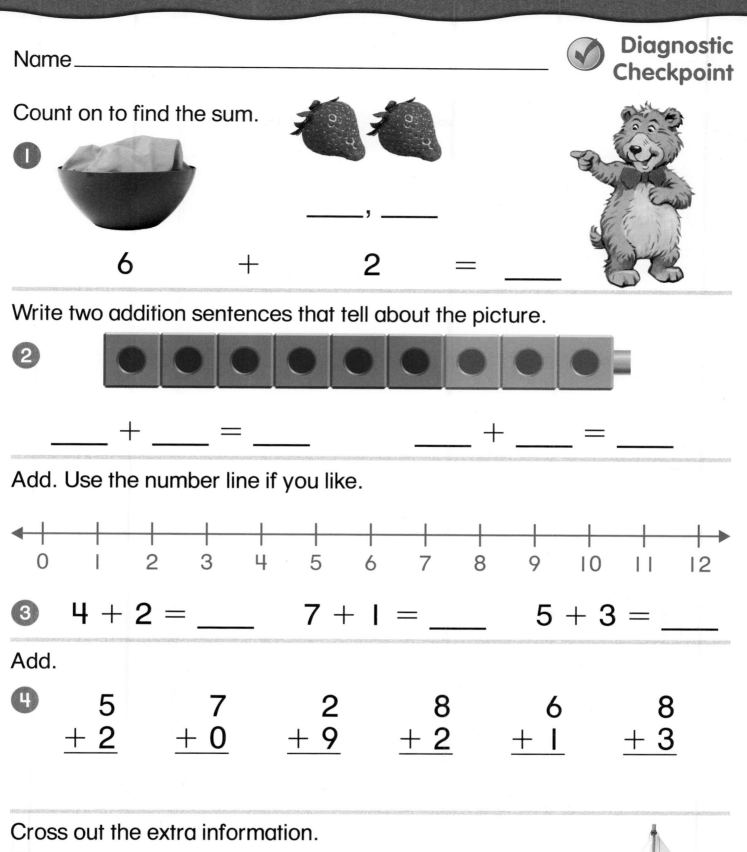

——, ——

6   +   2   = ___

Write two addition sentences that tell about the picture.

2

___ + ___ = ___   ___ + ___ = ___

Add. Use the number line if you like.

0 1 2 3 4 5 6 7 8 9 10 11 12

3 4 + 2 = ___   7 + 1 = ___   5 + 3 = ___

Add.

4
5   7   2   8   6   8
+ 2   + 0   + 9   + 2   + 1   + 3

Cross out the extra information.
Then write a number sentence to solve the problem.

5 There are 7 boats in the bay.
4 girls are fishing in the bay.
2 more boats sail into the bay.
How many boats are there now?   ___ + ___ = ___ boats

What is the missing number?

1

9 is 9 and _____.

0	2	4	6
Ⓐ	Ⓑ	Ⓒ	Ⓓ

2

11 is 3 and _____.

3	4	5	8
Ⓐ	Ⓑ	Ⓒ	Ⓓ

3 Which number is less than 4?

3	5	7	9
Ⓐ	Ⓑ	Ⓒ	Ⓓ

Solve the problem.

4 5 turtles are on a rock.
I turtle swims away.
How many turtles are
on the rock now?

I turtle	2 turtles	3 turtles	4 turtles
Ⓐ	Ⓑ	Ⓒ	Ⓓ

5 How many more mice are there than cats?

I more mouse	6 more mice	7 more mice	8 more mice
Ⓐ	Ⓑ	Ⓒ	Ⓓ

Visualize

You can picture what is happening in a story problem.

 Read this story problem. Picture it in your mind.

There are 5 oranges on the tree.
There are 5 oranges under the tree.
How many oranges are there in all?

❷ Finish the picture of the story problem by drawing the oranges.

How many oranges are on the tree? _____

How many oranges are under the tree? _____

❸ Write an addition sentence for the story problem. Count the oranges in the picture to find the sum.

_____ + _____ = _____ oranges

Think About It   Reasoning

How can you use the picture to check that your answer is correct?

Draw a picture.

Then write a number sentence.

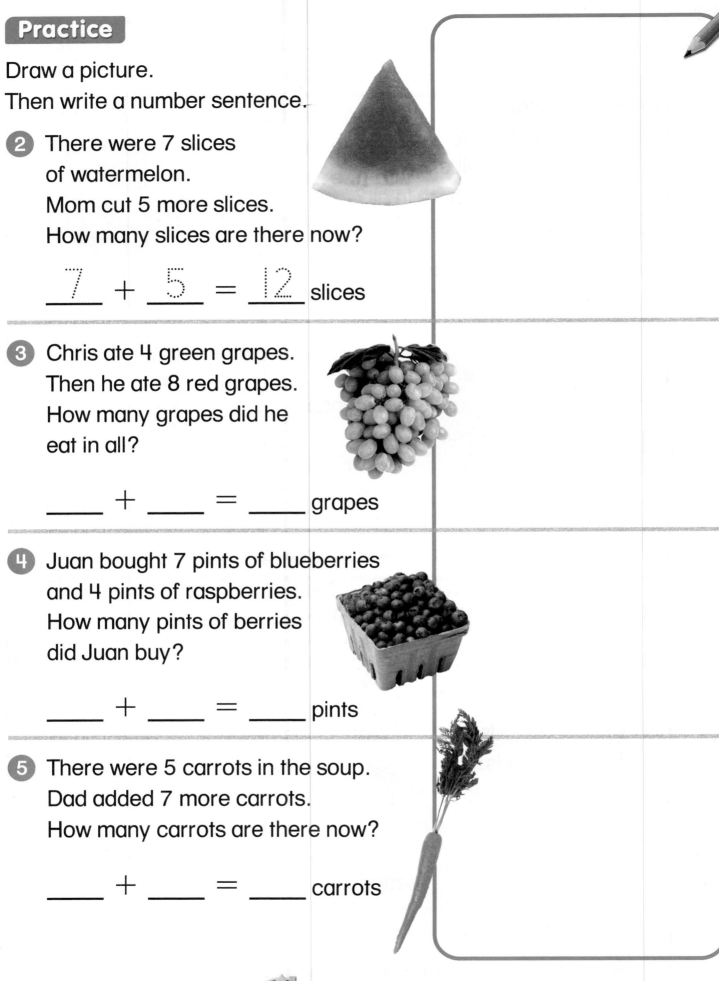

2 There were 7 slices
of watermelon.
Mom cut 5 more slices.
How many slices are there now?

__7__ + __5__ = __12__ slices

3 Chris ate 4 green grapes.
Then he ate 8 red grapes.
How many grapes did he
eat in all?

_____ + _____ = _____ grapes

4 Juan bought 7 pints of blueberries
and 4 pints of raspberries.
How many pints of berries
did Juan buy?

_____ + _____ = _____ pints

5 There were 5 carrots in the soup.
Dad added 7 more carrots.
How many carrots are there now?

_____ + _____ = _____ carrots

Home Connection Your child drew simple pictures to solve problems.
Home Activity Give your child an addition problem and ask him or her to
draw a picture to help solve it.

Name_____

Dorling Kindersley

Do You Know...
that rabbits like to eat lettuce and clover?

1 4 rabbits is _____ more than 3 rabbits.

2 2 rabbits are brown.
1 rabbit is white.
How many rabbits are there in all?

_____ rabbits

3 There are 10 rabbits.
5 of them are brown.
The rest are white.
How many rabbits are white?

___ + 5 = 10 rabbits

Fun Fact!
Tiny baby rabbits are called kittens.

4 5 big rabbits are eating.
2 ants are eating.
3 little rabbits are eating.
How many rabbits are eating?

____ + ____ = ____ rabbits

5 4 rabbits hop in the grass.
5 more rabbits join them.
How many rabbits are there in all?

There are _____ rabbits in all.

Very long rabbit ears pick up at sounds of danger!

6 3 rabbits are resting.
3 more rabbits sit with them.
How many rabbits are there in all?

There are _____ rabbits in all.

7 10 rabbits are in the garden.
The rabbits are in two groups.
One group has 7 rabbits.
How many rabbits are in the other group?

There are _____ rabbits in the other group.

8 **Writing in Math**

Draw a picture to show 10 rabbits in two groups.
Write an addition sentence for your picture.

© Pearson Education, Inc.

Home Connection Your child learned to solve problems by applying his or her math skills. **Home Activity** Talk to your child about how he or she solved the problems on these two pages.

Name_____

Use doubles to add.

1 2 + 2 = ___

2 + 3 = ___

2 3 + 3 = ___

3 + 4 = ___

Write each addition sentence.

3
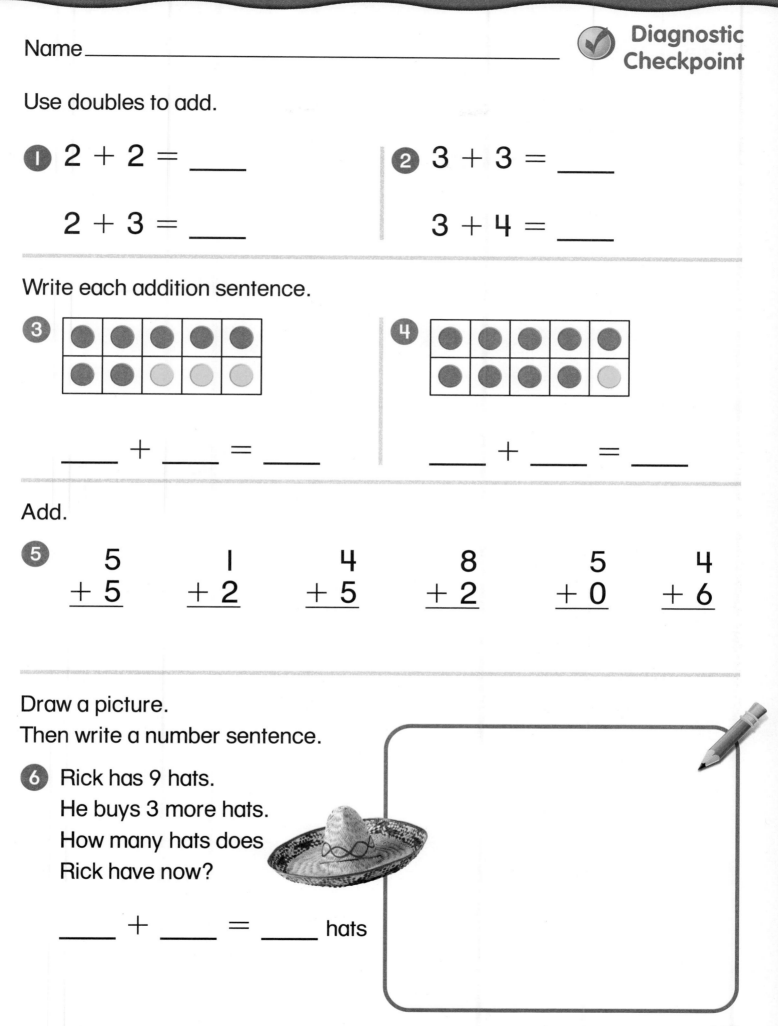

___ + ___ = ___

4

___ + ___ = ___

Add.

5

5	1	4	8	5	4
+ 5	+ 2	+ 5	+ 2	+ 0	+ 6

Draw a picture.
Then write a number sentence.

6 Rick has 9 hats.
He buys 3 more hats.
How many hats does
Rick have now?

___ + ___ = ___ hats

What is the missing number?

1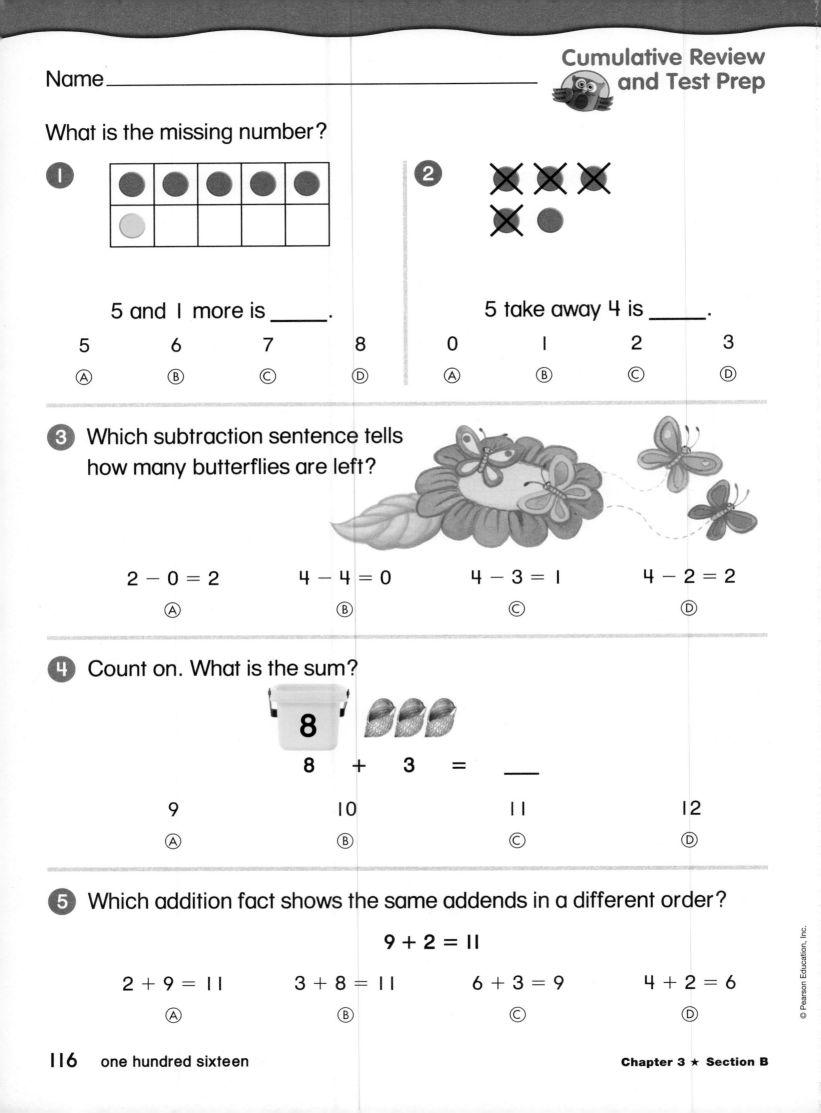

5 and 1 more is _____.

5	6	7	8
Ⓐ	Ⓑ	Ⓒ	Ⓓ

2

5 take away 4 is _____.

0	1	2	3
Ⓐ	Ⓑ	Ⓒ	Ⓓ

3 Which subtraction sentence tells how many butterflies are left?

$2 - 0 = 2$	$4 - 4 = 0$	$4 - 3 = 1$	$4 - 2 = 2$
Ⓐ	Ⓑ	Ⓒ	Ⓓ

4 Count on. What is the sum?

8

$8 + 3 = $ ___

9	10	11	12
Ⓐ	Ⓑ	Ⓒ	Ⓓ

5 Which addition fact shows the same addends in a different order?

$9 + 2 = 11$

$2 + 9 = 11$	$3 + 8 = 11$	$6 + 3 = 9$	$4 + 2 = 6$
Ⓐ	Ⓑ	Ⓒ	Ⓓ

Following Directions

Follow the directions.
Then tell where the children land.

1 Alex starts on 3.
Double it.

(thought bubble:) 3 + 3 = 6

Go back 5.

Alex is at ____.

2 Benito starts on 10.
Go back 9.
Add 3.

Benito is at ____.

3 Carla starts on 3.
Go back 2.
Add 5.

Carla is at ____.

4 Daniel starts on Carla's number.
Double it.
Count on 2.

Daniel is at ____.

5 **Writing in Math**

Start on 8. Write three directions so that
you land between Benito and Carla.

Home Connection Your child followed directions to solve problems.
Home Activity Give your child a series of directions to follow. Check to see
that he or she listens carefully.

Name_____

Add 1, 2, or 3 Using a Calculator

You can use a calculator to add 1, 2, or 3.

Press ON/C. Press the keys that you see below.
Then write the number you see in the display.

1. 7 + 1 = 8

2. 4 + 2 = ____

3. 5 + 2 = ____

4. 8 + 3 = ____

Press ON/C. Press the keys that you see below.
Write what the display shows each time you press = .

5. 7 + 3 = = =

Display: ____ ____ ____

6. 9 + 2 = = =

Display: ____ ____ ____

7. 1 0 + 2 = = = = = = = =

Display: ____ ____ ____ ____ ____ ____ ____ ____

Think About It   Number Sense

In Exercise 5, what number did you add
each time you pressed = ? Explain.

Home Connection Your child used a calculator to add 1, 2, or 3 to a
greater addend. **Home Activity** Ask your child to explain how to use a
calculator to find the sum of 5 + 3.

Plan How to Find the Answer

Sometimes you need to decide when to add and when to subtract.

Test-Taking Strategies

Understand the Question

Get Information for the Answer

Plan How to Find the Answer

Make Smart Choices

Use Writing in Math

1 Shannon has 7 dolls. She buys 3 more dolls. Which number sentence tells how many dolls she has now?

Ⓐ $7 + 3 = 10$

Ⓑ $7 + 2 = 9$

Ⓒ $7 - 3 = 4$

Ⓓ $10 - 3 = 7$

Plan to **add** if you are joining two groups together.

Plan to **subtract** if you are separating two groups.

Also plan to subtract if you are comparing two groups.

What does this question ask you to do?

Your Turn

Do you need to add or subtract?

Fill in the correct answer bubble.

 2 Tony has 6 markers. Maria has 8 markers. Which number sentence tells how many more markers Maria has?

Ⓐ $2 + 8 = 10$

Ⓑ $8 + 6 = 14$

Ⓒ $8 - 1 = 7$

Ⓓ $8 - 6 = 2$

 Home Connection Your child prepared for standardized tests by determining whether to add or subtract to solve a given math problem.
Home Activity Ask your child how he or she determined whether to add or subtract in Exercise 2.

Name _____

DISCOVERY CHANNEL **SCHOOL**

Read Together

Got Math?

Have you ever been to a dairy farm?
Cows are raised on dairy farms.
From cows we get the milk we drink.

"Moo"ving the Milk

Write number sentences to learn more about how
milk moves from the dairy farm to the grocery store.

1 Most dairy cows produce 7 gallons of milk a day.
One cow produced only 5 gallons.
How many more gallons does she need
to produce to catch up to the other cows?

_____ − _____ = _____ more gallons

2 Each dairy cow is milked every 12 hours.
One cow was milked 8 hours ago.
How many more hours will go by
before that cow is milked again?

_____ − _____ = _____ more hours

3 Milk goes from the dairy farm to a factory.
From there, the milk is taken to the grocery store.
How many different places is that?

_____ + _____ + _____ = _____ different places

Take It to the NET
Video and Activities
www.scottforesman.com

Home Connection Your child solved problems about milk production by
writing number sentences. **Home Activity** Ask your child to solve math
problems about drinking milk at home. For example, ask your child to find
the total number of cups of milk he or she drank in the past two days.

Count on to find the sum.

1

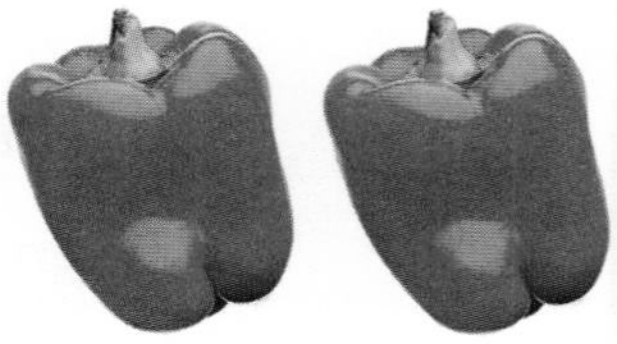

_____ , _____

5   +   2   = _____

Add. Use the number line if you like.

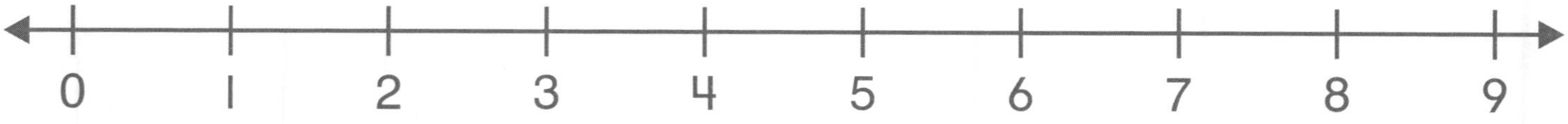

0   1   2   3   4   5   6   7   8   9

2 7 + 2 = _____   6 + 1 = _____   2 + 3 = _____

Add.

3

```
  6        8        8        7        4        9
+ 2      + 0      + 3      + 1      + 2      + 3
```

Draw a picture.
Then write a number sentence.

4 Olga has 6 dolls.
She gets 3 more dolls.
How many dolls does
Olga have now?

____ + ____ = ____ dolls

Name_____

Learn!

You can use a number line to **count back**.
Count back to subtract.

Start on 8.
Count back 2: 7, 6.

$$8 - 2 = \underline{6}$$

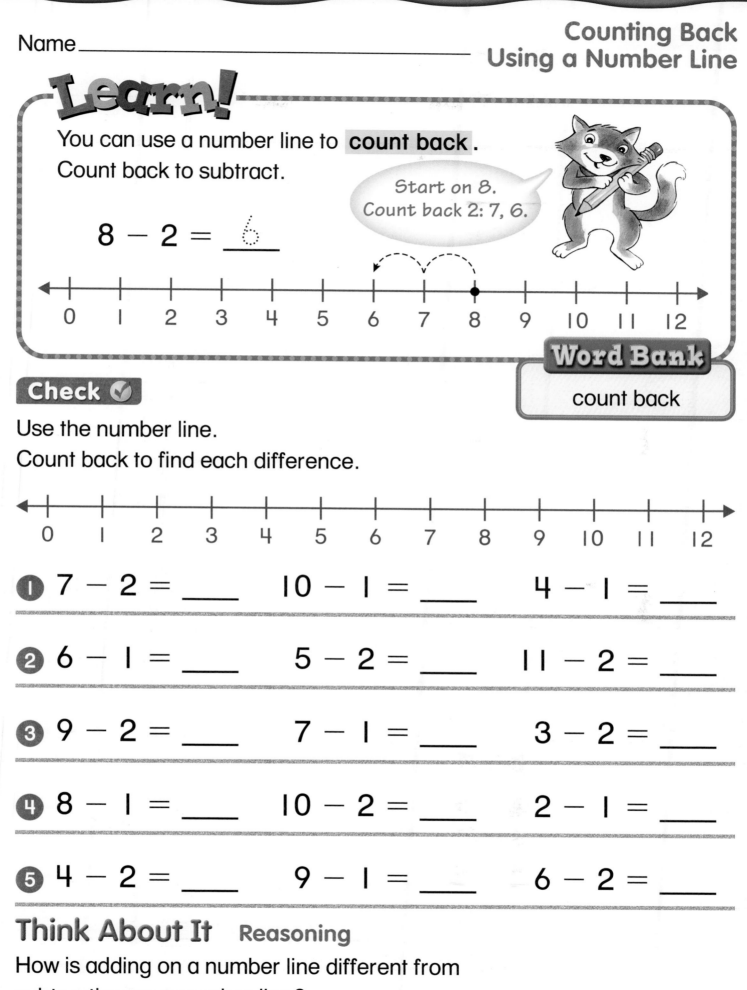

0 1 2 3 4 5 6 7 8 9 10 11 12

Word Bank

count back

Check ✓

Use the number line.
Count back to find each difference.

0 1 2 3 4 5 6 7 8 9 10 11 12

1 $7 - 2 = $ ___ $10 - 1 = $ ___ $4 - 1 = $ ___

2 $6 - 1 = $ ___ $5 - 2 = $ ___ $11 - 2 = $ ___

3 $9 - 2 = $ ___ $7 - 1 = $ ___ $3 - 2 = $ ___

4 $8 - 1 = $ ___ $10 - 2 = $ ___ $2 - 1 = $ ___

5 $4 - 2 = $ ___ $9 - 1 = $ ___ $6 - 2 = $ ___

Think About It   Reasoning

How is adding on a number line different from
subtracting on a number line?

Count back to subtract.
Use the number line if you like.

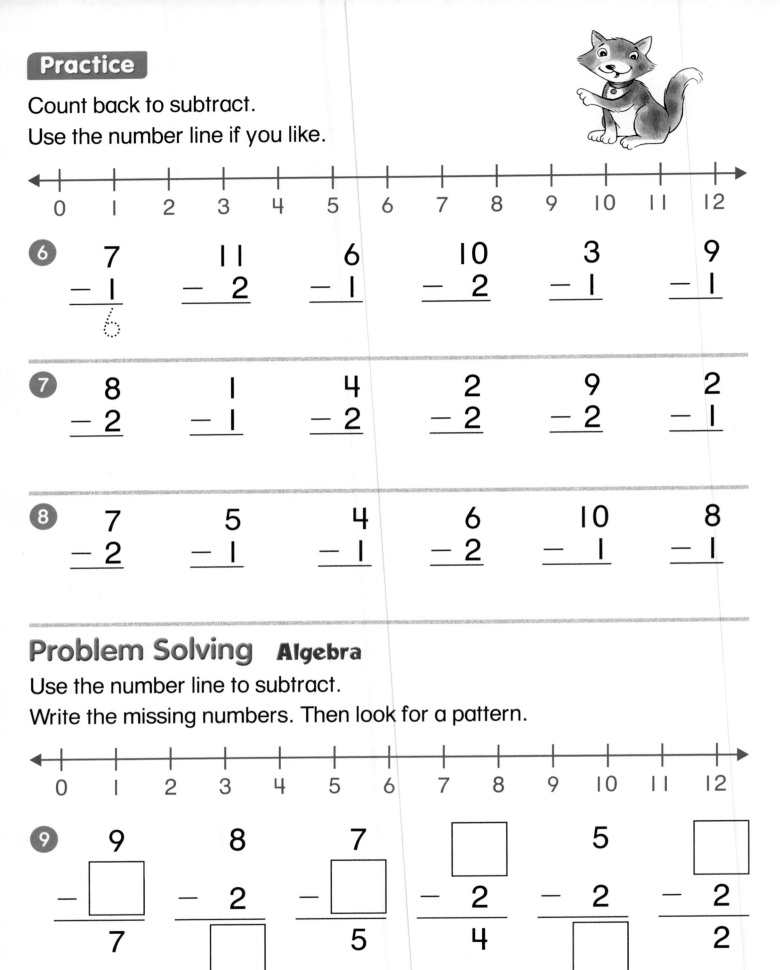

Number line: 0 1 2 3 4 5 6 7 8 9 10 11 12

6.

$$7 - 1 = 6$$ $$11 - 2$$ $$6 - 1$$ $$10 - 2$$ $$3 - 1$$ $$9 - 1$$

7.

$$8 - 2$$ $$1 - 1$$ $$4 - 2$$ $$2 - 2$$ $$9 - 2$$ $$2 - 1$$

8.

$$7 - 2$$ $$5 - 1$$ $$4 - 1$$ $$6 - 2$$ $$10 - 1$$ $$8 - 1$$

Problem Solving   Algebra

Use the number line to subtract.
Write the missing numbers. Then look for a pattern.

Number line: 0 1 2 3 4 5 6 7 8 9 10 11 12

9.

$$9 - \square = 7$$ $$8 - 2 = \square$$ $$7 - \square = 5$$ $$\square - 2 = 4$$ $$5 - 2 = \square$$ $$\square - 2 = 2$$

Home Connection Your child used a number line to count back 1 and 2.
Home Activity Point to a number greater than 2 on the number line at the top of this page. Ask your child to count back 1 or 2 from that number.

126   one hundred twenty-six

Name_____

Learn!

You can count back to subtract 1 or 2.

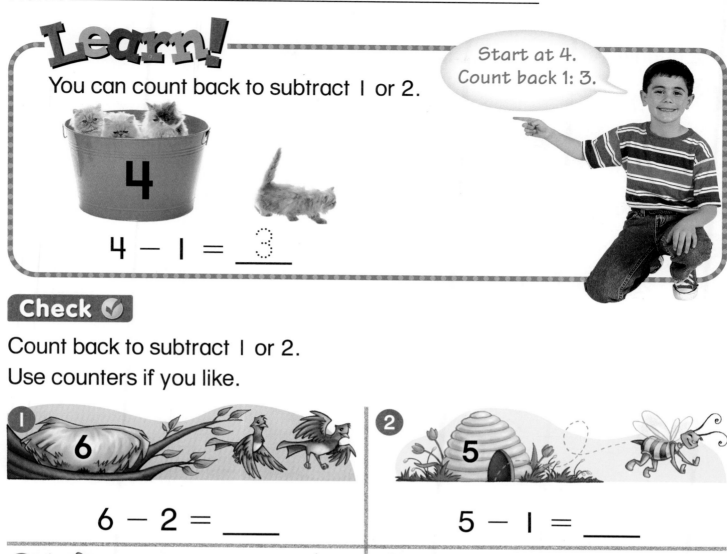

Start at 4.
Count back 1: 3.

$4 - 1 = \underline{3}$

Check ✓

Count back to subtract 1 or 2.
Use counters if you like.

1 6

$6 - 2 = \underline{}$

2 5

$5 - 1 = \underline{}$

3 8

$8 - 2 = \underline{}$

4 3

$3 - 2 = \underline{}$

5 10

$10 - 2 = \underline{}$

6 7

$7 - 1 = \underline{}$

Think About It   Reasoning

Is it easier to count back for $7 - 2$ or $7 - 4$? Explain.

Count back to subtract.
Use counters if you like.

Start at 9.
Count back 1: 8.

7

$$
\begin{array}{r} 9 \\ -\ 1 \\ \hline 8 \end{array}
$$

9

8

$$
\begin{array}{r} 6 \\ -\ 2 \\ \hline \end{array}
$$
$$
\begin{array}{r} 5 \\ -\ 1 \\ \hline \end{array}
$$
$$
\begin{array}{r} 2 \\ -\ 2 \\ \hline \end{array}
$$
$$
\begin{array}{r} 8 \\ -\ 1 \\ \hline \end{array}
$$
$$
\begin{array}{r} 4 \\ -\ 2 \\ \hline \end{array}
$$
$$
\begin{array}{r} 1 \\ -\ 1 \\ \hline \end{array}
$$

9

$$
\begin{array}{r} 6 \\ -\ 1 \\ \hline \end{array}
$$
$$
\begin{array}{r} 11 \\ -\ 2 \\ \hline \end{array}
$$
$$
\begin{array}{r} 10 \\ -\ 1 \\ \hline \end{array}
$$
$$
\begin{array}{r} 3 \\ -\ 1 \\ \hline \end{array}
$$
$$
\begin{array}{r} 7 \\ -\ 2 \\ \hline \end{array}
$$
$$
\begin{array}{r} 7 \\ -\ 1 \\ \hline \end{array}
$$

10

$$
\begin{array}{r} 2 \\ -\ 1 \\ \hline \end{array}
$$
$$
\begin{array}{r} 5 \\ -\ 2 \\ \hline \end{array}
$$
$$
\begin{array}{r} 8 \\ -\ 2 \\ \hline \end{array}
$$
$$
\begin{array}{r} 9 \\ -\ 2 \\ \hline \end{array}
$$
$$
\begin{array}{r} 4 \\ -\ 1 \\ \hline \end{array}
$$
$$
\begin{array}{r} 10 \\ -\ 2 \\ \hline \end{array}
$$

Problem Solving   Number Sense

Use the clues to answer each question.

11 Joy counted back 2.
Her answer was 7.
On what number did
Joy start?

_____

12 Mick counted back 1.
His answer was 9.
On what number did
Mick start?

_____

© Pearson Education, Inc.

Home Connection Your child counted back to subtract 1 or 2.
Home Activity Ask your child to explain how to count back to show 8 − 2.

128   one hundred twenty-eight

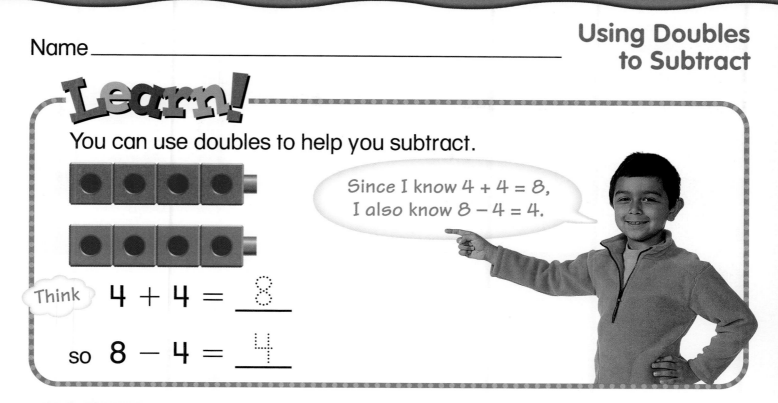

Learn!

You can use doubles to help you subtract.

Since I know $4 + 4 = 8$,
I also know $8 - 4 = 4$.

Think $4 + 4 = \underline{8}$

so $8 - 4 = \underline{4}$

Check ✓

Add the doubles.

Then use the doubles to help you subtract.

1

Think $3 + 3 = \underline{}$

so $6 - 3 = \underline{}$

2

Think $5 + 5 = \underline{}$

so $10 - 5 = \underline{}$

3

Think $6 + 6 = \underline{}$

so $12 - 6 = \underline{}$

4

Think $2 + 2 = \underline{}$

so $4 - 2 = \underline{}$

Think About It   Number Sense

Can doubles help you subtract $12 - 5$? Explain.

Add the doubles.

Then use the doubles to help you subtract.

If 5 + 5 = 10,
then 10 − 5 = 5.

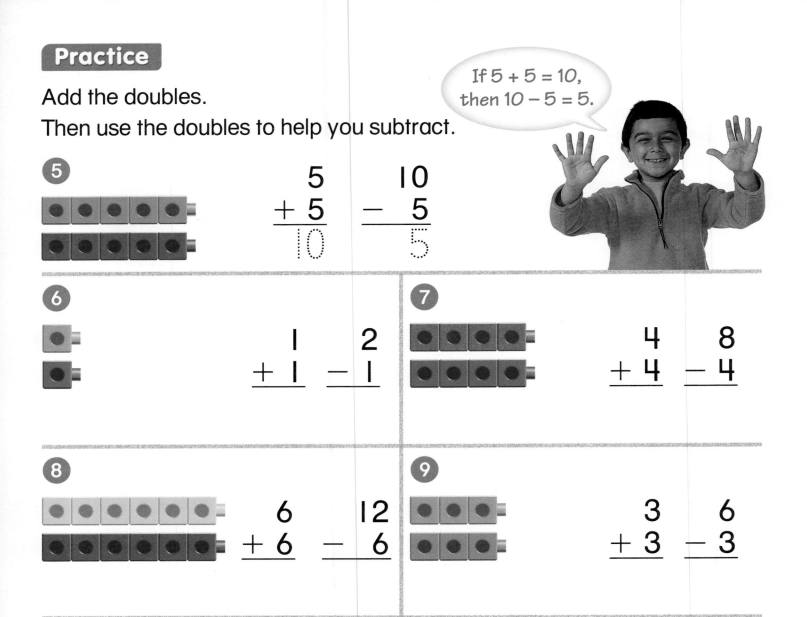

5

$$\begin{array}{r} 5 \\ + 5 \\ \hline 10 \end{array}$$
$$\begin{array}{r} 10 \\ - 5 \\ \hline 5 \end{array}$$

6

$$\begin{array}{r} 1 \\ + 1 \\ \hline \end{array}$$
$$\begin{array}{r} 2 \\ - 1 \\ \hline \end{array}$$

7

$$\begin{array}{r} 4 \\ + 4 \\ \hline \end{array}$$
$$\begin{array}{r} 8 \\ - 4 \\ \hline \end{array}$$

8

$$\begin{array}{r} 6 \\ + 6 \\ \hline \end{array}$$
$$\begin{array}{r} 12 \\ - 6 \\ \hline \end{array}$$

9

$$\begin{array}{r} 3 \\ + 3 \\ \hline \end{array}$$
$$\begin{array}{r} 6 \\ - 3 \\ \hline \end{array}$$

Problem Solving   Visual Thinking

Write an addition sentence and a
subtraction sentence for the picture.

10

___ + ___ = ___

___ − ___ = ___

Home Connection Your child used doubles to subtract. **Home Activity**
Ask your child to use buttons or other small objects to show a doubles fact.
Then have him or her name the subtraction problem that can be solved
using the doubles fact.

Reading for Math Success

Identify the Main Idea

Knowing the main idea in a story problem can help you solve it.

1 Read this story problem.

**There were 8 apples in a bowl.
Mike ate 2 apples.
How many apples are left?**

2 Circle what this story is all about.

a bowl

apples

a girl

3 Circle the main idea in the story problem.

   a. Mike likes apples.

   b. How many apples are left?

   c. Apples are in a bowl.

4 How many apples were in the bowl? _____

How many apples did Mike eat? _____

5 Solve this story problem.
   Write a subtraction sentence about the main idea.

   _____ − _____ = _____ apples

Think About It Reasoning

Why did you subtract to solve this
story problem?

6 Read this story problem.

A farmer had 6 pumpkins.
He sold 5 pumpkins.
How many pumpkins are left?

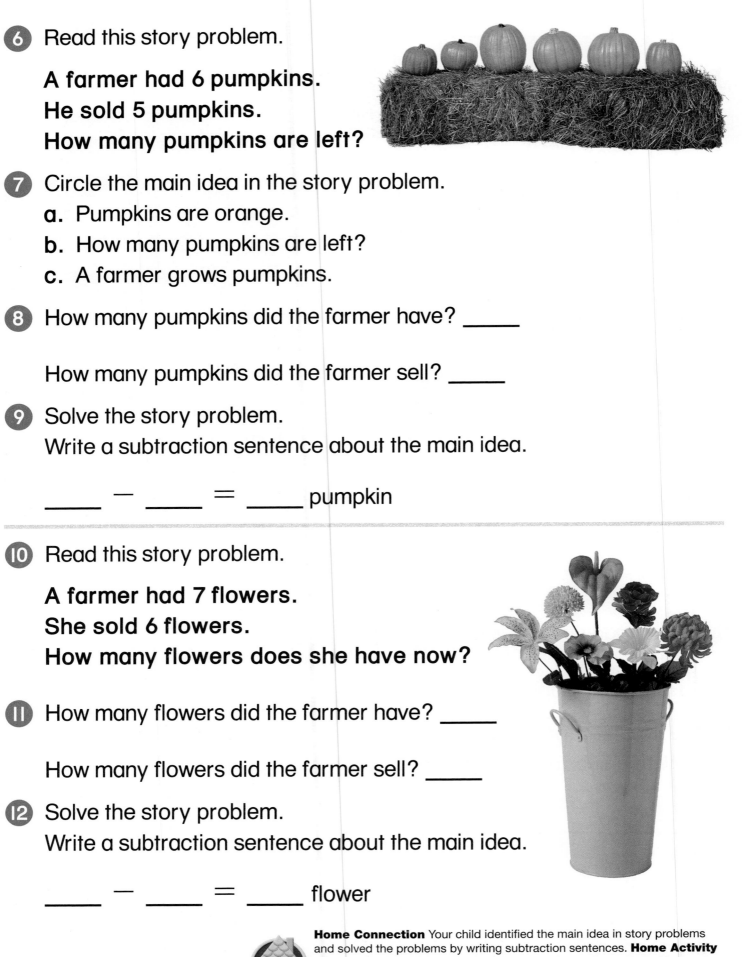

7 Circle the main idea in the story problem.
  a. Pumpkins are orange.
  b. How many pumpkins are left?
  c. A farmer grows pumpkins.

8 How many pumpkins did the farmer have? _____

How many pumpkins did the farmer sell? _____

9 Solve the story problem.
Write a subtraction sentence about the main idea.

_____ — _____ = _____ pumpkin

---

10 Read this story problem.

A farmer had 7 flowers.
She sold 6 flowers.
How many flowers does she have now?

11 How many flowers did the farmer have? _____

How many flowers did the farmer sell? _____

12 Solve the story problem.
Write a subtraction sentence about the main idea.

_____ — _____ = _____ flower

Write a Number Sentence

Learn! Algebra

There are 8 children on the bus.
2 children get off the bus.
How many children are left?

Read and Understand

You need to find how many children are left on the bus.

Plan and Solve

Write a subtraction sentence.
Count back to find the difference.

___8___ — ___2___ = ___6___ children

Look Back and Check

Does your answer make sense?

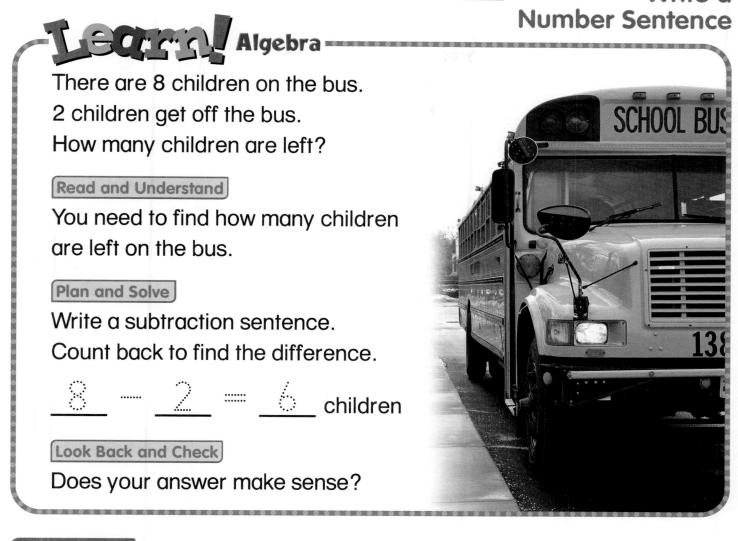

Check ✓

Write a subtraction sentence to answer the question.

1 There are 5 children playing with jacks.
2 children are playing with clay.
How many more children are
playing with jacks than with clay?

_____ — _____ = _____ more children

Think About It   Reasoning

How can you prove that your answer is correct?

Write a subtraction sentence to answer each question.

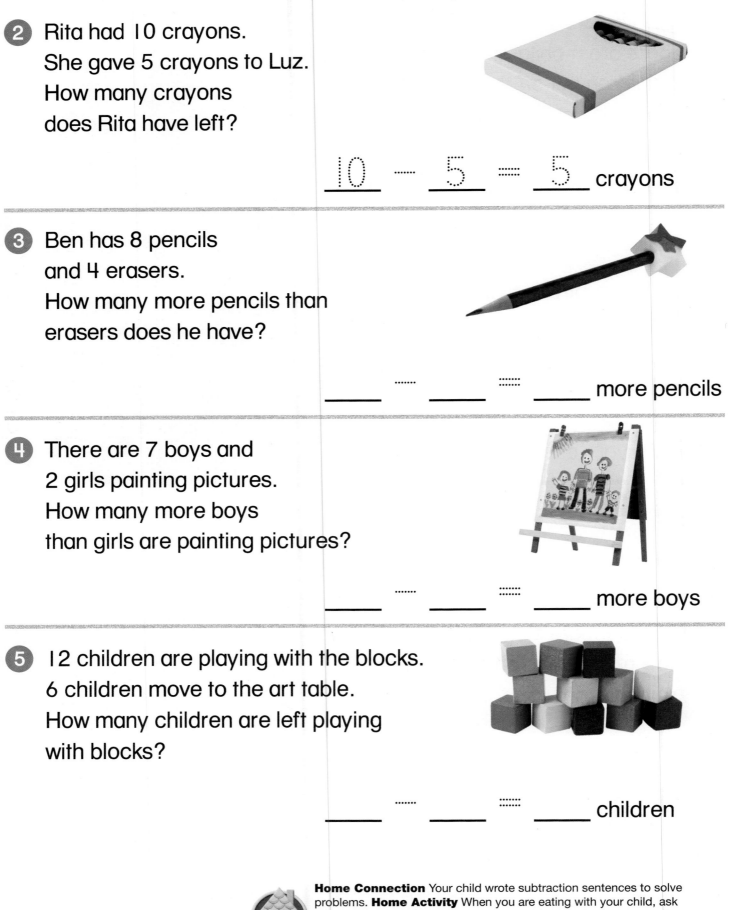

2 Rita had 10 crayons.
She gave 5 crayons to Luz.
How many crayons
does Rita have left?

$\underline{10} - \underline{5} = \underline{5}$ crayons

3 Ben has 8 pencils
and 4 erasers.
How many more pencils than
erasers does he have?

_____ − _____ = _____ more pencils

4 There are 7 boys and
2 girls painting pictures.
How many more boys
than girls are painting pictures?

_____ − _____ = _____ more boys

5 12 children are playing with the blocks.
6 children move to the art table.
How many children are left playing
with blocks?

_____ − _____ = _____ children

© Pearson Education, Inc.

Home Connection Your child wrote subtraction sentences to solve
problems. **Home Activity** When you are eating with your child, ask
questions such as, "How many crackers did you have? How many did you
eat? How many do you have left?" Have your child write subtraction
sentences for each problem.

Name_____

Count back to subtract.
Use counters if you like.

①

3 − 2 = ___

②

8 − 1 = ___

Add the doubles.
Then use the doubles to help you subtract.

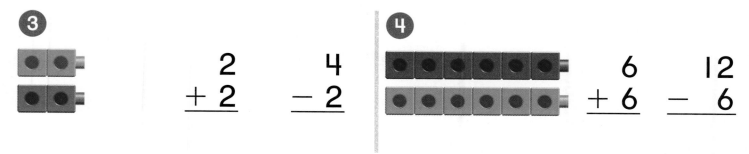

③

$$\begin{array}{r} 2 \\ +2 \\ \hline \end{array}$$
$$\begin{array}{r} 4 \\ -2 \\ \hline \end{array}$$

④

$$\begin{array}{r} 6 \\ +6 \\ \hline \end{array}$$
$$\begin{array}{r} 12 \\ -6 \\ \hline \end{array}$$

Count back to subtract.
Use the number line if you like.

←—|—|—|—|—|—|—|—|—|—|—|—|—|→
  0 1 2 3 4 5 6 7 8 9 10 11 12

⑤ 7 − 2 = ___   10 − 1 = ___   2 − 2 = ___

Write a subtraction sentence to answer the question.

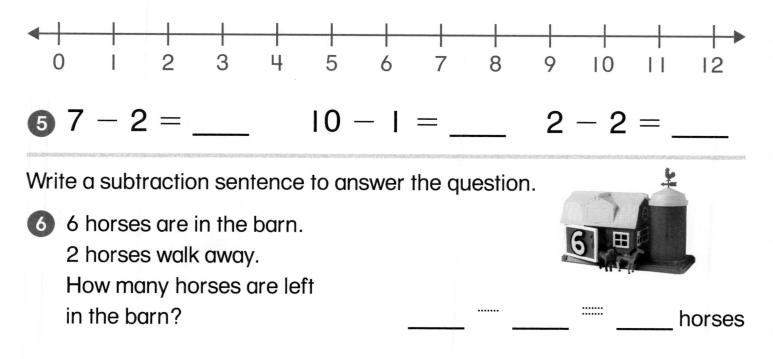

⑥ 6 horses are in the barn.
2 horses walk away.
How many horses are left
in the barn?

___ ___ ___ horses

Name_____

What is the missing number?

1

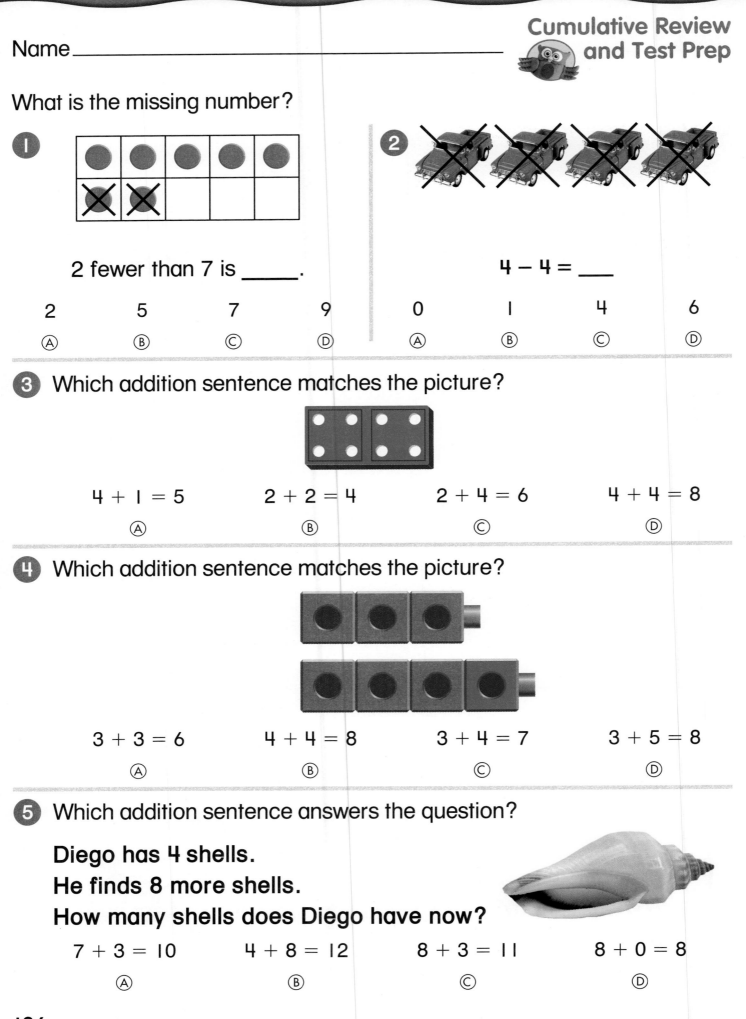

2 fewer than 7 is _____.

2	5	7	9
Ⓐ	Ⓑ	Ⓒ	Ⓓ

2

$4 - 4 = $ ___

0	1	4	6
Ⓐ	Ⓑ	Ⓒ	Ⓓ

3 Which addition sentence matches the picture?

$4 + 1 = 5$	$2 + 2 = 4$	$2 + 4 = 6$	$4 + 4 = 8$
Ⓐ	Ⓑ	Ⓒ	Ⓓ

4 Which addition sentence matches the picture?

$3 + 3 = 6$	$4 + 4 = 8$	$3 + 4 = 7$	$3 + 5 = 8$
Ⓐ	Ⓑ	Ⓒ	Ⓓ

5 Which addition sentence answers the question?

Diego has 4 shells.
He finds 8 more shells.
How many shells does Diego have now?

$7 + 3 = 10$	$4 + 8 = 12$	$8 + 3 = 11$	$8 + 0 = 8$
Ⓐ	Ⓑ	Ⓒ	Ⓓ

Name_____

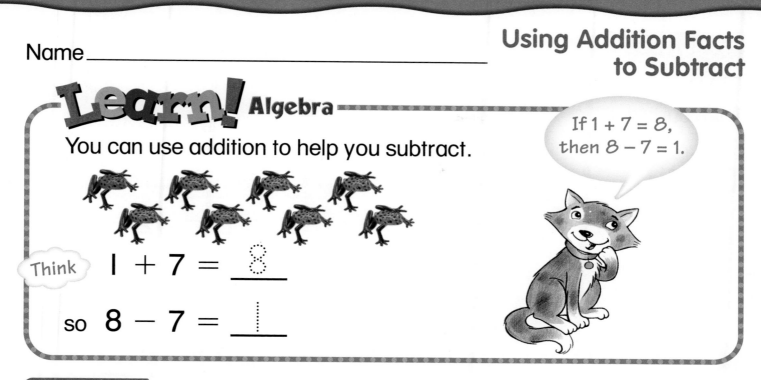

Learn! Algebra

You can use addition to help you subtract.

If 1 + 7 = 8,
then 8 − 7 = 1.

Think   1 + 7 = 8

so 8 − 7 = 1

Check ✓

Add.

Then use the addition fact to help you subtract.

1

Think   5 + 7 = ___

so 12 − 5 = ___

2

Think   9 + 2 = ___

so 11 − 9 = ___

3

Think   8 + 3 = ___

so 11 − 8 = ___

4

Think   9 + 3 = ___

so 12 − 9 = ___

Think About It   Number Sense

Which two addition facts could help you subtract 7 − 4?

Circle the addition fact that will help you subtract.
Then subtract.

5 | 10 − 4 = __6__
(4 + 6 = 10)
3 + 8 = 11

6 | 11 − 7 = ___
9 + 3 = 12
4 + 7 = 11

7 | 12 − 9 = ___
9 + 3 = 12
7 + 1 = 8

8 | 12 − 5 = ___
5 + 7 = 12
5 + 6 = 11

9 | 5 − 4 = ___
5 + 3 = 8
4 + 1 = 5

10 | 6 − 5 = ___
5 + 1 = 6
6 + 1 = 7

11 | 10 − 9 = ___
9 + 1 = 10
2 + 8 = 10

12 | 9 − 8 = ___
8 + 1 = 9
1 + 7 = 8

Problem Solving   Mental Math

13 Dan had 11 stamps.

He gave away 6 stamps.

How many stamps does Dan have left?   _____ stamps

Many Names for a Number

There are many ways to name 6. Can you think of another way?

12 − 6   2 + 4   9 − 3

Circle all of the names for each number.

1 11

(2 + 9)   5 + 6   8 + 3
1 + 1   7 + 4   10 − 1

2 7

4 + 5   10 − 3   7 − 0
12 − 6   1 + 6   3 + 4

3 9

12 − 3   4 + 4   7 + 2
11 − 2   5 − 4   1 + 8

4 12

6 + 6   9 + 3   1 + 2
10 − 2   7 + 5   8 + 4

5 Writing in Math

Make a list of different ways to name 10.
How many ways can you find?

Home Connection Your child found many ways to name different numbers.
Home Activity Have your child tell three different ways to name 8.

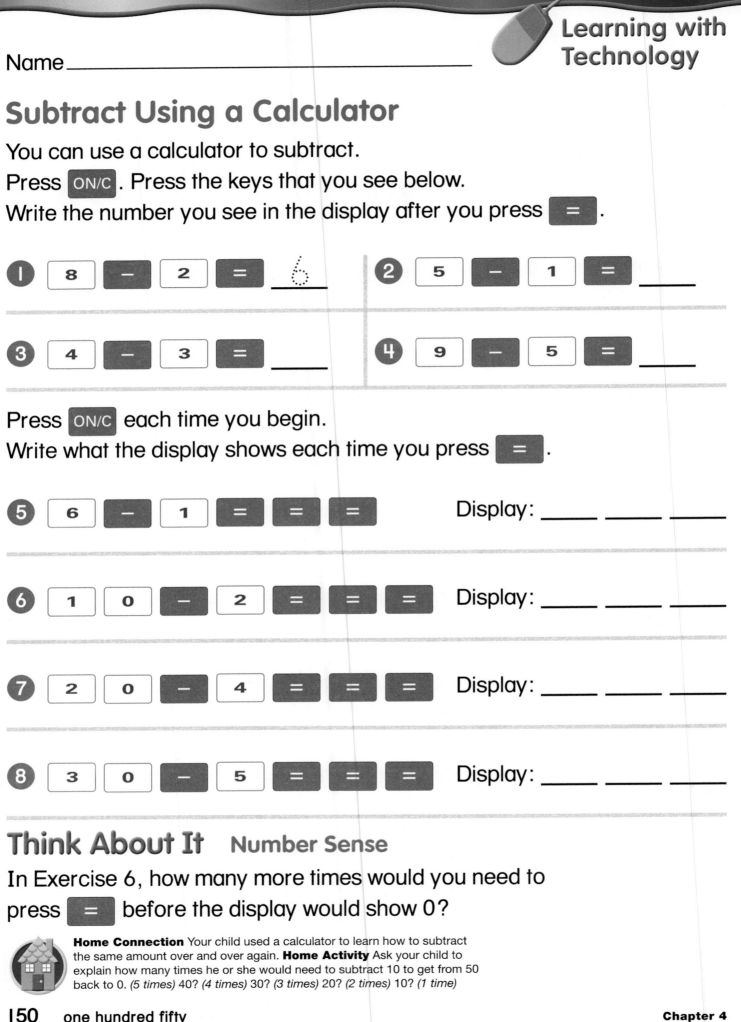

Subtract Using a Calculator

You can use a calculator to subtract.

Press ON/C. Press the keys that you see below.

Write the number you see in the display after you press =.

1 8 − 2 = 6

2 5 − 1 = ____

3 4 − 3 = ____

4 9 − 5 = ____

Press ON/C each time you begin.

Write what the display shows each time you press =.

5 6 − 1 = = =   Display: ____ ____ ____

6 1 0 − 2 = = =   Display: ____ ____ ____

7 2 0 − 4 = = =   Display: ____ ____ ____

8 3 0 − 5 = = =   Display: ____ ____ ____

Think About It   Number Sense

In Exercise 6, how many more times would you need to

press = before the display would show 0?

Home Connection Your child used a calculator to learn how to subtract the same amount over and over again. **Home Activity** Ask your child to explain how many times he or she would need to subtract 10 to get from 50 back to 0. *(5 times)* 40? *(4 times)* 30? *(3 times)* 20? *(2 times)* 10? *(1 time)*

Name_____

Make Smart Choices

When you take a math test,
you need to make good choices
and mark your answers correctly.

Test-Taking Strategies
Understand the Question
Get Information for the Answer
Plan How to Find the Answer
Make Smart Choices
Use Writing in Math

1 Use the number line.
Count back to subtract.
Fill in the answer bubble.

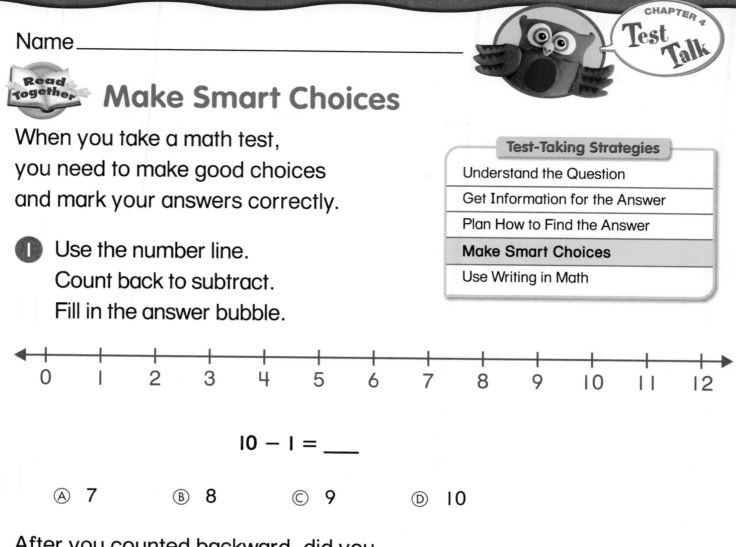

$$10 - 1 = \underline{}$$

Ⓐ 7   Ⓑ 8   Ⓒ 9   Ⓓ 10

After you counted backward, did you
fill in the correct answer bubble?

Your Turn

Solve the problem and fill in the answer bubble.

2 Use the number line. Count back to subtract.

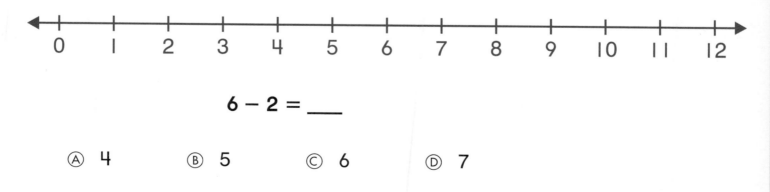

$$6 - 2 = \underline{}$$

Ⓐ 4   Ⓑ 5   Ⓒ 6   Ⓓ 7

Home Connection Your child prepared for standardized tests by learning how to
mark answer choices. **Home Activity** Ask your child how he or she knows that
the answer bubble for Exercise 2 was filled in correctly. *(Possible answer: I colored
in the bubble completely and didn't make any marks outside of the bubble.)*

Name _____

Discover Math in Your World

Countdown!

Have you ever watched a Space Shuttle launch on TV? Pretend that you are going on a flight.

Subtracting ... 3, 2, 1

Solve each problem. Use the number line to help you.

1 Your mission is supposed to last 10 days. But on Day 6, one of the computers has a problem. Mission Control tells you to land on Day 7. How many more days was your mission supposed to last?

__10__ − __7__ = ____ more days

2 There are going to be 12 flights this year. Your team is on the 10th flight. How many more flights will there be this year?

__12__ − __10__ = ____ more flights

3 There are 7 people on your mission. 1 is the commander, 1 is the pilot, and 2 are mission specialists. The rest are payload specialists. How many people are payload specialists?

__1__ + __1__ + __2__ + ____ = __7__ people in all

____ people are payload specialists.

15
14
13
12
11
10
9
8
7
6
5
4
3
2
1
0

 **Take It to the NET**
Video and Activities
www.scottforesman.com

 Home Connection Your child solved problems about an imaginary Space Shuttle mission by using a number line and by writing number sentences. **Home Activity** Ask your child to explain how using a number line helps him or her solve subtraction problems.

Chapter 4

Name _____

Count back to subtract.
Use the number line if you like.

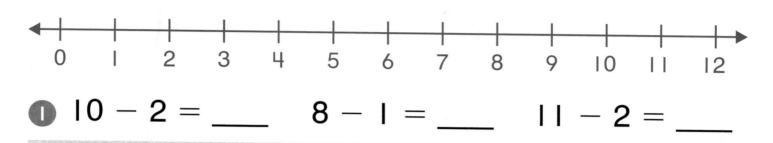

1 10 − 2 = ___   8 − 1 = ___   11 − 2 = ___

Write related addition and subtraction facts
for the picture.

2

___ + ___ = ___

___ − ___ = ___

Count back to subtract.
Use counters if you like.

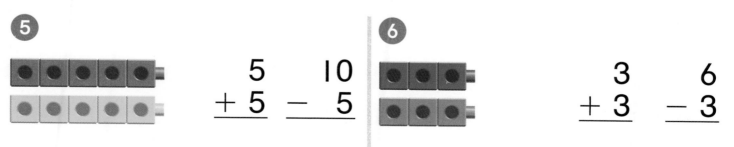

3

5 − 2 = ___

4

10 − 1 = ___

Add the doubles.
Then use the doubles to help you subtract.

5

$\begin{array}{r} 5 \\ + 5 \\ \hline \end{array}$ $\begin{array}{r} 10 \\ - 5 \\ \hline \end{array}$

6

$\begin{array}{r} 3 \\ + 3 \\ \hline \end{array}$ $\begin{array}{r} 6 \\ - 3 \\ \hline \end{array}$

Circle the addition fact that will help you subtract.
Then subtract.

7 $12 - 7 = \underline{}$

$5 + 1 = 6$

$5 + 7 = 12$

8 $11 - 8 = \underline{}$

$5 + 3 = 8$

$3 + 8 = 11$

Write the fact family.

9

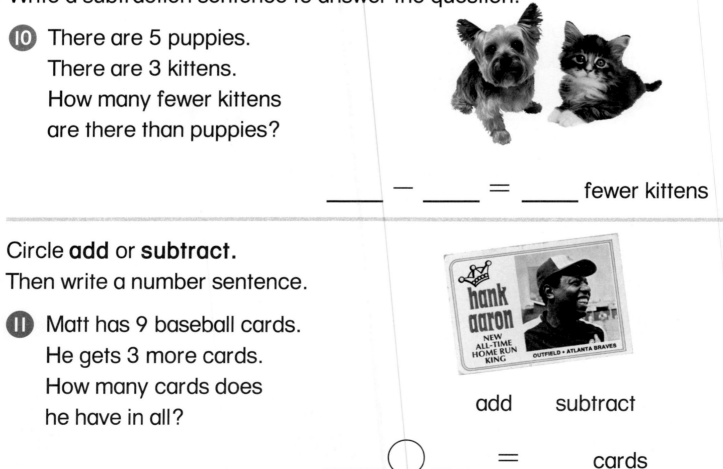

$\underline{} + \underline{} = \underline{}$ $\underline{} - \underline{} = \underline{}$

$\underline{} + \underline{} = \underline{}$ $\underline{} - \underline{} = \underline{}$

Write a subtraction sentence to answer the question.

10 There are 5 puppies.
There are 3 kittens.
How many fewer kittens
are there than puppies?

$\underline{} - \underline{} = \underline{}$ fewer kittens

Circle **add** or **subtract**.
Then write a number sentence.

11 Matt has 9 baseball cards.
He gets 3 more cards.
How many cards does
he have in all?

hank aaron
NEW ALL-TIME HOME RUN KING   OUTFIELD · ATLANTA BRAVES

add   subtract

$\underline{} \bigcirc \underline{} = \underline{}$ cards

1 Which letters show the same pattern as the toys?

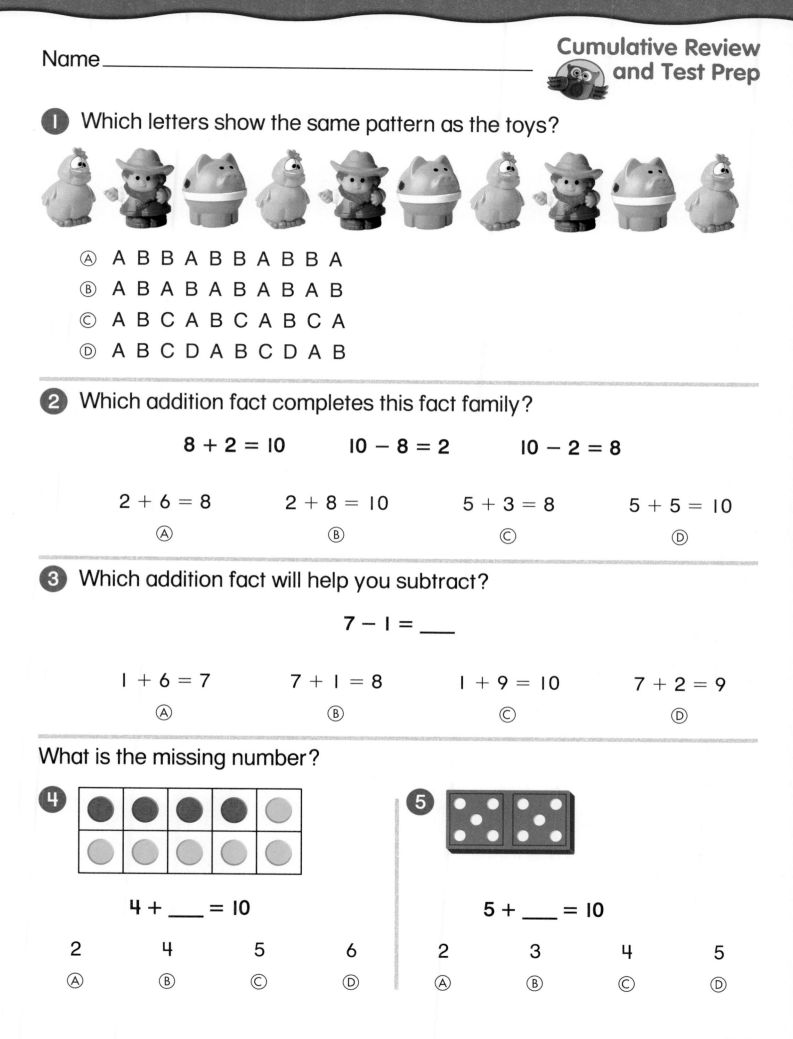

- Ⓐ A B B A B B A B B A
- Ⓑ A B A B A B A B A B
- Ⓒ A B C A B C A B C A
- Ⓓ A B C D A B C D A B

2 Which addition fact completes this fact family?

8 + 2 = 10   10 − 8 = 2   10 − 2 = 8

2 + 6 = 8   2 + 8 = 10   5 + 3 = 8   5 + 5 = 10
Ⓐ   Ⓑ   Ⓒ   Ⓓ

3 Which addition fact will help you subtract?

7 − 1 = ___

1 + 6 = 7   7 + 1 = 8   1 + 9 = 10   7 + 2 = 9
Ⓐ   Ⓑ   Ⓒ   Ⓓ

What is the missing number?

4

4 + ___ = 10

2   4   5   6
Ⓐ   Ⓑ   Ⓒ   Ⓓ

5

5 + ___ = 10

2   3   4   5
Ⓐ   Ⓑ   Ⓒ   Ⓓ

How many fewer red cubes than blue cubes?

6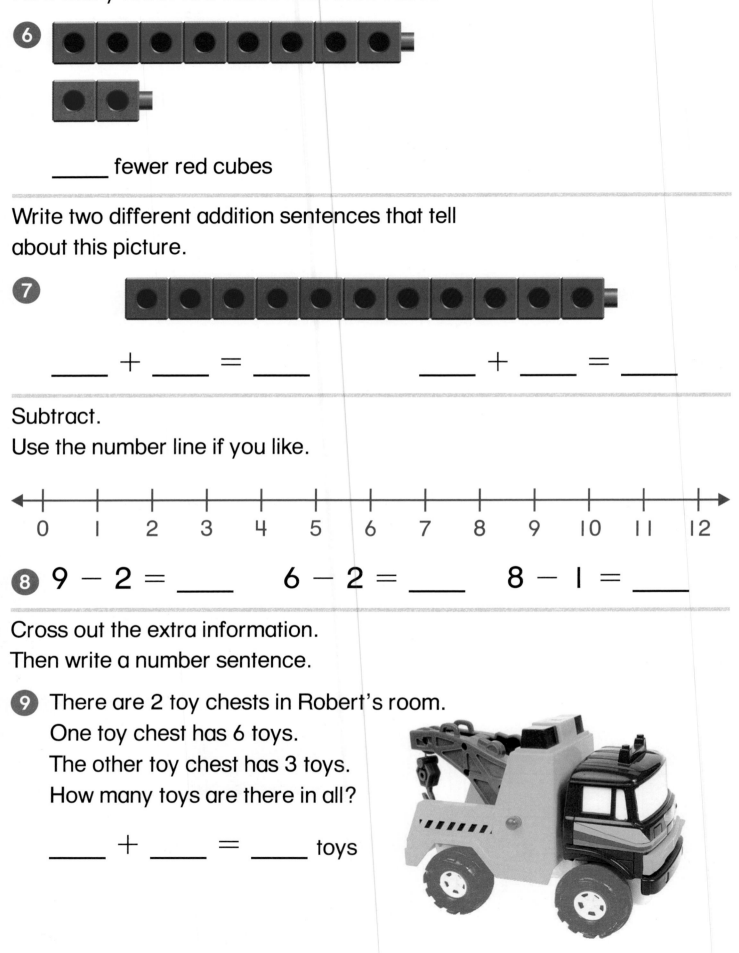

_____ fewer red cubes

Write two different addition sentences that tell
about this picture.

7

___ + ___ = ___   ___ + ___ = ___

Subtract.
Use the number line if you like.

```
◄──┼───┼───┼───┼───┼───┼───┼───┼───┼───┼───┼───┼───►
   0   1   2   3   4   5   6   7   8   9   10  11  12
```

8 9 − 2 = ___   6 − 2 = ___   8 − 1 = ___

Cross out the extra information.
Then write a number sentence.

9 There are 2 toy chests in Robert's room.
One toy chest has 6 toys.
The other toy chest has 3 toys.
How many toys are there in all?

___ + ___ = ___ toys

No Problem!

Written by Andrew Shields

Illustrated by Will Terry

This Math Storybook belongs to

_____

Life was easy for these two brothers.

If there was only I banana,
each brother got half a banana.

No problem!

5B

If there were a dozen strawberries, each brother got half a dozen.

No problem!

Even when their new baby
sister was born, no problem.

She was too little to eat fruit.

5D

But then one day, while the two brothers were sharing a dozen grapes, their little sister said,

"Hey! Where's mine?"

Uh-oh! Big problem!

But they solved it. Here's how.

If there were a dozen grapes, they did this:

If there was only | banana, they did this:

No problem!

Home-School Connection

Dear Family,

Today my class started Chapter 5, **Geometry and Fractions**. I will learn about solid figures like a cube and a cone, and also about plane shapes like a triangle and a square. I will learn about fractions and talk about halves, thirds, and fourths. Here are some of the math words I will be learning and some things we can do to help me with my math.

Love,

_____

Math Activity to Do at Home

Help your child create a plane-shapes collage. Cut out several triangles, rectangles, circles, and squares. Have your child color the shapes and use them to make a picture. Glue the shapes to a sheet of paper.

Books to Read Together

Reading math stories reinforces concepts. Look for these titles in your local library:

Rabbit and Hare Divide an Apple
By Harriet Ziefert
(Viking Penguin, 1997)

Shape Space
By Cathryn Falwell
(Houghton, 1992)

Take It to the NET
More Activities
www.scottforesman.com

My New Math Words

solid figures A solid figure is a 3-D shape.

cube   sphere   cone   rectangular prism   cylinder

plane shape A plane shape is a flat shape.

triangle   rectangle   circle   square

symmetry Two parts that match show symmetry.

line of symmetry

vertex A vertex is a corner of a solid figure or a plane shape.

face A face is the flat side of a cube or a prism.

Fraction Concentration

What You Need

12 paper squares ■

How to Play

1. Place the squares on the gameboard.
2. Take turns. Remove 2 squares.
3. If you find a match, keep both squares.
4. If you do not find a match, put the squares back.
5. Keep playing until you have made all of the matches.
6. Don't forget to concentrate!

Name _____

1 Circle all of the cylinders.

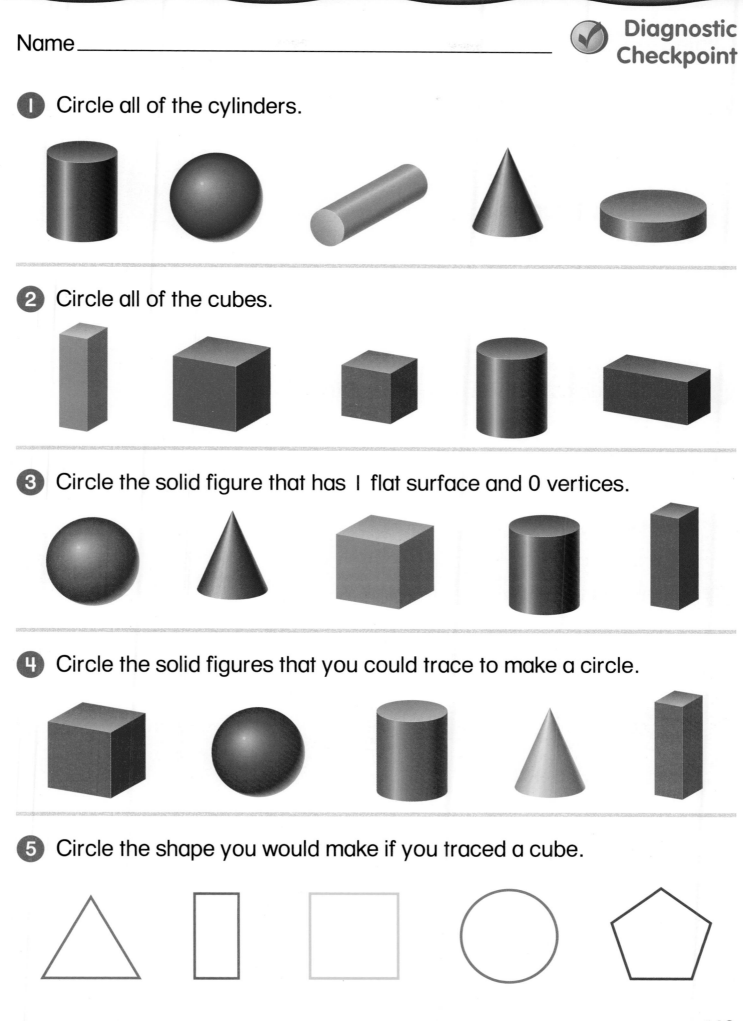

2 Circle all of the cubes.

3 Circle the solid figure that has 1 flat surface and 0 vertices.

4 Circle the solid figures that you could trace to make a circle.

5 Circle the shape you would make if you traced a cube.

1 Which number sentence answers the question?

Tim has 5 oranges.
Sally has 4 oranges.
Mom has 3 apples.
How many oranges are there in all?

$5 + 4 = 9$ $5 + 3 = 8$ $4 + 3 = 7$ $4 + 4 = 8$

Ⓐ Ⓑ Ⓒ Ⓓ

---

2 Which doubles fact will help you subtract?

$8 - 4 = $ ___

Ⓐ $2 + 2 = 4$

Ⓑ $3 + 3 = 6$

Ⓒ $4 + 4 = 8$

Ⓓ $5 + 5 = 10$

---

3 Which fact is a related subtraction fact?

$3 + 4 = 7$

Ⓐ $9 - 2 = 7$

Ⓑ $10 - 6 = 4$

Ⓒ $8 - 3 = 5$

Ⓓ $7 - 4 = 3$

---

4 Which fact completes this fact family?

$5 + 3 = 8$
$3 + 5 = 8$
$8 - 5 = 3$

Ⓐ $8 + 3 = 11$

Ⓑ $8 - 3 = 5$

Ⓒ $5 + 5 = 10$

Ⓓ $8 - 8 = 0$

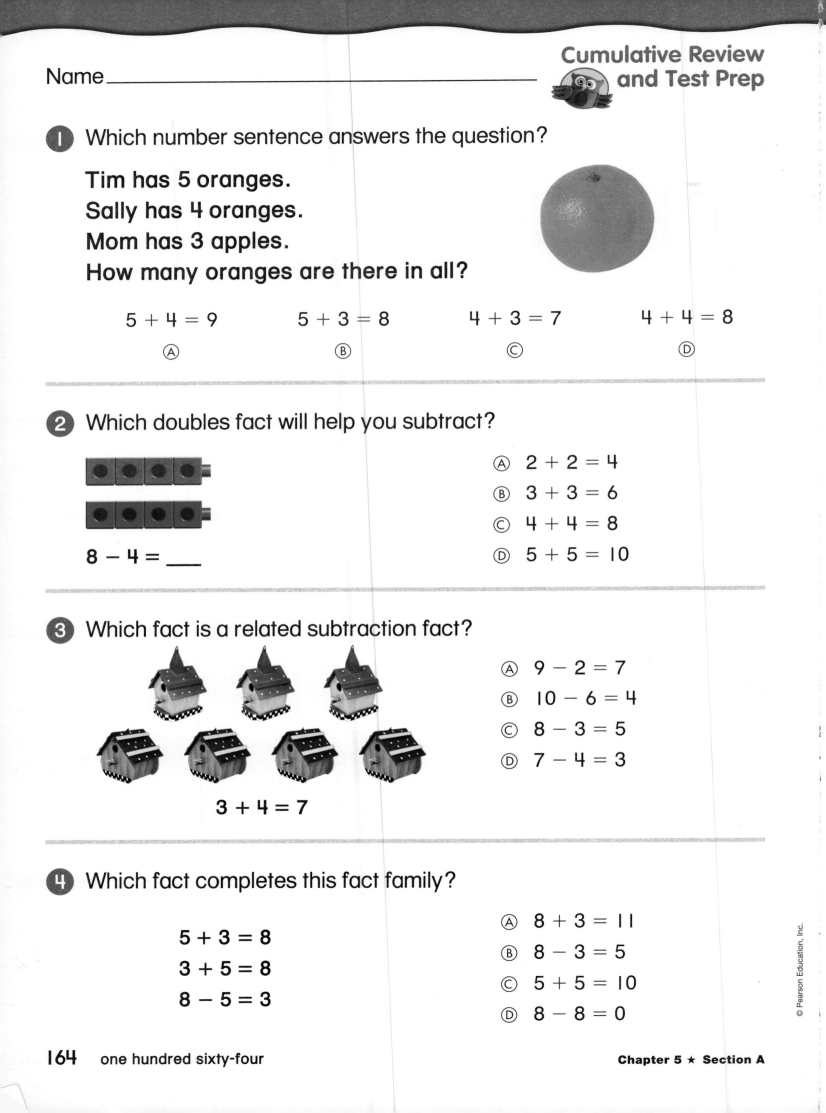

Learn!

Flat shapes are called **plane shapes** .

We see them everywhere!

triangle rectangle circle square

Word Bank

plane shape
triangle
rectangle
circle
square

Check ✓

1 Color all of the circles.

2 Color all of the squares.

3 Color all of the triangles.

4 Color all of the rectangles.

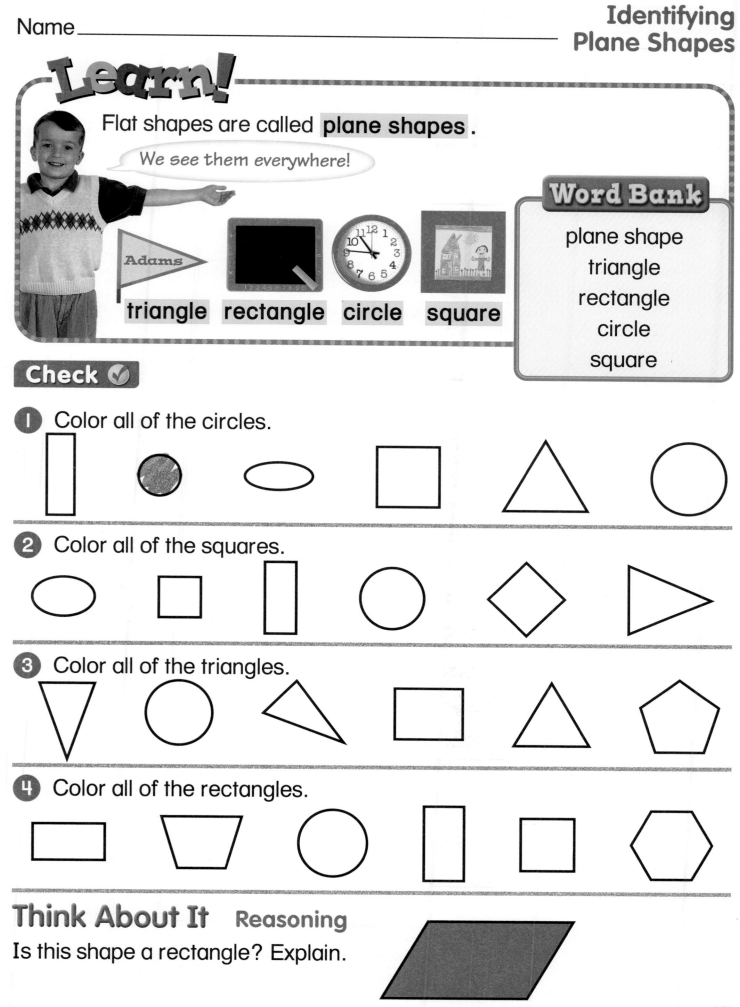

Think About It Reasoning

Is this shape a rectangle? Explain.

5 Draw a square.

6 Draw a circle.

7 Draw a rectangle.

8 Draw a triangle.

Problem Solving   Algebra

Draw the shape that comes next in the pattern.

9
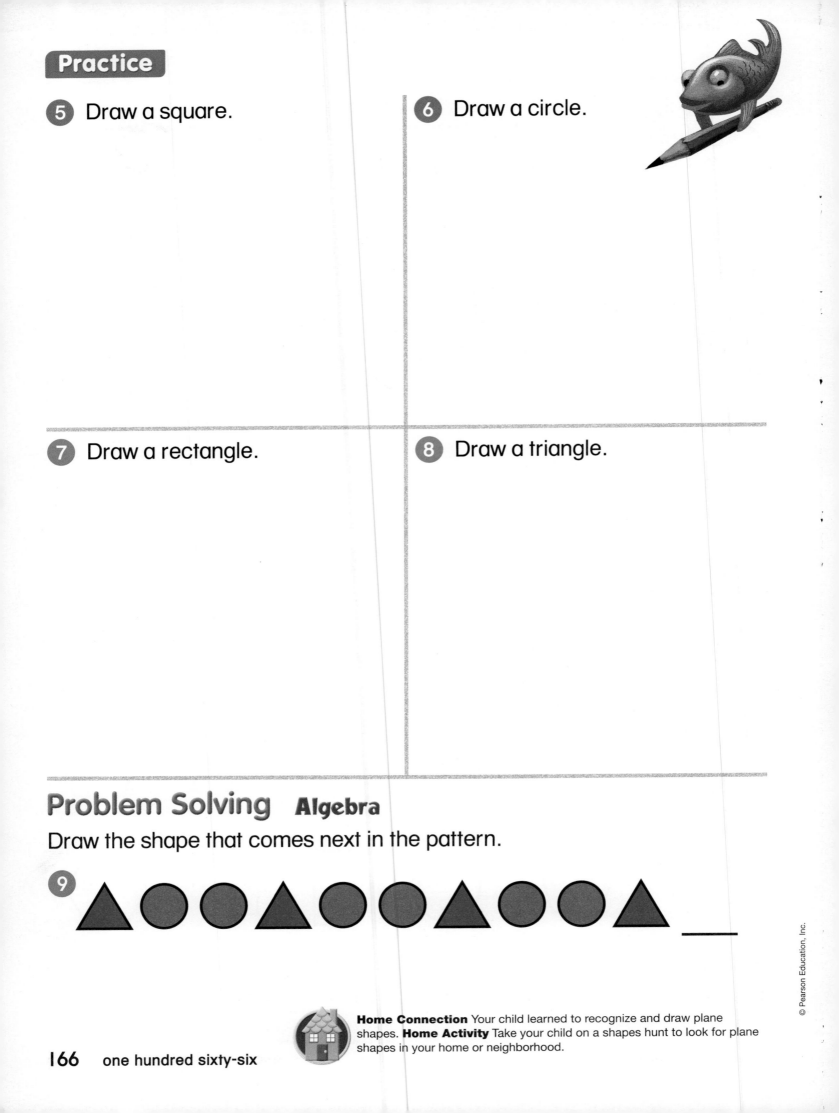

Home Connection Your child learned to recognize and draw plane shapes. **Home Activity** Take your child on a shapes hunt to look for plane shapes in your home or neighborhood.

© Pearson Education, Inc.

Name_____

Understand Graphic Sources: Lists

Look at these flowers.
How many of each flower did the children pick?

The answers are in the list below.
Read the list with your teacher.

Flowers Picked			
	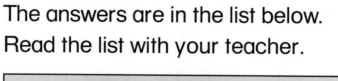		
Anna	1	2	3
Pedro	2	3	1
Yukio	3	1	2

1 How many  did Anna pick? _____

2 How many did Pedro pick? _____

3 How many did Yukio pick? _____

Think About It   Reasoning

Why might you put information in a list?

Use this list to answer the questions.

Leaves Collected			

Thomas	4	3	2
Carmen	3	2	4
Jade	2	4	3

4 How many 🍂 did Carmen collect? _____

5 How many 🍁 did Thomas collect? _____

6 How many 🍃 did Jade collect? _____

Use this list to answer the questions.

Shells Collected			
Luis	1	3	5
Alvin	3	5	1
Pam	5	1	3

7 How many 🐚 did Pam collect? _____

8 How many 🦪 did Luis collect? _____

9 How many 🐚 did Alvin collect? _____

 Home Connection Your child used information found in lists to answer questions. **Home Activity** Ask your child to explain some of the information in each list.

Learn!

1 How many ways can you make this shape using pattern blocks?

Read and Understand

You need to find all the ways to use pattern blocks to make the shape.

Plan and Solve

Make a list to keep track of the different ways you find.

Ways to Make  🔷			
	🔷	 ◆	 🔺
Way 1	1	0	0
Way 2			
Way 3			

Write how many of each shape you use.

Look Back and Check

Did you find all the ways?
How do you know?

Think About It   Reasoning

How does making an organized list help you?

2 How many ways can you make this shape using pattern blocks? Complete the list.

Ways to Make ⬡				
	⬡	⬢	◆	▲
Way 1	1	0	0	0
Way 2				
Way 3				
Way 4				
Way 5				
Way 6				
Way 7				
Way 8				

Writing in Math

3 How many ways can you use the pattern blocks to make ▲? Explain.

_____

_____

Home Connection Your child made a list of all the solutions to a problem.
Home Activity Ask your child to explain how he or she made the list in Exercise 2, above.

© Pearson Education, Inc.

Name _____

1 Circle the shape that has 3 straight sides and 3 vertices.

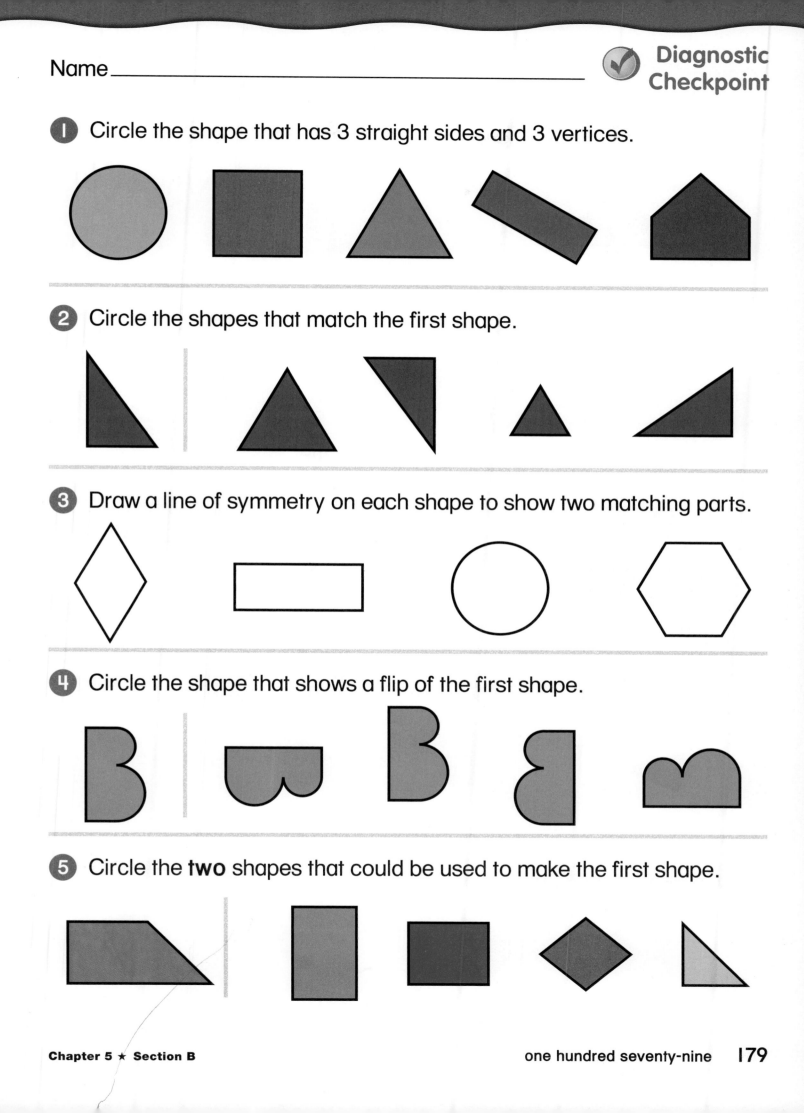

2 Circle the shapes that match the first shape.

3 Draw a line of symmetry on each shape to show two matching parts.

4 Circle the shape that shows a flip of the first shape.

5 Circle the **two** shapes that could be used to make the first shape.

Name_____

What is the missing number?

1

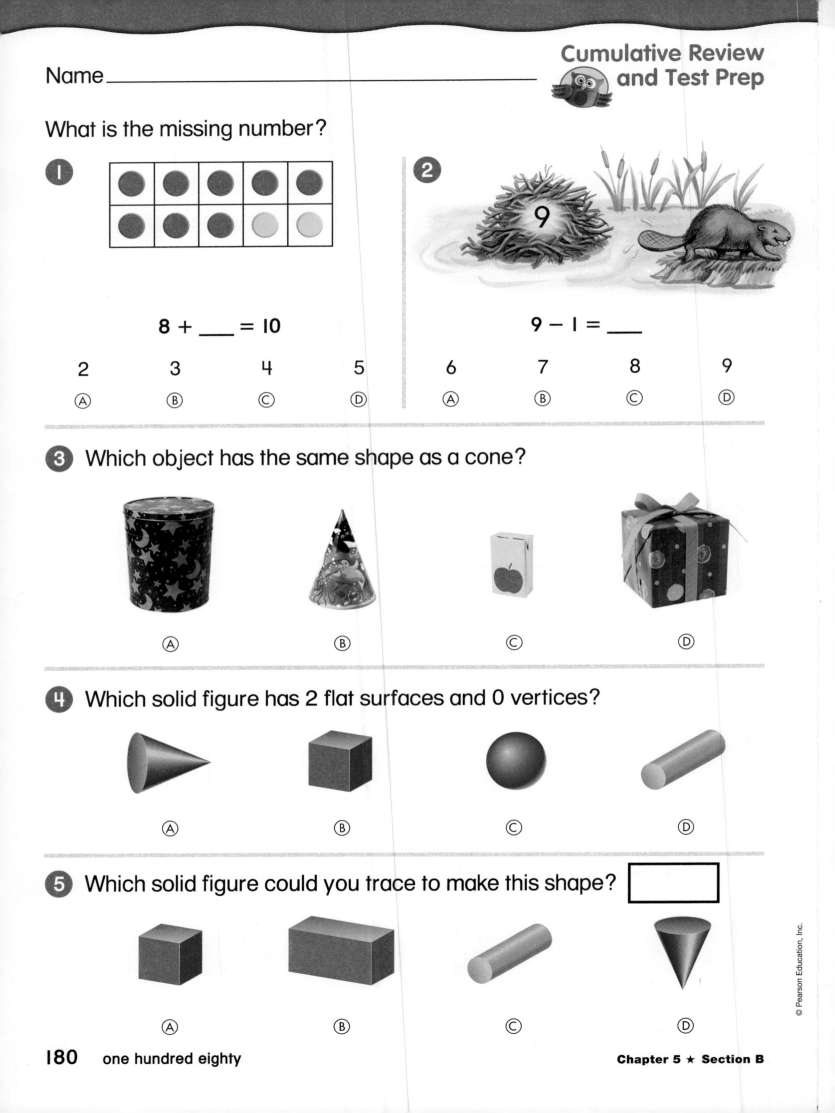

8 + ___ = 10

2	3	4	5
Ⓐ	Ⓑ	Ⓒ	Ⓓ

2

9

9 – 1 = ___

6	7	8	9
Ⓐ	Ⓑ	Ⓒ	Ⓓ

3 Which object has the same shape as a cone?

Ⓐ   Ⓑ   Ⓒ   Ⓓ

4 Which solid figure has 2 flat surfaces and 0 vertices?

Ⓐ   Ⓑ   Ⓒ   Ⓓ

5 Which solid figure could you trace to make this shape?

Ⓐ   Ⓑ   Ⓒ   Ⓓ

Name_____

Learn!

Fractions can name more than one equal part.

I shaded two fourths green.

So did I.

Check ✓

Circle the fraction that tells how much is colored.

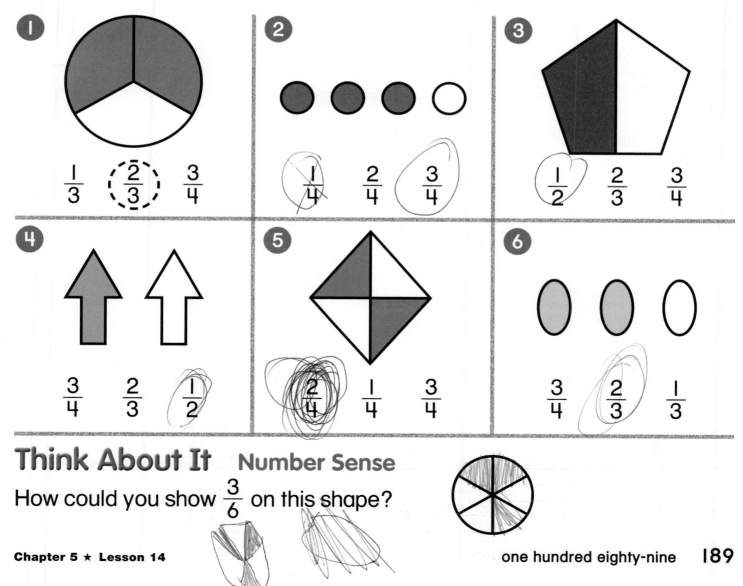

1

$\frac{1}{3}$ $\frac{2}{3}$ $\frac{3}{4}$

2

$\frac{1}{4}$ $\frac{2}{4}$ $\frac{3}{4}$

3

$\frac{1}{2}$ $\frac{2}{3}$ $\frac{3}{4}$

4

$\frac{3}{4}$ $\frac{2}{3}$ $\frac{1}{2}$

5

$\frac{2}{4}$ $\frac{1}{4}$ $\frac{3}{4}$

6

$\frac{3}{4}$ $\frac{2}{3}$ $\frac{1}{3}$

Think About It Number Sense

How could you show $\frac{3}{6}$ on this shape?

Write the fraction that tells how much is colored.

7

Both show $\frac{2}{3}$!

$\frac{2}{3}$

$\frac{2}{3}$

8

$\frac{}{}$

9

$\frac{}{}$

10

$\frac{}{}$

11

$\frac{}{}$

Problem Solving   Number Sense

12 Color to show $\frac{3}{8}$ of both.

 Home Connection Your child named fractions for shapes and for groups of objects. **Home Activity** Have your child tell how he or she solved the problems on this page.

Learn! Algebra

We can use a chart to help solve problems.

How can you give an **equal share** of erasers to each of 3 children?

The chart shows that there are 12 erasers.

Use 12 counters.

Give them out equally.

School Supplies	
Erasers	12
Pencils	8
Crayons	9
Brushes	12

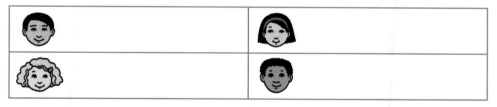

Each child gets ___4___ erasers.

Word Bank

equal share

Check ✓

Use the chart and counters to solve.
Draw the equal shares.

 1 4 children want to share the pencils equally.

Each child gets _____ pencils.

Think About It   Number Sense

Could 2 children share the crayons equally?
Explain?

6 Fill in the missing shapes in the quilt pattern.

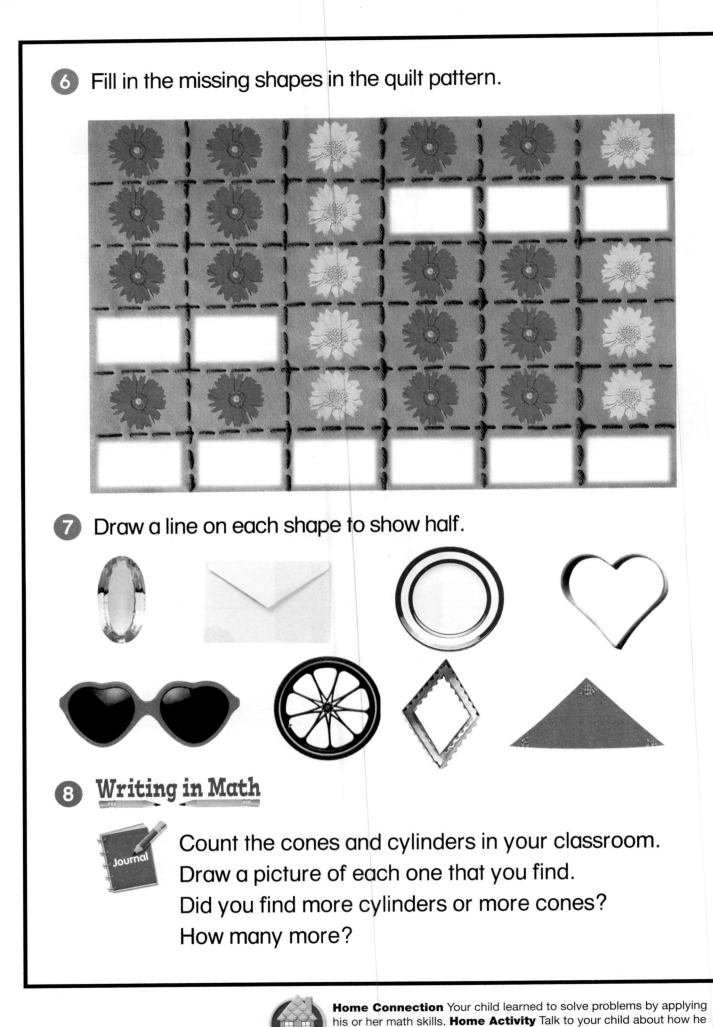

7 Draw a line on each shape to show half.

8 Writing in Math

Count the cones and cylinders in your classroom.
Draw a picture of each one that you find.
Did you find more cylinders or more cones?
How many more?

Home Connection Your child learned to solve problems by applying his or her math skills. **Home Activity** Talk to your child about how he or she solved the problems on these two pages.

Name _____

1 Circle the shapes that show one half shaded.

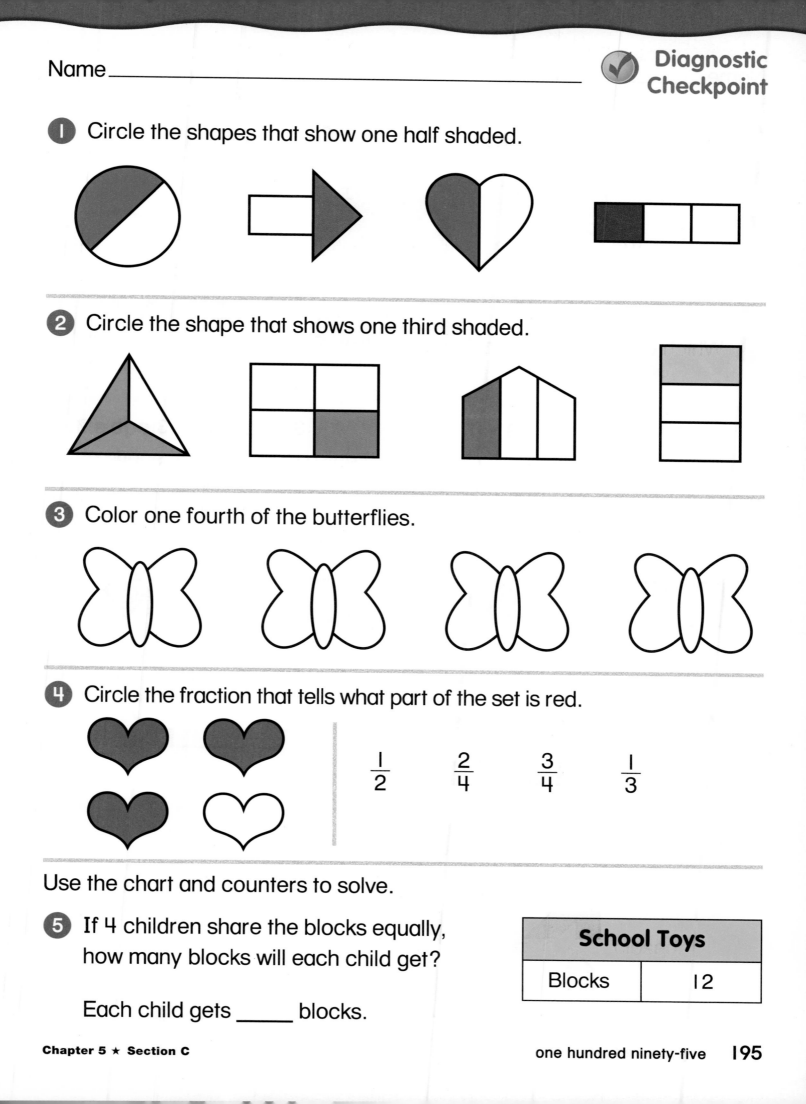

2 Circle the shape that shows one third shaded.

3 Color one fourth of the butterflies.

4 Circle the fraction that tells what part of the set is red.

$\frac{1}{2}$ $\frac{2}{4}$ $\frac{3}{4}$ $\frac{1}{3}$

Use the chart and counters to solve.

5 If 4 children share the blocks equally, how many blocks will each child get?

Each child gets _____ blocks.

School Toys	
Blocks	12

Name _____

Slide, Flip, and Turn Shapes Using a Computer

You can use a computer to slide, flip, and turn a shape.

1 Go to the Geometry Shapes eTool.

2 Pick a shape. Place it in the workspace. Draw it on your paper.

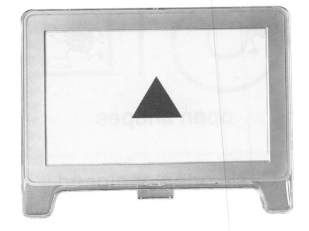

3 Flip the shape. Draw your screen. Label the shape as a **flip.**

4 Turn the shape. Draw your screen. Label the shape as a **turn.**

5 Slide the shape. Draw your screen. Label the shape as a **slide.**

6 Turn your paper over and repeat Steps 2–5, using a different shape.

Think About It   Reasoning

How are a turn and a slide the same?
How are they different?

Home Connection Your child used a computer to move shapes by flipping, sliding, and turning them. **Home Activity** Ask your child to draw a shape and then to draw the shape after it has been flipped, turned, and slid.

Name_____

 Read Together

Understand the Question

Some math problems have special words such as NOT.

① Which shape does not have $\frac{1}{3}$ shaded?

Ⓐ   Ⓑ   Ⓒ   Ⓓ

Circle the word NOT in this question. Choose the shape that is **not** divided into 3 equal parts. Fill in the answer bubble.

Test-Taking Strategies

Understand the Question
Get Information for the Answer
Plan How to Find the Answer
Make Smart Choices
Use Writing in Math

Your Turn

Underline the word NOT in this math problem. Solve the problem. Fill in the answer bubble.

② Which shape does not show a line of symmetry?

Ⓐ   Ⓑ   Ⓒ   Ⓓ

I need to think about this!

 Home Connection Your child prepared for standardized tests by identifying and applying the meaning of the word NOT to math problems. **Home Activity** Ask your child what the word NOT means in Exercise 2.

one hundred ninety-nine   **199**

Name _____

Discover Math in Your World

 Read Together

Math Music

Today you will play in the Hand-Clap Band.
Your teacher will divide the class
into three groups.

First, the whole class will practice
counting 1 - 2 - 3 - 4, 1 - 2 - 3 - 4.
Try to count the numbers, or beats,
at the same pace. Now ...

Musical Parts

1 Group 1 will clap only on beat 1.
Group 1 will be clapping 1 out of
every 4 beats. Write this as a fraction.

_____

2 Group 2 will clap only on beats 1 and 3.
Group 2 will be clapping 2 out of every 4 beats.
Write this as a fraction.

_____

3 Group 3 will clap on **every** beat.
Group 3 will be clapping 4 out of every 4 beats.
Write this as a fraction.

_____

Take It to the NET
Video and Activities
www.scottforesman.com

 Home Connection Your child solved problems about music by writing fractions. **Home Activity** Ask your child what fraction he or she would write to show clapping 3 out of every 4 beats. ($\frac{3}{4}$)

1 Circle the rectangular prism.

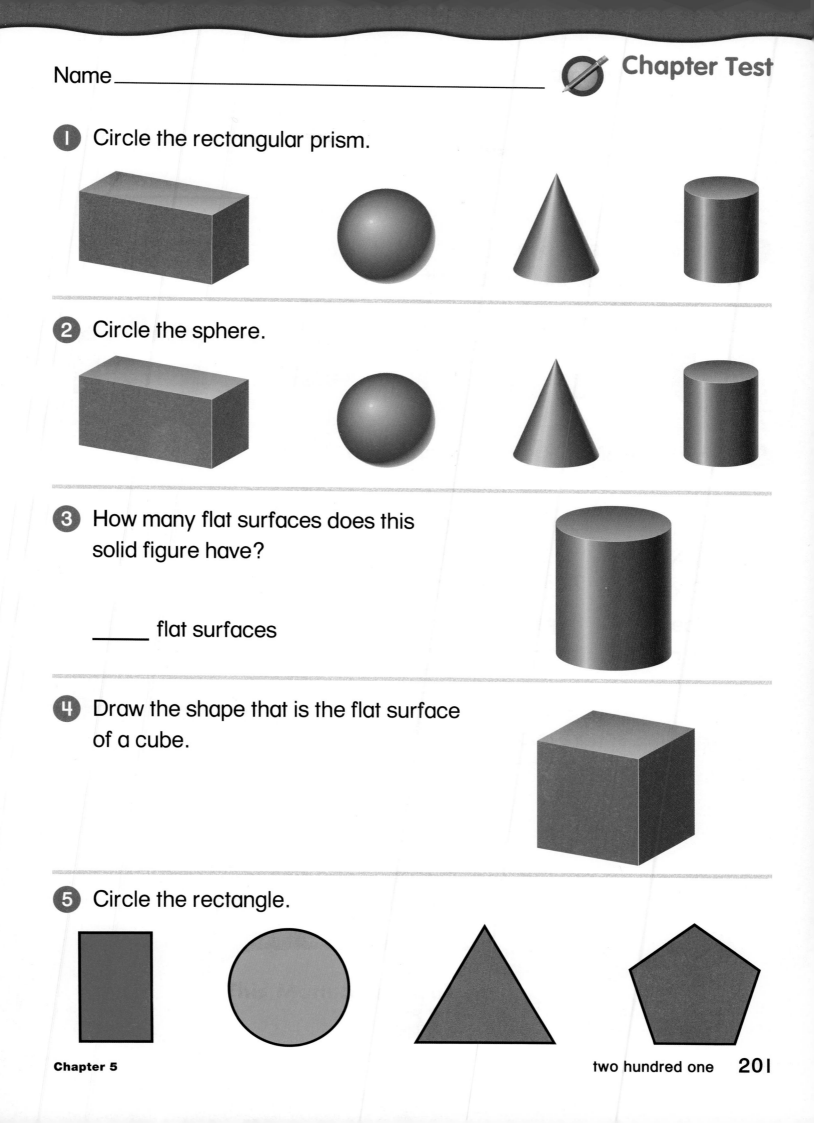

2 Circle the sphere.

3 How many flat surfaces does this solid figure have?

_____ flat surfaces

4 Draw the shape that is the flat surface of a cube.

5 Circle the rectangle.

"Where are my socks?
Where are my shoes?
I can't find anything!"

Oh, no! It was already 7:30.

Bunny hopped down the stairs.
She was almost out of breath.

"It's time for breakfast," said Bunny.
"I have to hurry! It's already 8:00!"

Then Bunny remembered. It was Saturday!

"There is no school today!" said Bunny.
"Silly, silly me! Oh, well."

Bunny ate her breakfast and read some
books until her mom and dad woke up.

6F

Name_____

Draw the hands on each clock face.
Then write the time on the other clock.

1 8 o'clock

2 1 o'clock

Write the same time.

3

4

How long does this activity take?
Circle the correct answer.

5

less than 1 minute

more than 1 minute

Write the starting time and the ending time.
Then draw the hands on the clock to show the ending time.

6

_____ o'clock ⟶ 2 hours ⟶ _____ o'clock

Name_____

1 Which subtraction sentence tells how many birds are left?

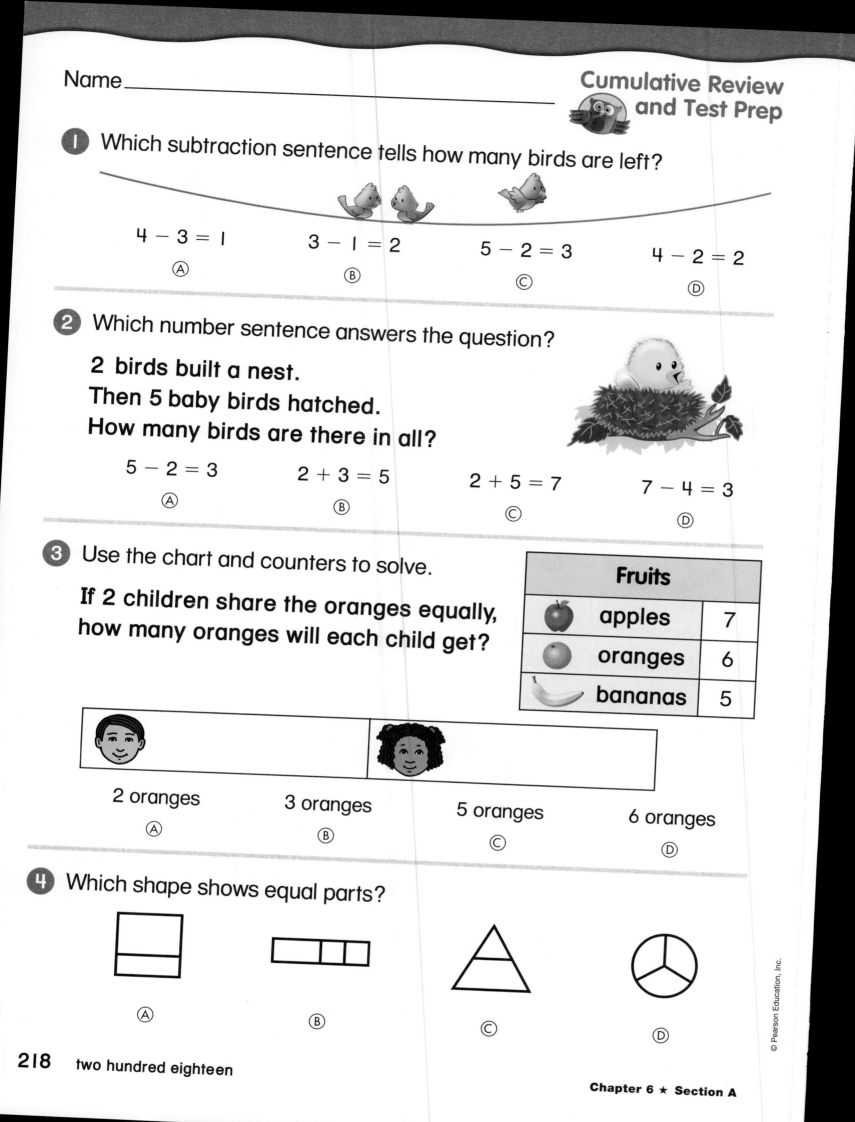

$4 - 3 = 1$ $3 - 1 = 2$ $5 - 2 = 3$ $4 - 2 = 2$

Ⓐ   Ⓑ   Ⓒ   Ⓓ

2 Which number sentence answers the question?

2 birds built a nest.
Then 5 baby birds hatched.
How many birds are there in all?

$5 - 2 = 3$ $2 + 3 = 5$ $2 + 5 = 7$ $7 - 4 = 3$

Ⓐ   Ⓑ   Ⓒ   Ⓓ

3 Use the chart and counters to solve.

If 2 children share the oranges equally, how many oranges will each child get?

Fruits	
apples	7
oranges	6
bananas	5

2 oranges   3 oranges   5 oranges   6 oranges

Ⓐ   Ⓑ   Ⓒ   Ⓓ

4 Which shape shows equal parts?

Ⓐ   Ⓑ   Ⓒ   Ⓓ

Name_____

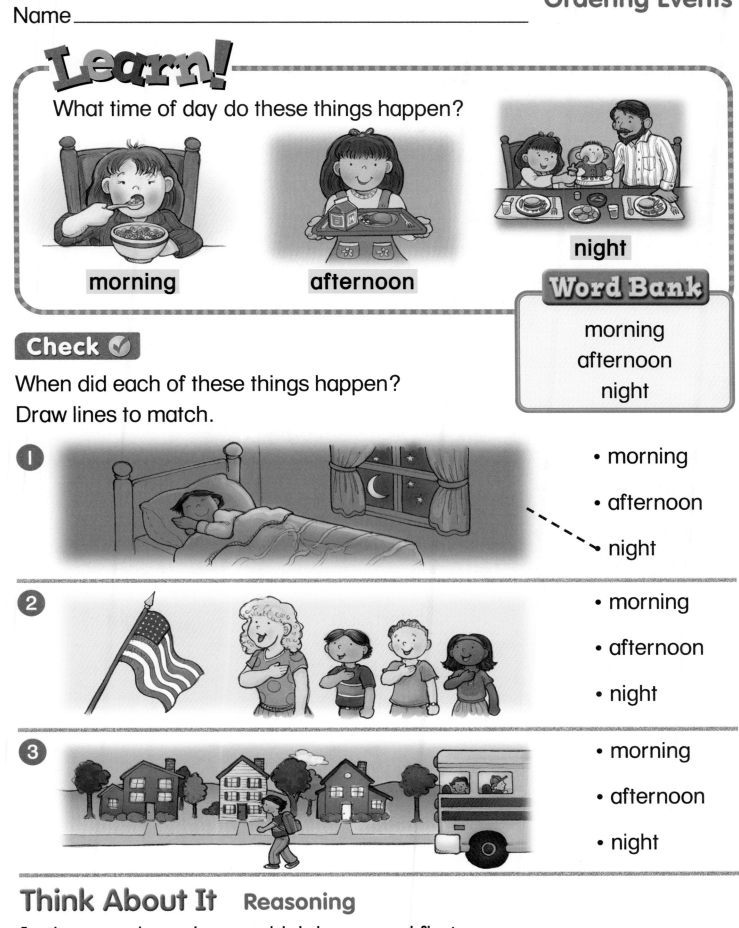

Learn!

What time of day do these things happen?

morning

afternoon

night

Word Bank

morning
afternoon
night

Check ✓

When did each of these things happen?
Draw lines to match.

1
• morning

• afternoon

• night

2
• morning

• afternoon

• night

3
• morning

• afternoon

• night

Think About It   Reasoning

In the exercises above, which happened first,
next, and last?

When did each of these things happen?
Draw lines to match.

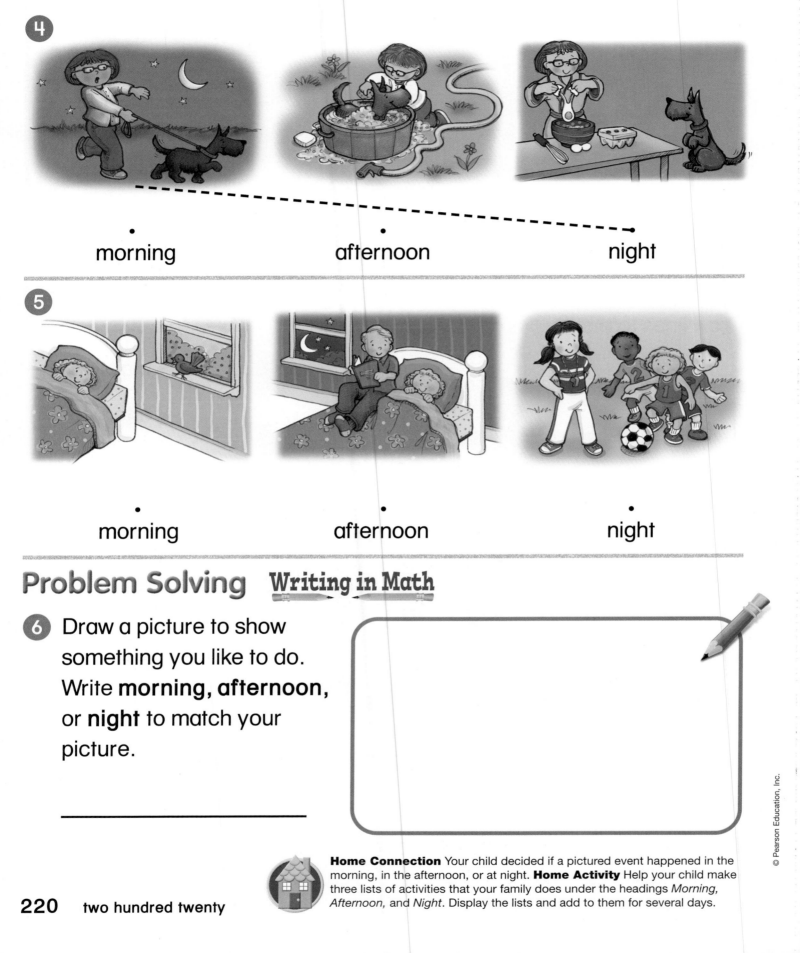

4

morning   afternoon   night

5

morning   afternoon   night

Problem Solving Writing in Math

6 Draw a picture to show
something you like to do.
Write **morning, afternoon,**
or **night** to match your
picture.

_____

Name_____

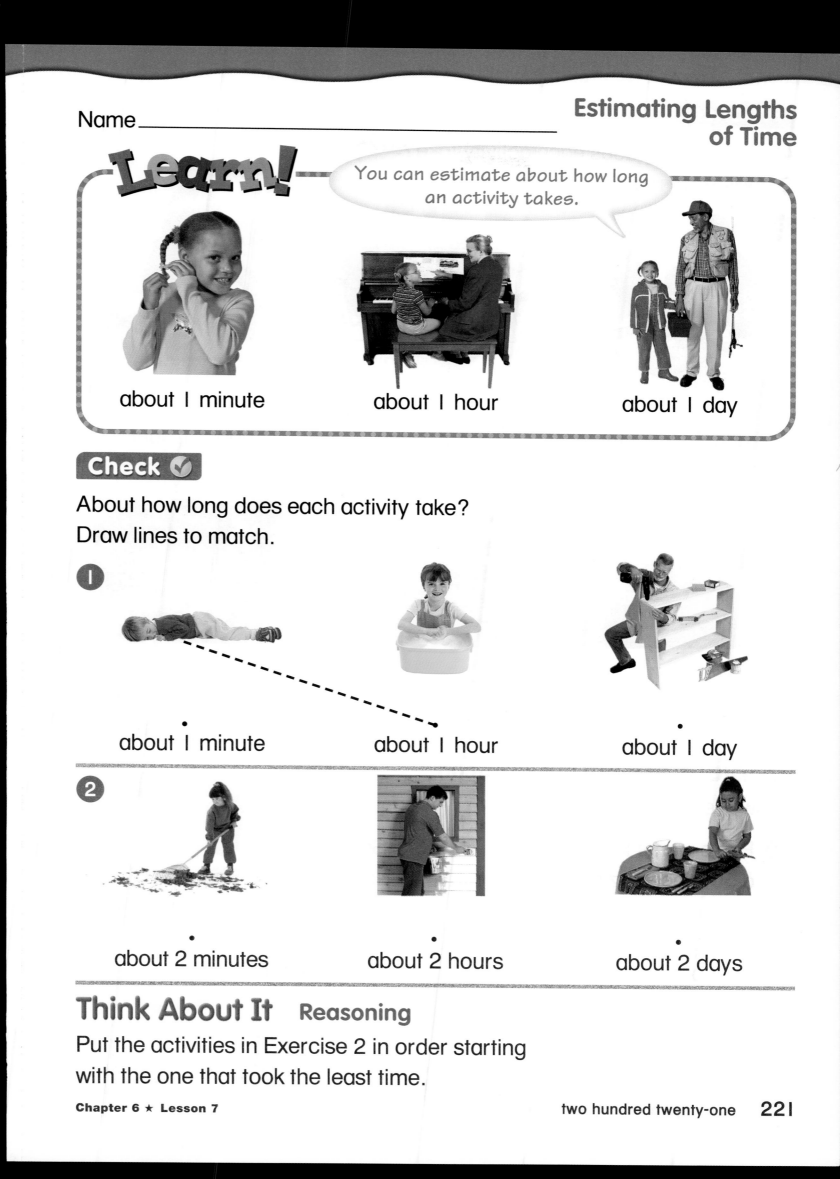

Learn! You can estimate about how long an activity takes.

about 1 minute   about 1 hour   about 1 day

Check ✓

About how long does each activity take?
Draw lines to match.

1

about 1 minute   about 1 hour   about 1 day

2

about 2 minutes   about 2 hours   about 2 days

Think About It   Reasoning

Put the activities in Exercise 2 in order starting
with the one that took the least time.

Use the schedule to answer the questions.

Mrs. Lopez's Class Schedule	
Time	Activity
8:00	Calendar Time
8:30	Reading
9:00	Centers
9:30	Math
10:00	Recess

4 What activity do children do just before recess?

_____

5 What does the class do just after reading?

_____

6 What time does math begin?

_____

Reasonableness

Use the schedule to solve the problem.

7 The class is about to start centers.
Jan wants to know how long it is until recess.
Peg says it is 2 hours.
Is she correct?

_____

Home Connection Your child used a schedule to answer questions.
Home Activity Work with your child to make a schedule of activities that you might do on a Saturday afternoon.

Name _____

This **calendar** shows the **days** and **weeks** in the **month** of November.

November

Sunday	Monday	Tuesday	Wednesday	Thursday	Friday	Saturday
	1	2	3	4	5	6
7	8	9	10	11	12	13
14	15	16	17	18	19	20
21	22	23	24	25	26	27
28	29	30				

Word Bank

calendar
day
week
month

Check ✓

Use the calendar above to answer the questions.

1. How many days are in 1 week? _____

2. How many days are in November? _____

3. On what day does this November begin? _____

4. If today is Thursday, what day will tomorrow be? _____

5. If today is Tuesday, what day was yesterday? _____

Think About It   Reasoning

On what day of the week will the next month begin? Explain.

6 Circle the names of the days of the week.

7 Color the Sundays green and the Thursdays blue.

8 Write the days of the week in order.

_____Sunday_____, _____Monday_____,

_____, _____,

_____, _____, _____

May						
Sunday	Monday	Tuesday	Wednesday	Thursday	Friday	Saturday
						1
2	3	4	5	6	7	8
9	10	11	12	13	14	15
16	17	18	19	20	21	22
23 / 30	24 / 31	25	26	27	28	29

Problem Solving   Visual Thinking

Find the pattern.

Then write the day that comes next.

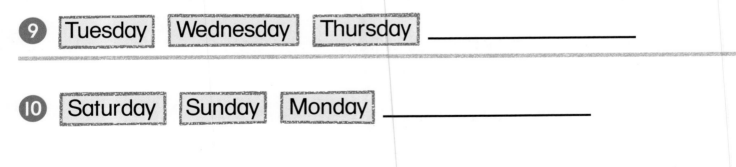

9 | Tuesday | Wednesday | Thursday | _____

10 | Saturday | Sunday | Monday | _____

Home Connection Your child learned about the calendar and named the days of the week. **Home Activity** Begin with Sunday and have your child name the days of the week in order. Look at the calendar for the current month. Talk about the dates on which your family has special plans.

Name _____

Learn!

There are 12 months in one **year** .

January
S	M	T	W	T	F	S
				1	2	3
4	5	6	7	8	9	10
11	12	13	14	15	16	17
18	19	20	21	22	23	24
25	26	27	28	29	30	31

February
S	M	T	W	T	F	S
1	2	3	4	5	6	7
8	9	10	11	12	13	14
15	16	17	18	19	20	21
22	23	24	25	26	27	28

March
S	M	T	W	T	F	S
1	2	3	4	5	6	7
8	9	10	11	12	13	14
15	16	17	18	19	20	21
22	23	24	25	26	27	28
29	30	31				

April
S	M	T	W	T	F	S
				1	2	3	4
5	6	7	8	9	10	11
12	13	14	15	16	17	18
19	20	21	22	23	24	25
26	27	28	29	30		

May
S	M	T	W	T	F	S
					1	2
3	4	5	6	7	8	9
10	11	12	13	14	15	16
17	18	19	20	21	22	23
24	25	26	27	28	29	30

June
S	M	T	W	T	F	S
	1	2	3	4	5	6
7	8	9	10	11	12	13
14	15	16	17	18	19	20
21	22	23	24	25	26	27
28	29	30				

July
S	M	T	W	T	F	S
			1	2	3	4
5	6	7	8	9	10	11
12	13	14	15	16	17	18
19	20	21	22	23	24	25
26	27	28	29	30	31	

August
S	M	T	W	T	F	S
						1
2	3	4	5	6	7	8
9	10	11	12	13	14	15
16	17	18	19	20	21	22
23/30	24/31	25	26	27	28	29

September
S	M	T	W	T	F	S
		1	2	3	4	5
6	7	8	9	10	11	12
13	14	15	16	17	18	19
20	21	22	23	24	25	26
27	28	29	30			

October
S	M	T	W	T	F	S
				1	2	3
4	5	6	7	8	9	10
11	12	13	14	15	16	17
18	19	20	21	22	23	24
25	26	27	28	29	30	31

November
S	M	T	W	T	F	S
1	2	3	4	5	6	7
8	9	10	11	12	13	14
15	16	17	18	19	20	21
22	23	24	25	26	27	28
29	30					

December
S	M	T	W	T	F	S
		1	2	3	4	5
6	7	8	9	10	11	12
13	14	15	16	17	18	19
20	21	22	23	24	25	26
27	28	29	30	31		

Check ✓

Word Bank

year

Use the calendar above to answer the questions.

1. How many months are in one year? _____

2. Which month comes before May? _____

3. Which month comes between January and March? _____

4. How many months have 31 days? _____

Think About It   Number Sense

Are there more months with 30 days or 31 days?

4 At 6:30 the baby tortoise walked out of the shell. Show 6:30 on both clocks.

5 How many hours passed from 4:30 to 6:30?

_____ hours

6 The baby tortoise started to hatch on Saturday. It walked out of the shell the next day. On which day did the baby tortoise walk out of the shell?

_____

7 Writing in Math

It takes 5 months for tortoise eggs to hatch. Use a calendar to show in which month the eggs will hatch if they are laid in March.

When did this activity happen?
Draw a line to match.

1

- morning

- afternoon

- night

About how long does each activity take?
Draw lines to match.

2

about I minute   about I day   about I hour

Use the schedule to answer the question.

3 What class does Tim have after music?

_____

Tim's Schedule	
11:00	Music
11:30	Art
12:00	Lunch

Answer the questions.

4 What days are missing?

Sunday, _____,
Tuesday, Wednesday,
_____, Friday, Saturday

_____ and _____

5 What day of the week will June 6 be?

June				
Sunday	Monday	Tuesday	Wednesday	Thursday
1	2	3	4	5
8	9	10	11	12

_____

Name_____

Create a Schedule Using a Computer

You can use a computer to show the times that you start your after-school activities.

 1 Make a list of 5 things you do after school. Write the activities in order on a separate sheet of paper.

2 On a computer, go to the Time eTool.

3 Choose a start time for your first activity by setting the hands of the clock.

4 Check the digital clock to make sure that it shows the time you want your first activity to start. Write this time next to the first activity on your sheet of paper.

5 Repeat Steps 3 and 4 for your other after-school activities.

Think About It   Reasoning

On which activity do you spend the greatest amount of time? On which activity do you spend the least amount of time?

 Home Connection Your child used a computer to show the starting times of different after-school activities and created a schedule for those activities.
Home Activity Ask your child questions about his or her weekday and weekend schedules.

Name_____

 ## Get Information for the Answer

You can get information from a table to help you solve math problems.

Test-Taking Strategies

Understand the Question

Get Information for the Answer

Plan How to Find the Answer

Make Smart Choices

Use Writing in Math

1. Which activity will Megan miss if she comes to the fair at 1:30?

Ⓐ Beanbag Toss

Ⓑ Face Painting

Ⓒ Cake Sale

Ⓓ Musical Chairs

Find the activity that starts before 1:30. Fill in the answer bubble.

School Fun Fair	
Activity	**Time**
Beanbag Toss	1:00
Face Painting	1:30
Cake Sale	2:00
Musical Chairs	2:30

Your Turn

Use the table to solve this problem.
Fill in the answer bubble.

2. At what time should Frank come to the fair if he does not want to miss anything?

Ⓐ 1:00

Ⓑ 1:30

Ⓒ 2:00

Ⓓ 2:30

 Home Connection Your child prepared for standardized tests by using information from a table to solve math problems. **Home Activity** Ask your child to explain how he or she used the table to solve the problem in Exercise 2.

Discover Math in Your World

Discovery CHANNEL
SCHOOL

Read Together

Time for Math!

Do you know at what time you wake up, have breakfast, and go to school? Do you know at what time you get home from school?

Right now it's time to do some math!

What Time Is It?

1 Carlos wakes up at 7:00 each morning. He arrives at school 1 hour later. At what time does Carlos get to school?

_____

2 At school, lunch begins at noon. It is now 10:00. In how many hours will lunch begin?

_____ hours

3 Jennifer gets home from school at the time shown on the clock. She will play for 1 hour. At what time will she finish playing?

_____

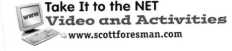
Take It to the NET
Video and Activities
www.scottforesman.com

Home Connection Your child solved problems about daily activities by telling time on analog (dial) and digital clocks. **Home Activity** Ask your child to tell at what time three daily activities begin or end, using both analog and digital clocks.

© Pearson Education, Inc.

How long does this activity take?
Circle the correct answer.

1

less than 1 minute

more than 1 minute

Draw the hands on each clock face.
Then write the time on the other clock.

2   5 o'clock

3   11 o'clock

Write the same time.

4

5

Answer the questions.

6 What day comes after Tuesday?

Sunday, Monday,
Tuesday,

_____

7 Which month comes after June?

January	February	March
April	May	June

_____

When did this activity happen?
Draw a line to match.

8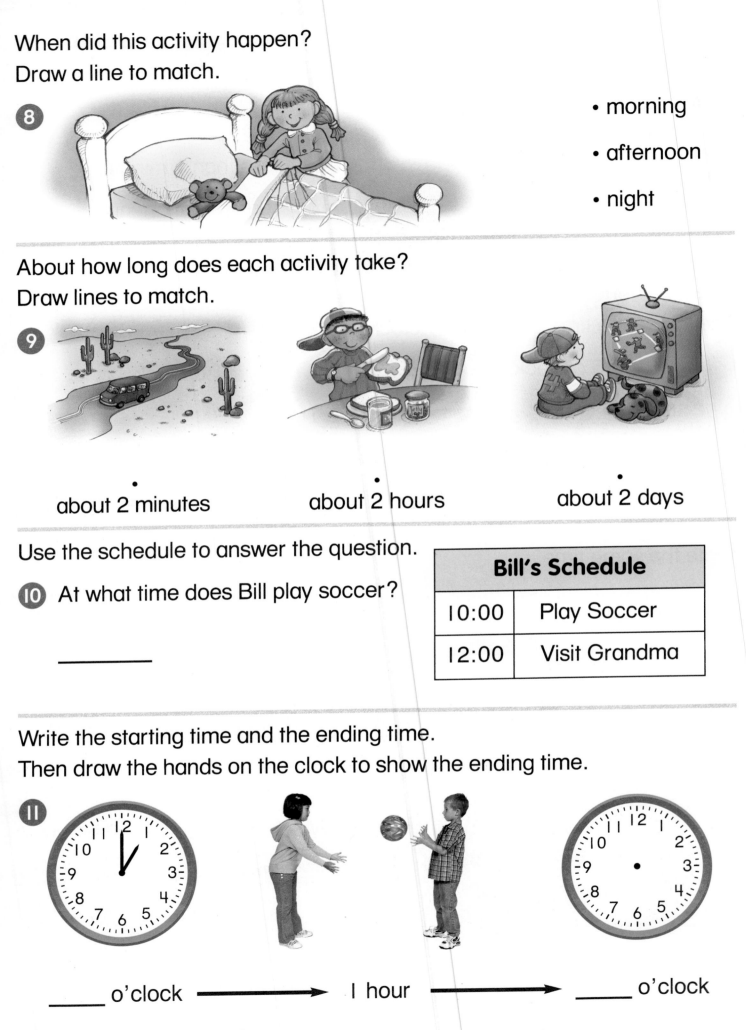

- morning

- afternoon

- night

About how long does each activity take?
Draw lines to match.

9

about 2 minutes   about 2 hours   about 2 days

Use the schedule to answer the question.

10 At what time does Bill play soccer?

_____

Bill's Schedule	
10:00	Play Soccer
12:00	Visit Grandma

Write the starting time and the ending time.
Then draw the hands on the clock to show the ending time.

11

_____ o'clock ⟶ I hour ⟶ _____ o'clock

Name_____

1 Which clock shows the same time?

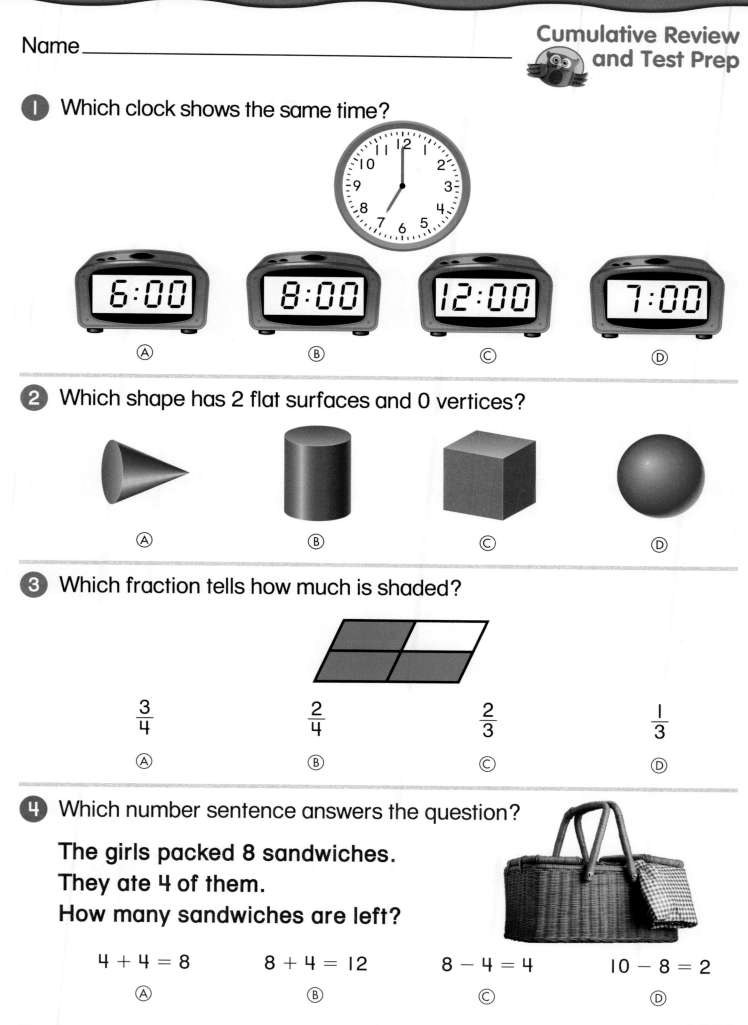

A 6:00
B 8:00
C 12:00
D 7:00

2 Which shape has 2 flat surfaces and 0 vertices?

A   B   C   D

3 Which fraction tells how much is shaded?

$\frac{3}{4}$ $\frac{2}{4}$ $\frac{2}{3}$ $\frac{1}{3}$

A   B   C   D

4 Which number sentence answers the question?

The girls packed 8 sandwiches.
They ate 4 of them.
How many sandwiches are left?

$4 + 4 = 8$ $8 + 4 = 12$ $8 - 4 = 4$ $10 - 8 = 2$

A   B   C   D

Add. Use a number line if you like.

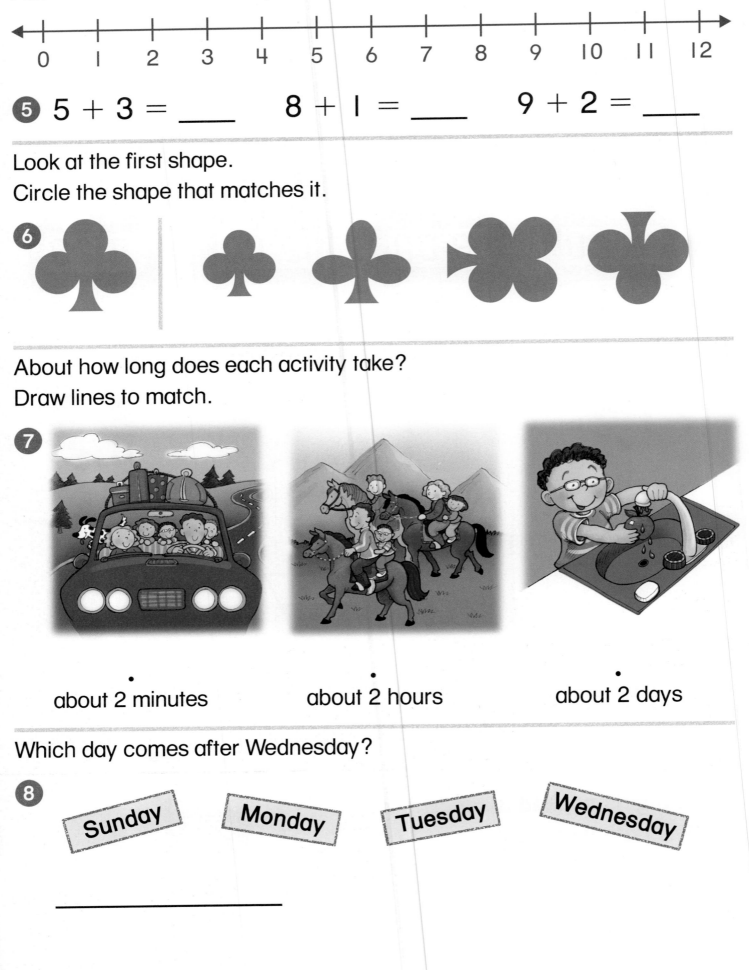

| | | | | | | | | | | | | |
0 1 2 3 4 5 6 7 8 9 10 11 12

⑤ 5 + 3 = ___   8 + 1 = ___   9 + 2 = ___

Look at the first shape.
Circle the shape that matches it.

⑥

About how long does each activity take?
Draw lines to match.

⑦

about 2 minutes   about 2 hours   about 2 days

Which day comes after Wednesday?

⑧   Sunday   Monday   Tuesday   Wednesday

_____

Four Little Chickens

A New Adaptation of An Old Rhyme About Ordinals

Illustrated by Amy Vangsguard

This Math Storybook belongs to

_____

Said the first little chicken
with an odd little squirm,

I wish I could find
a fat little worm.

Said the second little chicken
with an odd little shrug,

I wish I could find
a fat little bug.

Said the third little chicken
with an odd little tug,

I wish I could find
a fat little slug.

Said the fourth little chicken
with an odd little sigh,
I wish I could find
a fat little fly.

Said the old mother hen
from the green garden patch,

If you want any breakfast,
just come here and scratch!

Name_____

Learn!

16 is 10 and 6 left over.

Numbers from 11 to 19 can be made
with one group of 10 and some left over.

Check ✓

Use counters and Workmat 3.
Write each number as 10 and some left over.

1 | fifteen | 15 is __10__ and __5__.

2 | nineteen | 19 is _____ and _____.

3 | twelve | 12 is _____ and _____.

4 | fourteen | 14 is _____ and _____.

5 | seventeen | 17 is _____ and _____.

Think About It   Number Sense

If you have 2 toy cars, how many more do you
need to have 12? Tell how you know.

Practice

Use counters and Workmat 3.
Write each number as 10 and some left over.

6 | eleven | 11 is __10__ and __1__.

I think of these numbers as 10 and some left over!

7 | thirteen | 13 is _____ and _____.

8 | sixteen | 16 is _____ and _____.

9 | eighteen | 18 is _____ and _____.

10 | fifteen | 15 is _____ and _____.

Problem Solving Algebra

Write each missing number.

11 [ ] and 10 is 16.

12 1 and [ ] is 11.

13 10 and [ ] is 17.

14 [ ] and 9 is 19.

15 [ ] and 10 is 18.

16 10 and [ ] is 14.

17 5 and [ ] is 15.

18 [ ] and 2 is 12.

Home Connection Your child used counters to show numbers as a group of 10 and some left over. **Home Activity** Tell your child a number between 11 and 19. Ask him or her to say the number as 10 and some left over. For example, 17 is 10 and 7.

242 two hundred forty-two

© Pearson Education, Inc.

Name_____

Learn!

Sometimes counting by 10s is easier than counting by 1s.

4 groups of 10 is 40 in all!

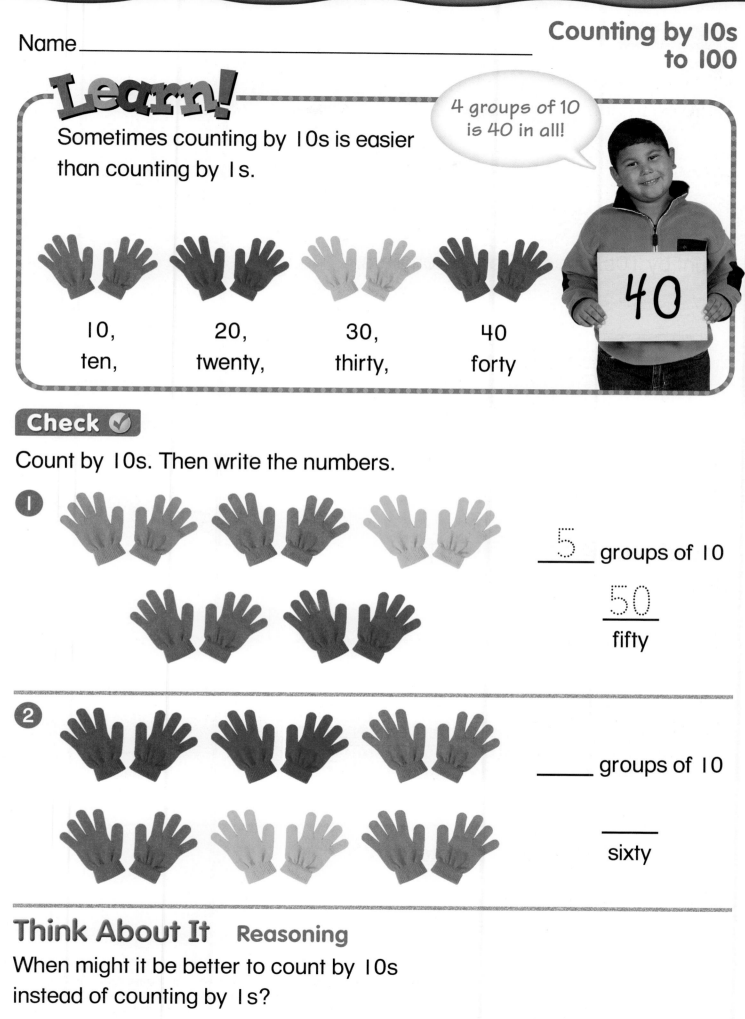

10,   20,   30,   40
ten,   twenty,   thirty,   forty

Check ✓

Count by 10s. Then write the numbers.

① _5_ groups of 10

_50_
fifty

② _____ groups of 10

_____
sixty

Think About It   Reasoning

When might it be better to count by 10s instead of counting by 1s?

10,	20,	30,	40,	50,
ten,	twenty,	thirty,	forty,	fifty,
60,	70,	80,	90,	100
sixty,	seventy,	eighty,	ninety,	one hundred

Count by 10s. Then write the numbers.

3

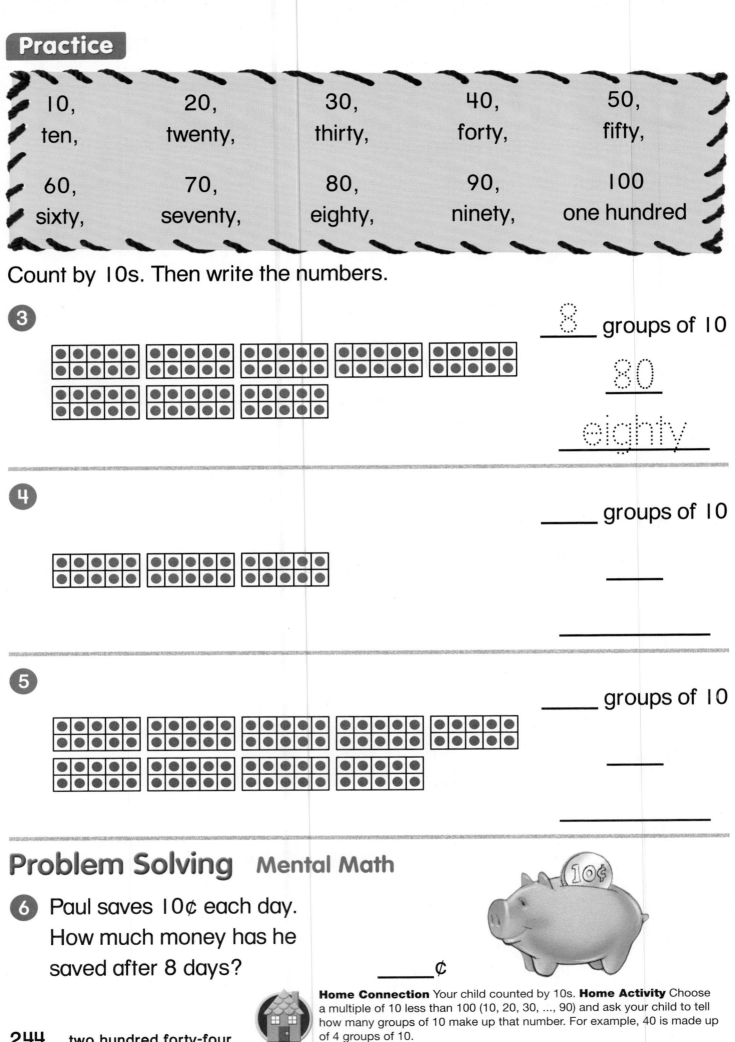

_8_ groups of 10

_80_

eighty

4

_____ groups of 10

____

_____

5

_____ groups of 10

____

_____

Problem Solving Mental Math

6 Paul saves 10¢ each day.
How much money has he
saved after 8 days?

_____¢

Home Connection Your child counted by 10s. **Home Activity** Choose
a multiple of 10 less than 100 (10, 20, 30, ..., 90) and ask your child to tell
how many groups of 10 make up that number. For example, 40 is made up
of 4 groups of 10.

Learn!

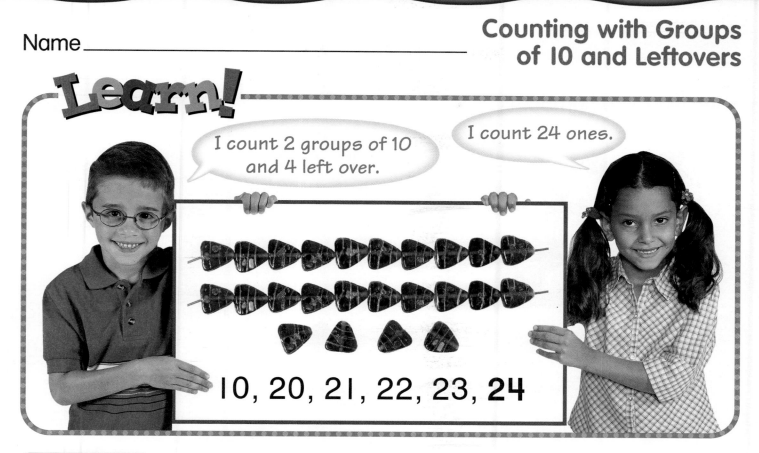

I count 2 groups of 10 and 4 left over.

I count 24 ones.

10, 20, 21, 22, 23, **24**

Check ✓

Circle groups of 10.
Then write the numbers.

❶
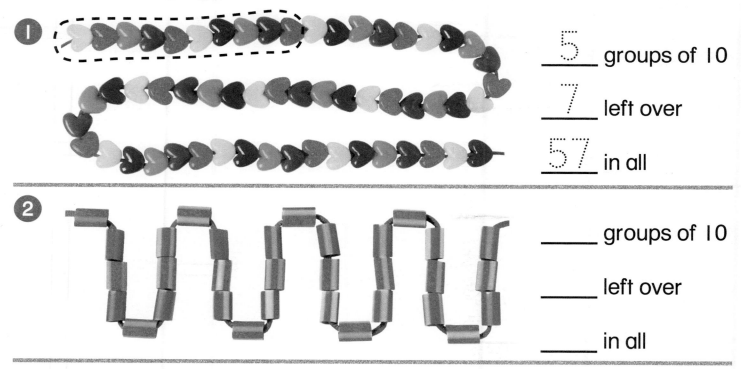

__5__ groups of 10

__7__ left over

__57__ in all

❷

____ groups of 10

____ left over

____ in all

Think About It Number Sense

Sam counted 8 groups of 10 stamps and 3 left over.
If he counts all of the stamps by 1s, how many will he count?

Circle groups of 10.
Then write the numbers.

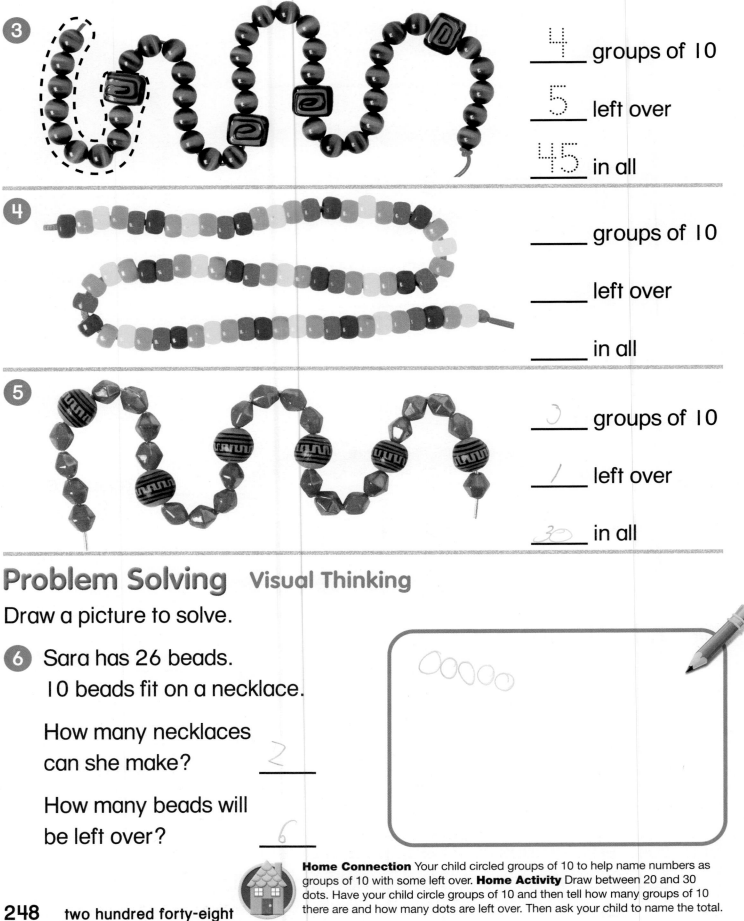

3

_____4_____ groups of 10

_____5_____ left over

_____45_____ in all

4

_____ groups of 10

_____ left over

_____ in all

5

_____3_____ groups of 10

_____1_____ left over

_____30_____ in all

Problem Solving   Visual Thinking

Draw a picture to solve.

6 Sara has 26 beads.
10 beads fit on a necklace.

How many necklaces
can she make? _____2_____

How many beads will
be left over? _____6_____

Home Connection Your child circled groups of 10 to help name numbers as groups of 10 with some left over. **Home Activity** Draw between 20 and 30 dots. Have your child circle groups of 10 and then tell how many groups of 10 there are and how many dots are left over. Then ask your child to name the total.

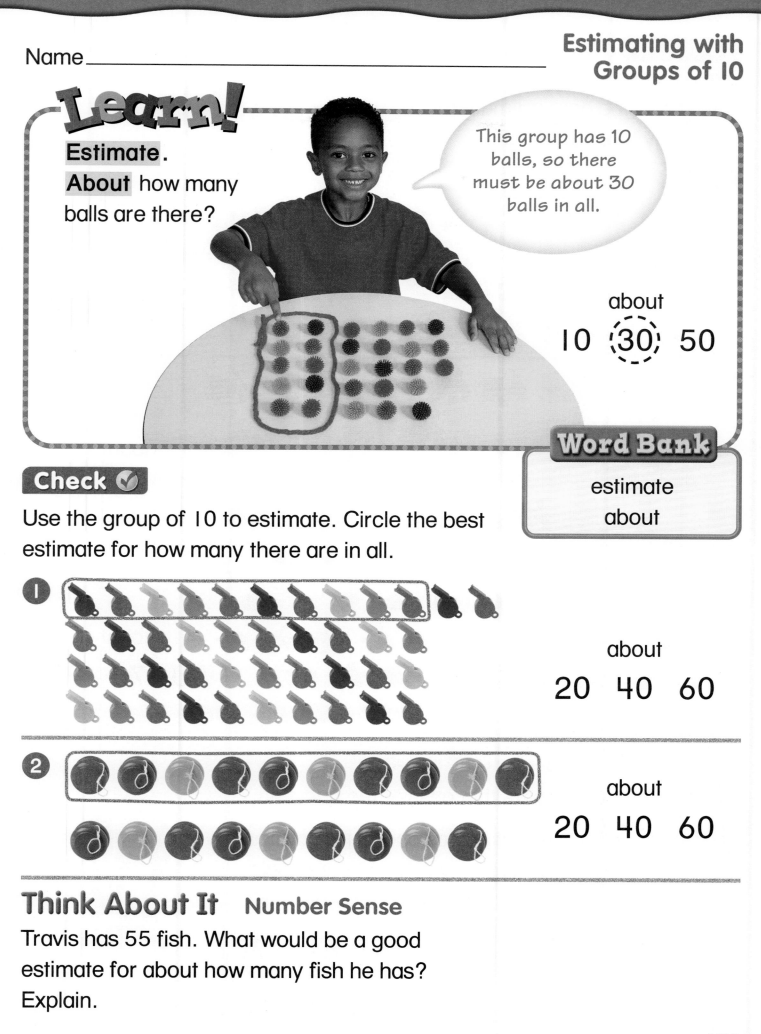

Learn!

Estimate.

About how many balls are there?

This group has 10 balls, so there must be about 30 balls in all.

about

10 (30) 50

Word Bank

estimate

about

Check ✓

Use the group of 10 to estimate. Circle the best estimate for how many there are in all.

1

about

20   40   60

2

about

20   40   60

Think About It   Number Sense

Travis has 55 fish. What would be a good estimate for about how many fish he has? Explain.

Circle a group of 10.
Then circle the best estimate for
how many there are in all.

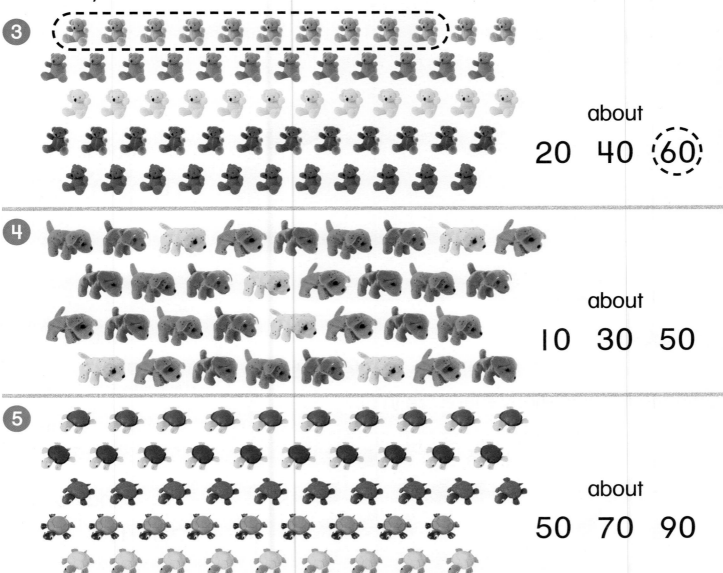

③ about

20 40 ⟨60⟩

④ about

10 30 50

⑤ about

50 70 90

Problem Solving Estimation

Circle all of the numbers that answer the question.

⑥ Martin estimates that he has about 40 marbles.
If 40 is a good estimate, which numbers could
show how many marbles Martin really has?

11 23 38 42 56 61 70

Home Connection Your child used a group of 10 to estimate a larger
quantity. **Home Activity** Draw between 35 and 45 dots. Ask your child to
circle a group of 10 and then tell whether he or she thinks there are about 20
dots or about 40 dots in all. *(About 40)*

Learn!

This **graph** shows how many of each kind of sticker there are.

Count by 10s to find how many stickers there are.

Our Stickers

Bugs	
Flowers	
Birds	

Word Bank

graph

Check ✓

Use the graph to answer each question.

1 How many bug stickers are there? _____

2 Of which kind of sticker are there the most? _____

3 Of which kind of sticker are there the fewest? _____

4 How many more bug stickers than flower stickers are there? _____

5 How many more bird stickers do we need to make 50? _____

Think About It   Reasoning

How do you use the graph to find out which group of stickers has the most?

Our Stamp Collection		
Red Stamps	**Yellow Stamps**	**Green Stamps**

Use the graph to answer each question.

6 Of which color stamp are there the most? _____

7 Of which color stamp are there the fewest? _____

8 How many more green stamps than yellow stamps are there? _____

9 How many red and yellow stamps are there altogether? _____

Writing in Math

10 Write your own question about the graph.

_____

_____

Home Connection Your child read and interpreted graphs. **Home Activity** Ask your child to look at the graph on this page and to tell how many of each color stamp there are. *(Red: 40; Yellow: 20; Green: 50)*

Name _____

Write each number as 10 and some left over.

1 18 is 10 and _____.

2 13 is 10 and _____.

Count by 10s. Then write the numbers.

3 _____ groups of 10

_____

Count on or count back by 1s.
Use a hundred chart if you like.

4 47, 48, 49, _____, _____, _____, _____, _____, _____

5 65, 64, 63, _____, _____, _____, _____, _____, _____

Circle groups of 10. Then write the numbers.

6 _____ groups of 10

_____ left over

_____ in all

Circle a group of 10.
Then circle the best estimate for
how many there are in all.

7

about

20   40   60

Name_____

1 What is the difference?

$9 - 4 = $ ___

(A) 0
(B) 4
(C) 5
(D) 7

$$\begin{array}{r} 9 \\ -\ 4 \\ \hline \end{array}$$

2 What fraction of the cherries is red?

$\dfrac{1}{4}$ $\dfrac{1}{2}$ $\dfrac{2}{3}$ $\dfrac{3}{4}$

(A) (B) (C) (D)

Use the schedule for Exercises 3, 4, and 5.

Camp Daisy Schedule	
Time	**Activity**
9:00	Art
10:30	Swimming
12:00	Lunch
1:00	Gardening
2:30	Hiking

3 What do the campers do at 10:30?

Art   Swimming   Lunch   Hiking
(A)   (B)   (C)   (D)

4 At what time does lunch begin?

10:30   12:00   1:00   2:30
(A)   (B)   (C)   (D)

5 What do the campers do just after Gardening?

Hiking   Lunch   Art   Swimming
(A)   (B)   (C)   (D)

Name_____

Learn! Algebra

There are lots of patterns on the hundred chart!
Write the numbers to continue the pattern.

I am beginning to see a pattern.

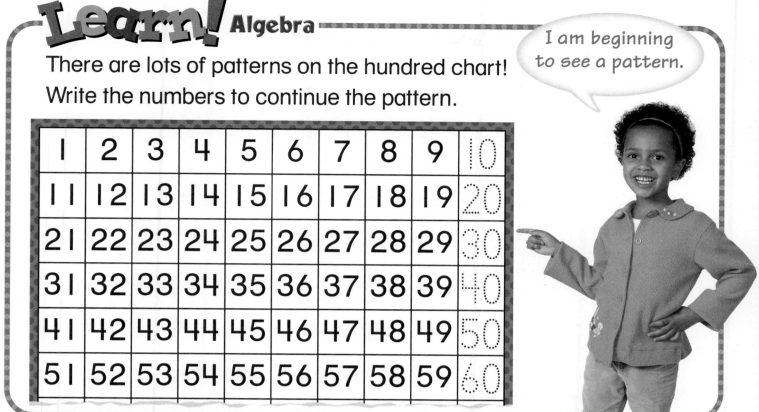

1	2	3	4	5	6	7	8	9	10
11	12	13	14	15	16	17	18	19	20
21	22	23	24	25	26	27	28	29	30
31	32	33	34	35	36	37	38	39	40
41	42	43	44	45	46	47	48	49	50
51	52	53	54	55	56	57	58	59	60

Check ✓

1 Skip count by 5s to continue the pattern.
Write the numbers.

1	2	3	4	5	6	7	8	9	10
11	12	13	14		16	17	18	19	
21	22	23	24		26	27	28	29	
31	32	33	34		36	37	38	39	

Think About It   Reasoning

How is the pattern for counting by 5s like the
pattern for counting by 10s? How is it different?

2 Color the numbers you say when you count by 2s.

1	2	3	4	5	6	7	8	9	10
11	12	13	14	15	16	17	18	19	20
21	22	23	24	25	26	27	28	29	30
31	32	33	34	35	36	37	38	39	40
41	42	43	44	45	46	47	48	49	50
51	52	53	54	55	56	57	58	59	60
61	62	63	64	65	66	67	68	69	70
71	72	73	74	75	76	77	78	79	80
81	82	83	84	85	86	87	88	89	90
91	92	93	94	95	96	97	98	99	100

What pattern do you see?

3 Color the numbers you say when you count by 5s.

41	42	43	44	45	46	47	48	49	50
51	52	53	54	55	56	57	58	59	60
61	62	63	64	65	66	67	68	69	70
71	72	73	74	75	76	77	78	79	80

Problem Solving   Visual Thinking

Finish coloring the calendar. Then write **yes** or **no**.

4 Kendra has a soccer game every 3 days.
Does she have a game on April 21? _____

April						
Sunday	Monday	Tuesday	Wednesday	Thursday	Friday	Saturday
1	2	3	4	5	6	7
8	9	10	11	12	13	14
15	16	17	18	19	20	21

Home Connection Your child used a hundred chart to skip count by 2s, 5s, and 10s. **Home Activity** Have your child use the hundred chart on this page to count by 5s, starting at 20.

Reading for Math Success

Predict

Read this beginning of a story.

The sky is full of big, dark clouds.
Thunder booms, and lightning flashes.

1 What do you think will happen next?

_____

_____

_____

_____

The rain stops, so Isso, Alex, John, and Marco want to play in the puddles. They go to find their boots.

2 How many boots do they need to find altogether?

Complete the chart.

Number of Boys	1	2	3	4
Number of Boots	2	4		

The boys need to find _____ boots altogether.

Think About It   Reasoning

How did you complete the chart?

Read the beginning of another story.

As the boys go outside, the sun begins to shine.

3 What do you think will happen to the puddle?

_____

_____

_____

_____

The boys decide to pick flowers. Each boy picks 3 flowers.

4 How many flowers do the boys pick altogether?

Complete the chart.

Number of Boys	1	2	3	4
Number of Flowers	3			

The boys pick _____ flowers altogether.

Home Connection Your child predicted what would happen next in two stories and completed charts to show which numbers came next in patterns. **Home Activity** Using this page and the previous page, ask your child to tell how many boots 6 boys would need and how many flowers 6 boys would pick. *(12 boots; 18 flowers)*

Learn! Algebra

1 The horses need new shoes.
Each horse has 4 hooves.
How many shoes will be needed for all of the horses?

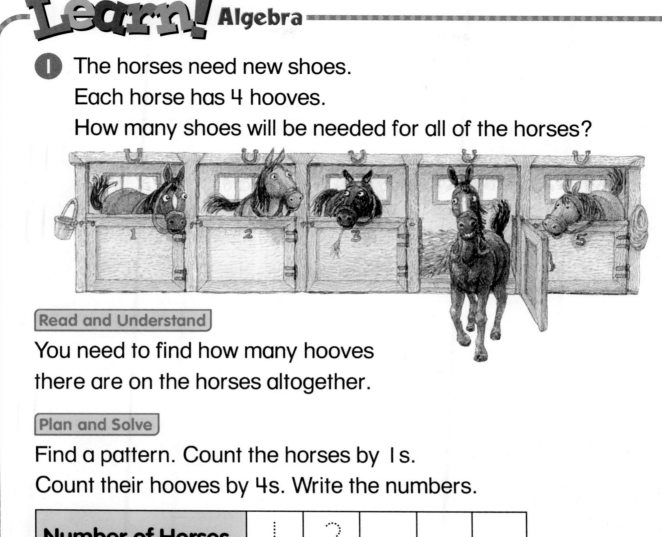

Read and Understand

You need to find how many hooves
there are on the horses altogether.

Plan and Solve

Find a pattern. Count the horses by 1s.
Count their hooves by 4s. Write the numbers.

Number of Horses	1	2			
Number of Hooves	4	8			

_____ shoes will be needed for all of the horses.

Look Back and Check

Does your answer make sense?

Think About It   Reasoning

How could you use the pattern to find how
many shoes would be needed for 8 horses?

Find a pattern. Then write the numbers.

2 There are 6 dogs.

Each dog has 2 ears.

How many ears are on the dogs altogether?

Number of Dogs	1					
Number of Ears	2					

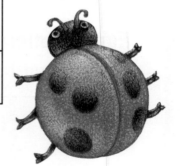

There are _____ ears in all on the dogs.

3 There are 5 ladybugs.

Each ladybug has 6 legs.

How many legs are on the ladybugs altogether?

Number of Ladybugs					
Number of Legs					

There are _____ legs in all on the ladybugs.

4 There are 5 hens.

Each hen lays 3 eggs.

How many eggs do the hens lay altogether?

Number of Hens				
Number of Eggs				

The hens lay _____ eggs in all.

Home Connection Your child used number patterns to solve problems.
Home Activity Draw a blank chart like the one in Exercise 4. Have your child show how to find the number of eggs if each hen lays 2 eggs.

© Pearson Education, Inc.

Name_____

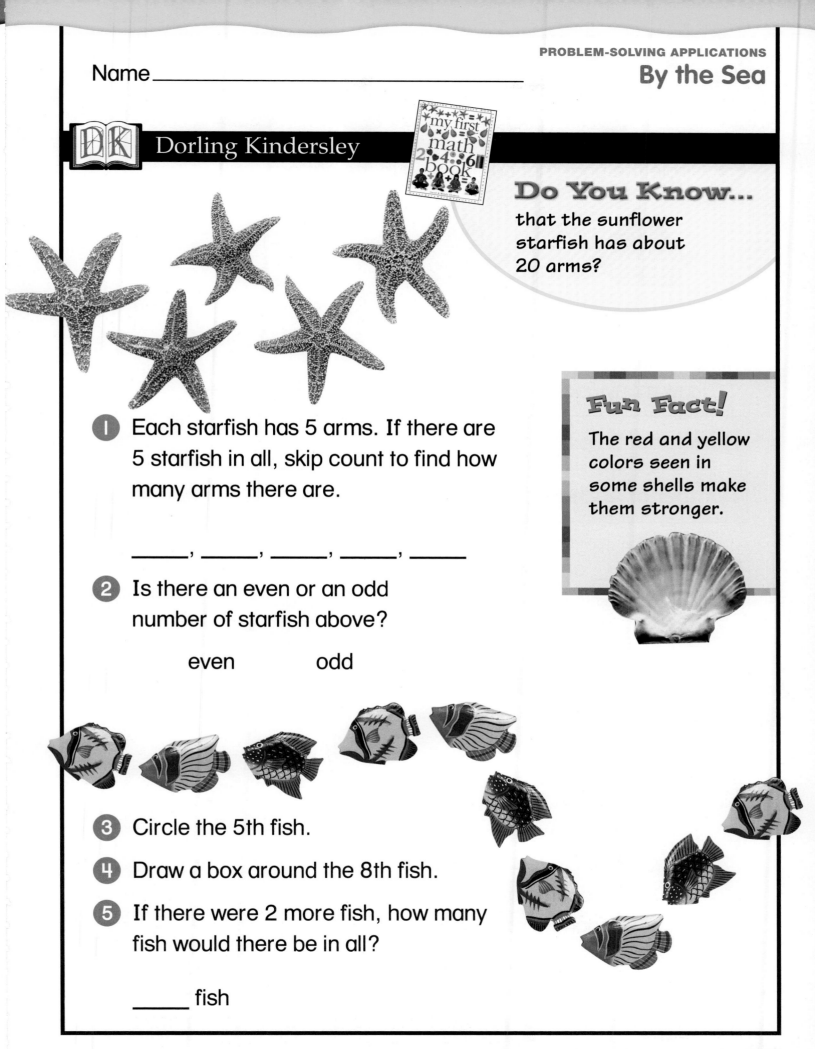

Dorling Kindersley

my first math book

Do You Know...
that the sunflower starfish has about 20 arms?

Fun Fact!
The red and yellow colors seen in some shells make them stronger.

1. Each starfish has 5 arms. If there are 5 starfish in all, skip count to find how many arms there are.

_____, _____, _____, _____, _____

2. Is there an even or an odd number of starfish above?

even   odd

3. Circle the 5th fish.

4. Draw a box around the 8th fish.

5. If there were 2 more fish, how many fish would there be in all?

_____ fish

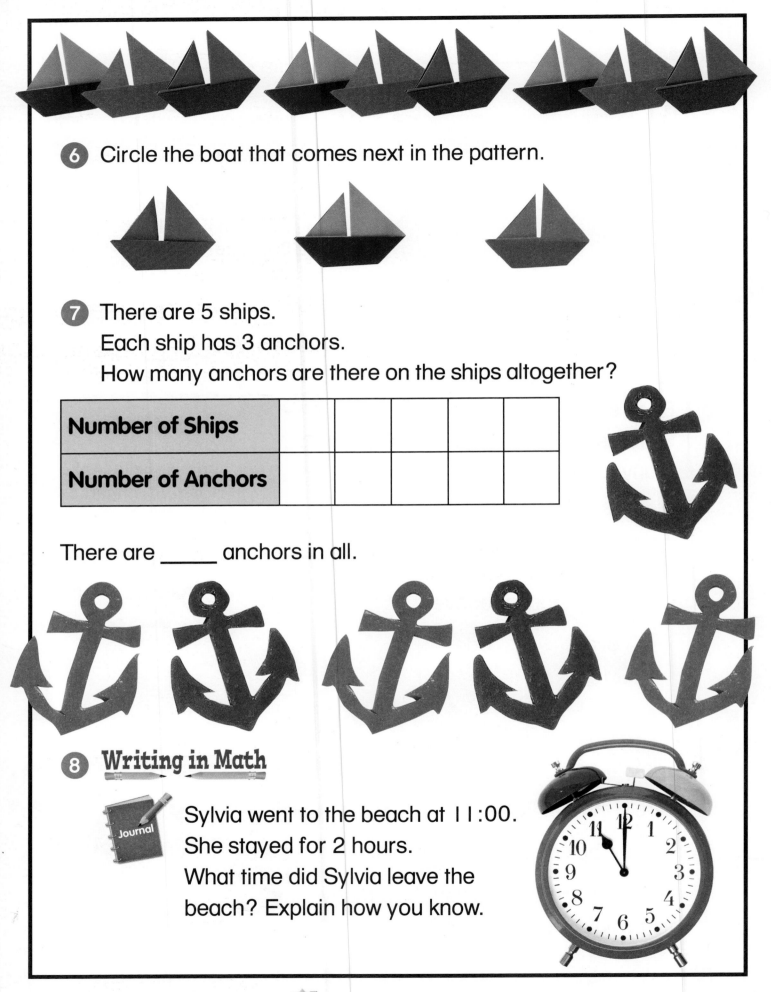

6 Circle the boat that comes next in the pattern.

7 There are 5 ships.
Each ship has 3 anchors.
How many anchors are there on the ships altogether?

Number of Ships					
Number of Anchors					

There are _____ anchors in all.

8 **Writing in Math**

Sylvia went to the beach at 11:00.
She stayed for 2 hours.
What time did Sylvia leave the
beach? Explain how you know.

Name_____

Color the numbers you say when you count by 2s.

1

51	52	53	54	55	56	57	58	59	60
61	62	63	64	65	66	67	68	69	70
71	72	73	74	75	76	77	78	79	80

How many cans of vegetables are there?
Count by 5s.

2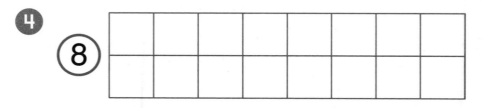

_____, _____, _____, _____, _____, _____

Find a pattern. Then write the numbers.

3 There are 5 sailboats.

Each boat has 3 sails.

How many sails are on the boats altogether?

Number of Boats					
Number of Sails					

There are _____ sails in all on the sailboats.

Draw circles to show the number.
Try to make equal rows.
Then circle **odd** or **even**.

4

⑧

odd

even

1 What is the sum?

$$\begin{array}{r} 6 \\ + 6 \\ \hline \end{array}$$

0	6	10	12
Ⓐ	Ⓑ	Ⓒ	Ⓓ

2 What is the missing number?

_____ groups of 10

1	2	5	10
Ⓐ	Ⓑ	Ⓒ	Ⓓ

3 Use the group of 10 to estimate.
What is the best estimate for how many there are in all?

Ⓐ about 20

Ⓑ about 40

Ⓒ about 60

Ⓓ about 80

4 Which day of the week answers the question?

On Thursday a baby bird leaves the nest.
It hops and tries to fly.
It is strong enough to fly away 2 days later.
On what day can the baby bird fly away?

Thursday	Friday	Saturday	Sunday
Ⓐ	Ⓑ	Ⓒ	Ⓓ

Writing in Math

5 What is something you do in the morning?
What is something you do in the evening?

_____

_____

Enrichment

Counting by 10s from Any Number

If you use a hundred chart, it is easy to count by 10s from any number.

1	2	3	4	5	6	7	8	9	10
11	12	13	14	15	16	17	18	19	20
21	22	23	24	25	26	27	28	29	30
31	32	33	34	35	36	37	38	39	40
41	42	43	44	45	46	47	48	49	50
51	52	53	54	55	56	57	58	59	60
61	62	63	64	65	66	67	68	69	70
71	72	73	74	75	76	77	78	79	80
81	82	83	84	85	86	87	88	89	90
91	92	93	94	95	96	97	98	99	100

6, __16__, __26__, __36__, __46__,

__56__, __66__, __76__, __86__, __96__

Start at the number given and count by 10s.
Use the hundred chart if you like.

1 3, _____, _____, _____, _____, _____, _____, _____, _____, _____

2 29, _____, _____, _____, _____, _____, _____, _____

3 14, _____, _____, _____, _____, _____, _____, _____, _____

4 38, _____, _____, _____, _____, _____, _____

5 **Writing in Math**

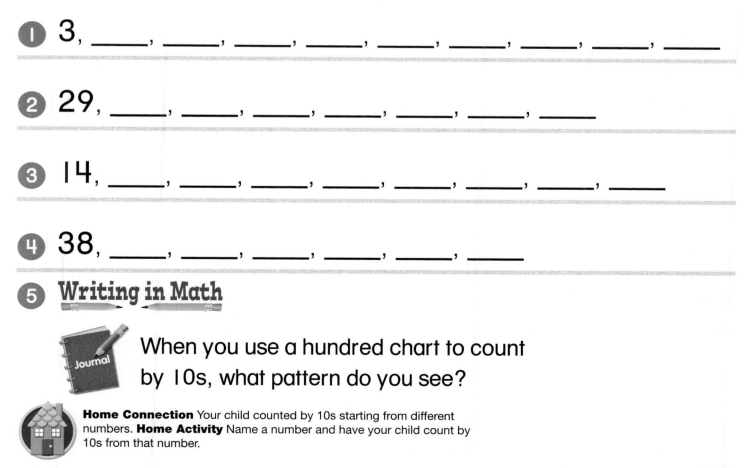

When you use a hundred chart to count by 10s, what pattern do you see?

Home Connection Your child counted by 10s starting from different numbers. **Home Activity** Name a number and have your child count by 10s from that number.

Name _____

Skip Count Using a Calculator

You can use a calculator to skip count.

Press `ON/C`. Press the keys that are shown.

Write what the display shows each time you press `=`.

① `2` `+` `2` `=` 4 `=` ___ `=` ___

The pattern is counting by ___2s___.

② `1` `0` `+` `1` `0` `=` ___ `=` ___ `=` ___

The pattern is counting by _____.

③ `4` `0` `+` `5` `=` ___ `=` ___ `=` ___

The pattern is counting by _____.

④ `8` `5` `+` `1` `0` `=` ___ `=` ___ `=` ___

The pattern is counting by _____.

Think About It   Number Sense

In Exercise 4, which calculator key would you press to find the next number in the pattern? Explain.

Home Connection Your child used a calculator to skip count by 2s, 5s, and 10s. **Home Activity** Ask your child to explain how to use a calculator to skip count by 3s. *(Sample answer: I would press 3 + 3 = = = .)*

Name_____

Plan How to Find the Answer

Read Together

You can use problem-solving strategies
to help you find answers to math problems.

Test-Taking Strategies

Understand the Question

Get Information for the Answer

Plan How to Find the Answer

Make Smart Choices

Use Writing in Math

1. Liz learns 2 new songs every day.
How many new songs does she
learn in 5 days?

Ⓐ 2 songs   Ⓑ 10 songs   Ⓒ 8 songs   Ⓓ 12 songs

Use problem-solving strategies. Make a table.
Look for a pattern. Count the songs by twos.

Number of Days	1	2	3	4	5
Number of Songs	2	4	6	8	10

In 5 days, Liz learns __10__ new songs. Fill in the answer bubble.

Your Turn

Use problem-solving strategies to solve this problem.
Fill in the answer bubble.

2. Derrick plays the piano 3 hours a week.
How many hours does he play the piano in 6 weeks?

Ⓐ 3 hours   Ⓑ 14 hours   Ⓒ 10 hours   Ⓓ 18 hours

Home Connection Your child prepared for standardized tests by using problem-solving strategies to answer math questions. **Home Activity** Ask your child to describe the strategies he or she used to solve Exercise 2. *(Possible answers: Make a table; look for a pattern; use objects)*

Name _____

Animal Families

How big is your family? Some families are small.
Some families are big.

Many animals live in groups. These groups are a lot
like families. Some of them are small. Some of them
are big. You can count groups of 10 to find out how
many animals there are in an animal family.

Family Pride

1 A group of lions is called a **pride.**
How many groups of 10 are in a pride of 30 lions?

_____ groups of 10

How many lions are left over? _____ lions

2 A group of sheep is called a **flock.**
How many groups of 10 are in a flock of 93 sheep?

_____ groups of ten

How many sheep are left over? _____ sheep

3 A group of monkeys is called a **troop.**
How many groups of 10 are in a troop of 11 monkeys?

_____ group of ten

How many monkeys are left over? _____ monkey

Take It to the NET
Video and Activities
www.scottforesman.com

Home Connection Your child solved problems about different kinds of
animal groups by counting groups of 10. **Home Activity** Show your
child a group of 20 to 60 small objects and ask him or her to count the
objects by groups of 10, to tell how many objects (if any) are left over,
and to write the total number of objects.

Write each number as 10 and some left over.

1 14 is 10 and _____.

2 19 is 10 and _____.

Count by 10s. Then write the numbers.

3 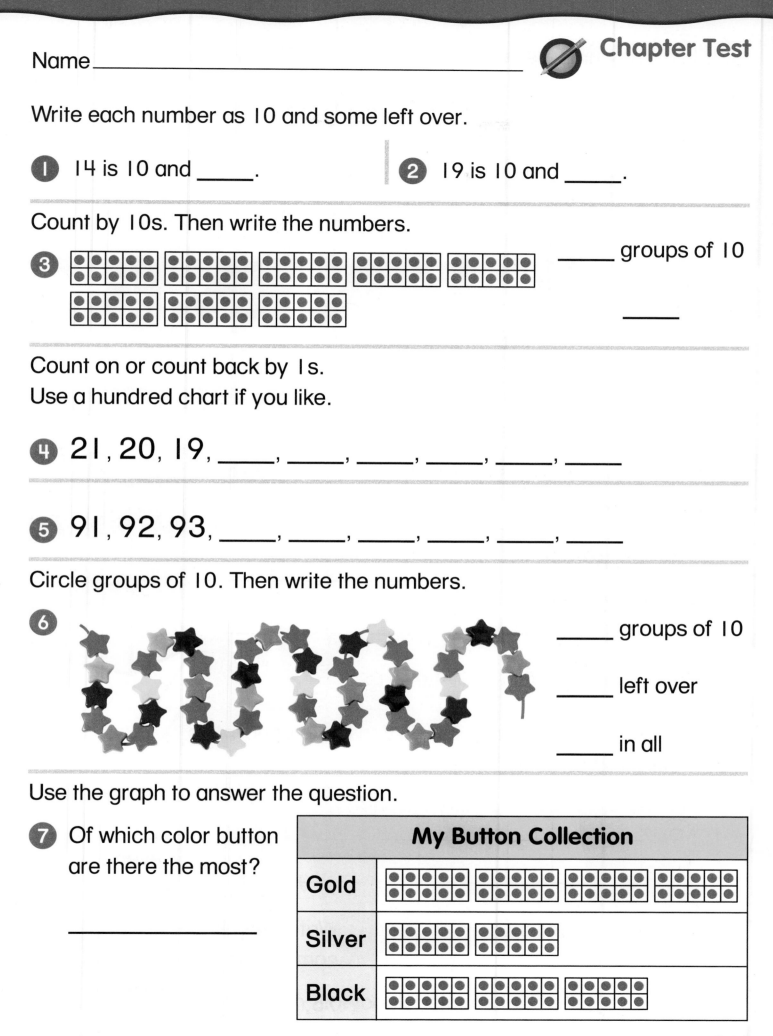 _____ groups of 10

_____

Count on or count back by 1s.
Use a hundred chart if you like.

4 21, 20, 19, _____, _____, _____, _____, _____, _____

5 91, 92, 93, _____, _____, _____, _____, _____, _____

Circle groups of 10. Then write the numbers.

6

_____ groups of 10

_____ left over

_____ in all

Use the graph to answer the question.

7 Of which color button are there the most?

_____

My Button Collection	
Gold	
Silver	
Black	

Use cubes or clips in sets of tens
on a grid that's **10** by **10**.

Toss a number cube, please do.
Then take that many **tens** for you.

This is how you play the game.
Making **100** is your aim.

Aa Bb Cc Dd Ee Ff Gg Hh Ii
I have 1 ten, but I've just begun.
When I get 9 more, I will have won!

We raced to **100**. We found **3** ways.
1 ten and **9** tens
2 tens and **8** tens
3 tens and **7** tens

How about you? Can you find some others?

Home-School Connection

Dear Family,

Today my class started Chapter 8, **Place Value, Data, and Graphs.** I will learn about numbers made with tens and ones. I will also learn how to use data to make different kinds of graphs. Here are some of the math words I will be learning and some things we can do to help me with my math.

Love,

_____

Math Activity to Do at Home

Play a number guessing game with your child. Think of a number between 10 and 100. Give your child clues, using math words. For example, if your number is 37, you might say: "I am thinking of an *odd number* between 35 and 39."

Books to Read Together

Reading math stories reinforces concepts. Look for these titles in your local library:

100th Day Worries
By Margery Cuyler
(Simon and Schuster, 2000)

One Hundred Hungry Ants
By Elinor J. Pinczes
(Houghton Mifflin, 1993)

Take It to the NET
More Activities
www.scottforesman.com

My New Math Words

The number **135** can be shown with these models:

1 **hundred**   3 **tens**   5 **ones**

Symbols are used to compare numbers.

20 **<** 30   30 **>** 20   30 **=** 30

is less than   **is greater than**   **equals**

Graphs are used to display data.

bar graph

picture graph

Race to One Hundred

How to Play

1. Play with a partner.
2. Take turns tossing the cube.
3. Color that many sets of ten on one of your grids. Say the number (for example, "6 tens is 60").
4. Keep playing until all of the grids have been colored in.

© Pearson Education, Inc.

What You Need

I dot cube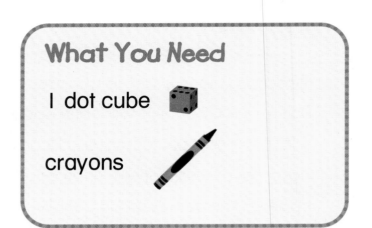

crayons

Learn!

You can show 32 in different ways.

You can break apart a ten to make 10 ones.

Tens	Ones

$32 = 30 + 2$

Tens	Ones

$32 = 20 + 12$

Check ✓

Use cubes and Workmat 4.

Follow the directions to show a different way to make the number.

1

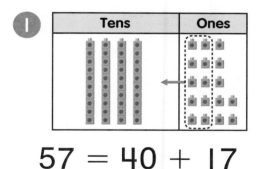

$57 = 40 + 17$

Make a ten with 10 ones:

$57 = \underline{50} + \underline{7}$

2

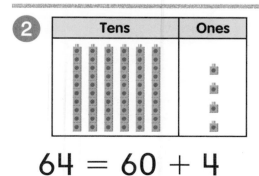

$64 = 60 + 4$

Break apart a ten into 10 ones:

$64 = \underline{} + \underline{}$

Think About It   Number Sense

Why is 2 tens and 7 ones the same as 1 ten and 17 ones?

Use cubes and Workmat 4.
Follow the directions to show a different
way to make the number.

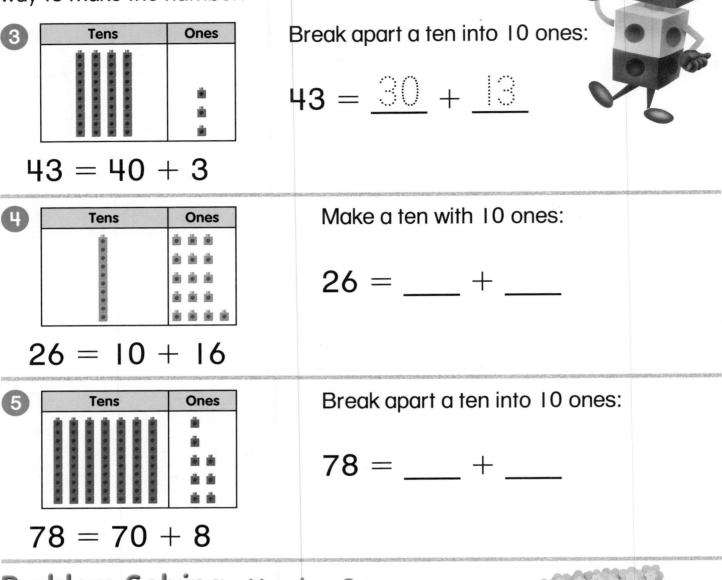

3

Tens	Ones

$43 = 40 + 3$

Break apart a ten into 10 ones:

$43 = \underline{30} + \underline{13}$

4

Tens	Ones

$26 = 10 + 16$

Make a ten with 10 ones:

$26 = \underline{} + \underline{}$

5

Tens	Ones

$78 = 70 + 8$

Break apart a ten into 10 ones:

$78 = \underline{} + \underline{}$

Problem Solving   Number Sense

Use cubes to solve.
Circle **yes** or **no**.

6 On Lori's workmat there are 2 tens and 11 ones.
On Beth's workmat there are 3 tens and 2 ones.

Are the girls showing the same number
on each of their workmats?

yes

no

Home Connection Your child showed numbers in different ways.
Home Activity Choose a number between 21 and 99. Ask your
child to tell you two different ways to make that number. For example,
$53 = 50 + 3$ and $53 = 40 + 13$.

Name_____

Understand Graphic Sources: Pictures

Read this story problem.
Use the picture to help you.

Mateo and Emily are selling wrapping paper.
Mateo has 24 rolls.
Emily has 22 rolls.
How many rolls do they have in all?

1 How many tens and ones are in
Mateo's group of rolls?

There are _____ tens and _____ ones.

2 How many tens and ones are in
Emily's group of rolls?

There are _____ tens and _____ ones.

3 How many tens and ones are there in all?

There are _____ tens and _____ ones in all.

4 How many rolls do Mateo and Emily have in all?

_____ rolls

Think About It   Reasoning

If you didn't have the picture, how could you find
how many rolls there are in all?

Read another story problem.
Use the picture to help you.

Amy and her mom went to a used-book sale.
Amy bought 27 books.
Her mom bought 32 books.
How many books did they buy in all?

5 Find the number of tens and ones
in each group.

Amy has _____ tens and _____ ones.

Amy's mom has _____ tens and _____ ones.

6 Find the number of tens and ones in all.

There are _____ tens and _____ ones in all.

7 How many books did Amy and her mom
buy in all?

_____ books

© Pearson Education, Inc.

Name _____

Learn!

Lars collects pine cones.
He has 15 big pine cones
and 23 small pine cones.
How many pine cones
does Lars have in all?

Read and Understand

You need to find how many
pine cones Lars has altogether.

Plan and Solve

Make each number with cubes.
Join the two groups of cubes.
Find how many there are in all.

There are ___3___ tens and ___8___ ones in all.

Lars has ___38___ pine cones.

Look Back and Check

How can you check that your answer is correct?

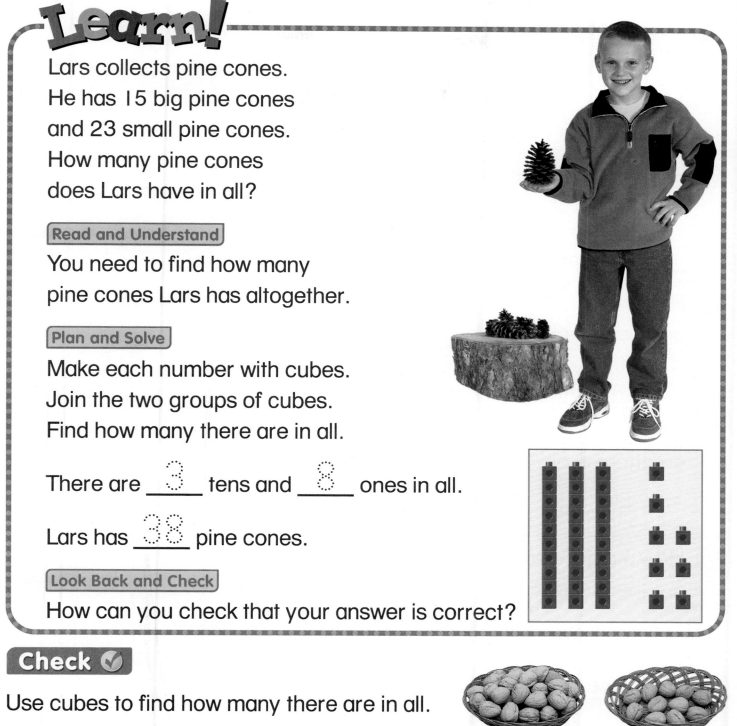

Check ✓

Use cubes to find how many there are in all.

1 Katie has 42 small walnuts
   and 14 large walnuts.
   How many walnuts does she have in all?

| 42 walnuts | 14 walnuts |

_____ walnuts

Think About It   Reasoning

How could you use cubes to find how
many walnuts there are in both baskets?

Use cubes to find how many there are in all.

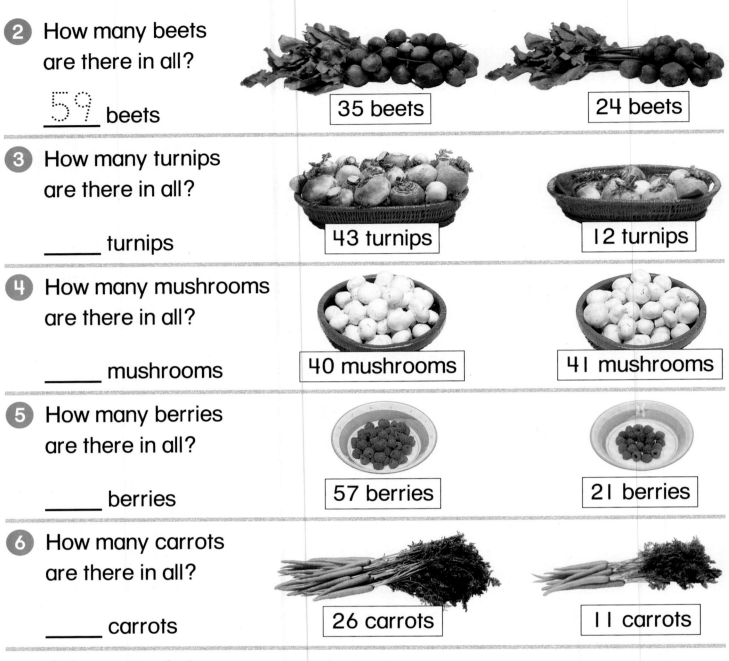

2 How many beets are there in all?

_59_ beets

35 beets   24 beets

3 How many turnips are there in all?

_____ turnips

43 turnips   12 turnips

4 How many mushrooms are there in all?

_____ mushrooms

40 mushrooms   41 mushrooms

5 How many berries are there in all?

_____ berries

57 berries   21 berries

6 How many carrots are there in all?

_____ carrots

26 carrots   11 carrots

Problem Solving   Algebra

Use cubes. Write the number of rice cakes below the basket.

7 There are 43 rice cakes in all.
31 rice cakes are in one basket.
How many rice cakes are in the other basket?

31 rice cakes   _____ rice cakes

Home Connection Your child put two groups of cubes together to find the total. **Home Activity** Give your child two groups of small objects, such as pennies or beans. Ask him or her to show each group as tens and ones and then to explain how to put the two groups together to find the total.

Count the tens. Then write the numbers.

1 ____ tens is ____.

2 ____ tens is ____.

Count the tens and ones. Then write the numbers.

3

Tens	Ones

➡

Tens	Ones

➡ ____

Draw the tens and ones. Then write the numbers.

4 27

Tens	Ones

____ tens + ____ ones = ____

____ + ____ = ____

Use cubes and Workmat 4 to show a different way to make the number.

5 58

Tens	Ones

$58 = 50 + 8$

Break apart a ten into 10 ones:

$58 = $ ____ $+$ ____

Use cubes to find how many there are in all.

6 How many pecans are there in all?

____ pecans

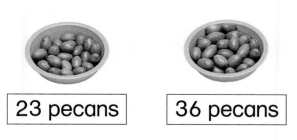

| 23 pecans | 36 pecans |

Use the hundred chart to answer the questions.

71	72	73	74	75	76	77	78	79	80
81	82	83		85	86	87	88	89	
91	92	93	94		96	97	98	99	100

1 What number is between 83 and 85?

    84   86   88   90

   Ⓐ   Ⓑ   Ⓒ   Ⓓ

2 What number is just before 91?

    81   89   90   91

   Ⓐ   Ⓑ   Ⓒ   Ⓓ

3 What number comes just after 94?

    94   95   96   97

   Ⓐ   Ⓑ   Ⓒ   Ⓓ

4 Which fraction tells how much is shaded?

    $\frac{1}{4}$ $\frac{1}{3}$ $\frac{2}{3}$ $\frac{3}{4}$

    Ⓐ   Ⓑ   Ⓒ   Ⓓ

Writing in Math

5 Write two number sentences that have a sum of 10.

$$\_\_ + \_\_ = 10$$

$$\_\_ + \_\_ = 10$$

Learn!

Take one cube away to show 1 less.

Add a ten to show 10 more.

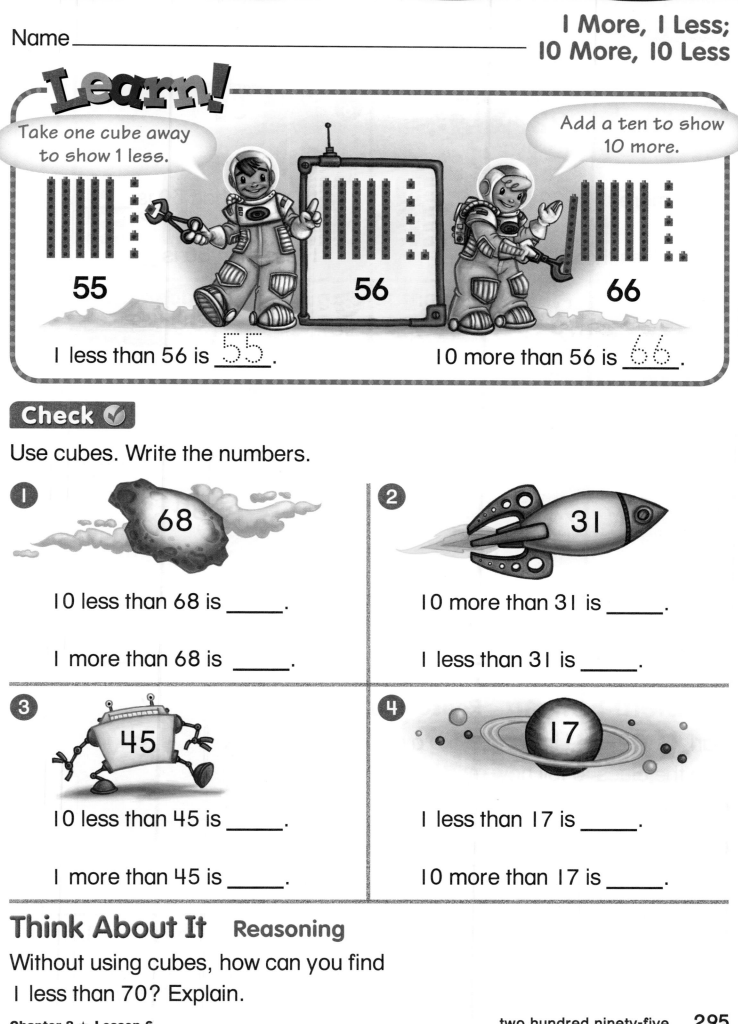

55

56

66

I less than 56 is __55__.

10 more than 56 is __66__.

Check ✓

Use cubes. Write the numbers.

1 68

10 less than 68 is _____.

1 more than 68 is _____.

2 31

10 more than 31 is _____.

1 less than 31 is _____.

3 45

10 less than 45 is _____.

1 more than 45 is _____.

4 17

1 less than 17 is _____.

10 more than 17 is _____.

Think About It   Reasoning

Without using cubes, how can you find
1 less than 70? Explain.

| < less than | > greater than | = equal to |

Write <, >, or =.

5 58 ◯(<) 70

6 13 ◯(<) 31

7 23 ◯(=) 23

8 86 ◯(>) 68

9 45 ◯(<) 54

10 29 ◯(<) 33

11 41 ◯(>) 39

12 93 ◯(=) 93

13 52 ◯(>) 25

14 77 ◯(<) 81

15 97 ◯(>) 79

16 15 ◯(<) 50

Problem Solving   Visual Thinking

17 Draw different models in the empty box.
Make both sides equal.

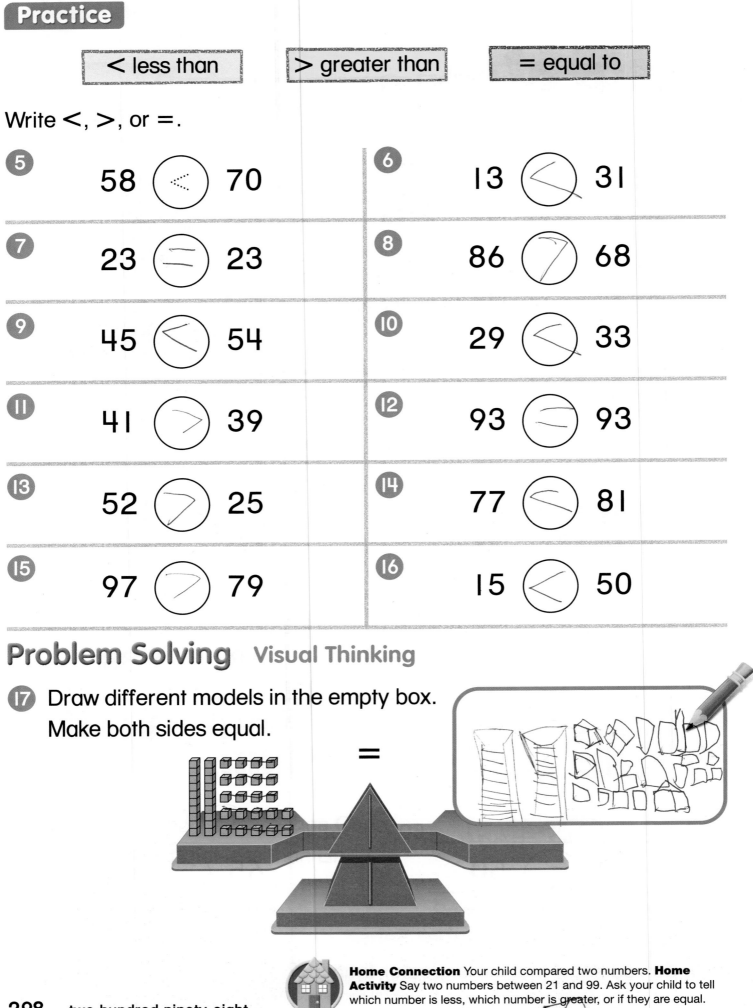

=

Home Connection Your child compared two numbers. **Home Activity** Say two numbers between 21 and 99. Ask your child to tell which number is less, which number is greater, or if they are equal.

Learn!

Draw lines to show where the numbers go on the number line.

Each number has its own place on the number line.

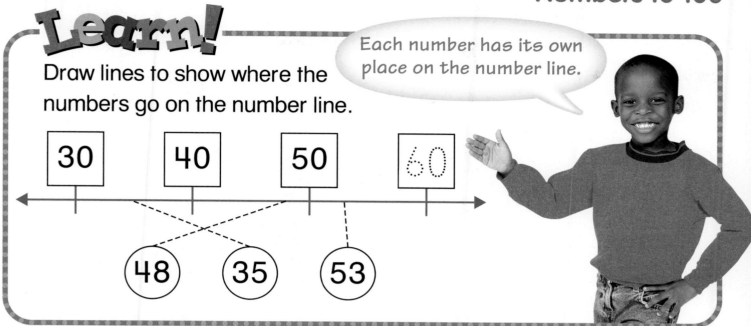

| 30 | 40 | 50 | 60 |

48   35   53

Check ✓

Complete the number line.
Then draw lines to show where the numbers go.

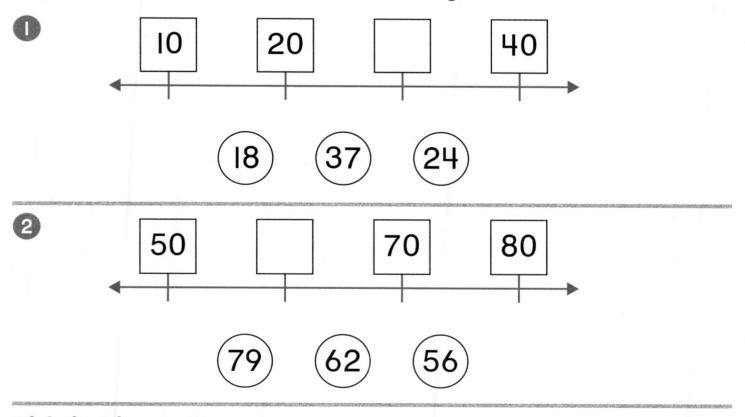

1

| 10 | 20 | | 40 |

18   37   24

2

| 50 | | 70 | 80 |

79   62   56

Think About It   Number Sense

Is 75 closer to 70 or to 80? Explain.

Complete the number line.
Then draw lines to show where the numbers go.

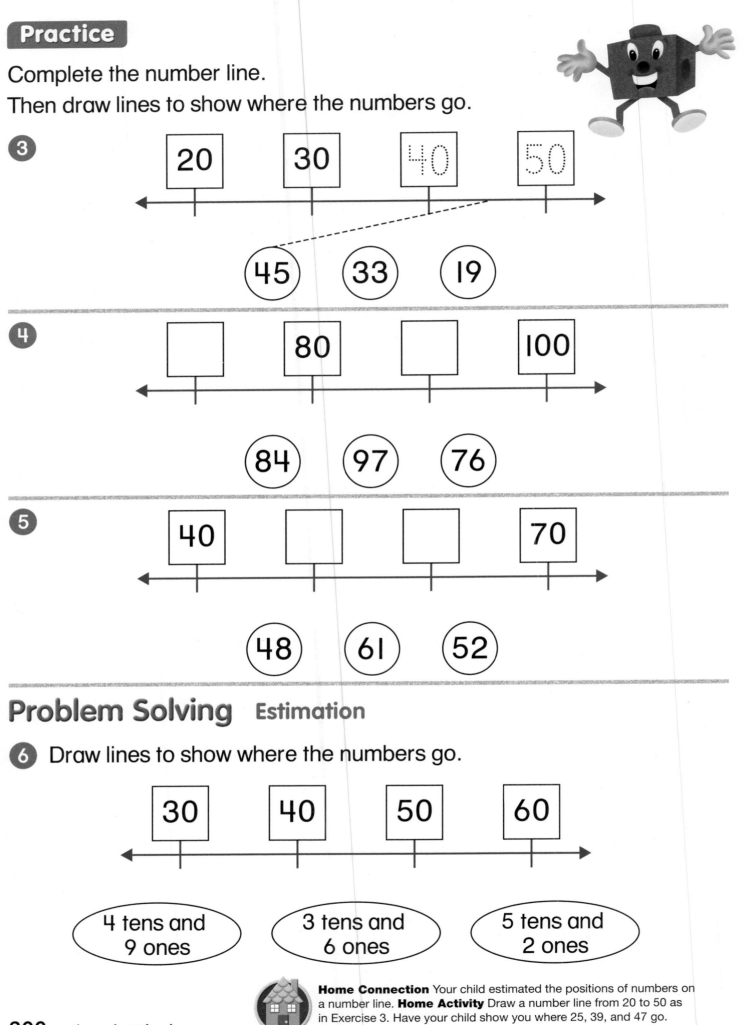

3

| 20 | 30 | 40 | 50 |

(45) (33) (19)

4

| | 80 | | 100 |

(84) (97) (76)

5

| 40 | | | 70 |

(48) (61) (52)

Problem Solving   Estimation

6 Draw lines to show where the numbers go.

| 30 | 40 | 50 | 60 |

(4 tens and 9 ones)   (3 tens and 6 ones)   (5 tens and 2 ones)

Home Connection Your child estimated the positions of numbers on a number line. **Home Activity** Draw a number line from 20 to 50 as in Exercise 3. Have your child show you where 25, 39, and 47 go.

Name_____

You can put these numbers in order from least to greatest.

least   greatest

Word Bank

least

greatest

Check ✔

Write the numbers in order from **least** to **greatest**.
Use Workmat 6 if you like.

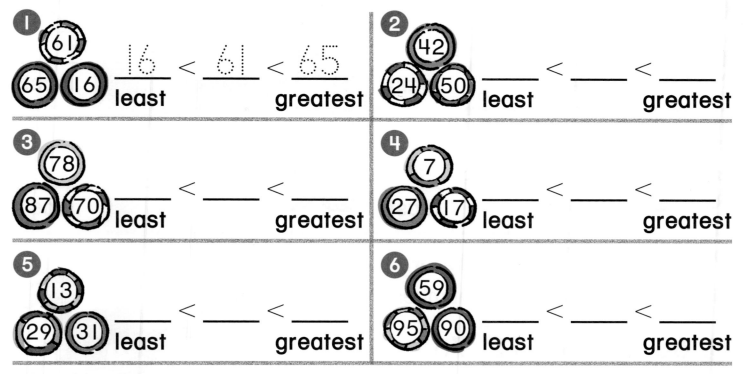

1 16 < 61 < 65
     least   greatest

2 ___ < ___ < ___
     least   greatest

3 ___ < ___ < ___
     least   greatest

4 ___ < ___ < ___
     least   greatest

5 ___ < ___ < ___
     least   greatest

6 ___ < ___ < ___
     least   greatest

Think About It   Number Sense

How can you tell which of these
numbers is the greatest?

41
43   14

What is the missing number?

1

10 is 6 and _____.

0	4	5	6
Ⓐ	Ⓑ	Ⓒ	Ⓓ

2

13 is 10 and _____.

0	2	3	4
Ⓐ	Ⓑ	Ⓒ	Ⓓ

3 What time is it?

Ⓐ 1 o'clock

Ⓑ 2 o'clock

Ⓒ 11 o'clock

Ⓓ 12 o'clock

4 Which group shows an even number?

Ⓐ   Ⓑ   Ⓒ   Ⓓ

5 What is the missing number?

Tens	Ones

Tens	Ones
2	7

___

20	27	70	72
Ⓐ	Ⓑ	Ⓒ	Ⓓ

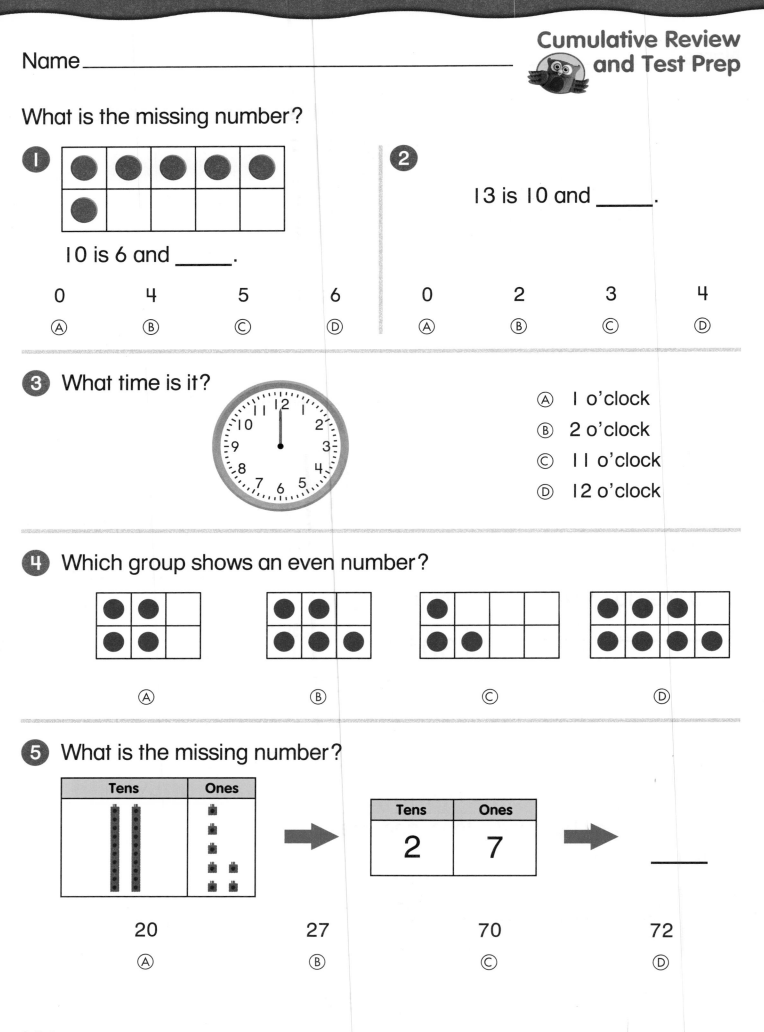

Name_____

Learn!

How are these fish sorted?

In what other ways could you **sort** them?

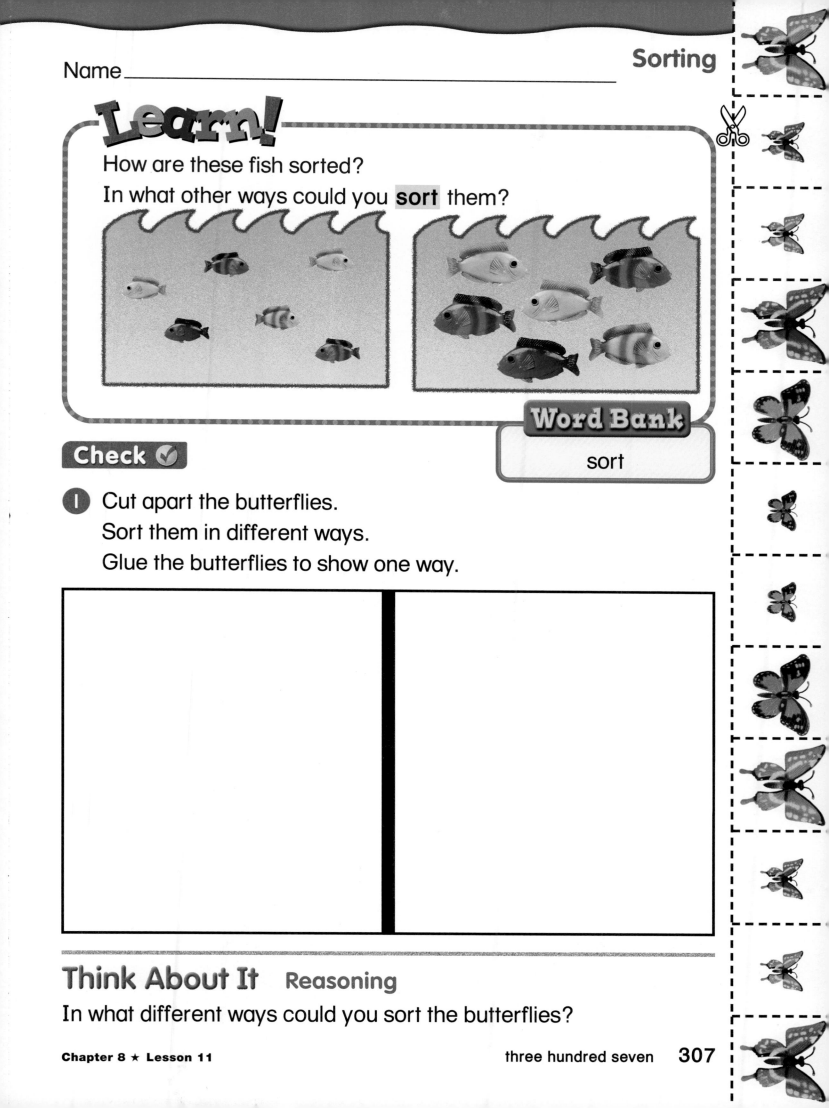

Word Bank

sort

Check ✓

1 Cut apart the butterflies.

Sort them in different ways.

Glue the butterflies to show one way.

Think About It   Reasoning

In what different ways could you sort the butterflies?

2 How could you sort these shapes?
Draw and color to show two groups
you could make.

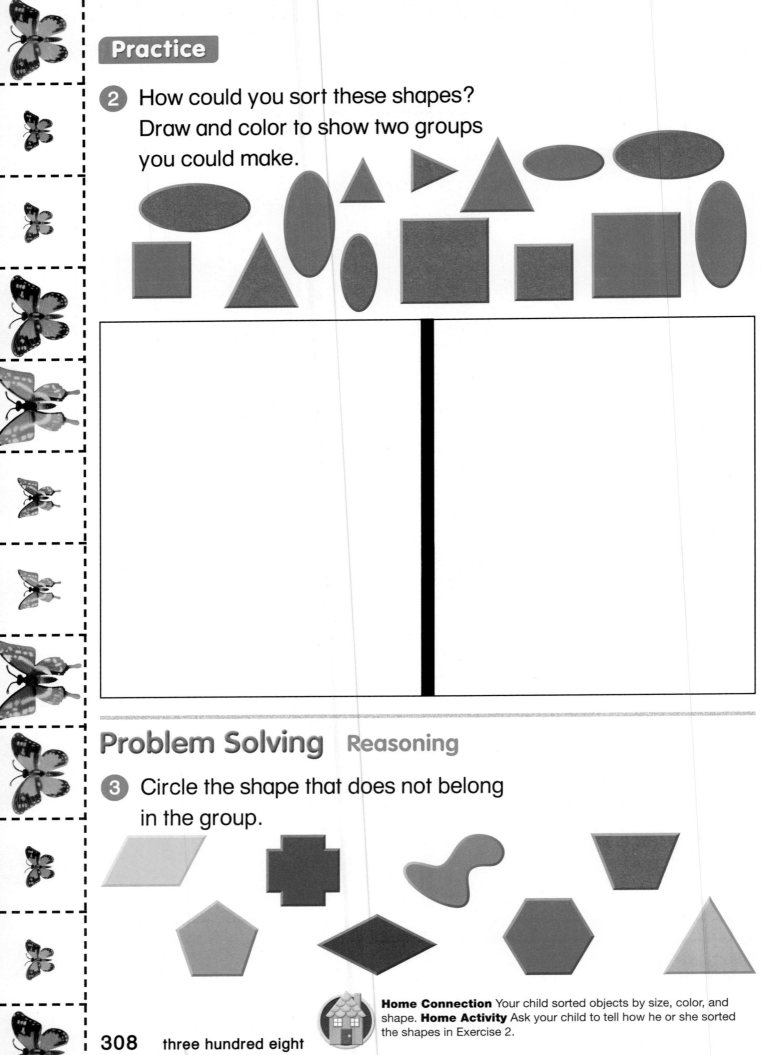

Problem Solving Reasoning

3 Circle the shape that does not belong
in the group.

© Pearson Education, Inc.

Home Connection Your child sorted objects by size, color, and
shape. **Home Activity** Ask your child to tell how he or she sorted
the shapes in Exercise 2.

Name_____

Learn!

You can show information in a **picture graph**.

Which toy is the favorite?

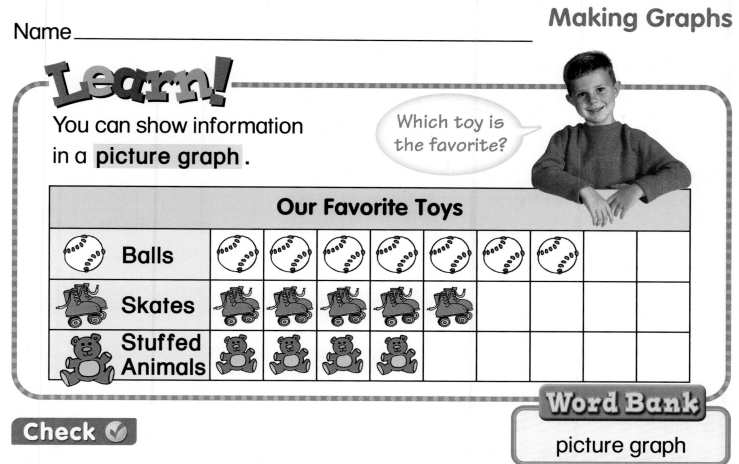

Our Favorite Toys

⚾	**Balls**	⚾	⚾	⚾	⚾	⚾	⚾	⚾		
🛼	**Skates**	🛼	🛼	🛼	🛼	🛼				
🧸	**Stuffed Animals**	🧸	🧸	🧸	🧸					

Check ✓

Word Bank

picture graph

1 Ask your classmates to choose their favorite lunches.
Draw to make a picture graph.

Our Favorite Lunches

🍲	**Soup**										
🥪	**Sandwich**										
🍕	**Pizza**										

Now use your graph to answer the questions.

2 Which lunch is the favorite? _____

3 Which lunch is the least favorite? _____

Think About It   Reasoning

How does the picture graph help
you keep track of the choices?

4 Ask your classmates to choose their favorite fruits.
Draw to make a picture graph.
Then answer the questions.

5 Which fruit is the
favorite of the class?

_____

6 Which fruit is the
least favorite?

_____

7 How many children
would have selected oranges
if 1 more child had
selected oranges?

_____

Our Favorite Fruits		
Apples	Bananas	Oranges

Problem Solving Writing in Math

8 Write a question about the picture graph above.

_____

_____

Home Connection Your child made picture graphs to show information
about the preferences of his or her classmates. **Home Activity** Have your
child explain the information in the graph on this page.

Name_____

Learn!

Read the **bar graph**.
Which sport is the favorite?

I chose soccer.

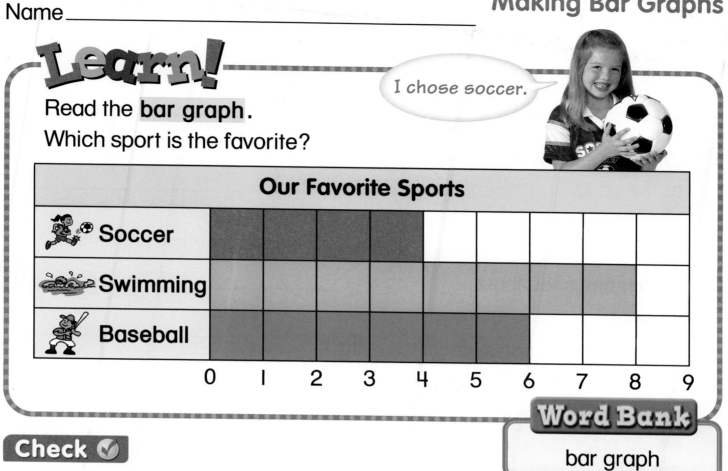

Our Favorite Sports

	0	1	2	3	4	5	6	7	8	9
Soccer										
Swimming										
Baseball										

Check ✓

Word Bank

bar graph

1 Ask your classmates to choose their favorite places.
Color to make a bar graph.

Our Favorite Places to Go

	0	1	2	3	4	5	6	7	8	9
Park										
Library										
Zoo										

Use the bar graph to answer the question.

2 Which place is the favorite of your class? _____

Think About It   Reasoning

How is a bar graph like a picture graph?
How is it different?

3 Ask your classmates to choose their favorite pets.
Color to make a bar graph.
Then answer the questions.

4 Which pet is the favorite
of the class?

_____

5 Which pet is the least
favorite?

_____

6 How many children
would have selected cats
if 2 more children
had selected them?

_____

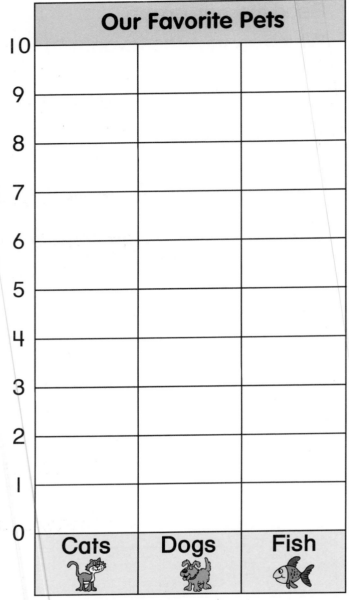

Our Favorite Pets

	Cats	Dogs	Fish

Problem Solving Number Sense

Put the pets in order from **least** to **greatest**
according to the number of spaces colored.
Write the words **Dogs**, **Cats**, and **Fish**.

7 _____, _____, _____
        least   greatest

Home Connection Your child made bar graphs to show information about
the preferences of his or her classmates. **Home Activity** Ask your child
how the bar graphs in this lesson are the same as and different from the
picture graphs in the previous lesson.

Name_____

Learn!

You can use **tally marks** to record information.

I made one tally mark for each spin.

		Total
Green	||||	4
Yellow	卌 卌 卌 |	16

Word Bank

tally mark

Check ✓

1. Spin the spinner 20 times using a pencil and a paper clip.
Make a tally mark for each spin.
Then write the totals.

		Total
Blue		
Red		
Yellow		

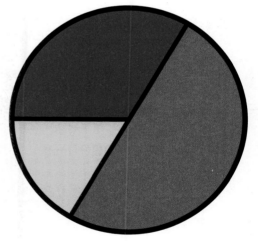

Use the tally chart to answer the questions.

2. Which color did you spin the most often? _____

3. Predict: If you spin one more time, on which color do you think the spinner will land? _____

Think About It Reasoning

How did you use the tally marks to help you predict the next color?

Make tally marks to show how many frogs
of each color there are. Then write the totals.

4

		Total
Green		
Yellow		
Orange		

Use the tally chart to answer the questions.

5 Of which color frogs are there the fewest? _____

6 How many green frogs and orange frogs
are there altogether? _____

7 How many more yellow frogs than
green frogs are there? _____

Problem Solving Writing in Math

8 Write your own question about the tally chart above.

_____

_____

Home Connection Your child made tally marks to record and count
information. **Home Activity** Have your child make tally marks to record the
number of males and females living in your house.

Name_____

Learn! Algebra

This is a map of Tory's town.

How would you get from Tory's house to the school?

Go 3 blocks right and 2 blocks up.

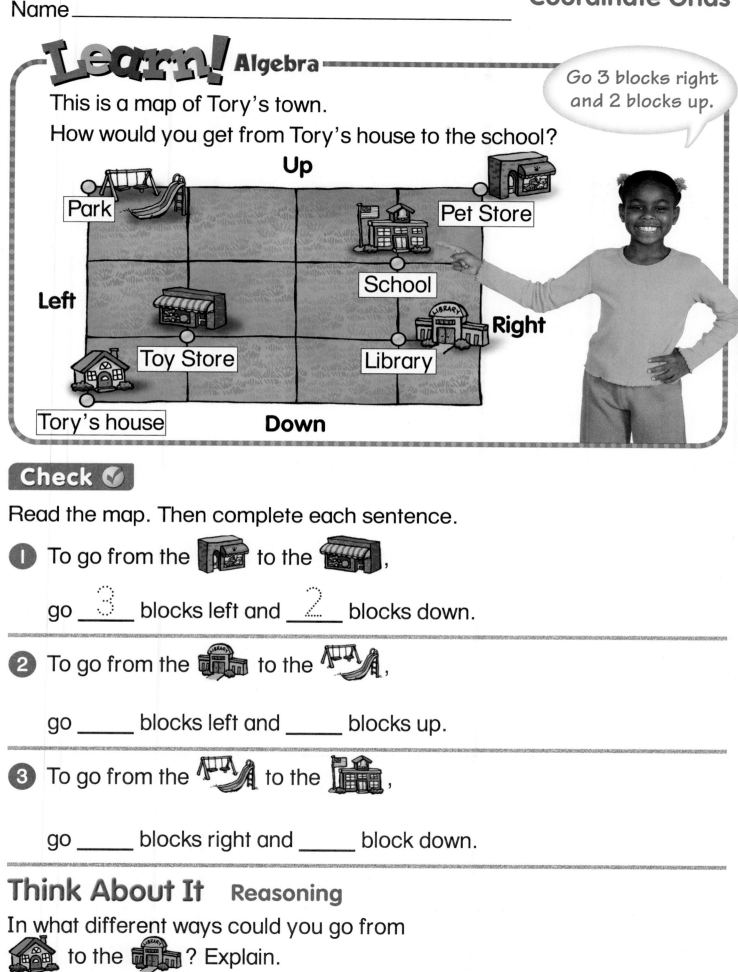

Check ✓

Read the map. Then complete each sentence.

1 To go from the [pet store] to the [toy store],

go __3__ blocks left and __2__ blocks down.

2 To go from the [library] to the [park],

go _____ blocks left and _____ blocks up.

3 To go from the [park] to the [school],

go _____ blocks right and _____ block down.

Think About It   Reasoning

In what different ways could you go from

[house] to the [library]? Explain.

Practice

This is a map of Bryan's town.

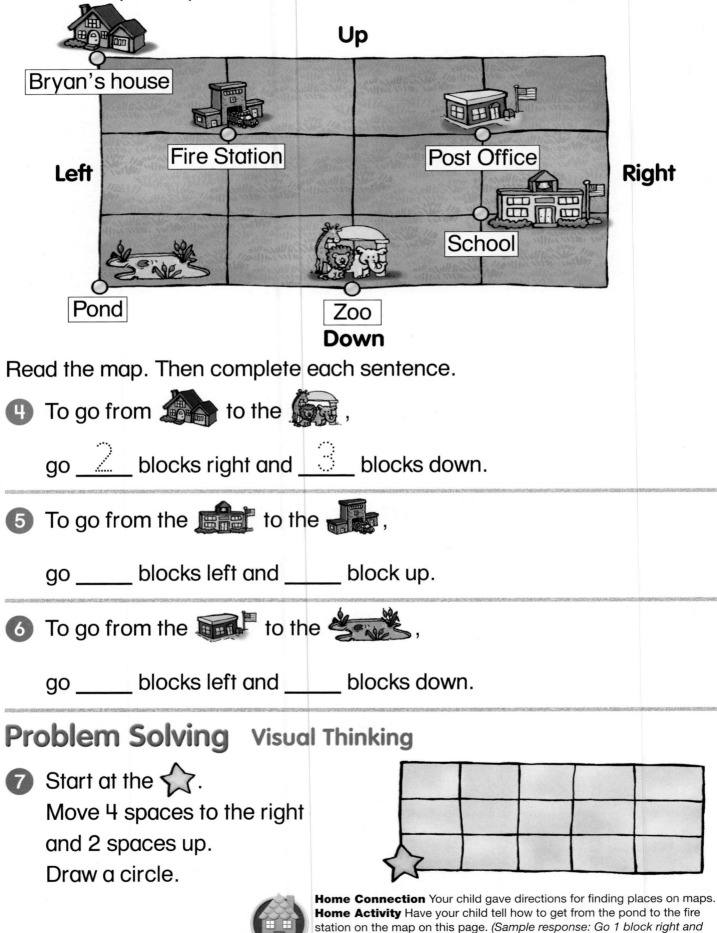

Read the map. Then complete each sentence.

4 To go from 🏠 to the 🐾 ,

go __2__ blocks right and __3__ blocks down.

5 To go from the 🏫 to the 🚒 ,

go _____ blocks left and _____ block up.

6 To go from the 🏤 to the 🌿 ,

go _____ blocks left and _____ blocks down.

Problem Solving Visual Thinking

7 Start at the ☆.
Move 4 spaces to the right
and 2 spaces up.
Draw a circle.

Home Connection Your child gave directions for finding places on maps.
Home Activity Have your child tell how to get from the pond to the fire station on the map on this page. *(Sample response: Go 1 block right and 2 blocks up.)*

Name_____

Learn!

This is a map of Lori's neighborhood. How many blocks is it from Lori's house to the ball field?

You can write an addition sentence to find out!

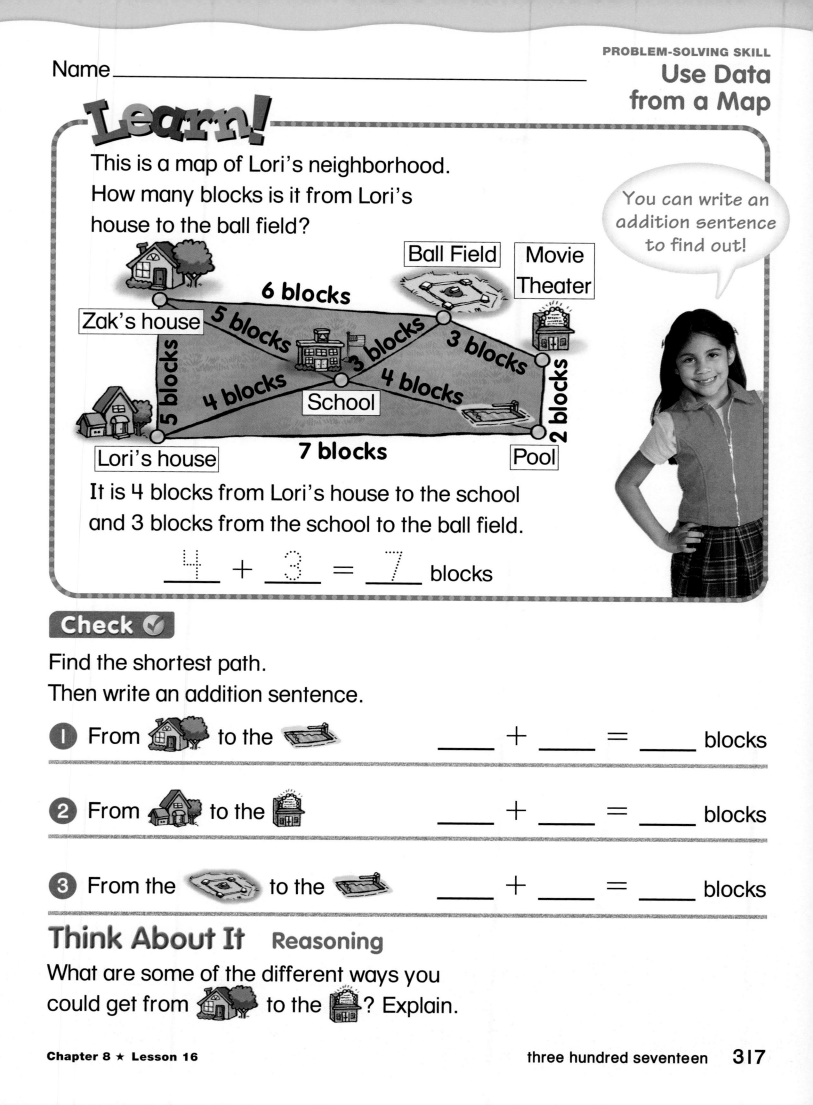

Zak's house

6 blocks

5 blocks

5 blocks

4 blocks

3 blocks

School

7 blocks

Lori's house

Ball Field

Movie Theater

3 blocks

4 blocks

2 blocks

Pool

It is 4 blocks from Lori's house to the school and 3 blocks from the school to the ball field.

__4__ + __3__ = __7__ blocks

Check ✓

Find the shortest path.
Then write an addition sentence.

1 From 🏠 to the ▭   ____ + ____ = ____ blocks

2 From 🏠 to the 🏛   ____ + ____ = ____ blocks

3 From the ⬡ to the ▭   ____ + ____ = ____ blocks

Think About It   Reasoning

What are some of the different ways you could get from 🏠 to the 🏛? Explain.

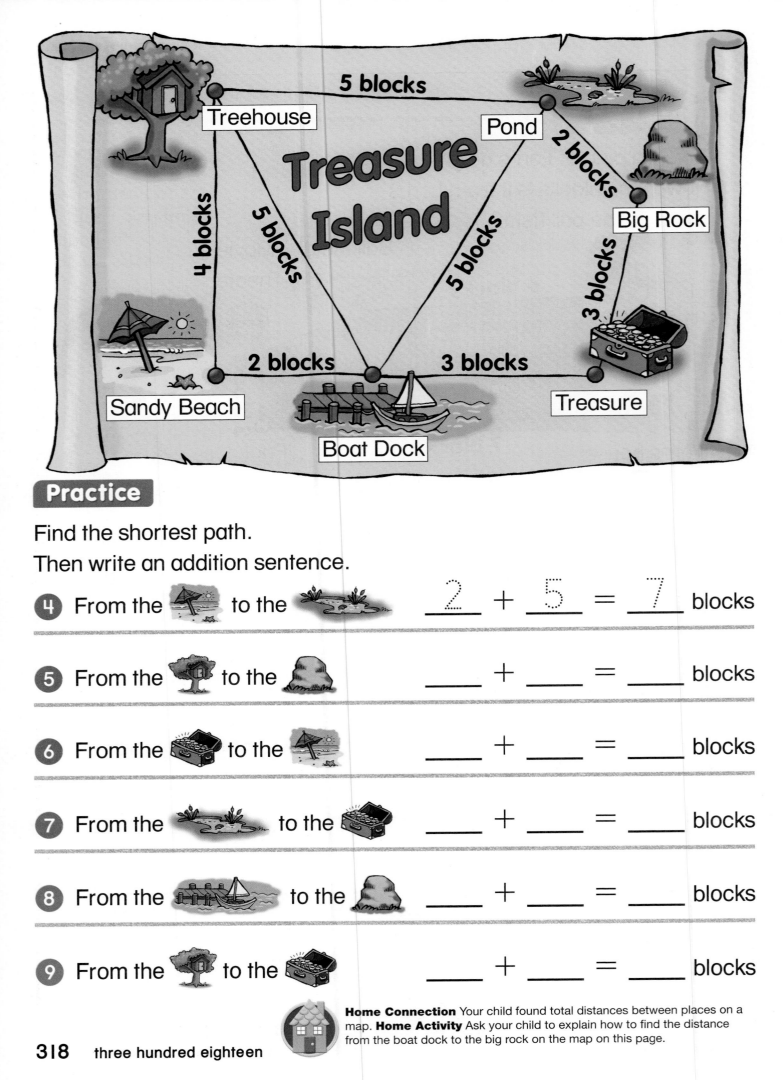

Treasure Island

5 blocks (Treehouse — Pond)

Treehouse

Pond

2 blocks (Pond — Big Rock)

Big Rock

4 blocks (Treehouse — Sandy Beach)

5 blocks (Treehouse — Boat Dock)

5 blocks (Pond — Boat Dock)

3 blocks (Big Rock — Treasure)

2 blocks (Sandy Beach — Boat Dock)

Sandy Beach

3 blocks (Boat Dock — Treasure)

Treasure

Boat Dock

Practice

Find the shortest path.

Then write an addition sentence.

4 From the 🏖 to the 🟩 $2 + 5 = 7$ blocks

5 From the 🌳 to the 🪨   ___ + ___ = ___ blocks

6 From the 💰 to the 🏖   ___ + ___ = ___ blocks

7 From the 🟩 to the 💰   ___ + ___ = ___ blocks

8 From the ⛵ to the 🪨   ___ + ___ = ___ blocks

9 From the 🌳 to the 💰   ___ + ___ = ___ blocks

Home Connection Your child found total distances between places on a map. **Home Activity** Ask your child to explain how to find the distance from the boat dock to the big rock on the map on this page.

Name_____

DK Dorling Kindersley

Do You Know...
that early Americans used dried asparagus for medicine?

Daryl is making soup.
He needs 10 carrots and 10 peppers.

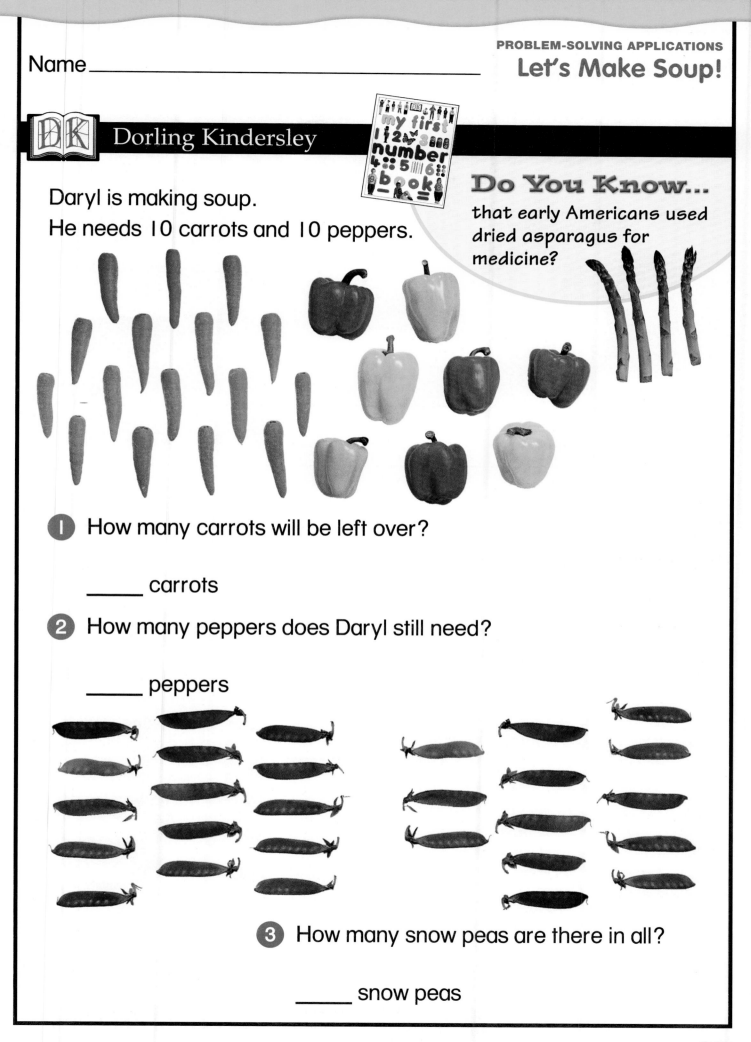

1 How many carrots will be left over?

_____ carrots

2 How many peppers does Daryl still need?

_____ peppers

3 How many snow peas are there in all?

_____ snow peas

4 Make tally marks to show how many vegetables. Then write the totals.

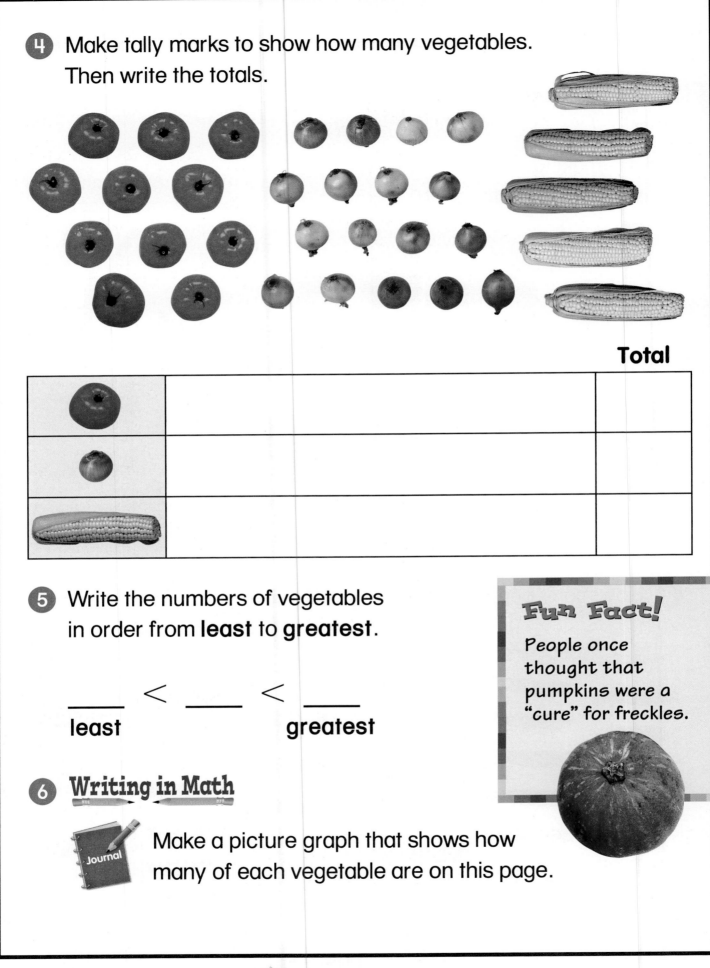

Total

🍅		
🧅		
🌽		

5 Write the numbers of vegetables in order from **least** to **greatest**.

____ < ____ < ____

least   greatest

6 **Writing in Math**

Make a picture graph that shows how many of each vegetable are on this page.

320 three hundred twenty

1 Sort the shapes.
Make a tally mark for each shape.

Total

Circles		
Squares		
Triangles		

Use the picture graph to answer the question.

2 Which snack is the favorite?

_____

Our Favorite Snacks

	Pretzels	⊗	⊗	⊗	⊗	⊗	⊗
	Muffins	🧁	🧁	🧁			
	Celery	🌿	🌿	🌿	🌿		

Use the bar graph to answer the question.

3 Which color is the least favorite?

_____

Our Favorite Colors

	0	1	2	3	4	5	6
Green							
Blue							
Red							

Read the map and complete the sentence.

4 To go from 🏠 to the 🏫,

go _____ blocks right

and _____ blocks down.

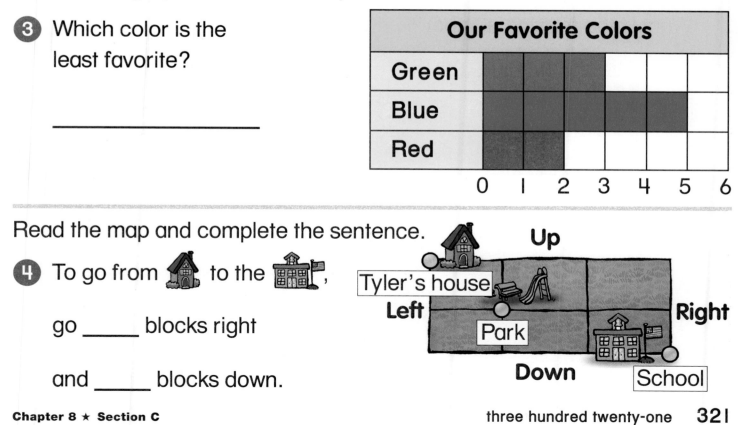

Up

Tyler's house

Left / Right

Park

Down

School

Name_____

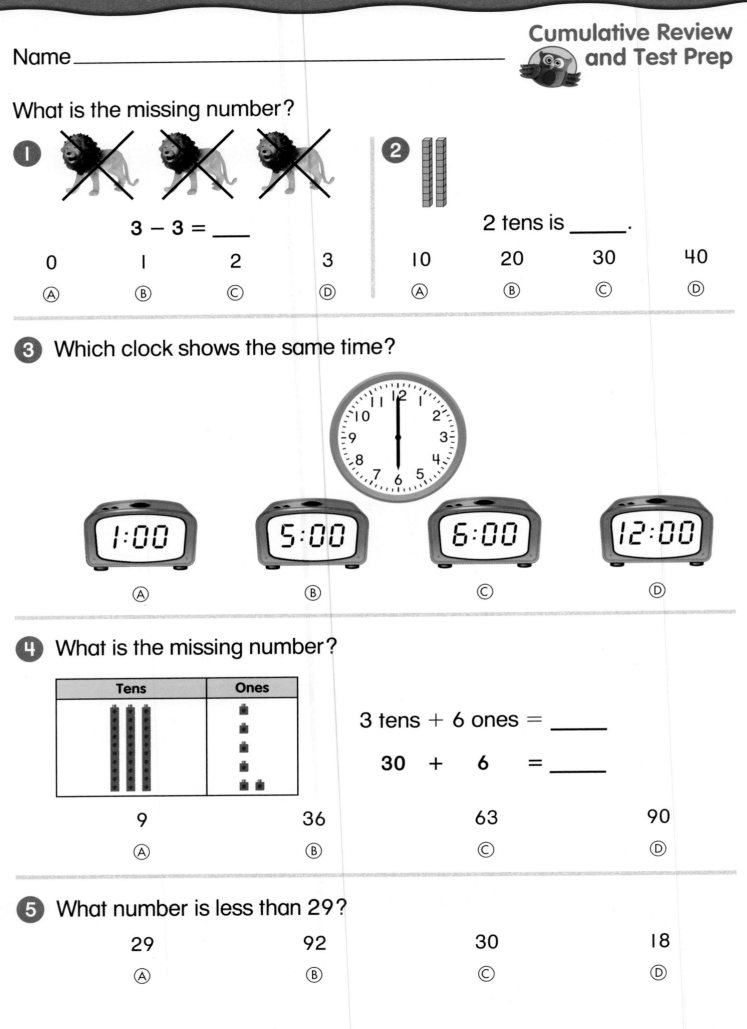

What is the missing number?

1

3 – 3 = ___

0   1   2   3
Ⓐ   Ⓑ   Ⓒ   Ⓓ

2

2 tens is ____.

10   20   30   40
Ⓐ   Ⓑ   Ⓒ   Ⓓ

3 Which clock shows the same time?

1:00   5:00   6:00   12:00
Ⓐ   Ⓑ   Ⓒ   Ⓓ

4 What is the missing number?

Tens	Ones

3 tens + 6 ones = ____

30 + 6 = ____

9   36   63   90
Ⓐ   Ⓑ   Ⓒ   Ⓓ

5 What number is less than 29?

29   92   30   18
Ⓐ   Ⓑ   Ⓒ   Ⓓ

Name_____

Rounding Numbers

Is 30 closer to 0 or to 100?

You can use the number line to find out.

> 30 is 70 away from 100, but only 30 away from 0.

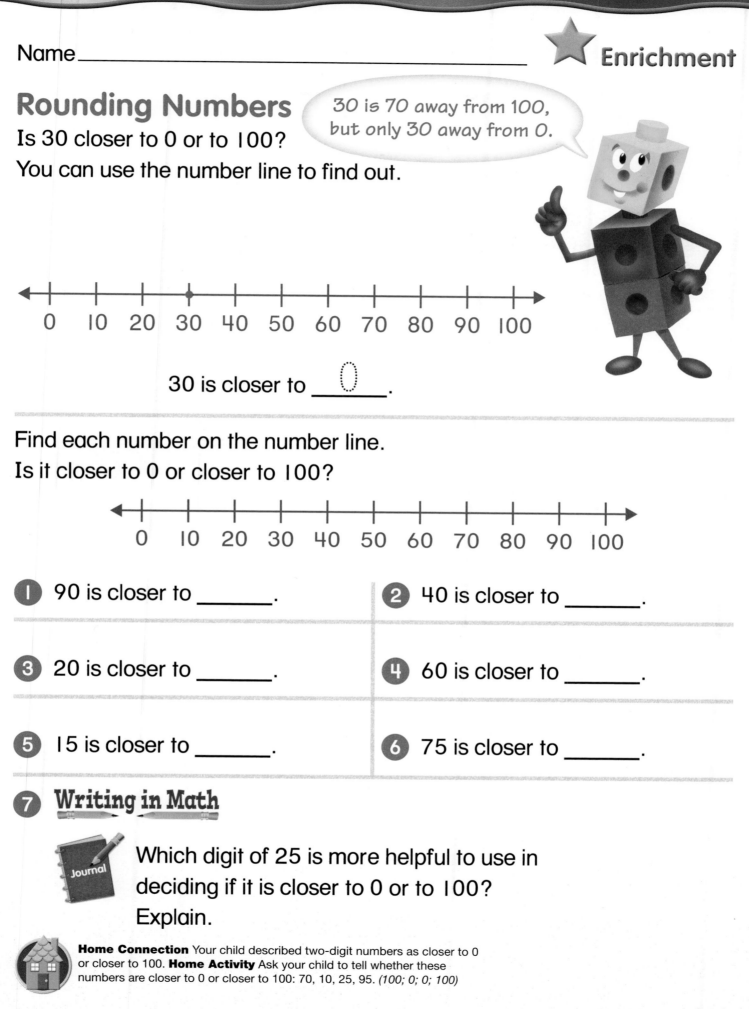

```
←——+——+——+——◆——+——+——+——+——+——+——→
   0  10  20  30  40  50  60  70  80  90  100
```

30 is closer to ____0____.

Find each number on the number line.
Is it closer to 0 or closer to 100?

```
←——+——+——+——+——+——+——+——+——+——+——→
   0   10  20  30  40  50  60  70  80  90  100
```

1 90 is closer to _____.

2 40 is closer to _____.

3 20 is closer to _____.

4 60 is closer to _____.

5 15 is closer to _____.

6 75 is closer to _____.

7 ✏️ **Writing in Math**

Which digit of 25 is more helpful to use in deciding if it is closer to 0 or to 100? Explain.

Home Connection Your child described two-digit numbers as closer to 0 or closer to 100. **Home Activity** Ask your child to tell whether these numbers are closer to 0 or closer to 100: 70, 10, 25, 95. *(100; 0; 0; 100)*

Make a Bar Graph on a Computer

You can make a graph that shows
your class's favorite seasons of the year.

1 On a sheet of paper, write the words **summer,
spring, winter,** and **fall.**

2 Put a tally mark next to your favorite season.

3 Ask each person which season is his or
her favorite. Put a tally mark next to it.

4 On a computer, go to the
Primary Spreadsheet in the
Spreadsheet/Data/Grapher eTool.

5 In the first box, type **summer.** Underneath
summer, type **spring, winter,** and **fall.**

6 Count the tallies on your paper and record the numbers
in the boxes next to each season's name on the computer.

7 Make a horizontal bar graph of your data.

Think About It   Reasoning

Which season is your class's favorite?
Which season is your class's least favorite?

I like all of them!

Home Connection Your child used a computer to record information and
make a bar graph. **Home Activity** Ask your child questions about the bar
graph he or she made about the class's favorite seasons. For example, ask how
many more children chose summer rather than winter as their favorite season.

Name_____

 Make Smart Choices

First, find the **wrong** answers.
Then, choose the **correct** answer.

Test-Taking Strategies

Understand the Question

Get Information for the Answer

Plan How to Find the Answer

Make Smart Choices

Use Writing in Math

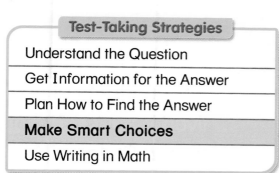

1 Which number is 10 less than 65?

Ⓐ 50

Ⓑ 70

Ⓒ 55

Ⓓ 75

You know that the correct answer should have a **5** in the ones place.

You know that the correct answer should be 10 **less** than 65.

Fill in the correct answer bubble.

Your Turn

First, find the wrong answers.
Then, fill in the correct answer bubble.

You can do it!

2 Which number is 10 more than 84?

Ⓐ 74

Ⓑ 94

Ⓒ 83

Ⓓ 85

 Home Connection Your child prepared for standardized tests by eliminating wrong answer choices to help find the correct answer choice. **Home Activity** Ask your child to explain why three of the answer choices are wrong in Exercise 2.

Add or subtract.

7.

$$\begin{array}{r} 7 \\ + 3 \\ \hline \end{array}$$
$$\begin{array}{r} 4 \\ + 8 \\ \hline \end{array}$$
$$\begin{array}{r} 11 \\ - 2 \\ \hline \end{array}$$
$$\begin{array}{r} 6 \\ + 0 \\ \hline \end{array}$$
$$\begin{array}{r} 7 \\ - 1 \\ \hline \end{array}$$
$$\begin{array}{r} 4 \\ - 4 \\ \hline \end{array}$$

Divide the group in half.

8.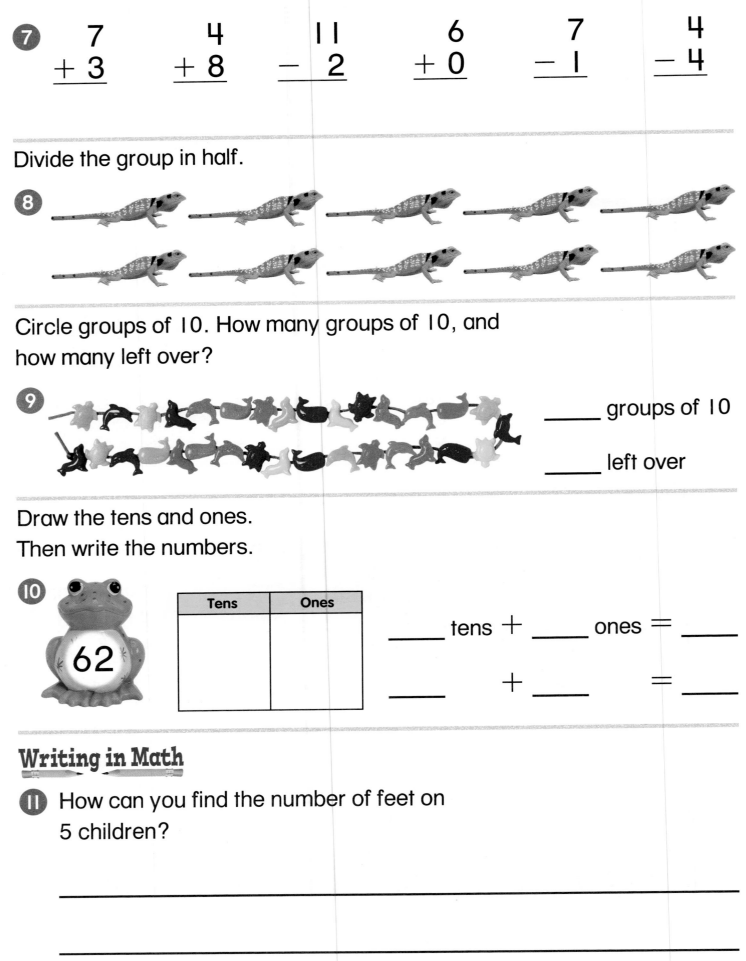

Circle groups of 10. How many groups of 10, and how many left over?

9.

_____ groups of 10

_____ left over

Draw the tens and ones.
Then write the numbers.

10.

62

Tens	Ones

_____ tens + _____ ones = _____

_____ + _____ = _____

Writing in Math

11. How can you find the number of feet on 5 children?

_____

_____

Rhyme Time

Written by Evie Lester   Illustrated by Laura Ovresat

This Math Storybook belongs to

_____

Penny, nickel, dollar, dime.
We can make change all the time.

9B

I had **5** pennies that I changed for a nickel.
Either will buy me a sweet, green pickle.

I had **4** quarters that I changed for a dollar.
Either will buy Rex a brand-new collar!

Name _____

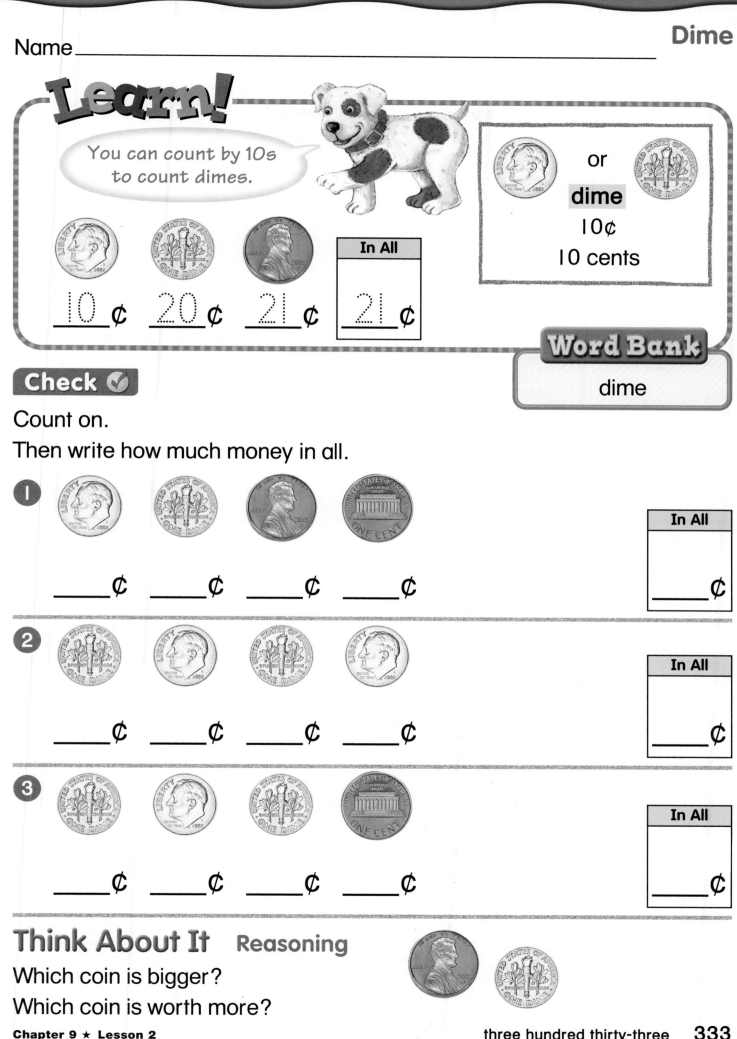

Learn!

You can count by 10s to count dimes.

__10__ ¢   __20__ ¢   __21__ ¢

In All
__21__ ¢

or

dime
10¢
10 cents

Check ✓

Count on.
Then write how much money in all.

1   ____¢ ____¢ ____¢ ____¢

In All
_____¢

2   ____¢ ____¢ ____¢ ____¢

In All
_____¢

3   ____¢ ____¢ ____¢ ____¢

In All
_____¢

Think About It   Reasoning

Which coin is bigger?
Which coin is worth more?

Circle the coins that match each price.

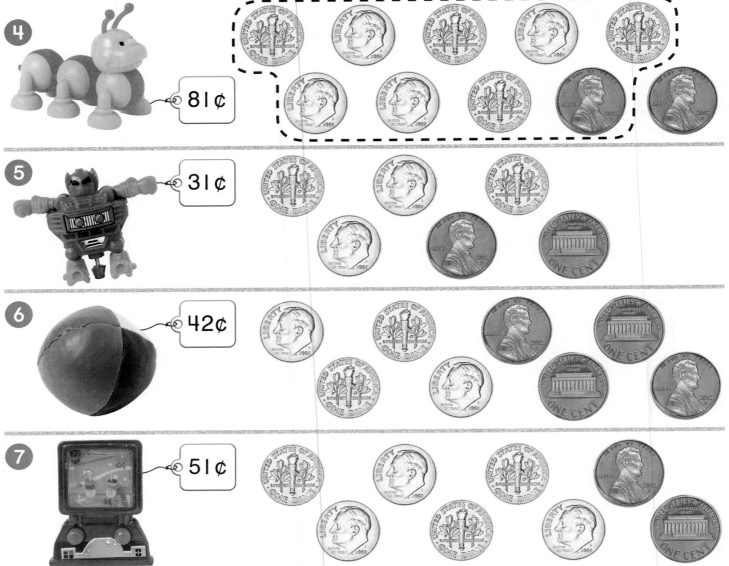

4   81¢

5   31¢

6   42¢

7   51¢

Problem Solving   Number Sense

Color each bank to make the sentences true.

8   The blue bank has the most money.
     The red bank has more money than the green bank.

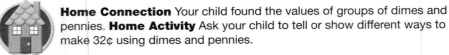
Home Connection Your child found the values of groups of dimes and pennies. **Home Activity** Ask your child to tell or show different ways to make 32¢ using dimes and pennies.

Learn!

Calvin buys an apple.
He gives 2 dimes to the clerk.
Will Calvin get **change**?

20¢ is more than 15¢.

yes

Menu

apple	15¢
cracker	4¢
melon	6¢
cheese	2¢

Word Bank

change

Check ✓

Use the menu above.
Write **yes** or **no**.

	You buy:	You use:	Will you get change?
1	melon	nickel, penny	
2	cracker	nickel	

Think About It   Reasoning

How can you decide if you will get change?

Use the menu.
Write **yes** or **no**.

Did you pay more than the price?

Menu

🍊	12¢
🍓	3¢
🧃	7¢
🥝🥝	13¢

	You buy:	You use:	Will you get change?
3	🍓	penny penny penny	
4	🧃	nickel nickel	
5	🥝🥝	dime nickel	

Writing in Math

6 Write a story problem using the information from the menu.

_____

_____

_____

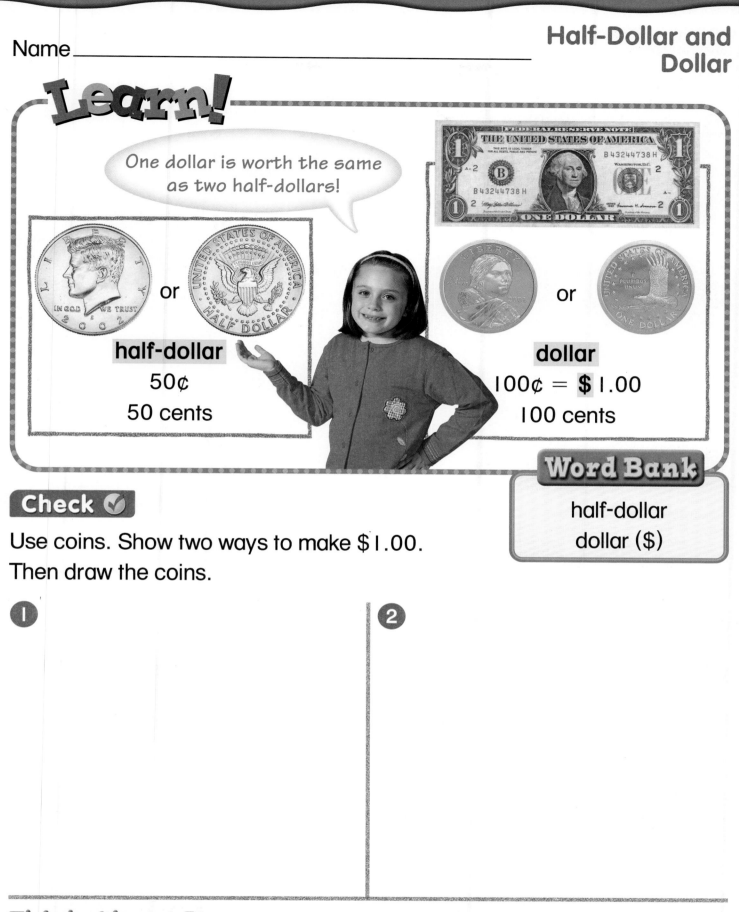

One dollar is worth the same as two half-dollars!

half-dollar
50¢
50 cents

dollar
100¢ = $1.00
100 cents

Check ✓

Use coins. Show two ways to make $1.00.
Then draw the coins.

Word Bank
half-dollar
dollar ($)

1

2

Think About It Number Sense

Does it take more dimes or more nickels
to make $1.00? Explain.

50 cents equals a half-dollar.
100 cents equals a dollar.

Write how much money in all.

3

In All
$1.00

4

In All

5

In All

Problem Solving   Reasoning

6   How can you show the same amount using only 3 coins?
Draw and label the coins in the empty bank.

Home Connection Your child identified and discussed the value of a half-dollar, a dollar bill, and a dollar coin. **Home Activity** Ask your child to show amounts that equal a dollar using coins or pictures of coins.

Predict and Verify

Read this story problem.

Erin has 12¢. She wants to spend
all of her money at a yard sale.
Which toys do you think Erin
will buy? Why do you think so?

1 What do you think will happen?

_____

_____

_____

2 Write a number sentence that shows the prices
of the toys you guessed.

___ + ___ = 12¢

3 Was your guess correct?

_____

4 If your guess was not correct, try again.

___ + ___ = 12¢

5¢ 2¢ 10¢

Think About It   Reasoning

Explain why you chose the toys you did.

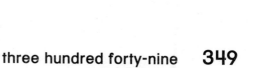

Read another story problem.

Grade I is having a sale.
Sam's job is to sell crayons.
Each crayon is 5¢.
A girl from preschool gives Sam 10¢.

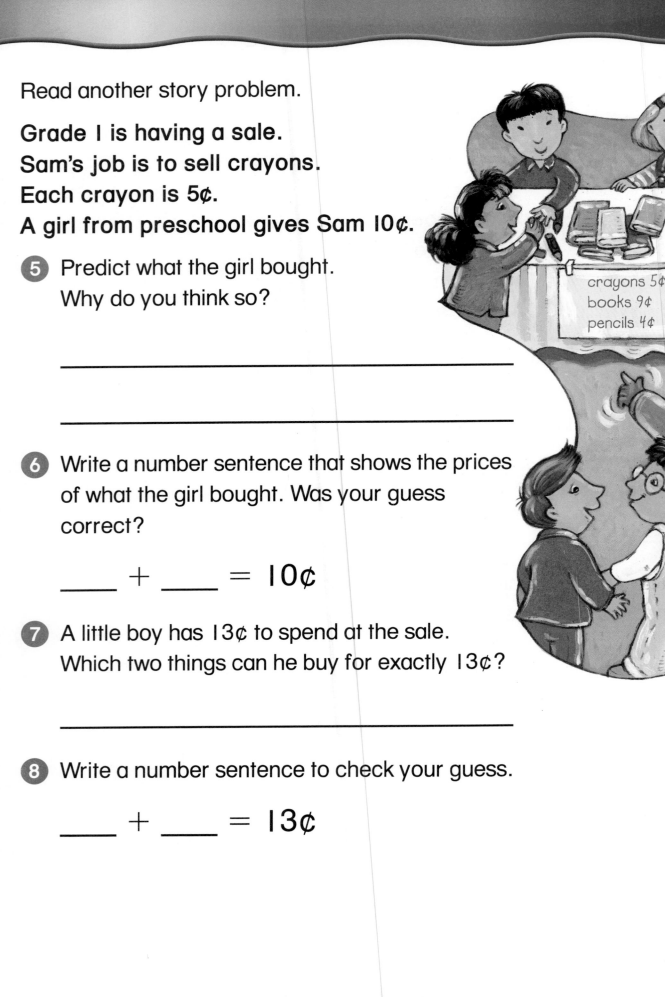

crayons 5¢
books 9¢
pencils 4¢

5 Predict what the girl bought.
Why do you think so?

_____

_____

6 Write a number sentence that shows the prices
of what the girl bought. Was your guess
correct?

___ + ___ = 10¢

7 A little boy has 13¢ to spend at the sale.
Which two things can he buy for exactly 13¢?

_____

8 Write a number sentence to check your guess.

___ + ___ = 13¢

Home Connection Your child made predictions about items that might be
purchased for a given amount and then checked his or her answer by writing
a number sentence. **Home Activity** Ask your child to explain how he or she
completed the problems on this page.

Learn!

1 Manolo bought 2 toys at a yard sale.
Together the toys cost 13¢.
Which toys did he buy?

5¢

Read and Understand

Choose 2 toys.
Find the sum of the prices.

6¢

Plan and Solve

Try [crocodile] and [octopus].

Test: ___5___ + ___6___ = ___11___ ¢

8¢

*11¢ is less than 13¢.
Try again.*

Try [crocodile] and [dolphin].

9¢

Test: ___5___ + ___8___ = ___13___ ¢

Look Back and Check

How can you check your guess?

Think About It   Reasoning

When your first try is too much, how do you
decide what to try next?

Practice

Circle the toys each child bought.
Then write an addition sentence to check your guess.

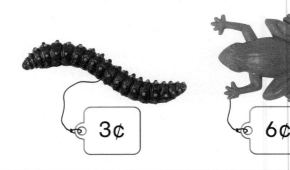  

| 3¢ | 6¢ | 7¢ | 9¢ |

---

2 Wendy bought 2 different toys.
Together they cost 12¢.
What did Wendy buy?

$\underline{3} + \underline{9} = \underline{12}$ ¢

---

3 Kendra bought 2 different toys.
Together they cost 15¢.
What did Kendra buy?

____ + ____ = ____ ¢

---

4 Tran bought 2 different toys.
Together they cost 13¢.
What did Tran buy?

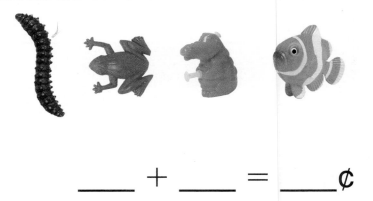

____ + ____ = ____ ¢

Name_____

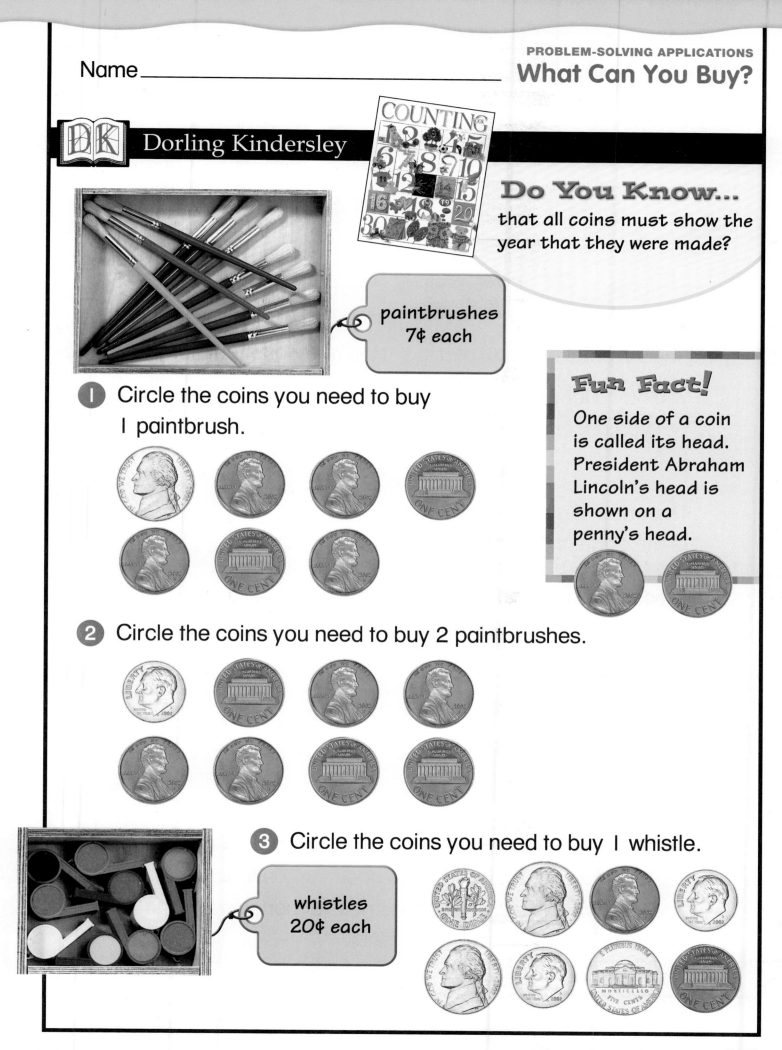

Dorling Kindersley

Do You Know...
that all coins must show the year that they were made?

paintbrushes
7¢ each

1 Circle the coins you need to buy
1 paintbrush.

Fun Fact!
One side of a coin is called its head. President Abraham Lincoln's head is shown on a penny's head.

2 Circle the coins you need to buy 2 paintbrushes.

3 Circle the coins you need to buy 1 whistle.

whistles
20¢ each

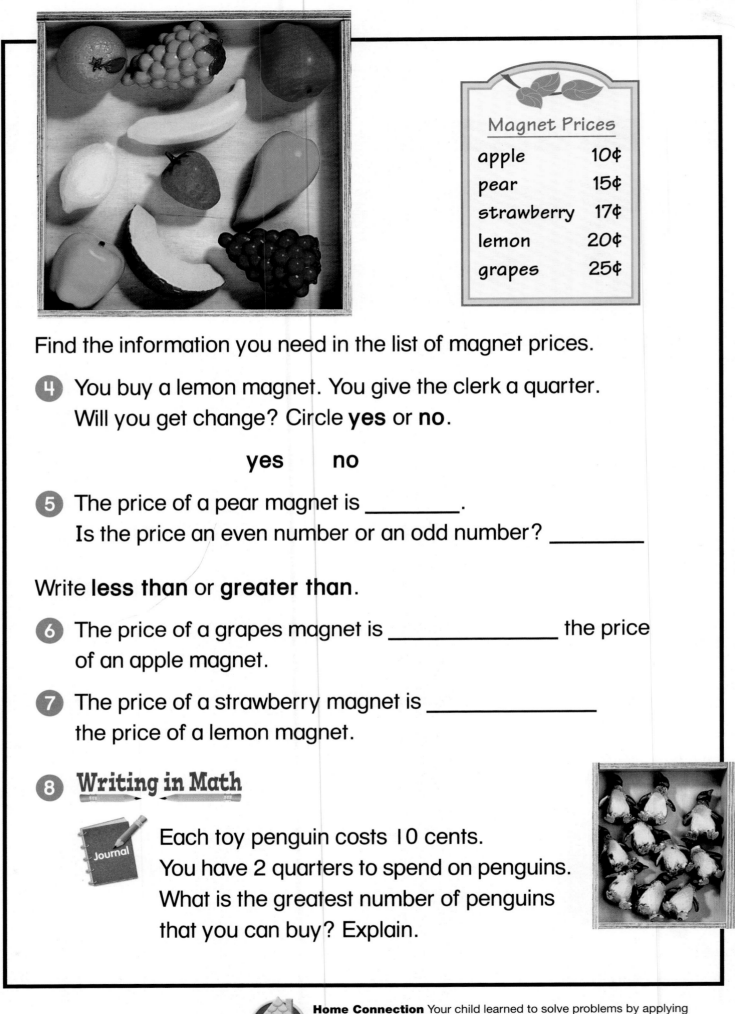

Magnet Prices	
apple	10¢
pear	15¢
strawberry	17¢
lemon	20¢
grapes	25¢

Find the information you need in the list of magnet prices.

4 You buy a lemon magnet. You give the clerk a quarter.
Will you get change? Circle **yes** or **no**.

yes   **no**

5 The price of a pear magnet is _____.
Is the price an even number or an odd number? _____

Write **less than** or **greater than**.

6 The price of a grapes magnet is _____ the price
of an apple magnet.

7 The price of a strawberry magnet is _____
the price of a lemon magnet.

8 **Writing in Math**

Each toy penguin costs 10 cents.
You have 2 quarters to spend on penguins.
What is the greatest number of penguins
that you can buy? Explain.

Home Connection Your child learned to solve problems by applying his or her math skills. **Home Activity** Talk to your child about how he or she solved the problems on these two pages.

Name_____

⭐ Enrichment

Counting Dollars, Dimes, and Pennies

Counting dollars, dimes, and pennies is just like counting hundreds, tens, and ones.

112¢ is the same as $1.12.

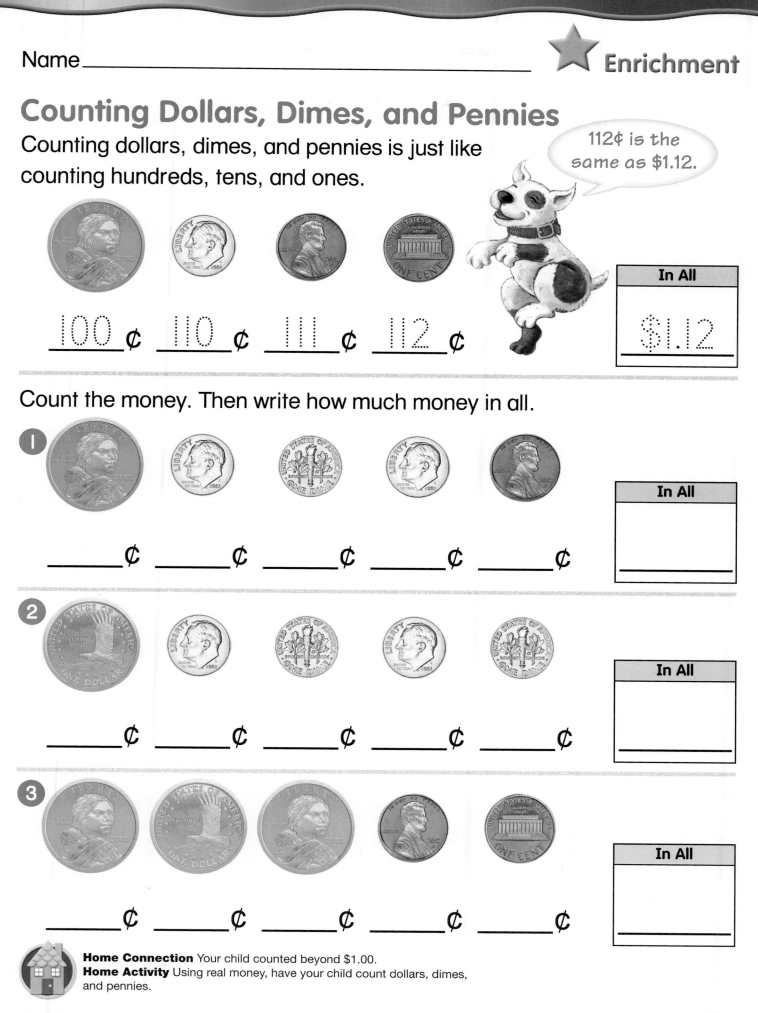

100 ¢   110 ¢   111 ¢   112 ¢

In All
$1.12

Count the money. Then write how much money in all.

1 _____ ¢ _____ ¢ _____ ¢ _____ ¢ _____ ¢

In All

2 _____ ¢ _____ ¢ _____ ¢ _____ ¢ _____ ¢

In All

3 _____ ¢ _____ ¢ _____ ¢ _____ ¢ _____ ¢

In All

🏠 **Home Connection** Your child counted beyond $1.00.
Home Activity Using real money, have your child count dollars, dimes, and pennies.

Golden Dollar Obverse. 1999 United States Mint. All Rights reserved. Used with permission/United States Mint.

Name_____

Count Sets of Coins Using a Calculator

You can use a calculator to find how much money in all.

Press ON/C each time you begin. Add the values of the coins.

Press 2 5 for a quarter. Press 1 0 for a dime.

Press 5 for a nickel. Press 1 for a penny.

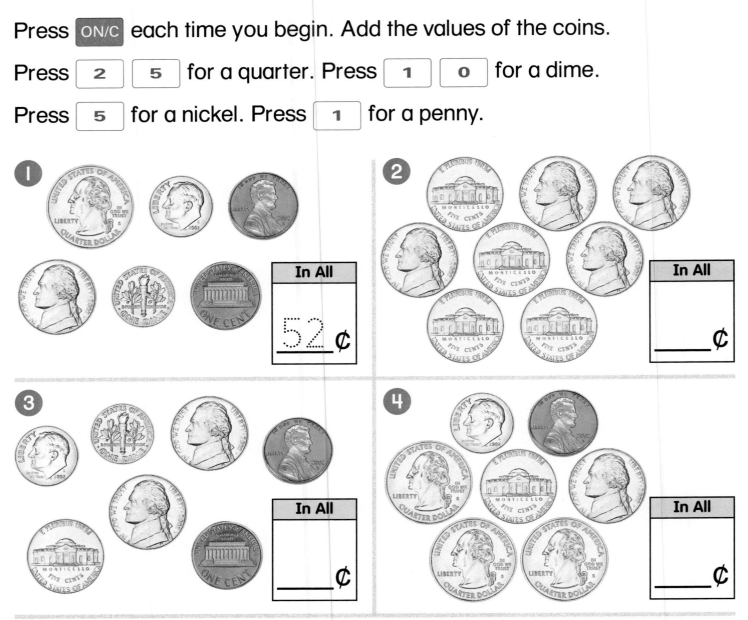

1	In All
	52 ¢

2	In All
	____ ¢

3	In All
	____ ¢

4	In All
	____ ¢

Think About It   Number Sense

In Exercise 2, what are two ways you could
use a calculator to check your addition?

Home Connection Your child used a calculator to find the total value of
each of four different groups of quarters, dimes, nickels, and pennies. **Home
Activity** Ask your child to explain how he or she used a calculator to check
his or her addition in Exercise 2. (Note that some, but not all calculators have a
constant function that allows you to repeat an operation with one keystroke.)

© Pearson Education, Inc.

Name_____

Get Information for the Answer

Looking at pictures can help you solve math problems.

Test-Taking Strategies

Understand the Question

Get Information for the Answer

Plan How to Find the Answer

Make Smart Choices

Use Writing in Math

1 How much money in all is in this picture? Count on to add the coins. Then fill in the answer bubble.

Ⓐ 42¢   Ⓑ 50¢   Ⓒ 52¢   Ⓓ 62¢

Your Turn

Read the question. Look at all four of the pictures.
Count on to add the coins in each picture.
Then fill in the answer bubble.

2 Which group of coins has a total value of 25¢?

Home Connection Your child prepared for standardized tests by learning to get information from pictures. **Home Activity** Ask your child to count on to find the total value of the coins in each set in Exercise 2, beginning with the coin or coins of greatest value and then proceeding sequentially to the coin or coins of least value. Use real coins, if possible.

Name _____

Discover Math in Your World

 **Read Together**

Saving Makes Cents!

Your class has been saving money in three piggy banks. How much money has your class saved so far?

Counting Coins

1 Max, Jackie, and Rachel opened each bank and counted the coins. Write how much money was in each bank.

_____¢ was in the red bank.

_____¢ was in the blue bank.

_____¢ was in the green bank.

2 Which bank contained the most money?

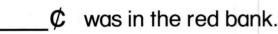

_____

3 How much money has your class saved so far?

 _____¢ or $_____

4 Can your class think of other combinations of coins that add up to this amount of money?

 **Take It to the NET**
Video and Activities
www.scottforesman.com

 Home Connection Your child solved problems about saving money by finding the total value of each group of coins and the combined value of the three groups. **Home Activity** Ask your child to explain how he or she found the answers in Exercise 3. Also, help your child read both answers: "119 cents" and "1 dollar and 19 cents."

© Pearson Educa

Chapter 9

Circle the coins that match the price.

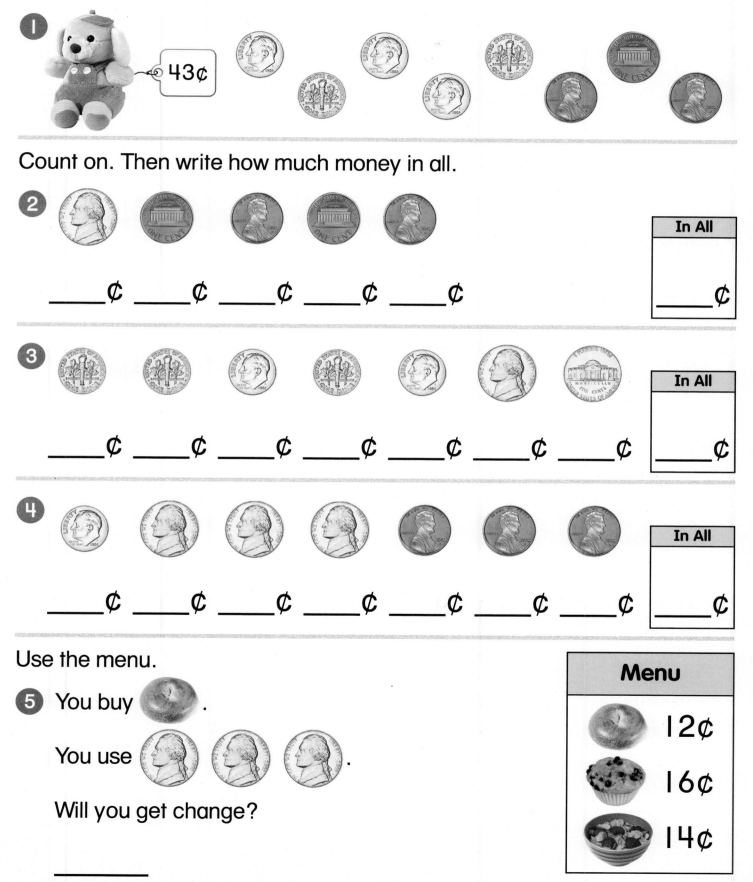

1

43¢

Count on. Then write how much money in all.

2

____¢ ____¢ ____¢ ____¢ ____¢

In All
____¢

3

____¢ ____¢ ____¢ ____¢ ____¢ ____¢ ____¢

In All
____¢

4

____¢ ____¢ ____¢ ____¢ ____¢ ____¢ ____¢

In All
____¢

Use the menu.

5 You buy .

You use .

Will you get change?

_____

Menu
12¢
16¢
14¢

Circle the coins that equal 25¢.

6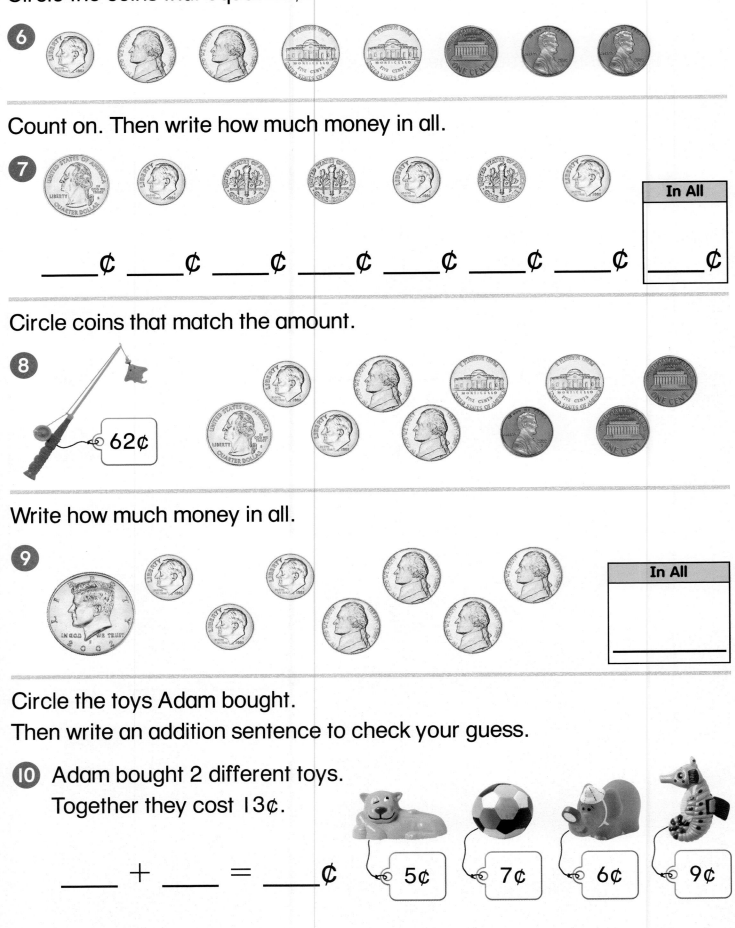

Count on. Then write how much money in all.

7

_____ ¢ _____ ¢ _____ ¢ _____ ¢ _____ ¢ _____ ¢ _____ ¢

In All
_____ ¢

Circle coins that match the amount.

8

62¢

Write how much money in all.

9

In All
_____

Circle the toys Adam bought.

Then write an addition sentence to check your guess.

10 Adam bought 2 different toys.
Together they cost 13¢.

_____ + _____ = _____ ¢

5¢   7¢   6¢   9¢

Read Together

One Very Smart Chicken

By Anne Miranda

Illustrated by Bridget Starr Taylor

SPEED 25 LIMIT

623

This Math Storybook belongs to

_____

10A

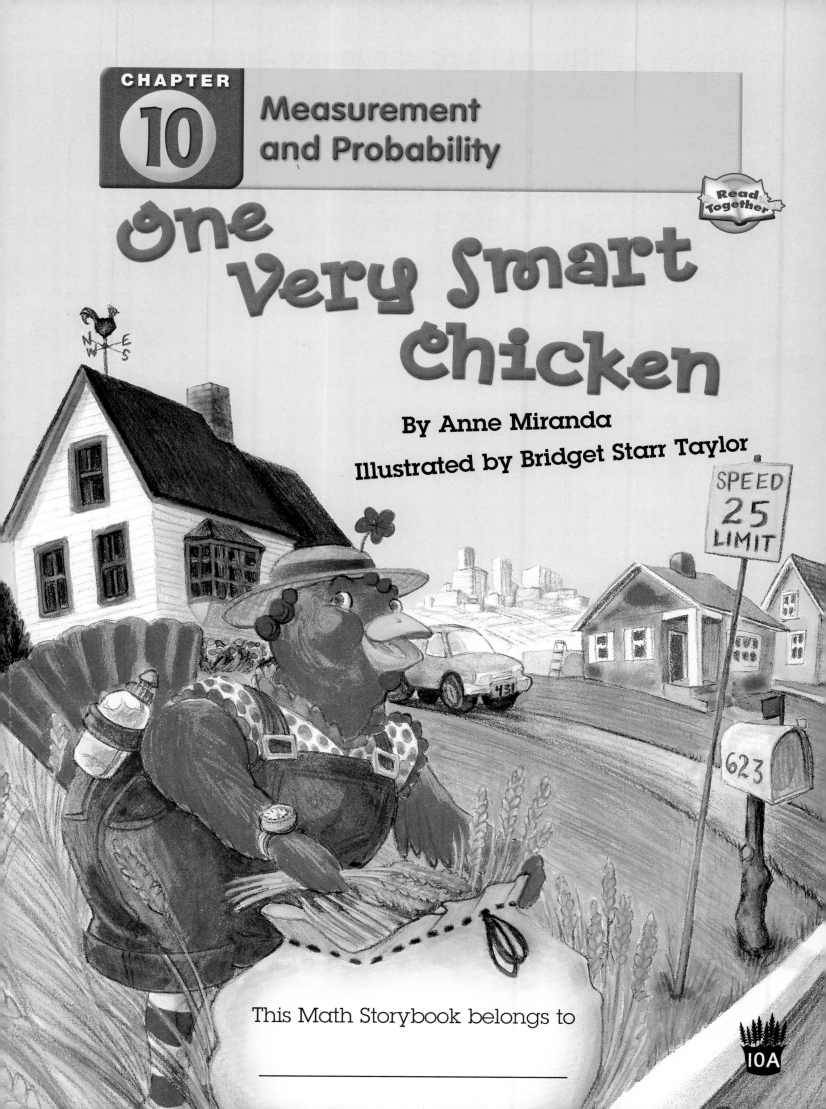

"Who will help me make the bread?"
asked the little red hen.

"Not I," said the duck.
"Not I," said the pig.
"Not I," said the horse.

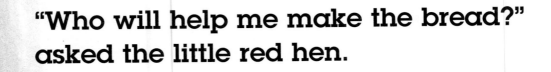

WORK TO DO:
Duck–Grind
Pig–Mix
Horse–Bake

"OK," said the little red hen.
"Here's how it's going to be.
If you want to EAT the bread,
you have to help me MAKE the bread.
Got it?"

"Got it," sighed the duck, the pig,
and the horse.

"OK, that's more like it,"
said the little red hen.
"Now, here's a chart
that tells you what to do."

10C

So the duck helped grind the wheat.
It was hard work,
but when she was done
there were **5** cups of flour.

The pig helped make the dough.
That was hard work too.
He added about **2** cups of water
to the flour.
Then he put in some
sugar and some yeast.

And the horse put the bread
into the oven.
That was hard work too.
Each loaf weighed about 1 pound,
and this horse had not been
getting much exercise.
(Too much TV.)

10E

Everybody ate the bread.
Everybody enjoyed the bread.

"Now, who will help me do the dishes?"
asked the little red hen.

What do YOU think will happen next?

Are the duck, the pig, and the horse
likely or unlikely to jump up and
help the little red hen with the dishes?

Home-School Connection

Dear Family,

Today my class started Chapter 10, **Measurement and Probability.** I will learn to estimate and measure length, capacity, weight, and temperature. I will also learn to predict how likely or unlikely it is for an event to happen. Here are some of the math words I will be learning and some things we can do to help me with my math.

Love,

_____

Math Activity to Do at Home

Have some fun measuring with pieces of cereal! Try measuring the length of a spoon by laying the cereal pieces end to end beside the spoon. Then fill a cup with cereal and count the cereal pieces to see how many pieces it took to fill the cup.

Books to Read Together

Reading math stories reinforces concepts. Look for these titles in your local library:

Me and the Measure of Things
By Joan Sweeney
(Crown, 2001)

Measuring Penny
By Loreen Leedy
(Holt, 2000)

Take It to the NET
More Activities
www.scottforesman.com

My New Math Words

We measure length in inches, feet, and centimeters.

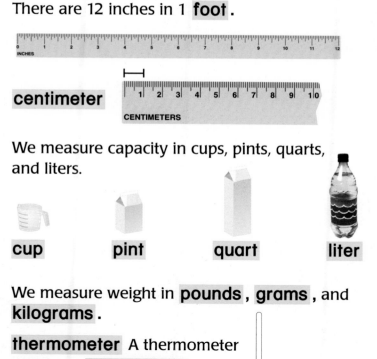

inch

There are 12 inches in 1 **foot**.

centimeter

We measure capacity in cups, pints, quarts, and liters.

cup   **pint**   **quart**   **liter**

We measure weight in **pounds**, **grams**, and **kilograms**.

thermometer A thermometer measures **temperature**.

Name _____

More likely or less likely?

© Pearson Education, Inc.

What You Need

paper clip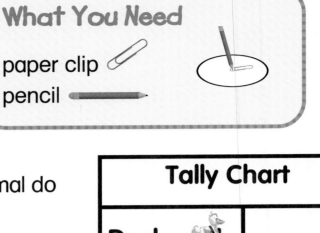
pencil

How to Play

1. When you spin the spinner, which animal do you think you will land on the most?
2. Spin 10 times.
3. On the Tally Chart, put a tally mark next to the animal you land on.
4. Find the animal you landed on **most often.**
5. Find the animal you landed on **least often.**
6. Tell someone why it is **more likely** that you will land on the hen than that you will land on the duck, the pig, or the horse.

Tally Chart		
Duck		
Pig		
Horse		
Hen		

Name _____

Learn!

About how long is the bug?

It measures exactly 3 cubes long.

It looks about 4 cubes long. 4 is a good estimate.

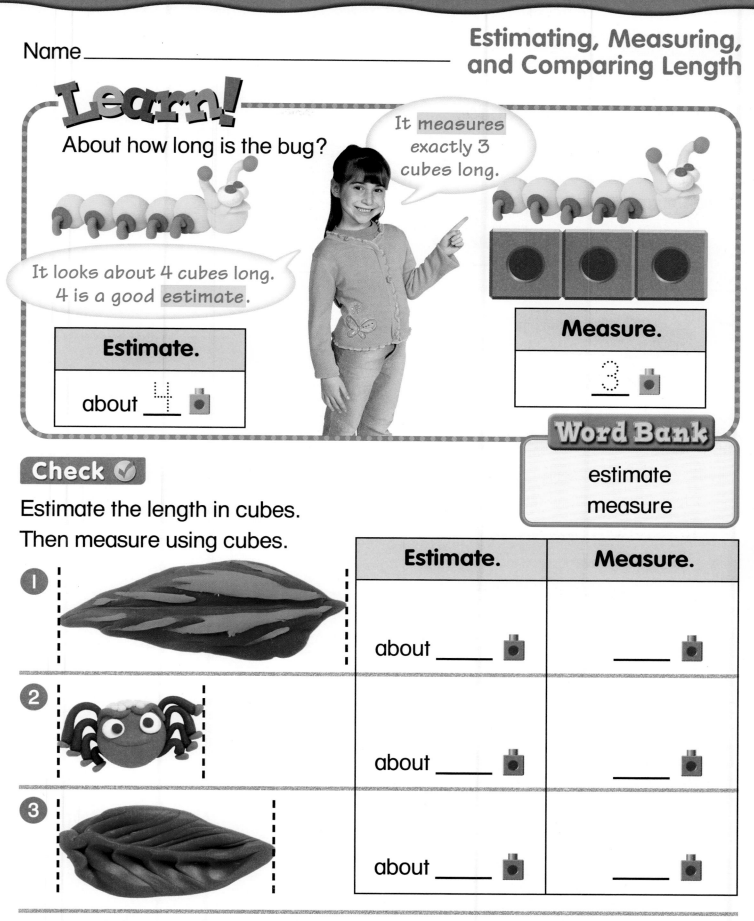

Estimate.
about __4__ 🔲

Measure.
__3__ 🔲

Word Bank

estimate

measure

Check ✓

Estimate the length in cubes.

Then measure using cubes.

	Estimate.	Measure.
1	about _____ 🔲	_____ 🔲
2	about _____ 🔲	_____ 🔲
3	about _____ 🔲	_____ 🔲

Think About It   Number Sense

Which is the longest object you measured?

How do you know?

Find each object in your classroom.
Estimate the length in cubes.
Then measure using cubes.

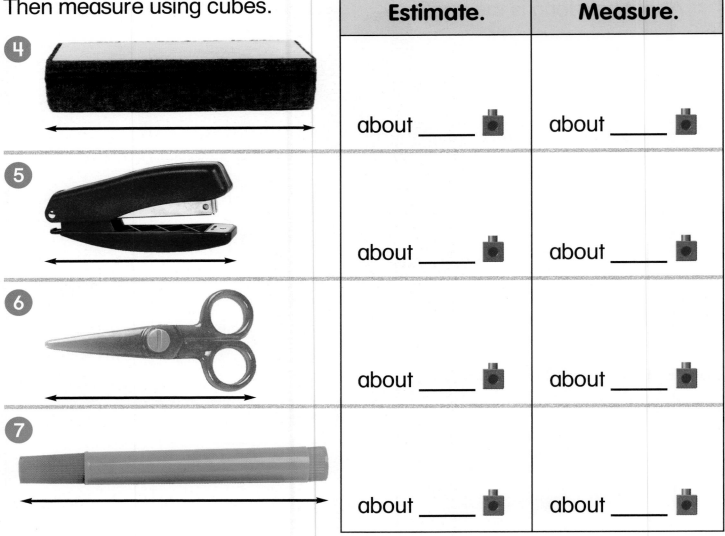

	Estimate.	Measure.
4	about _____ ▢	about _____ ▢
5	about _____ ▢	about _____ ▢
6	about _____ ▢	about _____ ▢
7	about _____ ▢	about _____ ▢

Problem Solving   Visual Thinking

8   Measure each turtle using cubes. Circle the
longest turtle. Mark an **X** on the shortest turtle.

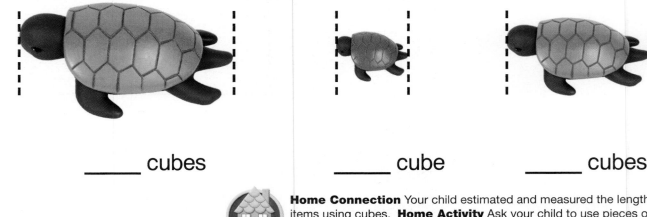

_____ cubes   _____ cube   _____ cubes

Home Connection Your child estimated and measured the lengths of
items using cubes. **Home Activity** Ask your child to use pieces of cereal
or pasta to measure the lengths of several small objects at home.

Draw Conclusions

Sharon measured 3 objects using ⬭ and ◾.
Here is what each object measured.

about 3 ⬭

about 5 ◾

1 What did she use **more** of to measure the grasshopper?

Circle your answer.   more ⬭   or   (more ◾)

about 2 ⬭

about 3 ◾

2 What did she use **more** of to measure the twig?

Circle your answer.   more ⬭   or   more ◾

about 4 ⬭

about 7 ◾

3 What did she use **more** of to measure the feather?

Circle your answer.   more ⬭   or   more ◾

Think About It   Reasoning

Why do you think it took more ◾ than ⬭ to
measure every object?

What do you need **fewer** of to measure each object?
Circle your answer.

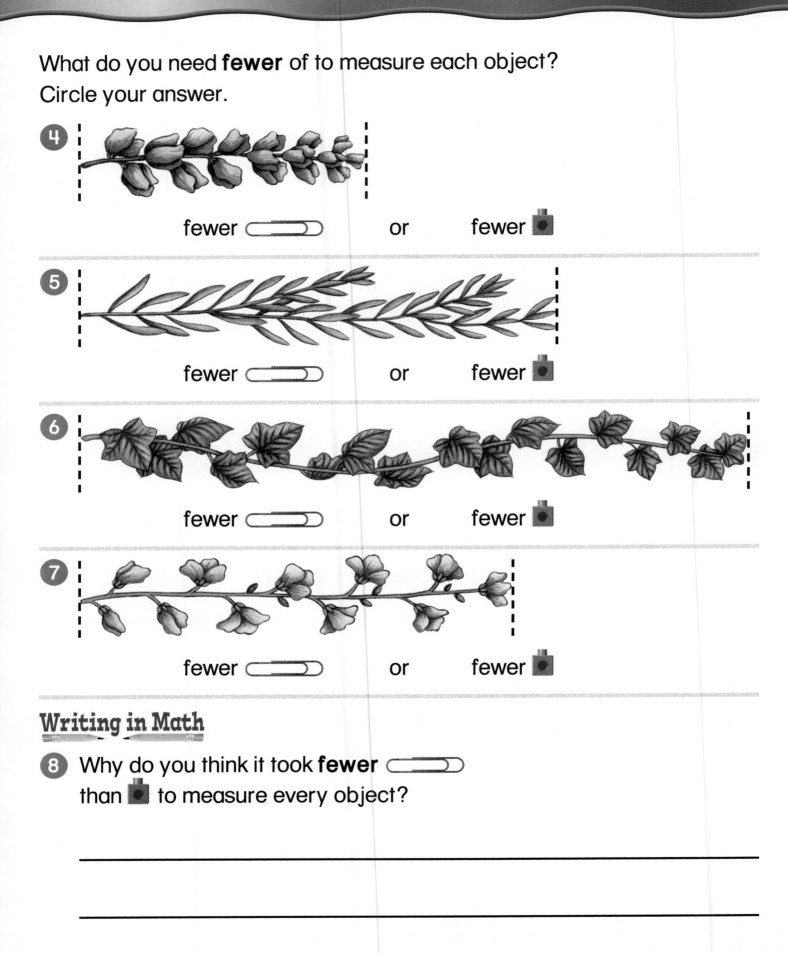

4

fewer ⬭   or   fewer ▪

5

fewer ⬭   or   fewer ▪

6

fewer ⬭   or   fewer ▪

7

fewer ⬭   or   fewer ▪

Writing in Math

8 Why do you think it took **fewer** ⬭
than ▪ to measure every object?

_____

_____

Home Connection Your child drew conclusions about whether it would take more paper clips or more cubes to measure the lengths of objects and then whether it would take fewer paper clips or cubes to measure the lengths of other objects. **Home Activity** Ask your child to explain his or her answer to Exercise 8.

Learn!

1 Predict: Will you need more  or more  to measure the shoe?

Read and Understand

You must find out if you need more ⌒⊃ or more ▣.

You can measure with the ⌒⊃ and the ▣ to check your prediction.

Plan and Solve

You can use reasoning to help you predict. The cubes are shorter, so you will need more cubes.

more ⌒⊃   (more ▣)

Look Back and Check

Measure to check your prediction. Was your prediction correct?

Measure.
about __4__ ⌒⊃
about __7__ ▣

Think About It   Reasoning

Would you need more drinking straws or more paper clips to measure a table? Why?

Will it take fewer 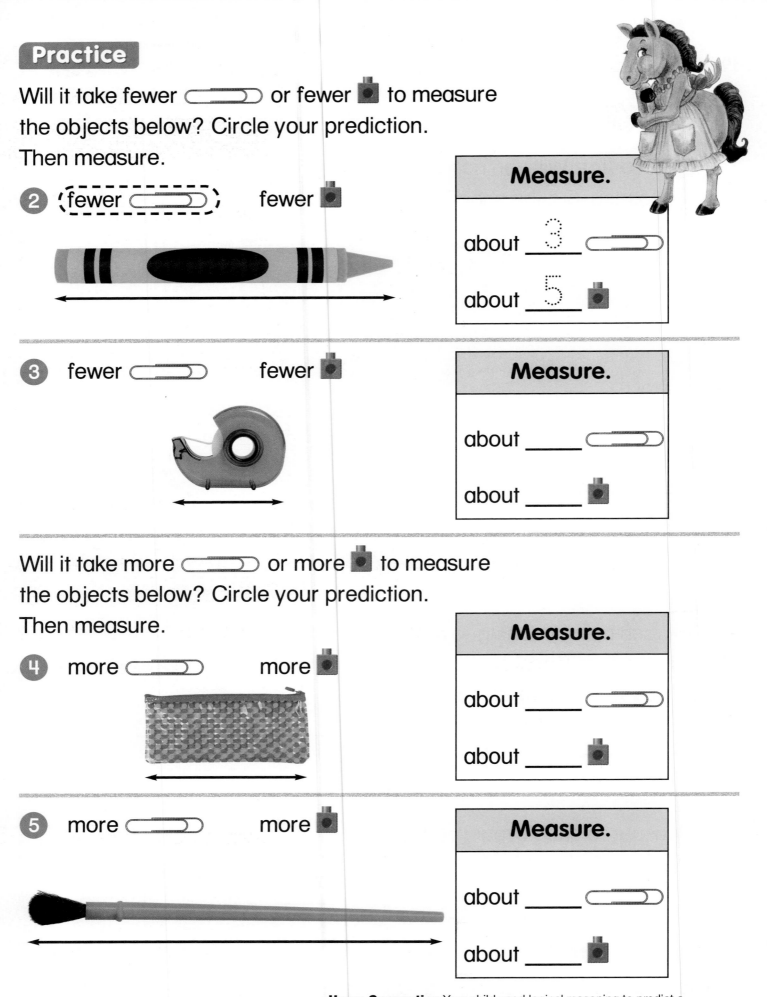 or fewer 🔲 to measure
the objects below? Circle your prediction.
Then measure.

2 (fewer ⬭)   fewer 🔲

Measure.

about __3__ ⬭

about __5__ 🔲

3   fewer ⬭   fewer 🔲

Measure.

about _____ ⬭

about _____ 🔲

Will it take more ⬭ or more 🔲 to measure
the objects below? Circle your prediction.
Then measure.

4   more ⬭   more 🔲

Measure.

about _____ ⬭

about _____ 🔲

5   more ⬭   more 🔲

Measure.

about _____ ⬭

about _____ 🔲

Home Connection Your child used logical reasoning to predict a
measurement. **Home Activity** Ask your child if it would take more crayons
or more paper clips to measure the length of a table. Have your child use
crayons and paper clips to check the prediction. If you do not have crayons
or paper clips, use other available items.

Learn!

How many cubes can you use to cover the shape?

3 are not enough. 5 cubes will cover the shape!

3 cubes
(5 cubes)

Does it make sense?

Check ✓

How many cubes will cover each shape?
Circle the answer that makes sense.

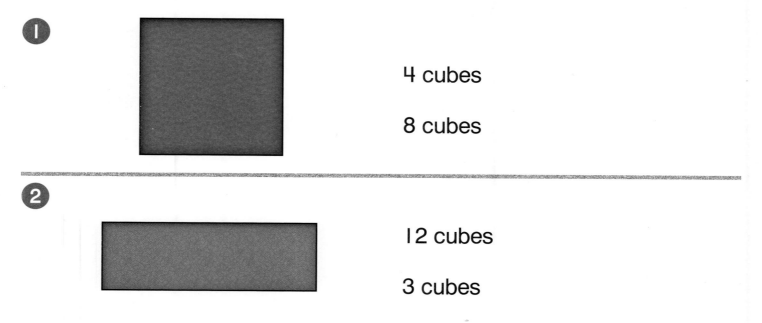

1

4 cubes

8 cubes

2

12 cubes

3 cubes

Think About It   Reasoning

Could you use pennies instead of cubes to cover the shapes above? Explain.

How many cubes will cover each shape?
Circle the answer that makes sense.

3

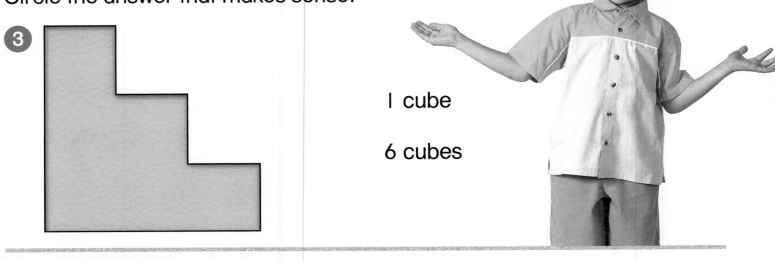

I cube

6 cubes

4

3 cubes

9 cubes

Problem Solving   Visual Thinking

5   Draw a different shape with the same number of square units.

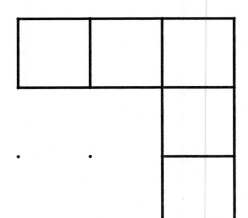

Home Connection Your child estimated how many cubes would cover a
shape. Then he or she chose an answer that made sense. **Home Activity**
Draw 20 dots like the ones shown in Exercise 5. Have your child draw and
color in a shape made up of 6 square units.

© Pearson Education, Inc.

Name_____

Estimate the length. Then measure using cubes.

1

Estimate.	Measure.
about _____ 🔲	_____ 🔲

Estimate the length. Then measure using an inch ruler.

2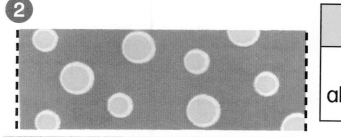

Estimate.	Measure.
about _____ inches	_____ inches

Estimate the length. Then measure using a centimeter ruler.

3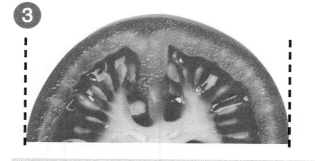

Estimate.	Measure.
about _____ centimeters	_____ centimeters

Count how many inches around this shape.

4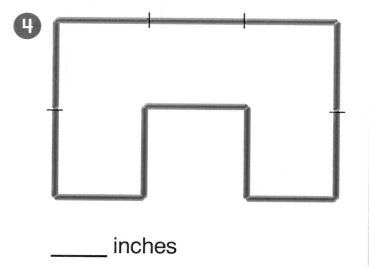

_____ inches

Write how many cubes will cover this shape.

5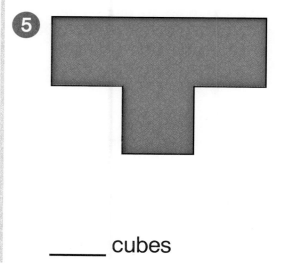

_____ cubes

How much money is there in all?

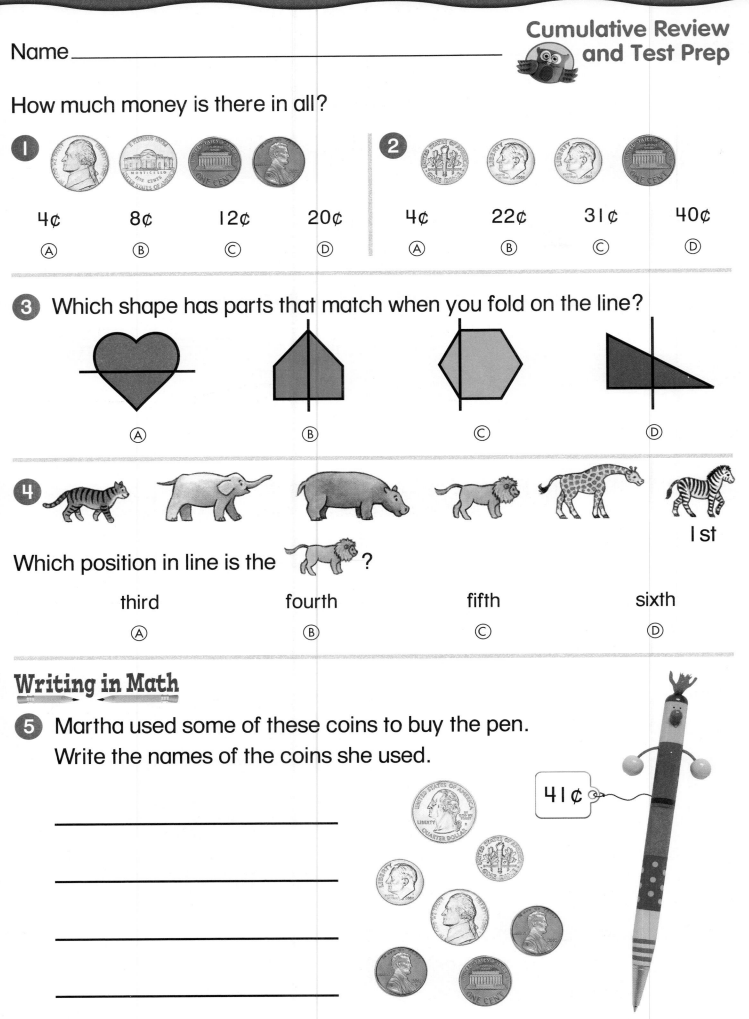

1

4¢   8¢   12¢   20¢

Ⓐ   Ⓑ   Ⓒ   Ⓓ

2

4¢   22¢   31¢   40¢

Ⓐ   Ⓑ   Ⓒ   Ⓓ

3 Which shape has parts that match when you fold on the line?

Ⓐ   Ⓑ   Ⓒ   Ⓓ

4

1st

Which position in line is the 🦁 ?

third   fourth   fifth   sixth

Ⓐ   Ⓑ   Ⓒ   Ⓓ

Writing in Math

5 Martha used some of these coins to buy the pen.
Write the names of the coins she used.

41¢

_____

_____

_____

_____

Learn!

About how many **cups** of rice will fill the bowl?

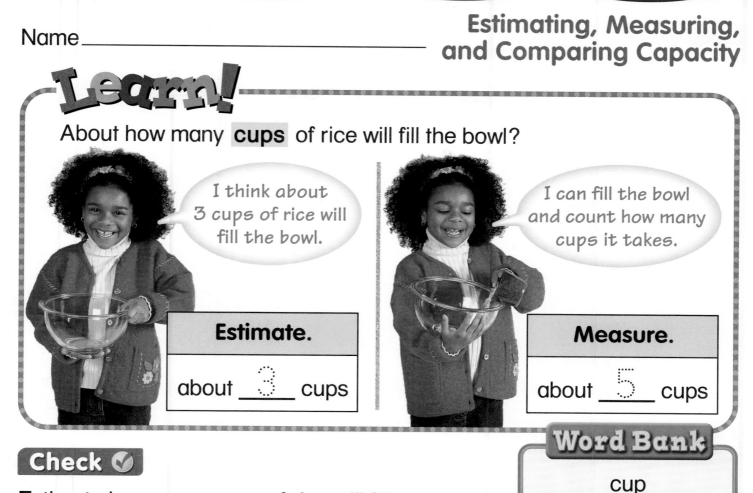

I think about 3 cups of rice will fill the bowl.

Estimate.

about ⋯3⋯ cups

I can fill the bowl and count how many cups it takes.

Measure.

about __5__ cups

Check ✓

Estimate how many cups of rice will fill each item.
Then measure.

Word Bank

cup

	Estimate.	Measure.
❶	about _____ cups	about _____ cups
❷	about _____ cups	about _____ cups

Think About It Number Sense

How would you put the bowl, the jar, and
the pitcher in order from the one that holds the
least to the one that holds the most?

Estimate how many cups of rice will fill each item.
Then measure.

	Estimate.	Measure.
3	about _____ cups	about _____ cups
4	about _____ cups	about _____ cups
5	about _____ cups	about _____ cups
6	about _____ cups	about _____ cups

Problem Solving Estimation

7 Circle the container that holds about 1 cup.

Home Connection Your child estimated and then measured how many cups of rice various containers hold. **Home Activity** Have your child measure the capacities of containers at home using cups of beans, cereal pieces, or water.

Name _____

Learn!

cup

pint

quart

How much red paint will fill the jar?

about 1

about 1

Word Bank

cup

pint

quart

Check ✓

Circle the best estimate.

1

about 1

about 1

2

about 1

about 1

3

about 1

about 1

4

about 1

about 1

Think About It   Reasoning

Would you use cups, pints, or quarts to tell how much water is in a fish tank? Explain.

qudrt

Practice

Circle the best estimate.

How much water will I need to fill the bathtub?

5  less than 1 quart

~~more than 1 quart~~ (circled)

6 more than 1 cup

(less than 1 cup) (circled)

7 more than 1 quart

(less than 1 quart) (circled)

8 (more than 1 pint) (circled)

less than 1 pint

9 (more than 1 cup) (circled)

less than 1 cup

Problem Solving Reasoning

Fill in each blank.

10 2 🥤 = 1 🥛

4  🥤 = ___2___ 🥛

11 2 🥛 = 1 🥛

4 🥛 = ___2___ 🥛

Learn!

Does this glass hold more or less than 1 **liter**?

| less than 1 liter |  about 1 liter |  more than 1 liter |

Word Bank

liter

Check ✓

Circle the best estimate.

1. 
(less than 1 liter)
more than 1 liter

2. 
less than 1 liter
more than 1 liter

3. 
less than 1 liter
more than 1 liter

4. 
less than 1 liter
more than 1 liter

Think About It   Number Sense

If a bottle of juice holds 2 liters, how much juice will you have if you buy 2 bottles?

Circle the best estimate.

5

less than 1 liter

(more than 1 liter)

6

less than 1 liter

more than 1 liter

7

less than 1 liter

more than 1 liter

8

less than 1 liter

more than 1 liter

9

less than 1 liter

more than 1 liter

10

less than 1 liter

more than 1 liter

Problem Solving Estimation

Circle the best estimate.

11

30 liters

3 liters

12

10 liters

1 liter

Home Connection Your child compared the capacities of various containers to the capacity of a liter. **Home Activity** Ask your child to identify items on the page that hold about 1 liter, less than 1 liter, and more than 1 liter.

Name_____

Circle the best estimate.

1 about 1

   about 1

2 less than 1 cup

   more than 1 cup

3 less than 1 liter

   more than 1 liter

4 grams

   kilograms

Number these things from lightest to heaviest.
Use 1 for the lightest and 4 for the heaviest.

5 ____   ____   ____   ____

Circle the thermometer that shows the temperature.

6

°F   °F

      85

20

Name _____

Use the map to answer the questions.

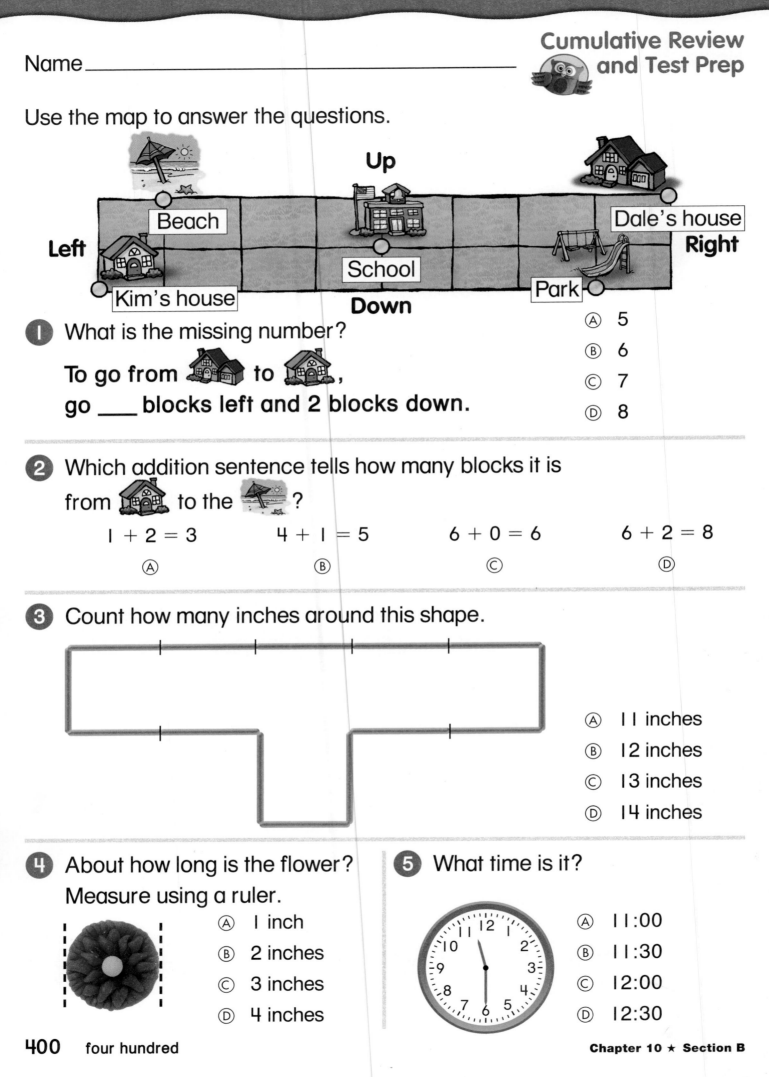

Up

Beach

Dale's house

Left

Right

School

Park

Kim's house

Down

1 What is the missing number?

To go from 🏠 to 🏠,
go ___ blocks left and 2 blocks down.

- Ⓐ 5
- Ⓑ 6
- Ⓒ 7
- Ⓓ 8

2 Which addition sentence tells how many blocks it is
from 🏠 to the ⛱?

$1 + 2 = 3$ $4 + 1 = 5$ $6 + 0 = 6$ $6 + 2 = 8$
  Ⓐ   Ⓑ   Ⓒ   Ⓓ

3 Count how many inches around this shape.

- Ⓐ 11 inches
- Ⓑ 12 inches
- Ⓒ 13 inches
- Ⓓ 14 inches

4 About how long is the flower?
Measure using a ruler.

- Ⓐ 1 inch
- Ⓑ 2 inches
- Ⓒ 3 inches
- Ⓓ 4 inches

5 What time is it?

- Ⓐ 11:00
- Ⓑ 11:30
- Ⓒ 12:00
- Ⓓ 12:30

© Pearson Education, Inc.

Name _____

Learn!

It is **more likely** that the spinner will land on green.

It is **less likely** that the spinner will land on purple.

Color	Tally
Green	ⱵⱵ IIII
Purple	III

Check ✓

Use a pencil and a paper clip to make a spinner.
Spin the spinner 10 times.
Mark a tally for each spin.

Word Bank

more likely
less likely

1

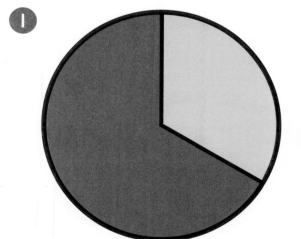

Color	Tally
Yellow	
Red	

2 **Predict:** On which color is the spinner more
likely to land next?

_____

Think About It   Reasoning

How did you use the tally chart to
help you predict?

Use each tally chart to answer the questions.

Color	Tally
Green	HHT HHT
Orange	HHT

3 **Predict:** On which color is the spinner **more likely** to land next? _____

Color	Tally
Blue	||||
Yellow	HHT ||||

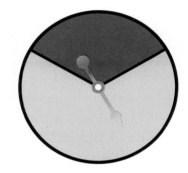

4 **Predict:** On which color is the spinner **less likely** to land next? _____

Problem Solving Algebra

Solve.

5 Liz spun this spinner 11 times. She landed on blue 8 times. How many times did she land on red?

_____ times

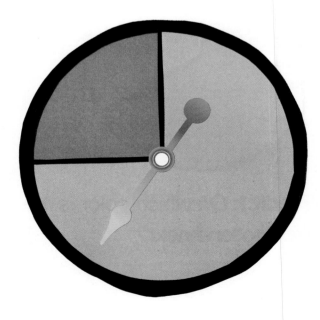

Home Connection Your child spun a spinner and predicted which color it would land on next. **Home Activity** Ask your child to explain how he or she made the predictions in Exercises 3 and 4.

Name_____

Dorling Kindersley

Chow mein is made by combining noodles and stir-fried vegetables.

Do You Know...
that more people have soy sauce in their homes than have milk?

1 Lin is making chow mein. He needs 1 cup of dry noodles. Is 1 cup more than 1 quart or less than 1 quart?

_____

2 A chopstick measures about 10 inches long. Is 10 inches more than 1 centimeter or less than 1 centimeter?

_____

3 Is 10 inches more than 1 foot or less than 1 foot?

_____

Fun Fact!
People started using chopsticks in China over 4,000 years ago.

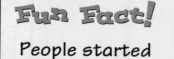

4 The carrots cost 20¢.
If Lin gave the clerk a quarter,
did he get change?

_____

5 Circle the thermometer that
shows the temperature at which
the chow mein will probably be
after Lin stir-fries it.

°F 110

°F 20

6 Lin started making chow mein at 5:00.
It takes a half hour to make chow mein.
At what time did Lin finish?

_____

7 Writing in Math

Ask 10 children in your class if
they have ever eaten chow mein.
Make a tally chart to show their answers.

Home Connection Your child learned to solve problems by applying
his or her math skills. **Home Activity** Talk to your child about how he
or she solved the problems on these two pages.

406 four hundred six

Name_____

Are you certain to pick a purple crayon, or is it impossible?
Circle your answer.

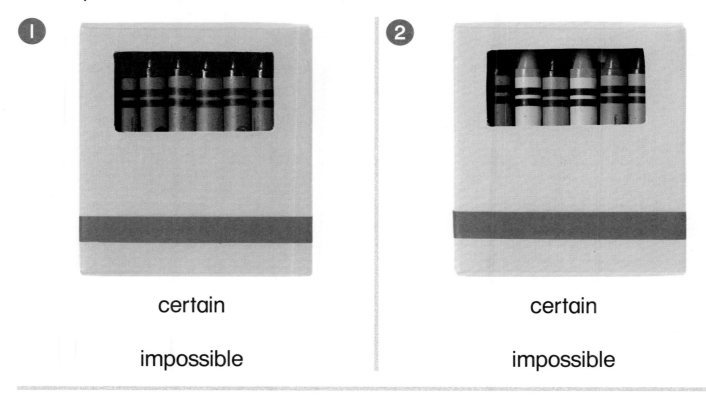

1

certain

impossible

2

certain

impossible

Use the spinner and the tally chart to answer
each question.

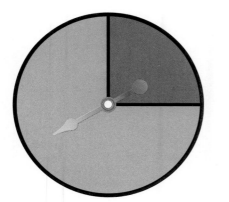

Color	Tally
Green	||||
Orange	ЖЖ ЖЖ

3 **Predict:** On which color is the spinner more likely
to land on the next spin?   _____

4 On which color is it less likely to land?   _____

1 How long is the watch?

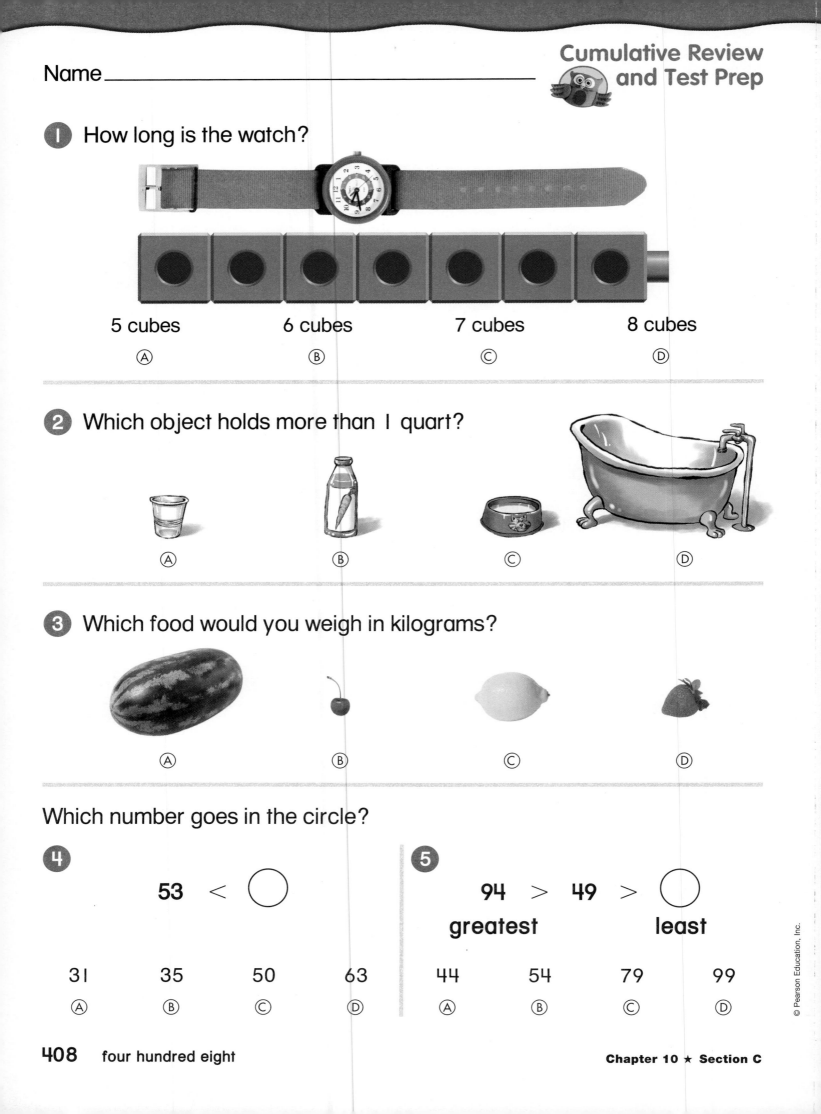

| 5 cubes | 6 cubes | 7 cubes | 8 cubes |
| Ⓐ | Ⓑ | Ⓒ | Ⓓ |

2 Which object holds more than 1 quart?

Ⓐ Ⓑ Ⓒ Ⓓ

3 Which food would you weigh in kilograms?

Ⓐ Ⓑ Ⓒ Ⓓ

Which number goes in the circle?

4

53 < ◯

| 31 | 35 | 50 | 63 |
| Ⓐ | Ⓑ | Ⓒ | Ⓓ |

5

94 > 49 > ◯
greatest   least

| 44 | 54 | 79 | 99 |
| Ⓐ | Ⓑ | Ⓒ | Ⓓ |

Standard and Nonstandard Units

Tim and Anna measured with paper clips.

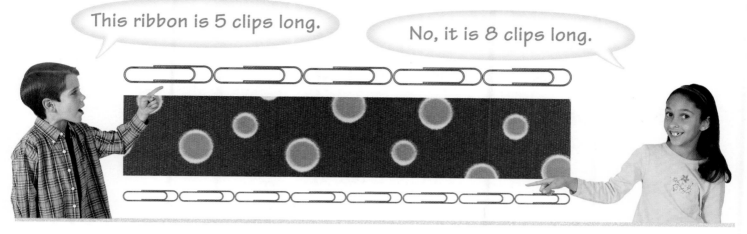

This ribbon is 5 clips long.

No, it is 8 clips long.

Use paper clips and an inch ruler
to measure the ribbons.

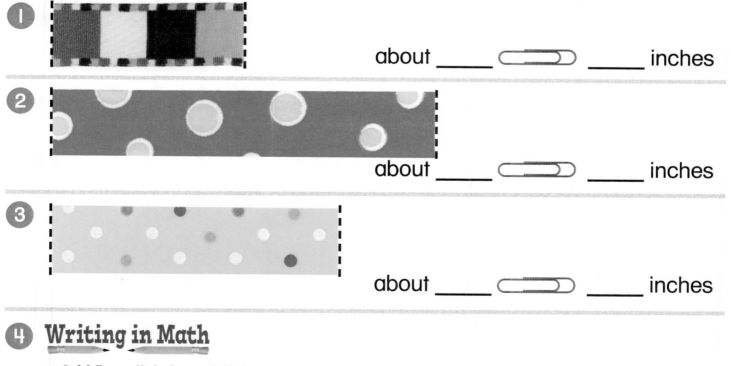

① about _____ ◠ _____ inches

② about _____ ◠ _____ inches

③ about _____ ◠ _____ inches

④ **Writing in Math**

Why did the children get different answers
when they measured with paper clips?

Home Connection Your child measured length with various sizes of paper clips. **Home Activity** Use your child's thumb and then your own thumb to measure a cookie sheet. Discuss the results.

Name_____

Make Predictions Using a Computer

1 Go to the Geometry Shapes eTool.
Place 10 squares and 5 triangles in the workspace.

2 Color 5 squares red and 5 squares blue.
Color 3 triangles red and 2 triangles yellow.

3 Which **shape** do you think you will pick
more often with your eyes closed? _____

4 Try it. Close your eyes and touch the screen.
Use tally marks. Do this 20 times.

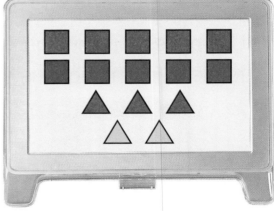

Shapes I Chose	
Square	
Triangle	

5 Which **color** do you think you will pick
most often with your eyes closed? _____

6 Try it 20 times.

Colors I Chose	
Red	
Blue	
Yellow	

Think About It   Reasoning

How did you make your predictions?

Home Connection Your child predicted which of two shapes and which of
three colors he or she would most likely choose and then completed tally charts
to show the results. **Home Activity** Ask your child to explain one of the tally
charts to you.

Plan How to Find the Answer

Read Together

Choosing the correct measurement tools can help you solve math problems.

Test-Taking Strategies

Understand the Question

Get Information for the Answer

Plan How to Find the Answer

Make Smart Choices

Use Writing in Math

1 Which tool would you use to find the length of your math book?

Ⓐ a balance scale

Ⓑ an inch ruler

Ⓒ a thermometer

Ⓓ a cup

Choose the tool that measures length.
Fill in the answer bubble.

Your Turn

Choose the correct tool. Fill in the answer bubble.

I know the answer!

2 Which tool would you use to find the temperature in your classroom?

Ⓐ a thermometer

Ⓑ a centimeter ruler

Ⓒ a balance scale

Ⓓ a one-liter container

Home Connection Your child prepared for standardized tests by determining which measurement tools he or she would use to solve different kinds of problems.
Home Activity Ask your child to identify the word in Exercise 2 that tells what needs to be measured. *(Temperature)* Then ask your child to explain how he or she chose the correct measurement tool.

four hundred eleven   **411**

Name _____

Light as a Feather?

Can you pick up an elephant? No way!
Some things are very heavy.
Others are very light.
How would you weigh a feather?

Measuring Weight

1. Work in a group. Choose something light to weigh.

2. Put your object on one side of a balance scale.

3. On the other side of the scale, add seeds
   or beans one at a time until the scale balances.

4. Record the weight of your object on a separate
   sheet of paper.

5. Repeat Steps 1–4 using two other light objects.

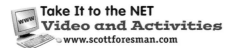
Take It to the NET
Video and Activities
www.scottforesman.com

Home Connection Your child weighed light objects by using
a balance scale and seeds or beans. **Home Activity** Ask your
child to explain how he or she found the weight of one of the
objects.

© Pearson Education, Inc.

Name_____

Estimate the length. Then measure using an inch ruler.

1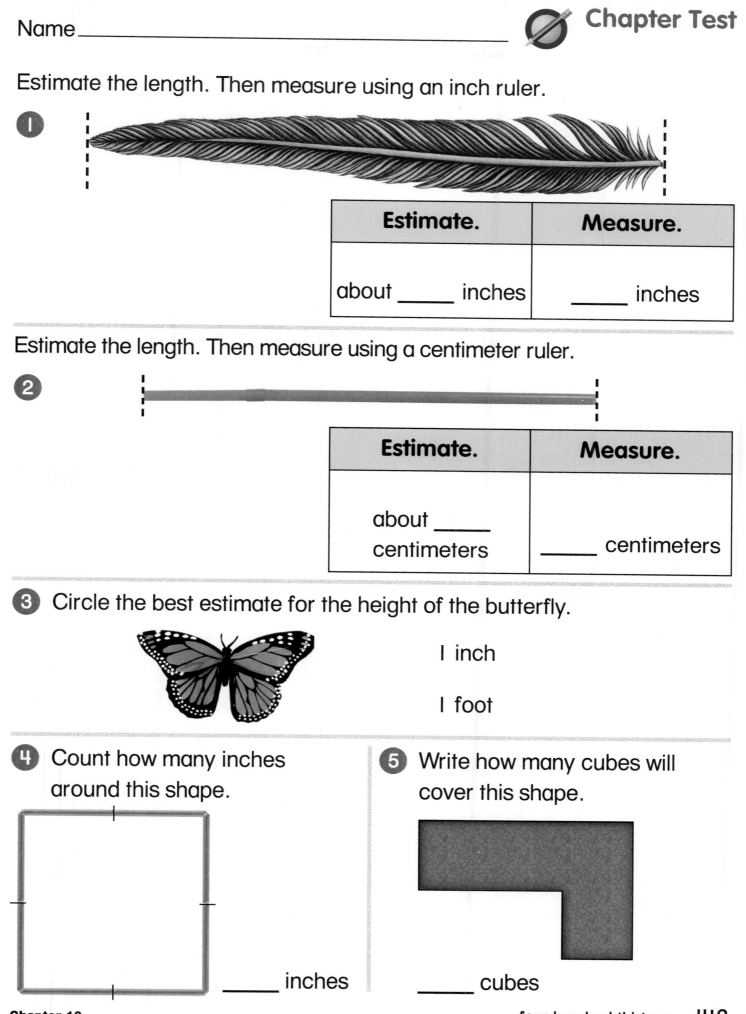

Estimate.	Measure.
about _____ inches	_____ inches

Estimate the length. Then measure using a centimeter ruler.

2

Estimate.	Measure.
about _____ centimeters	_____ centimeters

3 Circle the best estimate for the height of the butterfly.

I inch

I foot

4 Count how many inches around this shape.

_____ inches

5 Write how many cubes will cover this shape.

_____ cubes

Circle the best estimate.

6
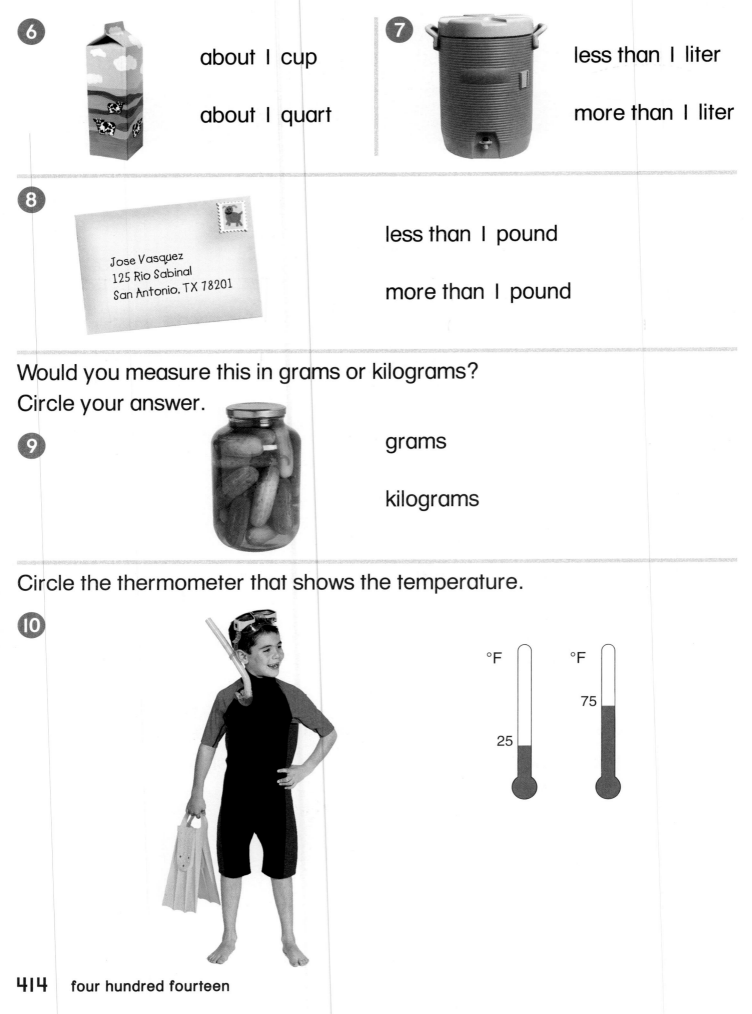
about 1 cup

about 1 quart

7
less than 1 liter

more than 1 liter

8
Jose Vasquez
125 Rio Sabinal
San Antonio, TX 78201

less than 1 pound

more than 1 pound

Would you measure this in grams or kilograms?
Circle your answer.

9
grams

kilograms

Circle the thermometer that shows the temperature.

10

°F
25

°F
75

1 Which addition sentence matches the picture?

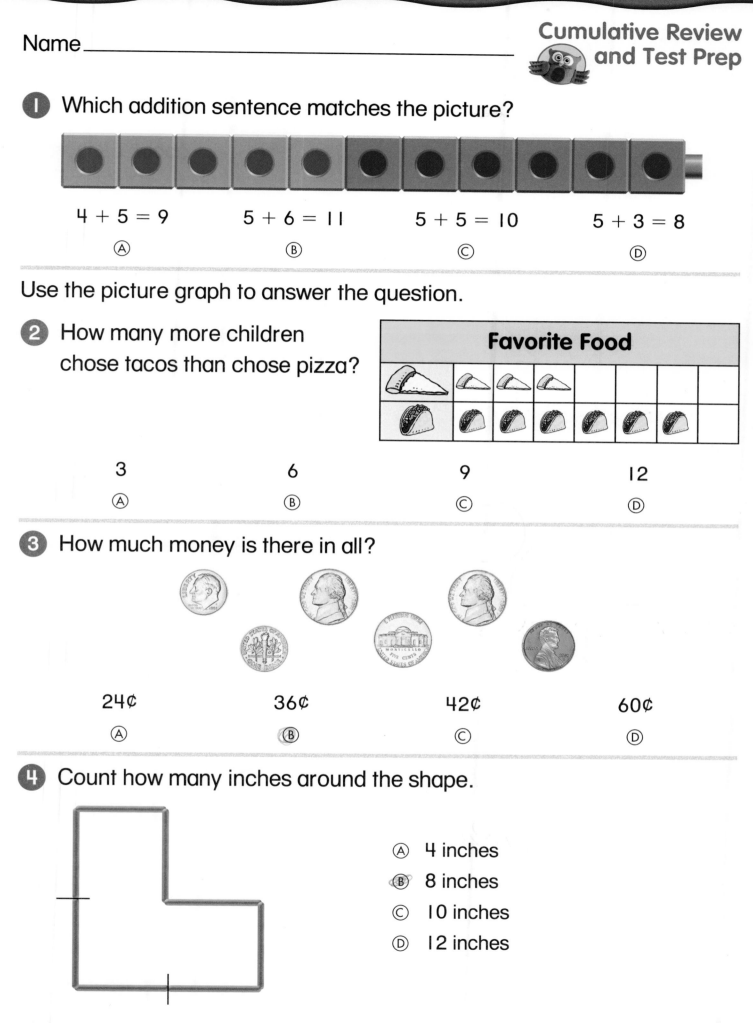

4 + 5 = 9   5 + 6 = 11   5 + 5 = 10   5 + 3 = 8
Ⓐ   Ⓑ   Ⓒ   Ⓓ

Use the picture graph to answer the question.

2 How many more children chose tacos than chose pizza?

Favorite Food

3   6   9   12
Ⓐ   Ⓑ   Ⓒ   Ⓓ

3 How much money is there in all?

24¢   36¢   42¢   60¢
Ⓐ   Ⓑ   Ⓒ   Ⓓ

4 Count how many inches around the shape.

Ⓐ 4 inches
Ⓑ 8 inches
Ⓒ 10 inches
Ⓓ 12 inches

Circle the best estimate.

5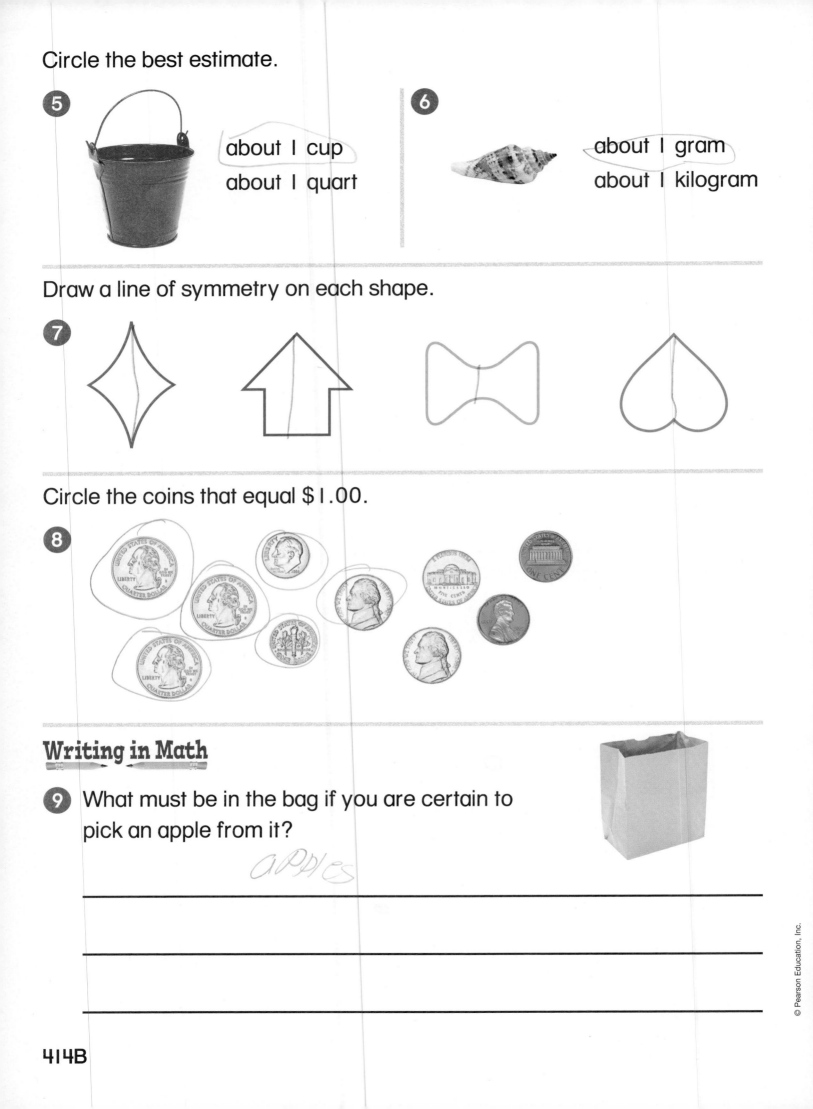

about I cup

about I quart

6

about I gram

about I kilogram

Draw a line of symmetry on each shape.

7

Circle the coins that equal $1.00.

8

Writing in Math

9 What must be in the bag if you are certain to pick an apple from it?

apples

_____

_____

_____

414B

Fuzzy Wuzzy

By Anne Miranda

Illustrated by Diane Greenseid

This Math Storybook belongs to

_____

Fuzzy Wuzzy was a farmer,
Fuzzy was a real bee charmer.

Fuzzy Wuzzy's bees gave honey,
which he sold to make some money.

HONEY FOR SALE
ONLY 5¢ a jar

In came Mac and Benny Rabbit.
Buying honey was their habit.

Mac gave Fuzzy **7** pennies,
plus the **6** cents that were Benny's.

Fuzzy Wuzzy sure could count.
He saw it was the wrong amount.

Fuzzy Wuzzy looked at Mac,
and then he gave him **3** cents back.

Y FOR SALE

5¢ a jar

Mac and Benny smiled because
they saw how clever Fuzzy was!

The pair of honey-loving bunnies
took their change and jars of honey.

With a wink they gave a hop,
thanked Fuzzy twice, and left his shop.

Fuzzy Wuzzy was a bear
who treated all his buyers fair.

His business grew, and grew, and grew.
That shows what being fair can do.

(Of course there was one other fact:
That bear knew how to add and subtract!)

Home-School Connection

Dear Family,

Today my class started Chapter 11, **Addition and Subtraction Facts to 18.** I will learn about addition fact strategies and subtraction fact strategies. Here are some of the math words I will be learning and some things we can do to help me with my math.

Love,

_____

Math Activity to Do at Home

Write 10 on a card. Then ask your child to write a doubles fact that has the sum of 10. Next, on the back of that card, together decide on a related subtraction fact to write. Continue with sums of 8, 6, and 4.

Books to Read Together

Reading math stories reinforces concepts. Look for these titles in your local library:

Mission: Addition
By Loreen Leedy
(Holiday House, 1997)

Two of Everything:
A Chinese Folktale
By Lily T. Hong
(Albert Whitman, 1993)

My New Math Words

related facts Addition and subtraction facts are related if they use the same numbers.

For example:

$$9 + 8 = 17$$
$$17 - 9 = 8$$

Related facts use the same numbers.

fact family A fact family is a group of related addition and subtraction facts. For example:

$7 + 6 = 13$
$6 + 7 = 13$
$13 - 6 = 7$
$13 - 7 = 6$

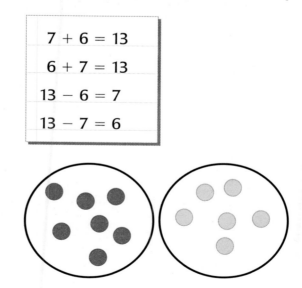

Name_____

Get That Honey!

What You Need

I dot cube 🎲

I marker for each player ⚪ ⚫

How to Play

1. Play with a partner. Put your markers on START.
2. Take turns tossing the cube. Move that number of spaces.
3. Read what it says on the space you land on.
   Do what it says on the space you land on.
4. Keep playing until both of you reach Fuzzy Wuzzy and his honey!

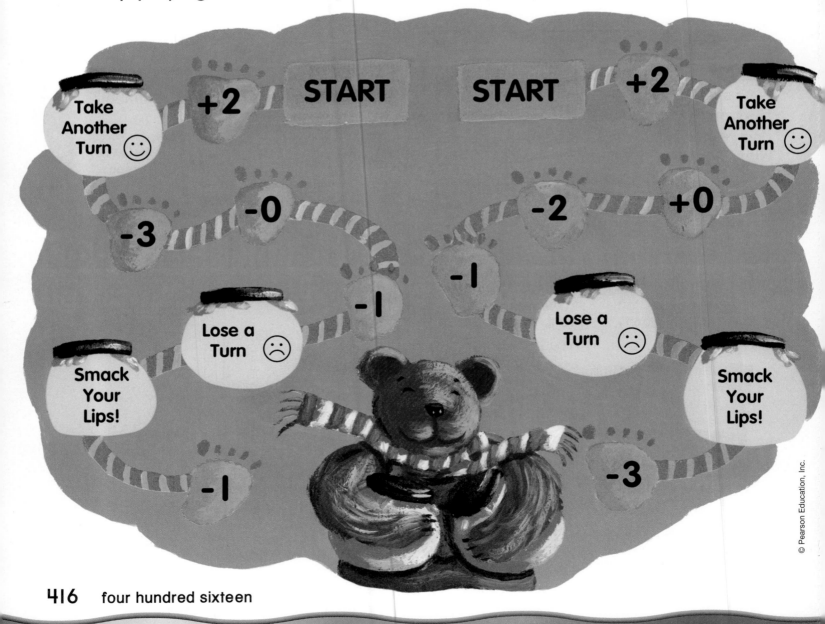

Learn!

You can use doubles to solve other problems.

Think 3 + 3 and 1 more.

Think 3 + 3 and 1 less.

$3 + 3 = \underline{6}$ $3 + 4 = \underline{7}$ $3 + 2 = \underline{5}$

Check ✔

Add the doubles.

Then use the doubles to help you add.

1

$5 + 5 = \underline{}$ $5 + 6 = \underline{}$ $5 + 4 = \underline{}$

2

$7 + 7 = \underline{}$ $7 + 8 = \underline{}$ $7 + 6 = \underline{}$

Think About It   Number Sense

Which two doubles facts could you use
to find the sum for 8 + 7? Explain.

Practice

Add the doubles.

Then use the doubles to help you add.

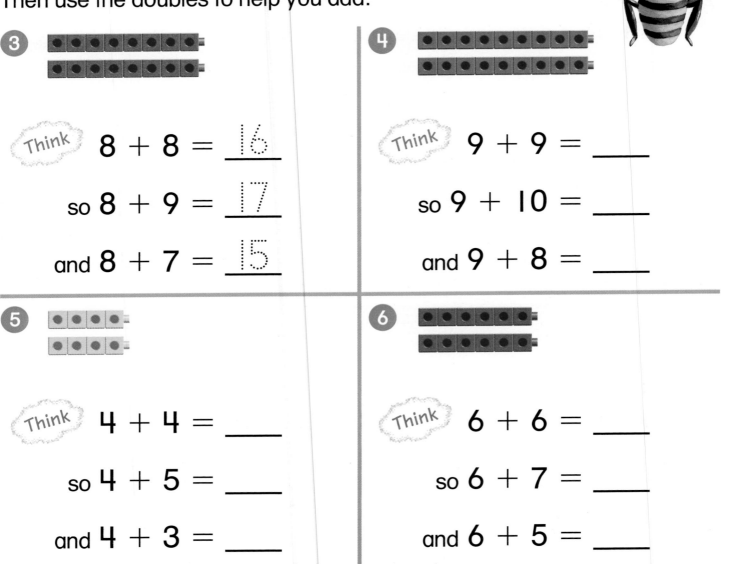

3

Think $8 + 8 = \underline{16}$

so $8 + 9 = \underline{17}$

and $8 + 7 = \underline{15}$

4

Think $9 + 9 = \underline{}$

so $9 + 10 = \underline{}$

and $9 + 8 = \underline{}$

5

Think $4 + 4 = \underline{}$

so $4 + 5 = \underline{}$

and $4 + 3 = \underline{}$

6

Think $6 + 6 = \underline{}$

so $6 + 7 = \underline{}$

and $6 + 5 = \underline{}$

Problem Solving Mental Math

Answer each question.

7 Carrie has 7 red balloons and 8 yellow balloons. How many balloons does Carrie have in all?

_____ balloons

8 Pepe has 6 baseball cards. Dad gives him 7 more cards. How many cards does Pepe have in all?

_____ baseball cards

Home Connection Your child used a doubles fact to solve other addition problems. **Home Activity** Ask your child to show a doubles fact using crayons or other small objects. Then ask him or her to show you a doubles-plus-1 fact and a doubles-minus-1 fact.

Name_____

Learn! Algebra

You can use a pattern when adding 10.

10 + 1 = 11   10 + 2 = 12   10 + 3 = 13

Check ✓

Draw the counters. Then find the sum.

1 10 + 5 = ___

2 10 + 8 = ___

3 10 + 4 = ___

4 10 + 6 = ___

Think About It Reasoning

Which addition fact can help you find the sum for 4 + 10?

How can you show the addition fact with a ten-frame?

Chapter 11 ★ Lesson 3   four hundred twenty-one   **421**

Write the addition sentence for each ten-frame.

5

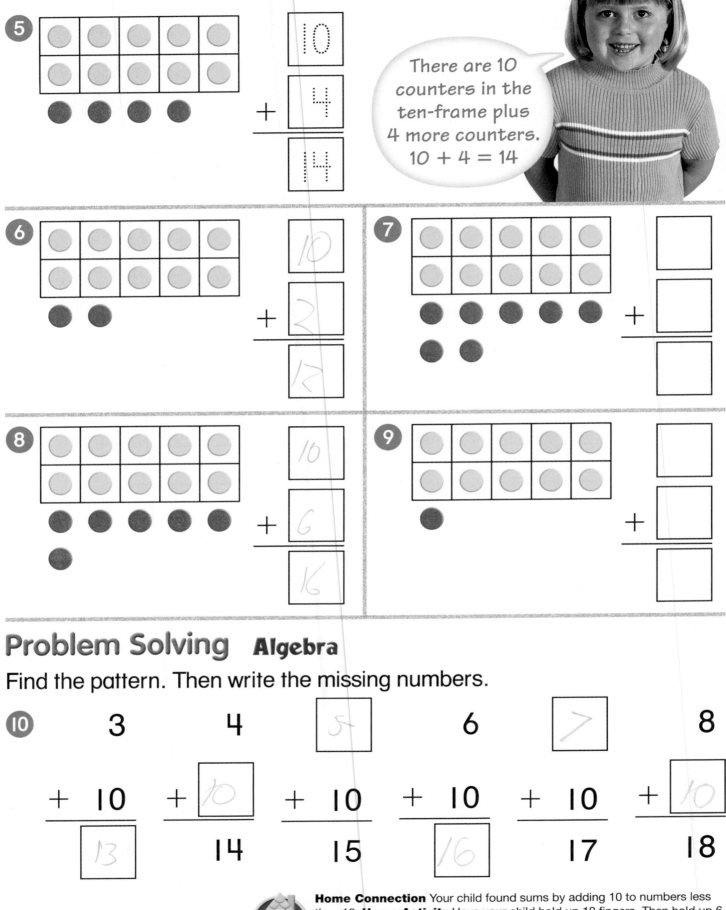

$$10$$
$$+ \quad 4$$
$$\overline{14}$$

There are 10 counters in the ten-frame plus 4 more counters.
$$10 + 4 = 14$$

6

$$10$$
$$+ \quad 2$$
$$\overline{12}$$

7

$$\square$$
$$+ \quad \square$$
$$\overline{\square}$$

8

$$10$$
$$+ \quad 6$$
$$\overline{16}$$

9

$$\square$$
$$+ \quad \square$$
$$\overline{\square}$$

Problem Solving **Algebra**

Find the pattern. Then write the missing numbers.

10

3	4	5	6	7	8
+ 10	+ 10	+ 10	+ 10	+ 10	+ 10
13	14	15	16	17	18

Home Connection Your child found sums by adding 10 to numbers less than 10. **Home Activity** Have your child hold up 10 fingers. Then hold up 6 of your fingers. Ask your child to tell how many fingers in all. Repeat with 10 and other numbers.

422   four hundred twenty-two

© Pearson Education, Inc.

Learn!

You can make a 10 to add other numbers.

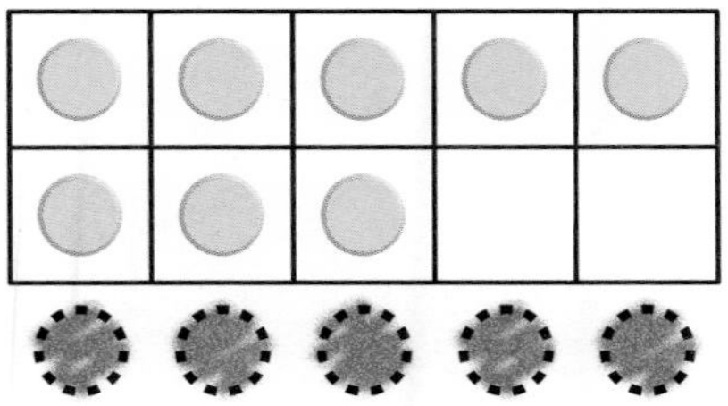

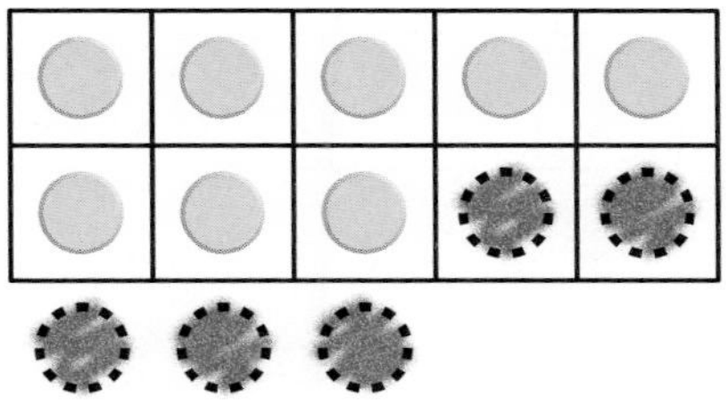

8
+ 5
———
13

8 + 5 is the same as 10 + 3.

10
+ 3
———
13

Check ✓

Use counters and Workmat 2.

Draw the counters. Then write the sums.

1

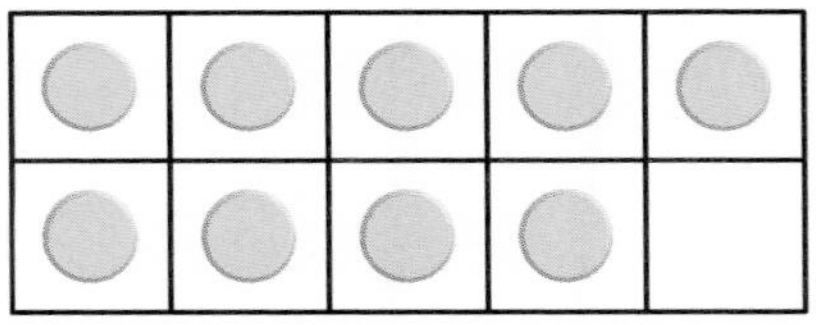

       9   10
   + 3   + 2

2

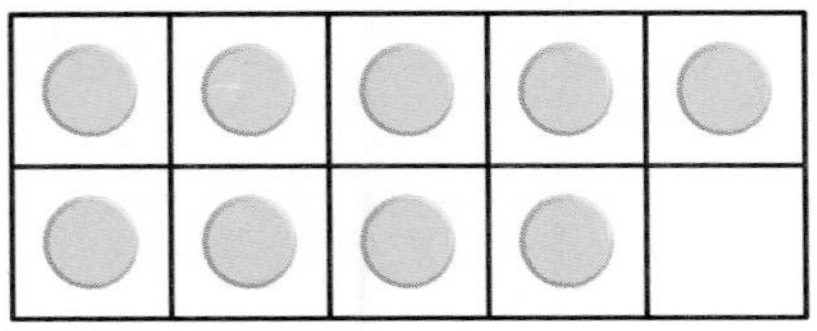

       9   10
   + 5   + 4

3

       8   10
   + 4   + 2

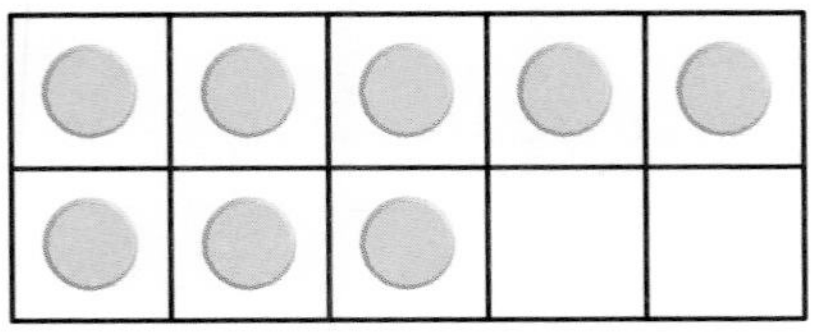

Think About It Number Sense

How would you make a 10 to find the sum of 4 + 9?

Draw the counters. Then write the sums.
Use counters and Workmat 2 if you like.

It is easy to make a 10 to add!

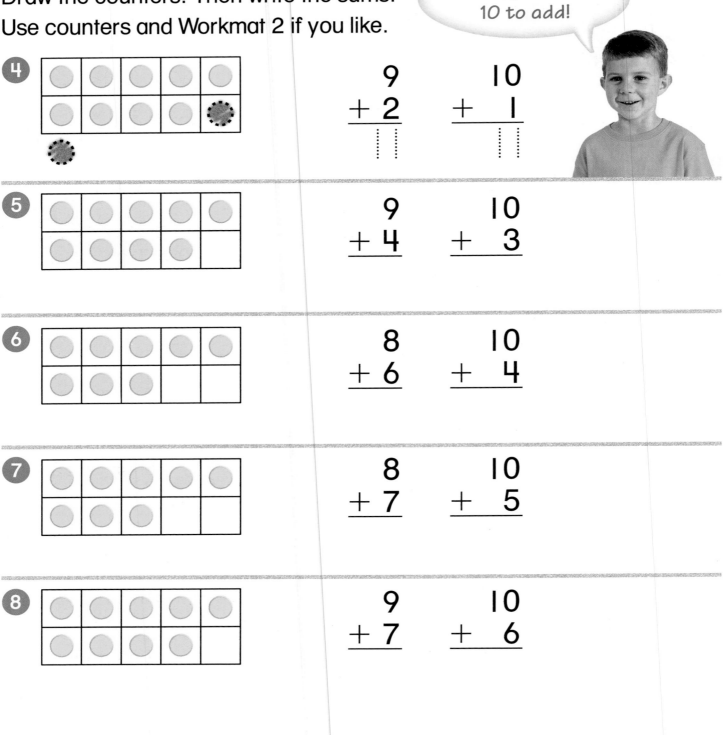

4

$$
\begin{array}{r}
9 \\
+\ 2 \\
\hline
\end{array}
\qquad
\begin{array}{r}
10 \\
+\ 1 \\
\hline
\end{array}
$$

5

$$
\begin{array}{r}
9 \\
+\ 4 \\
\hline
\end{array}
\qquad
\begin{array}{r}
10 \\
+\ 3 \\
\hline
\end{array}
$$

6

$$
\begin{array}{r}
8 \\
+\ 6 \\
\hline
\end{array}
\qquad
\begin{array}{r}
10 \\
+\ 4 \\
\hline
\end{array}
$$

7

$$
\begin{array}{r}
8 \\
+\ 7 \\
\hline
\end{array}
\qquad
\begin{array}{r}
10 \\
+\ 5 \\
\hline
\end{array}
$$

8

$$
\begin{array}{r}
9 \\
+\ 7 \\
\hline
\end{array}
\qquad
\begin{array}{r}
10 \\
+\ 6 \\
\hline
\end{array}
$$

Problem Solving Algebra

Complete the number sentence.

9 $9 + 8 = 10 + 7 = \boxed{}$

Home Connection Your child practiced making a 10 to add two numbers.
Home Activity Hold out 8 pennies in one hand and 5 in the other. Have your child move the pennies to show 10 in one hand and 3 in the other. Have your child explain why 8 + 5 is the same as 10 + 3. Repeat with other numbers.

Learn! Algebra

You can add three numbers in any order.

③+⑥+ 4 = _13_

3 +⑥+④= _13_

9

10

6 + 4 = 10
3 + 10 = 13

3 + 6 = 9
9 + 4 = 13

Check ✓

Find each sum.

❶ ②+⑦+ 3 = ___

2 +⑦+③= ___

❷ ⑤+⑤+ 4 = ___

5 +⑤+④= ___

❸ ③+⑥+ 2 = ___

3 +⑥+②= ___

Think About It Reasoning

Explain why both problems in

Exercise 3 have the same answer.

Circle the two numbers you choose to add first.
Then find each sum.

First add 6 + 4 = 10.
Then add 10 + 5 = 15.

4
(6)
5
+(4)   10

15

5
7
9
+ 1   ☐

5
2
+ 8   ☐

6
6
+ 3   ☐

6
3
7
+ 6   ☐

8
2
+ 2   ☐

7
3
+ 7   ☐

Problem Solving   Algebra

Find the missing numbers.

7   The three numbers on
each branch add up to 18.

© Pearson Education, Inc.

Name_____

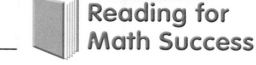

Understand Graphic Sources: Tables

1 Read this story problem.

Mia has dolls and teddy bears.
Each toy box will hold 2 toys.
Mia thought about all the ways to
put the toys in the toy boxes.

Way 1	Way 2	Way 3

She made a table to show the different ways.

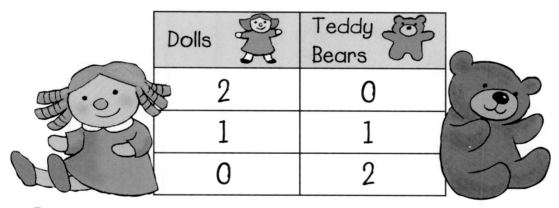

Dolls	Teddy Bears
2	0
1	1
0	2

2 Which way does the first row of the table show?

_____

3 Which way does the second row show? The third row?

_____ _____

Think About It Reasoning

Should there be another row in the table? Explain.

4 Read this story problem.

Mick has 2 kinds of stickers to put on envelopes. Each envelope will have 2 stickers on it. How many different ways can Mick put the stickers on the envelopes?

5 Draw the ways that Mick could put the stickers on the envelopes.

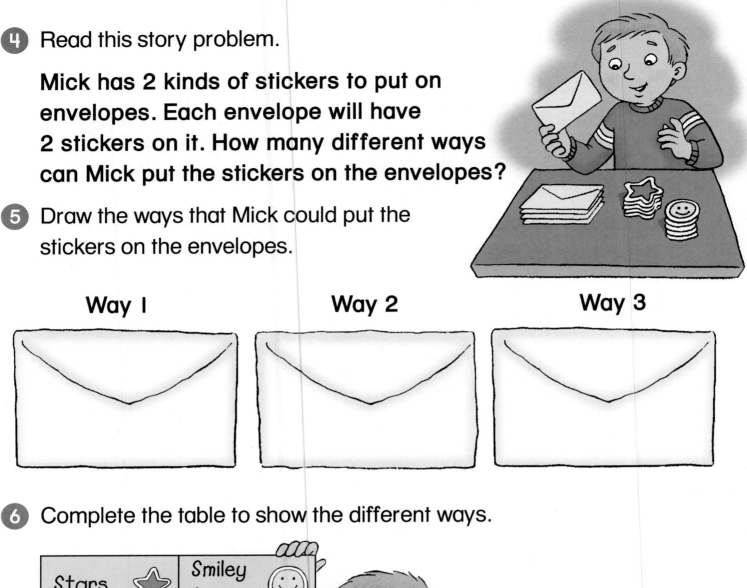

Way I

Way 2

Way 3

6 Complete the table to show the different ways.

Stars ⭐	Smiley faces 😊

7 How many different ways can Mick put 2 stickers on each envelope?

_____ ways

Home Connection Your child completed a table to help solve a story problem. **Home Activity** Think of problems similar to those on these pages, such as finding different ways to put two kinds of objects in a bag. Have your child fill a bag with two objects in three different ways and ask him or her to complete a table like the one above to show all of the possible solutions.

Name_____

Learn!

1 Sandra is making fruit baskets. She has pears, apples, and plums. Each basket holds 3 pieces of fruit. How many different baskets can Sandra make?

Read and Understand

You need to find how many different ways Sandra can fill a basket with 3 pieces of fruit.

Plan and Solve

You can make a table. Then you can count the ways.

There are _____ different ways.

Look Back and Check

Did you find all of the ways? How do you know?

Pears	Apples	Plums
3	0	0
0	3	0
0	0	3
2	1	0
2	0	1
1	2	0
0	2	1
1	0	2
0	1	2
1	1	1

Think About It   Reasoning

How did the table help you answer the question?

Make a table to solve the problem.

2 Dad is making gift bags. He has yo-yos, kazoos, and rings. Each bag holds 3 toys. How many different bags can Dad make?

Dad can make _____ different bags.

Yo-Yos	Kazoos	Rings
3	0	0

Reasoning

3 What do you notice about each row of the table?

_____

_____

Home Connection Your child made tables to help solve problems.
Home Activity Ask your child to explain how he or she filled in the table at the top of the page and to tell how the table helped solve the problem.

Name _____

Add the doubles.
Then use the doubles to help you add.

1 (Think) 7 + 7 = ____   so 7 + 8 = ____

and 7 + 6 = ____

Draw the counters.
Then write the sums.

2

●	●	●	●	●
●	●	●		

```
   8        10
+  6      +  4
```

Add.

3
```
    9        10        5        9        7        5
+   5      +   7     +  8     +  9        4        4
                                      +  3      +  5
```

Complete the table to answer the question.

4 A clown has orange balloons
and purple balloons.
How many different ways
can the clown hold 2 balloons at a time?

There are _____ different ways.

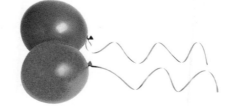

Orange	Purple

Name_____

Use the spinner and tally chart for Exercises 1 and 2.

1 Sam spun the spinner 18 times. He made a tally mark in the chart for each spin. How many times did the spinner land on green?

| Green | ⅢⅢ ⅢⅢ ‖ |
| Red | ⅢⅢ ‖ |

6   11   12   14
Ⓐ   Ⓑ   Ⓒ   Ⓓ

2 If Sam spins the spinner again, on which color is the spinner more likely to land?

green   red   yellow   blue
Ⓐ   Ⓑ   Ⓒ   Ⓓ

3 What is the temperature?

°F   °F   °F   °F
                                    95
                          60
               30
15
15°   30°   60°   95°
Ⓐ   Ⓑ   Ⓒ   Ⓓ

Writing in Math

4 If February 5 is a Thursday, what day will February 9 be? Tell how you found your answer.

_____

_____

Learn! Algebra

Related facts are addition and subtraction facts that have the same numbers.

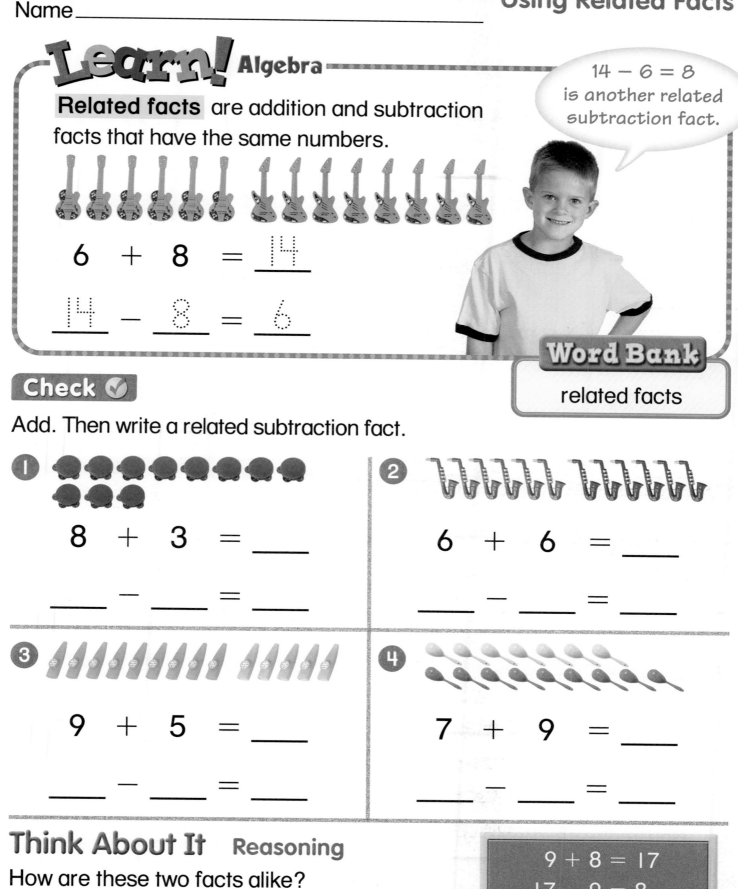

$6 + 8 = \underline{14}$

$\underline{14} - \underline{8} = \underline{6}$

$14 - 6 = 8$ is another related subtraction fact.

Word Bank

related facts

Check ✓

Add. Then write a related subtraction fact.

1

$8 + 3 = \underline{\hspace{1cm}}$

$\underline{\hspace{0.7cm}} - \underline{\hspace{0.7cm}} = \underline{\hspace{0.7cm}}$

2

$6 + 6 = \underline{\hspace{1cm}}$

$\underline{\hspace{0.7cm}} - \underline{\hspace{0.7cm}} = \underline{\hspace{0.7cm}}$

3

$9 + 5 = \underline{\hspace{1cm}}$

$\underline{\hspace{0.7cm}} - \underline{\hspace{0.7cm}} = \underline{\hspace{0.7cm}}$

4

$7 + 9 = \underline{\hspace{1cm}}$

$\underline{\hspace{0.7cm}} - \underline{\hspace{0.7cm}} = \underline{\hspace{0.7cm}}$

Think About It   Reasoning

How are these two facts alike?
How are they different?

$9 + 8 = 17$
$17 - 9 = 8$

Write related addition and subtraction facts for each picture.

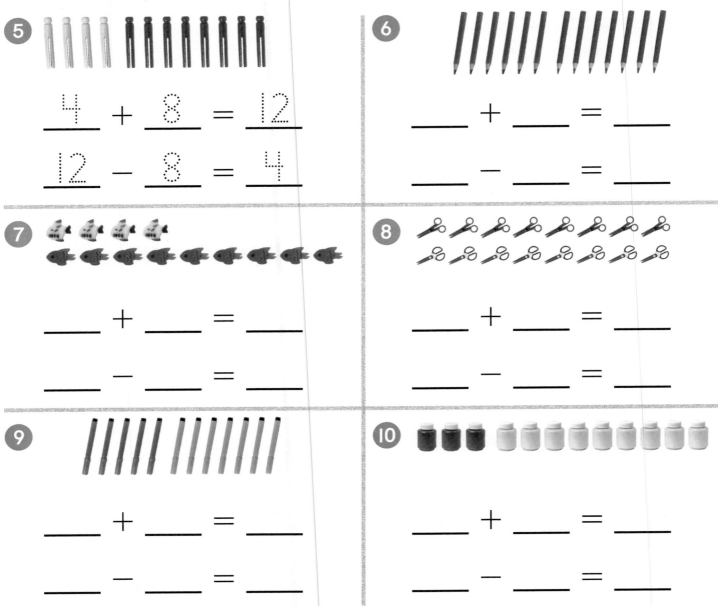

5 $\underline{4} + \underline{8} = \underline{12}$

$\underline{12} - \underline{8} = \underline{4}$

6 $\underline{} + \underline{} = \underline{}$

$\underline{} - \underline{} = \underline{}$

7 $\underline{} + \underline{} = \underline{}$

$\underline{} - \underline{} = \underline{}$

8 $\underline{} + \underline{} = \underline{}$

$\underline{} - \underline{} = \underline{}$

9 $\underline{} + \underline{} = \underline{}$

$\underline{} - \underline{} = \underline{}$

10 $\underline{} + \underline{} = \underline{}$

$\underline{} - \underline{} = \underline{}$

Problem Solving   Number Sense

Write two related facts to answer the questions.

11 8 boys and 6 girls are marching in a band.
How many children are there in all?
If 6 of the children go home,
how many children will be left?

$\underline{} + \underline{} = \underline{}$

$\underline{} - \underline{} = \underline{}$

Home Connection Your child wrote related addition and subtraction facts.
Home Activity Ask your child to use pennies or other small objects to show $8 + 7 = 15$ and $15 - 7 = 8$ and other pairs of related facts.

Learn! Algebra

These related addition and subtraction facts make a **fact family**.

They all use the same three numbers: 7, 9, and 16.

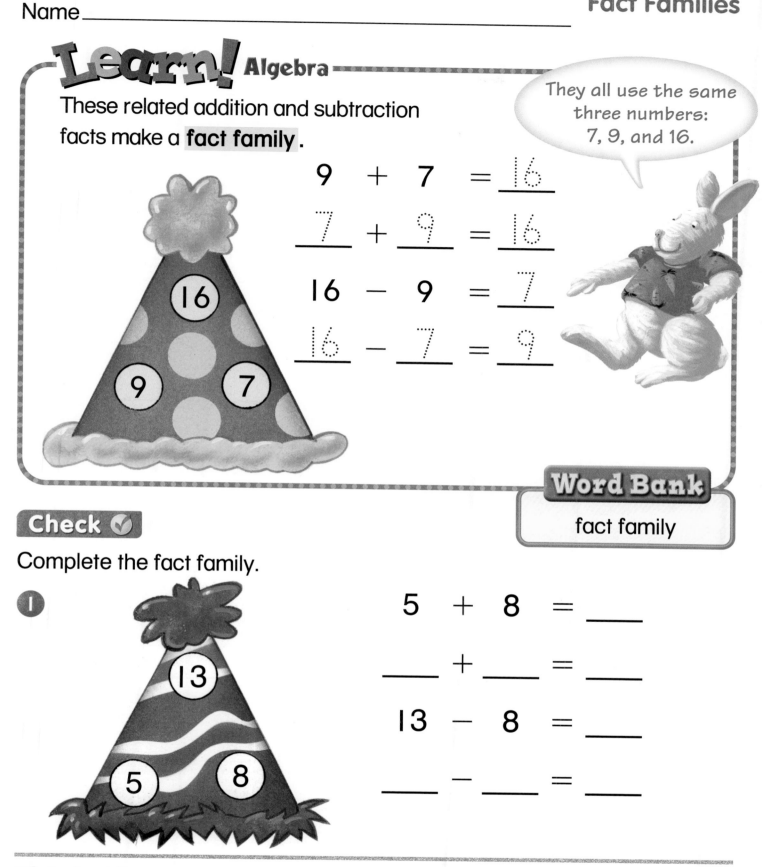

$9 + 7 = \underline{16}$

$\underline{7} + \underline{9} = \underline{16}$

$16 - 9 = \underline{7}$

$\underline{16} - \underline{7} = \underline{9}$

Word Bank

fact family

Check ✔

Complete the fact family.

① (13) (5) (8)

$5 + 8 = \underline{}$

$\underline{} + \underline{} = \underline{}$

$13 - 8 = \underline{}$

$\underline{} - \underline{} = \underline{}$

Think About It   Reasoning

Which fact families have only two facts? Explain.

Practice

Use the numbers on each hat to write a fact family.

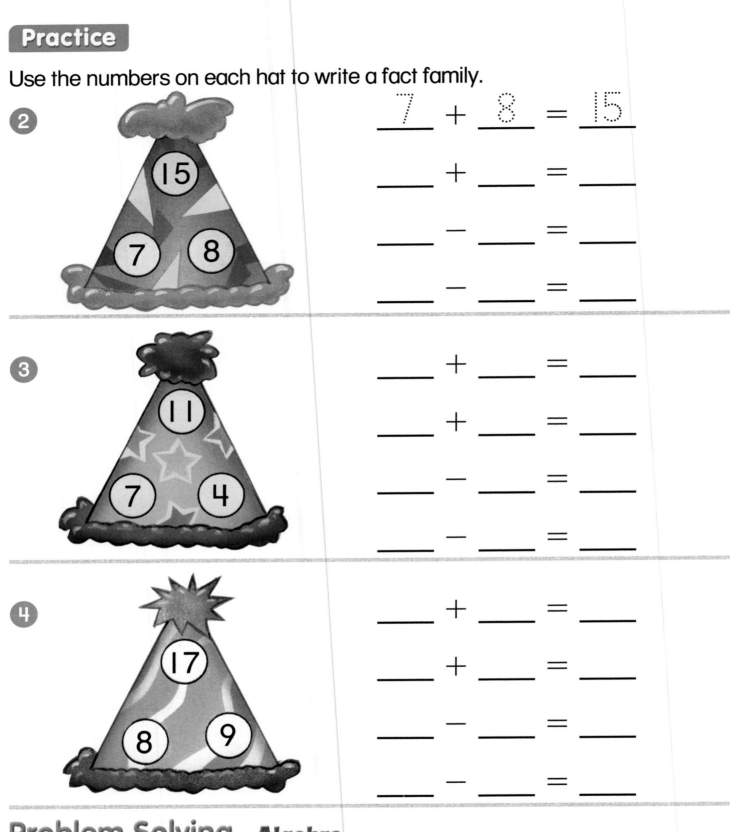

2

$$\underline{7} + \underline{8} = \underline{15}$$

$$\underline{} + \underline{} = \underline{}$$

$$\underline{} - \underline{} = \underline{}$$

$$\underline{} - \underline{} = \underline{}$$

3

$$\underline{} + \underline{} = \underline{}$$

$$\underline{} + \underline{} = \underline{}$$

$$\underline{} - \underline{} = \underline{}$$

$$\underline{} - \underline{} = \underline{}$$

4

$$\underline{} + \underline{} = \underline{}$$

$$\underline{} + \underline{} = \underline{}$$

$$\underline{} - \underline{} = \underline{}$$

$$\underline{} - \underline{} = \underline{}$$

Problem Solving Algebra

Write the missing number for each fact family.

5

6   12

6

4   9

Home Connection Your child wrote the related facts in a fact family.
Home Activity Remove the face cards from a deck of cards. Have your child pick 2 cards and write an addition fact, such as 7 + 8 = 15, using the numbers. Then ask your child to complete the fact family.

Name_____

Learn! Algebra

You can use addition to help you subtract.

If $5 + 8 = 13$,
then $13 - 8 = 5$.

Think $5 + 8 = \underline{13}$

so $13 - 8 = \underline{5}$

Check ✓

Add.

Then use the addition fact to help you subtract.

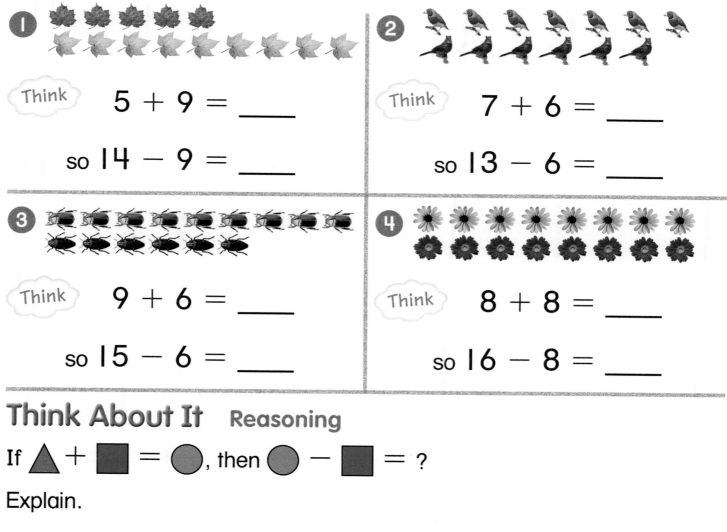

1

Think $5 + 9 = \underline{\hphantom{00}}$

so $14 - 9 = \underline{\hphantom{00}}$

2

Think $7 + 6 = \underline{\hphantom{00}}$

so $13 - 6 = \underline{\hphantom{00}}$

3

Think $9 + 6 = \underline{\hphantom{00}}$

so $15 - 6 = \underline{\hphantom{00}}$

4

Think $8 + 8 = \underline{\hphantom{00}}$

so $16 - 8 = \underline{\hphantom{00}}$

Think About It Reasoning

If $\triangle + \blacksquare = \bigcirc$, then $\bigcirc - \blacksquare = $?

Explain.

Circle the addition fact that will help you subtract.
Then subtract.

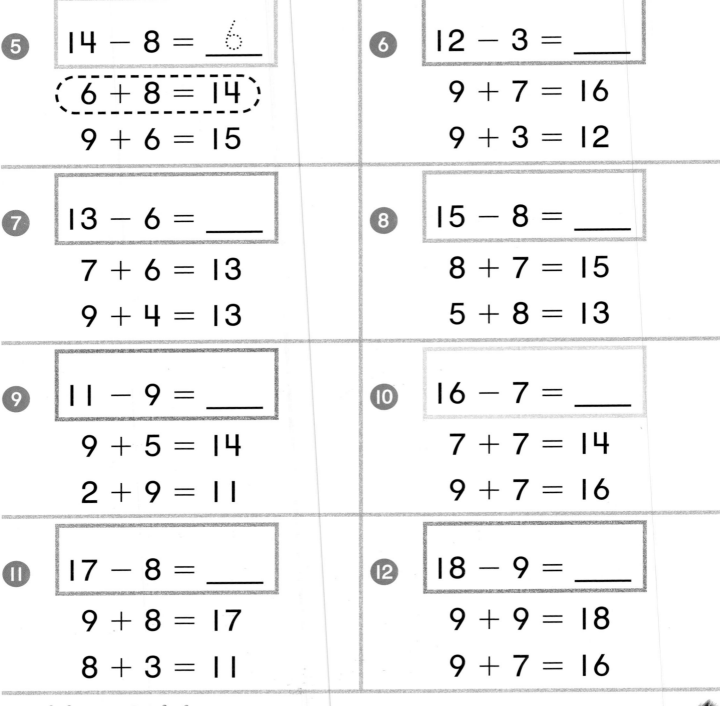

5 14 − 8 = _6_

(6 + 8 = 14)

9 + 6 = 15

6 12 − 3 = ___

9 + 7 = 16

9 + 3 = 12

7 13 − 6 = ___

7 + 6 = 13

9 + 4 = 13

8 15 − 8 = ___

8 + 7 = 15

5 + 8 = 13

9 11 − 9 = ___

9 + 5 = 14

2 + 9 = 11

10 16 − 7 = ___

7 + 7 = 14

9 + 7 = 16

11 17 − 8 = ___

9 + 8 = 17

8 + 3 = 11

12 18 − 9 = ___

9 + 9 = 18

9 + 7 = 16

Problem Solving   Mental Math

Solve.

13 The chipmunk stored 9 of its 17 acorns.
How many acorns does it still need to store?   _____ acorns

Home Connection Your child used addition facts to help with subtraction.
Home Activity Write 15 − 6 on a piece of paper. Ask your child to write a
related addition fact and then solve the subtraction problem. Continue with
other subtraction problems.

Name_____

Learn!

You can use a ten-frame to subtract.

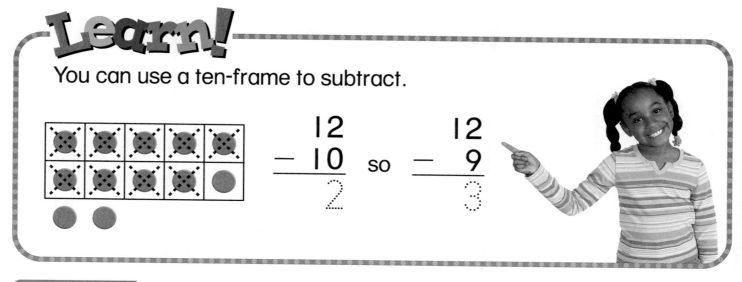

$$\begin{array}{r} 12 \\ -\ 10 \\ \hline 2 \end{array}$$ so $$\begin{array}{r} 12 \\ -\ 9 \\ \hline 3 \end{array}$$

Check ✓

Cross out to subtract.

Use a ten-frame and counters if you like.

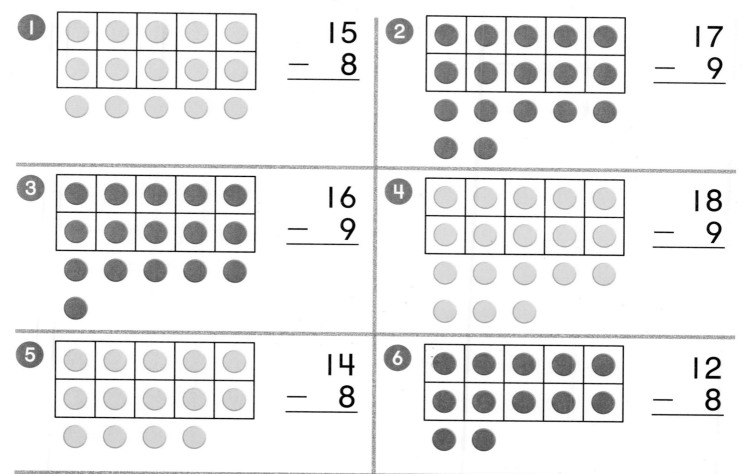

1. $$\begin{array}{r} 15 \\ -\ 8 \\ \hline \end{array}$$

2. $$\begin{array}{r} 17 \\ -\ 9 \\ \hline \end{array}$$

3. $$\begin{array}{r} 16 \\ -\ 9 \\ \hline \end{array}$$

4. $$\begin{array}{r} 18 \\ -\ 9 \\ \hline \end{array}$$

5. $$\begin{array}{r} 14 \\ -\ 8 \\ \hline \end{array}$$

6. $$\begin{array}{r} 12 \\ -\ 8 \\ \hline \end{array}$$

Think About It Number Sense

Which difference do you think will be
greater, $15 - 10$ or $15 - 8$? Explain.

Cross out to subtract.

Use a ten-frame and counters if you like.

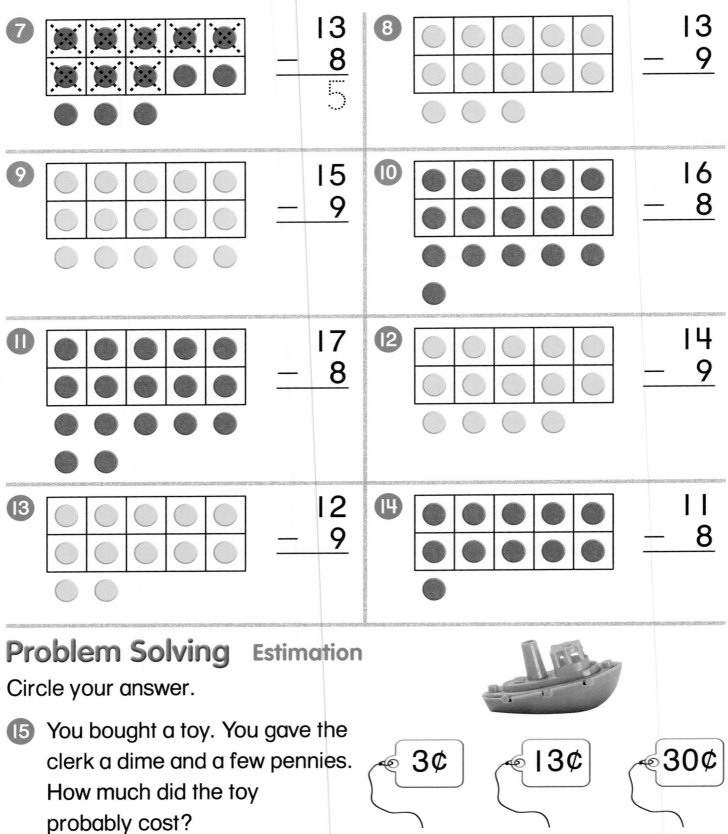

7 $\begin{array}{r} 13 \\ -\ 8 \\ \hline 5 \end{array}$

8 $\begin{array}{r} 13 \\ -\ 9 \\ \hline \end{array}$

9 $\begin{array}{r} 15 \\ -\ 9 \\ \hline \end{array}$

10 $\begin{array}{r} 16 \\ -\ 8 \\ \hline \end{array}$

11 $\begin{array}{r} 17 \\ -\ 8 \\ \hline \end{array}$

12 $\begin{array}{r} 14 \\ -\ 9 \\ \hline \end{array}$

13 $\begin{array}{r} 12 \\ -\ 9 \\ \hline \end{array}$

14 $\begin{array}{r} 11 \\ -\ 8 \\ \hline \end{array}$

Problem Solving   Estimation

Circle your answer.

15 You bought a toy. You gave the clerk a dime and a few pennies. How much did the toy probably cost?

3¢   13¢   30¢

© Pearson Education, Inc.

Home Connection Your child used a ten-frame to subtract. **Home Activity** For Exercises 7 and 10 on this page, ask your child to write a subtraction sentence that takes away one more. *(13 − 9 = 4; 16 − 9 = 7)*

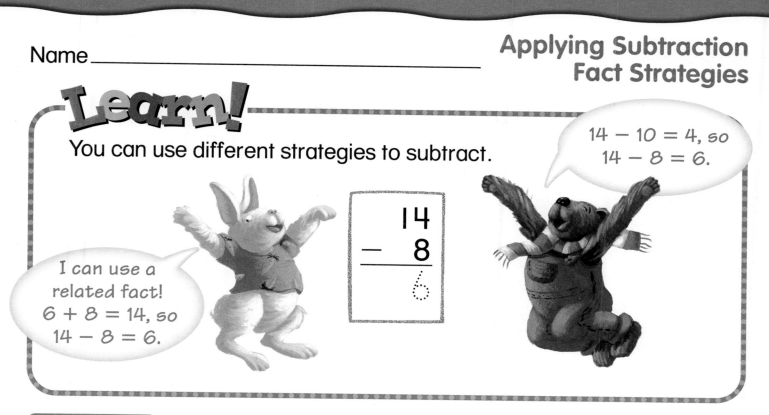

Learn!

You can use different strategies to subtract.

14 − 10 = 4, so
14 − 8 = 6.

$$\begin{array}{r} 14 \\ -\ 8 \\ \hline 6 \end{array}$$

I can use a
related fact!
6 + 8 = 14, so
14 − 8 = 6.

Check ✓

Subtract.

Then circle the strategy that you used.

① $\begin{array}{r} 15 \\ -\ 9 \\ \hline \end{array}$ use a related fact

use 10

② $\begin{array}{r} 11 \\ -\ 5 \\ \hline \end{array}$ use a related fact

use 10

③ $\begin{array}{r} 12 \\ -\ 8 \\ \hline \end{array}$ use a related fact

use 10

④ $\begin{array}{r} 14 \\ -\ 6 \\ \hline \end{array}$ use a related fact

use 10

⑤ $\begin{array}{r} 13 \\ -\ 7 \\ \hline \end{array}$ use a related fact

use 10

⑥ $\begin{array}{r} 16 \\ -\ 9 \\ \hline \end{array}$ use a related fact

use 10

Think About It   Reasoning

Which strategy do you use more often?

Explain why.

Subtract.

7
```
  13        14        17        15
-  9      -  7      -  8      -  6
   4
```

8
```
  16        13        14        17         9        15
-  8      -  8      -  8      -  9      -  9      -  9
```

9
```
  13        15        12        16        14        13
-  4      -  8      -  3      -  9      -  6      -  7
```

10
```
  15        14        13        10        18        14
-  7      -  9      -  6      -  7      -  9      -  5
```

11
```
  12         7        11         8        10        12
-  4      -  0      -  5      -  8      -  4      -  6
```

Problem Solving   Reasonableness

Circle your answer.

12 If Jay has 12 − 8 ribbons and May has
12 − 5 ribbons, then which sentence is true?

Jay has more ribbons than May.

May has more ribbons than Jay.

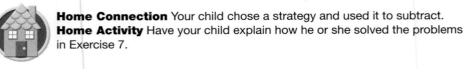

Home Connection Your child chose a strategy and used it to subtract.
Home Activity Have your child explain how he or she solved the problems
in Exercise 7.

Name_____

Learn! Algebra

Clifton has 7 bones. He gets 5 more bones. How many bones does Clifton have in all?

__7__ ⊕ __5__ = __12__ bones

I can use the answer to the first question to answer the second question.

If Clifton buries 6 of the bones, how many bones are not buried?

__12__ ⊖ __6__ = __6__ bones

Check ✓

Solve each problem.

1 Kitty has 4 cat toys. She gets 3 more toys. How many toys does Kitty have in all?

____ ◯ ____ = ____ toys

If Kitty gets 8 more cat toys, how many toys will she have then?

____ ◯ ____ = ____ toys

Think About It   Reasoning

Can you answer the second question before you answer the first question? Explain.

Solve each problem.

2 There are 13 bunnies in the yard.
7 bunnies are brown. The rest are white.
How many bunnies are white?

____ ◯ ____ = ____ bunnies

If 4 more white bunnies come into the yard,
how many white bunnies will there be in all?

____ ◯ ____ = ____ bunnies

3 In a cage are 7 yellow birds and 7 orange birds.
How many birds are there in all?

____ ◯ ____ = ____ birds

Pam takes 5 birds from the cage.
How many birds are left in the cage?

____ ◯ ____ = ____ birds

4 The pet store has 9 hamsters.
The store gets 7 more hamsters.
How many hamsters does the store have now?

____ ◯ ____ = ____ hamsters

If the store sells 8 hamsters,
how many hamsters will be left?

____ ◯ ____ = ____ hamsters

Home Connection Your child solved two-step story problems.
Home Activity Use spoons or forks to show an addition problem. Then
continue the problem by taking some away. Together with your child, write
the addition sentence and the subtraction sentence that solve the problem.

Name_____

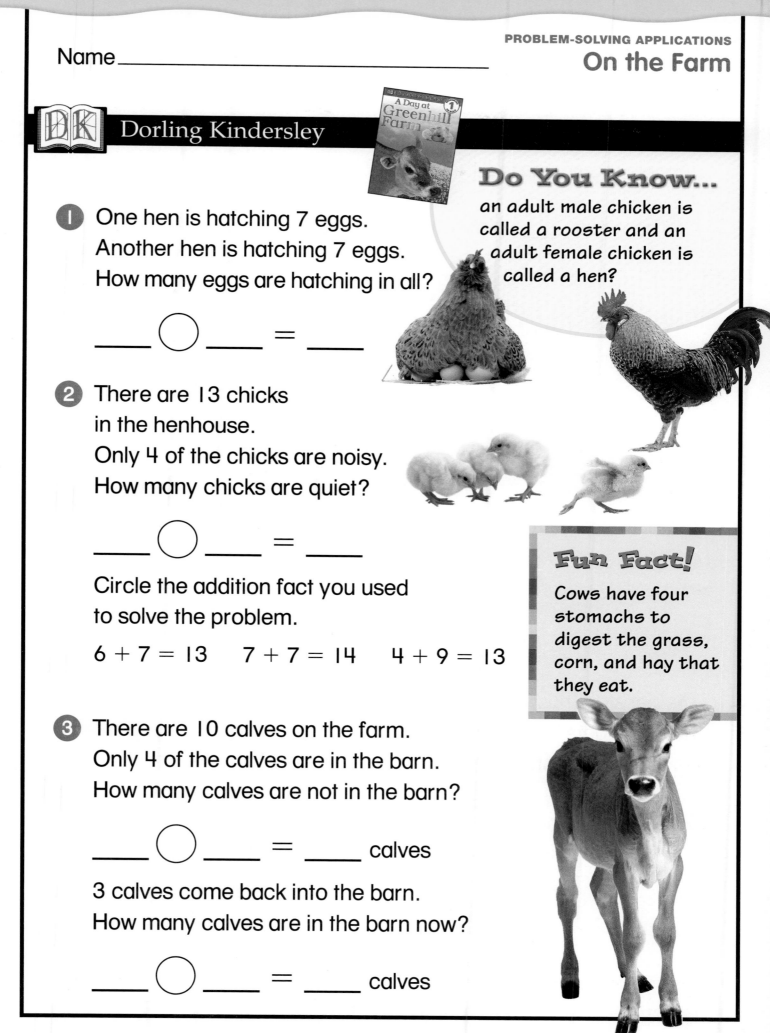

Dorling Kindersley

A Day at
Greenhill
Farm

Do You Know...
an adult male chicken is called a rooster and an adult female chicken is called a hen?

1 One hen is hatching 7 eggs.
Another hen is hatching 7 eggs.
How many eggs are hatching in all?

____ ◯ ____ = ____

2 There are 13 chicks
in the henhouse.
Only 4 of the chicks are noisy.
How many chicks are quiet?

____ ◯ ____ = ____

Circle the addition fact you used
to solve the problem.

$6 + 7 = 13$ $7 + 7 = 14$ $4 + 9 = 13$

Fun Fact!
Cows have four stomachs to digest the grass, corn, and hay that they eat.

3 There are 10 calves on the farm.
Only 4 of the calves are in the barn.
How many calves are not in the barn?

____ ◯ ____ = ____ calves

3 calves come back into the barn.
How many calves are in the barn now?

____ ◯ ____ = ____ calves

4 There are 6 pink pigs.
There are 4 spotted pigs.
There are 4 brown pigs.
How many pigs are there in all?

$$\begin{array}{r} 6 \\ 4 \\ + 4 \\ \hline \end{array}$$

There are _____ pigs in all.

5 If 1 pig is pink and 2 pigs are gray,
what fraction of the pigs is pink?

$$\frac{1}{2} \qquad \frac{1}{3} \qquad \frac{1}{4}$$

6 A farmer bought 45 bags of feed.
Now he has 10 fewer than 45 bags.
How many bags does he have now?

_____ bags

7 **Writing in Math**

Draw a picture of 18 piglets.
Write a subtraction story about your picture.
Then write a number sentence to go with your story.

____ ◯ ____ = ____

Home Connection Your child learned to solve problems by using his or her math skills. **Home Activity** Talk to your child about how he or she solved the problems on these two pages.

Name _____

Write an addition sentence and a subtraction sentence to go with the picture.

1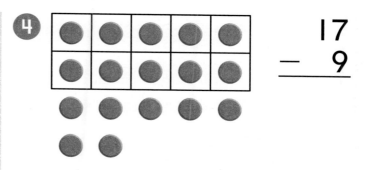

___ + ___ = ___

___ − ___ = ___

Use the numbers to write a fact family.

2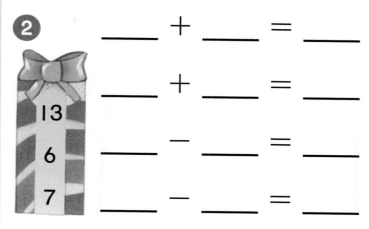

13

6

7

___ + ___ = ___

___ + ___ = ___

___ − ___ = ___

___ − ___ = ___

Add. Then use the addition fact to help you subtract.

3

$9 + 6 =$ ___

so $15 - 6 =$ ___

Cross out to subtract.

4

$\begin{array}{r} 17 \\ -\ 9 \\ \hline \end{array}$

Solve each problem.

5 Ann put 9 red cars on the track. Then she put on 7 yellow cars. How many cars were on the track?

___ ◯ ___ = ___ cars

If Ann takes away 8 cars, how many cars will be left on the track?

___ ◯ ___ = ___ cars

Name_____

Add.

1
```
    8
  + 8
```

14   15   16   17
Ⓐ   Ⓑ   Ⓒ   Ⓓ

2
```
    2
    7
  + 3
```

10   11   12   13
Ⓐ   Ⓑ   Ⓒ   Ⓓ

3 Which group of counters will help you
find 8 + 4?

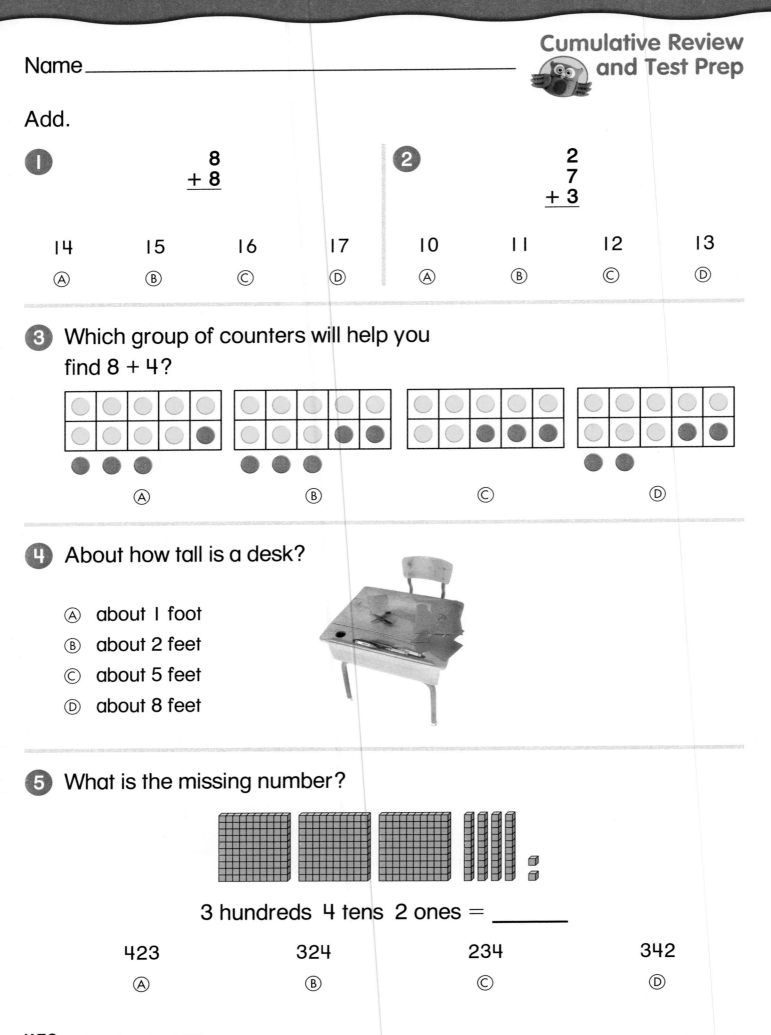

Ⓐ   Ⓑ   Ⓒ   Ⓓ

4 About how tall is a desk?

Ⓐ   about 1 foot

Ⓑ   about 2 feet

Ⓒ   about 5 feet

Ⓓ   about 8 feet

5 What is the missing number?

3 hundreds 4 tens 2 ones = _____

423   324   234   342
Ⓐ   Ⓑ   Ⓒ   Ⓓ

Multiplication as Repeated Addition

Sonia made this picture with more than 50 stickers.

Can you find the three 5s?

Complete the table.

How many stickers are in each shape?	How many stickers are there in all?		
① <u>5</u>	5 + 5 + 5	= <u>15</u>	
②		= <u> </u>	
③ <u> </u>		= <u> </u>	
④ <u> </u>		= <u> </u>	
⑤ <u> </u>		= <u> </u>	

Writing in Math

⑥ If three 5s are 15, then how many are four 5s?
Explain how you got your answer.

_____

_____

Home Connection Your child encountered the idea of multiplication by doing repeated addition. **Home Activity** Ask your child to use addition to tell what four 3s equal and what five 2s equal. *(3 + 3 + 3 + 3 = 12; 2 + 2 + 2 + 2 + 2 = 10)*

Make Fact Families Using a Calculator

You can use a calculator to make a fact family.
Write the numbers you press for each fact.
Write the number in the display for each fact.
Press ON/C each time you begin.

1 Make a fact family.

[7] [+] [   ] [=] __9__

[   ] [+] [7] [=] ____

[   ] [−] [   ] [=] __2__

[   ] [−] [   ] [=] ____

2 Make another fact family.

[   ] [+] [1] [=] __9__

[1] [+] [   ] [=] ____

[   ] [−] [   ] [=] ____

[   ] [−] [   ] [=] ____

3 Make a doubles fact family.

[4] [+] [   ] [=] __8__

[   ] [−] [   ] [=] ____

4 Make your own doubles fact family.

[   ] [+] [   ] [=] ____

[   ] [−] [   ] [=] ____

Think About It   Reasoning

How could you use a calculator to make a
bigger doubles fact family?

Home Connection Your child used a calculator to make fact families (groups of related facts). **Home Activity** Ask your child to explain how he or she would make a fact family for 11 on a calculator. *(Sample answer: I would press 6 + 5 =, 5 + 6 =, 11 − 5 =, and 11 − 6 =.)*

Make Smart Choices

What if you solve a problem, but your answer is not one of the choices? Try again!

Test-Taking Strategies

Understand the Question

Get Information for the Answer

Plan How to Find the Answer

Make Smart Choices

Use Writing in Math

1 Find the sum. Fill in the answer bubble.

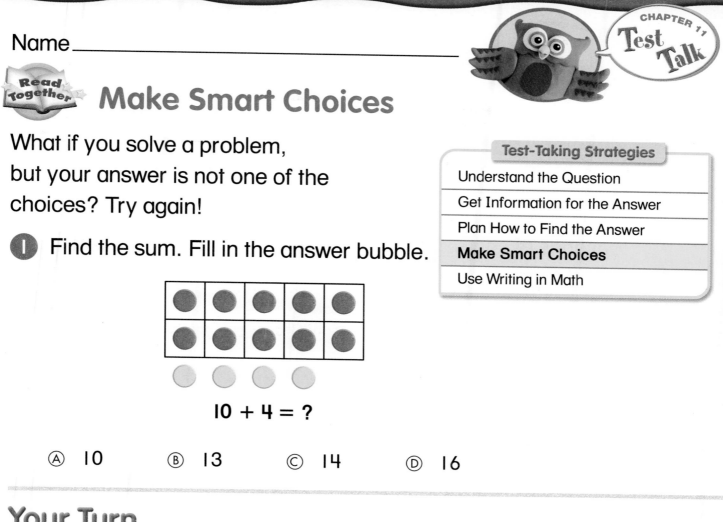

$$10 + 4 = ?$$

Ⓐ 10   Ⓑ 13   Ⓒ 14   Ⓓ 16

Your Turn

2 Find the sum. Fill in the answer bubble.

$$\begin{array}{r} 7 \\ 7 \\ + 3 \\ \hline ? \end{array}$$

Ⓐ 10   Ⓑ 14   Ⓒ 16   Ⓓ 17

You can do it!

Name _____

Read Together

Board Games

People have been playing board games for thousands of years. Pretend that you are playing a game with a friend.

Game Facts

Solve each problem. Watch out: The last one is tricky!

1 Your card says: Move 5 spaces. Your friend's card says: Move 5 spaces and then move 6 spaces. How many spaces will your friend move?

_____

2 Your next card says: Stay where you are. Your friend's card says: Go back 6 spaces. What space will your friend land on?

_____

3 Who is ahead now? Explain.

_____

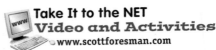
Take It to the NET
Video and Activities
www.scottforesman.com

Home Connection Your child solved problems about playing a game with a friend. **Home Activity** Ask your child to write a number sentence about playing a board game. For example, say to your child: "I moved 3 spaces on my first turn and 8 spaces on my second turn. How many spaces did I move altogether on those two turns?" *(3 + 8 = 11 spaces)*

Add.

1

$$\begin{array}{r} 9 \\ + 6 \\ \hline \end{array}$$
$$\begin{array}{r} 5 \\ + 6 \\ \hline \end{array}$$
$$\begin{array}{r} 4 \\ + 9 \\ \hline \end{array}$$
$$\begin{array}{r} 7 \\ + 7 \\ \hline \end{array}$$
$$\begin{array}{r} 8 \\ 3 \\ + 2 \\ \hline \end{array}$$
$$\begin{array}{r} 5 \\ 6 \\ + 6 \\ \hline \end{array}$$

Subtract.

2

$$\begin{array}{r} 16 \\ - 9 \\ \hline \end{array}$$
$$\begin{array}{r} 13 \\ - 8 \\ \hline \end{array}$$
$$\begin{array}{r} 12 \\ - 4 \\ \hline \end{array}$$
$$\begin{array}{r} 15 \\ - 7 \\ \hline \end{array}$$
$$\begin{array}{r} 16 \\ - 8 \\ \hline \end{array}$$
$$\begin{array}{r} 11 \\ - 5 \\ \hline \end{array}$$

Add the doubles.

Then use the doubles to help you add.

3   *Think* $7 + 7 =$ _____   so $7 + 8 =$ _____

and $7 + 6 =$ _____

Draw the counters. Then write the sums.

4

$$\begin{array}{r} 9 \\ + 6 \\ \hline \end{array}$$
$$\begin{array}{r} 10 \\ + 5 \\ \hline \end{array}$$

Write related addition and subtraction facts
to go with the picture.

5

____ + ____ = ____   ____ − ____ = ____

Add.

Then use the addition fact to help you subtract.

6

$$6 + 8 = \underline{\hspace{2em}}$$

so $14 - 8 = \underline{\hspace{2em}}$

Use the numbers to write a fact family.

7

$$\underline{\hspace{1.5em}} + \underline{\hspace{1.5em}} = \underline{\hspace{1.5em}}$$

$$\underline{\hspace{1.5em}} + \underline{\hspace{1.5em}} = \underline{\hspace{1.5em}}$$

$$\underline{\hspace{1.5em}} - \underline{\hspace{1.5em}} = \underline{\hspace{1.5em}}$$

$$\underline{\hspace{1.5em}} - \underline{\hspace{1.5em}} = \underline{\hspace{1.5em}}$$

Make a table to answer the question.

8 Eli has daisies and tulips.
The vase holds 2 flowers.
How many different ways can
Eli fill the vase?

There are _____ different ways.

Daisies	Tulips

Solve each problem.

9 Mrs. Green has 5 large pumpkins and 9 small
pumpkins. How many pumpkins does she have in all?

$$\underline{\hspace{2em}} \bigcirc \underline{\hspace{2em}} = \underline{\hspace{2em}} \text{ pumpkins}$$

Mrs. Green sells 7 pumpkins.
How many pumpkins does she have left?

$$\underline{\hspace{2em}} \bigcirc \underline{\hspace{2em}} = \underline{\hspace{2em}} \text{ pumpkins}$$

When Paco went shopping,
he saw exactly what he wanted.
A brand-new, bright red flying saucer!
The price tag read, "only **85** cents."
But Paco's piggy bank was empty.

How could he earn the money he needed?
"I guess I'll have to do some chores,"
he moaned and groaned.

Paco's mom gave him **30** cents to water the plants. Then she gave him another **30** cents to feed the hamster.

And then she gave him another **30** cents to take out the garbage.

"You should have enough money now," she said.

The woman behind the counter counted Paco's coins.
"You gave me too much money," she said. "I owe you some change."

"You do?" said Paco.

"I sure do," said the woman. "You gave me **90** cents, but your flying saucer costs only **85** cents. Here's your change."

Just then, Paco saw a shiny purple boomerang. The price tag read, "only **75** cents."

"WOW!" said Paco as the woman handed him his nickel in change.

"I'll be back as soon as I earn enough money for that boomerang!"

ONLY 85¢

ONLY 75¢

Learn!

How do you add 4 to 38?

When there are 10 or more ones, you can regroup.

Show 38.
Add 4.

Regroup 10 ones as 1 ten to find the sum.

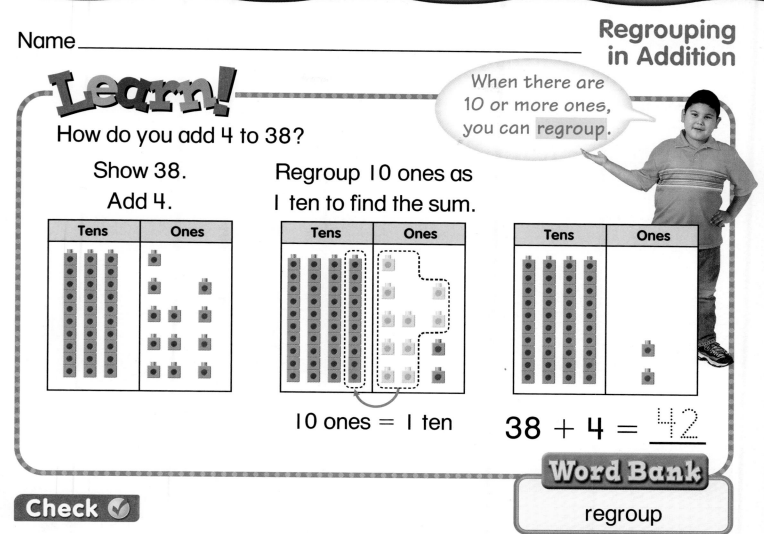

10 ones = 1 ten

$38 + 4 = \underline{42}$

Word Bank

regroup

Check ✓

Use cubes and Workmat 4. Do you need to regroup?
Circle **yes** or **no.** Then write the sum.

	Show.	Add.	Do you need to regroup?	Find the sum.
❶	15	8	(yes) no	$15 + 8 = \underline{}$
❷	34	3	yes no	$34 + 3 = \underline{}$
❸	65	5	yes no	$65 + 5 = \underline{}$
❹	77	6	yes no	$77 + 6 = \underline{}$

Think About It   Reasoning

How do you know when you need to regroup?

Use cubes and Workmat 4. Do you need to regroup?
Circle **yes** or **no**. Then write the sum.

Show.	Add.	Do you need to regroup?		Find the sum.
⑤ 47	5	(yes)	no	$47 + 5 = \underline{52}$
⑥ 62	8	yes	no	$62 + 8 = \underline{}$
⑦ 54	4	yes	no	$54 + 4 = \underline{}$
⑧ 23	6	yes	no	$23 + 6 = \underline{}$
⑨ 35	7	yes	no	$35 + 7 = \underline{}$
⑩ 16	9	yes	no	$16 + 9 = \underline{}$
⑪ 81	2	yes	no	$81 + 2 = \underline{}$
⑫ 78	3	yes	no	$78 + 3 = \underline{}$

Problem Solving   Number Sense

Use the number line to add.

```
<--+----+----+----+----+----+----+----+----+----+----+-->
  25   26   27   28   29   30   31   32   33   34   35
```

⑬ $26 + 5 = \underline{}$ ⑭ $32 + 3 = \underline{}$

⑮ $29 + 1 = \underline{}$ ⑯ $27 + 6 = \underline{}$

Home Connection Your child learned to add numbers with regrouping.
Home Activity Have your child explain how to find the sum of 13 and 8.
(21)

Learn!

When can you estimate to solve a problem?

1 Yukiko has 2 packages of muffins.
Each package contains 9 muffins.
There are 20 children in her class.
Are there enough muffins for all of the children?

Read and Understand

We need to know if 2 packages of muffins
are enough for 20 children. Do we need
an exact answer or an estimate?

Plan and Solve

9 is less than 10, so 9 + 9 is less
than 10 + 10. We can estimate
that 2 packages contain fewer
than 20 muffins.

exact answer   ⟨estimate⟩

Look Back and Check

Does your answer make sense?

Think About It   Reasoning

How did you decide whether you needed
an exact answer or an estimate?

Circle **exact answer** or **estimate**.

2 Mrs. Cruz wants to put math books on her shelf.
The shelf is 40 inches wide.
Each math book is 2 inches thick.
How many books will fit on her shelf?

Do we need an exact answer or an estimate?

(exact answer)   estimate

3 Lidie wants to buy 5 apples.
They cost 12¢ each. She has 50¢.
Does she have enough money?

Do we need an exact answer or an estimate?

exact answer   estimate

4 Sandy wants to buy 9 bananas.
They cost 8¢ each. She has 90¢.
Does she have enough money?

Do we need an exact answer or an estimate?

exact answer   estimate

Problem Solving Estimation

Circle the better estimate.

5 About how many
can you hold in one hand?

about 10   about 100

6 About how many
can you hold in one hand?

about 5   about 50

Home Connection Your child determined whether an estimate or an exact answer was needed to solve a problem. **Home Activity** Ask your child to choose a problem on this page and to explain how he or she decided the answer.

Name_____

Write each number sentence.

① ____ + ____ = ____

② 51 ____ + ____ = ____

Write each sum.

③

Tens	Ones
1	5
+ 2	4

Tens	Ones
3	3
+ 3	2

Tens	Ones
4	7
+ 5	2

Tens	Ones
6	1
+ 1	7

Use cubes and Workmat 4. Do you need to regroup?
Circle **yes** or **no**. Then write the sum.

Show.	Add.	Do you need to regroup?	Find the sum.
④ 35	5	yes no	35 + 5 = ____
⑤ 43	6	yes no	43 + 6 = ____

Circle **exact answer** or **estimate**.

⑥ Joe wants to buy 5 pencils.
They cost 11¢ each. He has 50¢.
Does he have enough money?

Do we need an exact answer or an estimate?

exact answer   estimate

How much money in all?

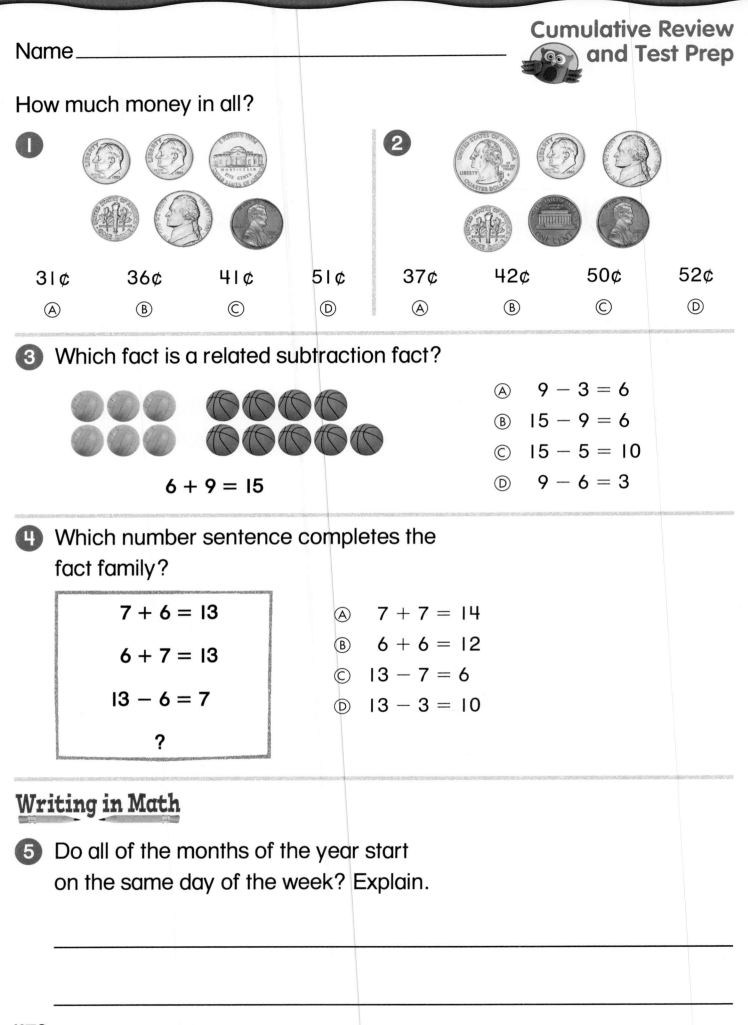

1

31¢	36¢	41¢	51¢
Ⓐ	Ⓑ	Ⓒ	Ⓓ

2

37¢	42¢	50¢	52¢
Ⓐ	Ⓑ	Ⓒ	Ⓓ

3 Which fact is a related subtraction fact?

6 + 9 = 15

Ⓐ   9 − 3 = 6

Ⓑ   15 − 9 = 6

Ⓒ   15 − 5 = 10

Ⓓ   9 − 6 = 3

4 Which number sentence completes the fact family?

7 + 6 = 13

6 + 7 = 13

13 − 6 = 7

?

Ⓐ   7 + 7 = 14

Ⓑ   6 + 6 = 12

Ⓒ   13 − 7 = 6

Ⓓ   13 − 3 = 10

Writing in Math

5 Do all of the months of the year start on the same day of the week? Explain.

_____

_____

Name_____

Learn!

Subtracting groups of 10 is like
subtracting numbers less than 10.

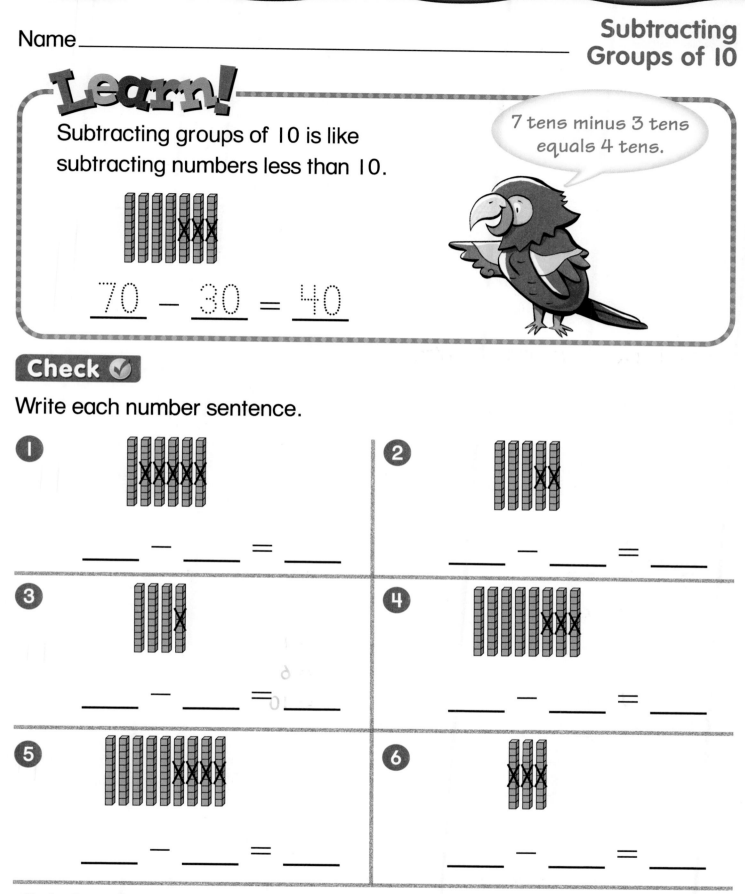

7 tens minus 3 tens
equals 4 tens.

70 – 30 = 40

Check ✓

Write each number sentence.

1

___ – ___ = ___

2

___ – ___ = ___

3

___ – ___ = ___

4

___ – ___ = ___

5

___ – ___ = ___

6

___ – ___ = ___

Think About It   Reasoning

How is subtracting tens like subtracting numbers
less than 10? How is it different?

Write each number sentence.

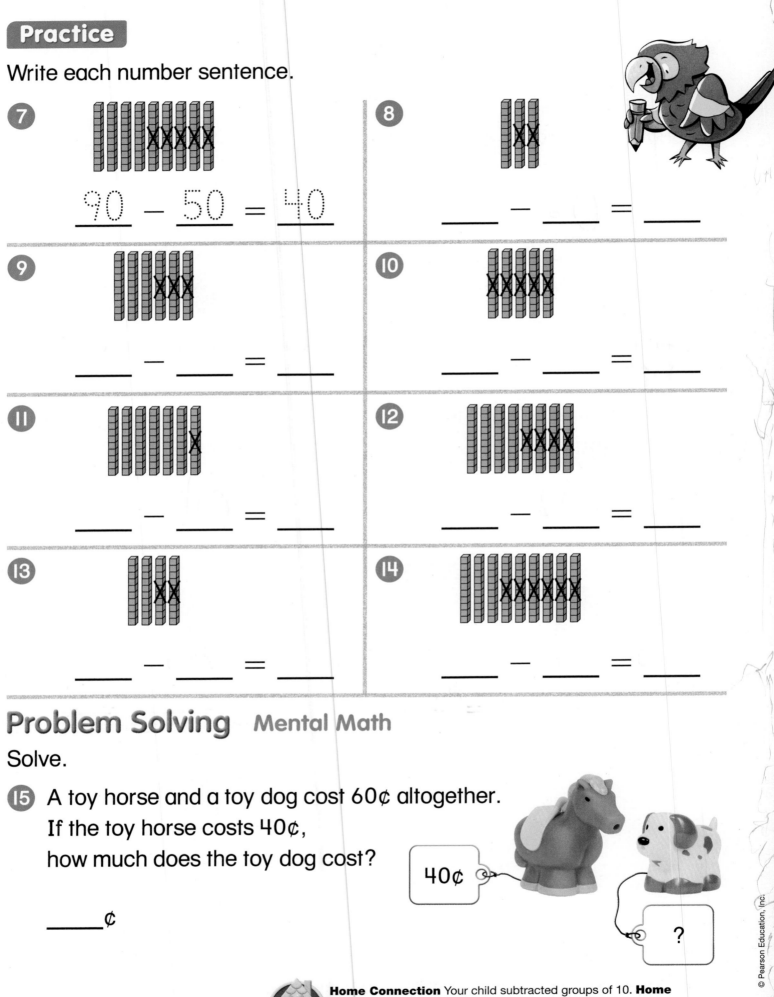

7

$$\underline{90} - \underline{50} = \underline{40}$$

8

___ − ___ = ___

9

___ − ___ = ___

10

___ − ___ = ___

11

___ − ___ = ___

12

___ − ___ = ___

13

___ − ___ = ___

14

___ − ___ = ___

Problem Solving Mental Math

Solve.

15 A toy horse and a toy dog cost 60¢ altogether.
If the toy horse costs 40¢,
how much does the toy dog cost?

40¢

?

_____¢

Home Connection Your child subtracted groups of 10. **Home Activity** Ask your child to draw a picture of models like those shown above to show 80 − 30 and then find the difference. *(50)*

Name_____

Learn!

Find the difference for the problem 43 − 8.

If you need more ones, you can regroup.

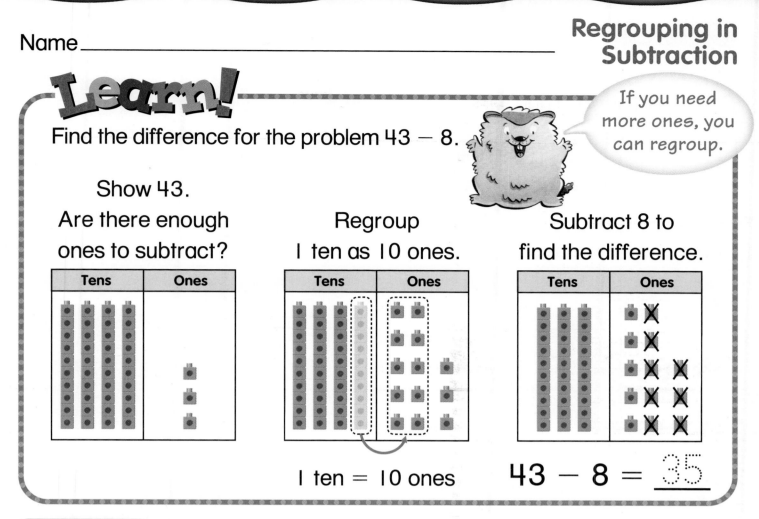

Show 43.
Are there enough ones to subtract?

| Tens | Ones |

Regroup
1 ten as 10 ones.

| Tens | Ones |

1 ten = 10 ones

Subtract 8 to find the difference.

| Tens | Ones |

43 − 8 = 35

Check ✓

Use cubes and Workmat 4. Do you need to regroup?
Circle **yes** or **no.** Then write the difference.

	Show.	Subtract.	Do you need to regroup?	Find the difference.
❶	32	5	(yes) no	32 − 5 = ___
❷	56	4	yes no	56 − 4 = ___
❸	75	9	yes no	75 − 9 = ___

Think About It Reasoning

How do you know when you need to regroup?

Use cubes and Workmat 4. Do you need to regroup?
Circle **yes** or **no**. Then write the difference.

Show.	Subtract.	Do you need to regroup?	Find the difference.
④ 47	8	(yes) no	47 – 8 = 39
⑤ 28	6	yes no	28 – 6 = ___
⑥ 86	9	yes no	86 – 9 = ___
⑦ 12	5	yes no	12 – 5 = ___
⑧ 34	3	yes no	34 – 3 = ___
⑨ 95	8	yes no	95 – 8 = ___
⑩ 53	7	yes no	53 – 7 = ___

Problem Solving   Visual Thinking

Use the number line to subtract.

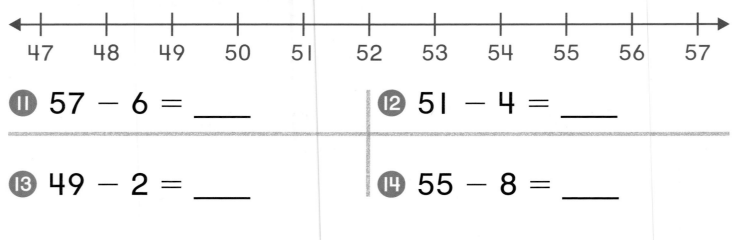

47   48   49   50   51   52   53   54   55   56   57

⑪ 57 – 6 = ___   ⑫ 51 – 4 = ___

⑬ 49 – 2 = ___   ⑭ 55 – 8 = ___

Home Connection Your child learned how to subtract numbers with regrouping. **Home Activity** Have your child explain how to find the difference for the problem 31 – 5. *(26)*

Name_____

Understand Graphic Sources: Graphs

1 Read this math problem.

Two first-grade classes collected soup labels to raise money for their school. The chart shows how many soup labels each class collected. Which class collected more?

Soup Labels Collected			
	Month 1	**Month 2**	**Month 3**
Room A	15	10	20
Room B	20	5	15

Then the classes made a graph to find out.

Soup Labels Collected	
Room A	
Room B	

0   5   10   15   20   25   30   35   40   45   50

2 How many soup labels did Room A collect? _____ soup labels

3 How many soup labels did Room B collect? _____ soup labels

Think About It   Reasoning

Which class collected more?

How can you use the graph to tell?

4 Read another math problem.

The first-grade classes also collected box tops to raise money for their school. The chart shows how many box tops each class collected. Which class collected more box tops?

Box Tops Collected			
	Month 1	Month 2	Month 3
Room A	20	10	50
Room B	30	40	20

5 Complete the graph below to show how many box tops each class collected.

Box Tops Collected										
Room A										
Room B										

0   10   20   30   40   50   60   70   80   90   100

6 How many box tops did each class collect?

Room A: _____ box tops

Room B: _____ box tops

7 Which class collected more box tops?

_____

Home Connection Your child completed a graph to help solve a word problem. **Home Activity** Ask your child to explain how he or she used the graph on this page to determine how many box tops each class collected and which class collected more.

Name_____

> You can make a graph to solve this problem.

1 Amy's class collected cans for recycling. Which team collected more cans?

Cans Collected

	Week 1	Week 2	Week 3	Week 4
Blue Team	5	15	10	5
Green Team	20	10	5	15

Read and Understand

The chart shows how many cans each team collected. We want to find which team collected the greater number of cans.

Plan and Solve

Use the information in the chart to make a graph. Color one box for every 5 cans.

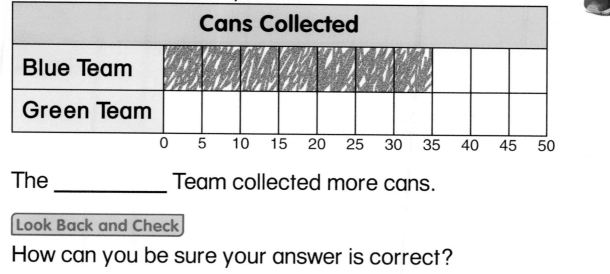

The _____ Team collected more cans.

Look Back and Check

How can you be sure your answer is correct?

Think About It   Reasoning

How could you show the same information using a tally chart or a picture graph?

Make a graph to solve the problem.

2 Miguel's class collected paper for recycling. The chart shows how many pounds of paper each team collected. Which team collected the most paper? **Color one box for every 10 pounds of paper.**

Paper Collected (in Pounds)				
	Week 1	Week 2	Week 3	Week 4
Yellow Team	10	20	20	30
Orange Team	20	30	30	20
Purple Team	20	20	10	30

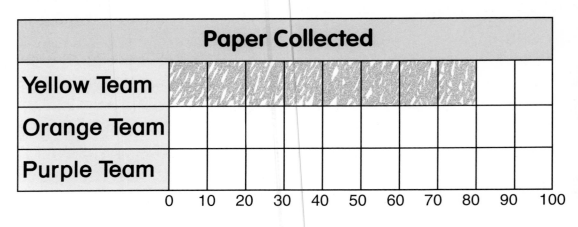

The _____ Team collected the most paper.

Writing in Math

3 Write another question that could be answered using the bar graph above.

_____

_____

Home Connection Your child made graphs to solve problems. **Home Activity** Ask your child to explain how he or she made and used the graph on this page to solve the problem above.

Name_____

Dorling Kindersley

1 Haruo fed his kitten 33 fish bits in the morning and 20 fish bits in the evening. How many fish bits did Haruo feed his kitten altogether?

____ ◯ ____ = ____ fish bits

2 The next day Haruo gave his kitten 44 fish bits. His kitten ate only 20 of them. How many fish bits were left?

____ ◯ ____ = ____ fish bits

3 The animal shelter had 8 tabby kittens and 5 ragdoll kittens. How many kittens did the shelter have in all?

____ ◯ ____ = ____ kittens

6 kittens were adopted. How many kittens were left?

____ ◯ ____ = ____ kittens

Do You Know...
that kittens should have regular checkups at the vet to help them stay healthy?

Fun Fact!
House cats belong to the same family as lions, tigers, and jaguars. They are all felines.

4 The pet store had 58 cat brushes.
The store sold 14 of them.
How many brushes were left?

Tens	Ones
5	8
− 1	4

_____ brushes

5 There were 21 kittens at the pet store.
The Morris family bought 2 kittens.
How many kittens were left?

$21 - 2 =$ _____ kittens

6 Luz has

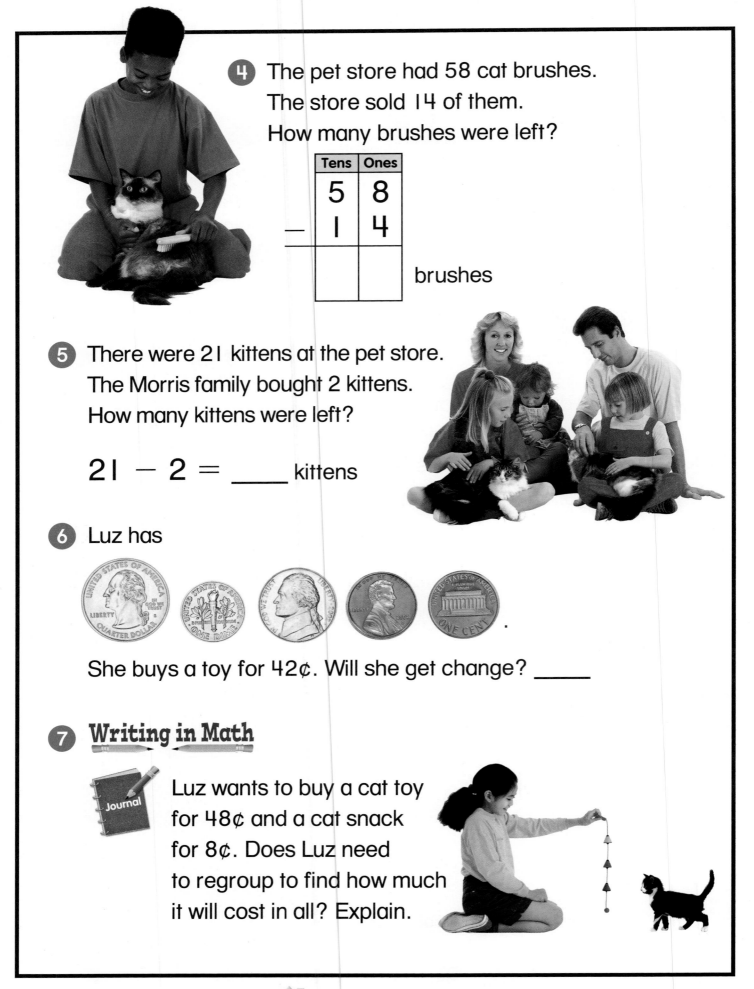

She buys a toy for 42¢. Will she get change? _____

7 **Writing in Math**

Luz wants to buy a cat toy
for 48¢ and a cat snack
for 8¢. Does Luz need
to regroup to find how much
it will cost in all? Explain.

Home Connection Your child learned to solve problems by applying his or her math skills. **Home Activity** Talk to your child about how he or she solved the problems on these two pages.

Write each number sentence.

1

_____ − _____ = _____

2

_____ − _____ = _____

3

_____ − _____ = _____

4

_____ − _____ = _____

Write each difference.

5

Tens	Ones
4	8
− 2	4

Tens	Ones
5	6
− 4	1

Tens	Ones
7	5
− 3	2

Tens	Ones
8	9
− 5	3

Use cubes and Workmat 4. Do you need to regroup?
Circle **yes** or **no.** Then write the difference.

Show.	Subtract.	Do you need to regroup?	Find the difference.
6 61	5	yes no	61 − 5 = ____
7 47	6	yes no	47 − 6 = ____

1 How many eyes are there? Count by twos.

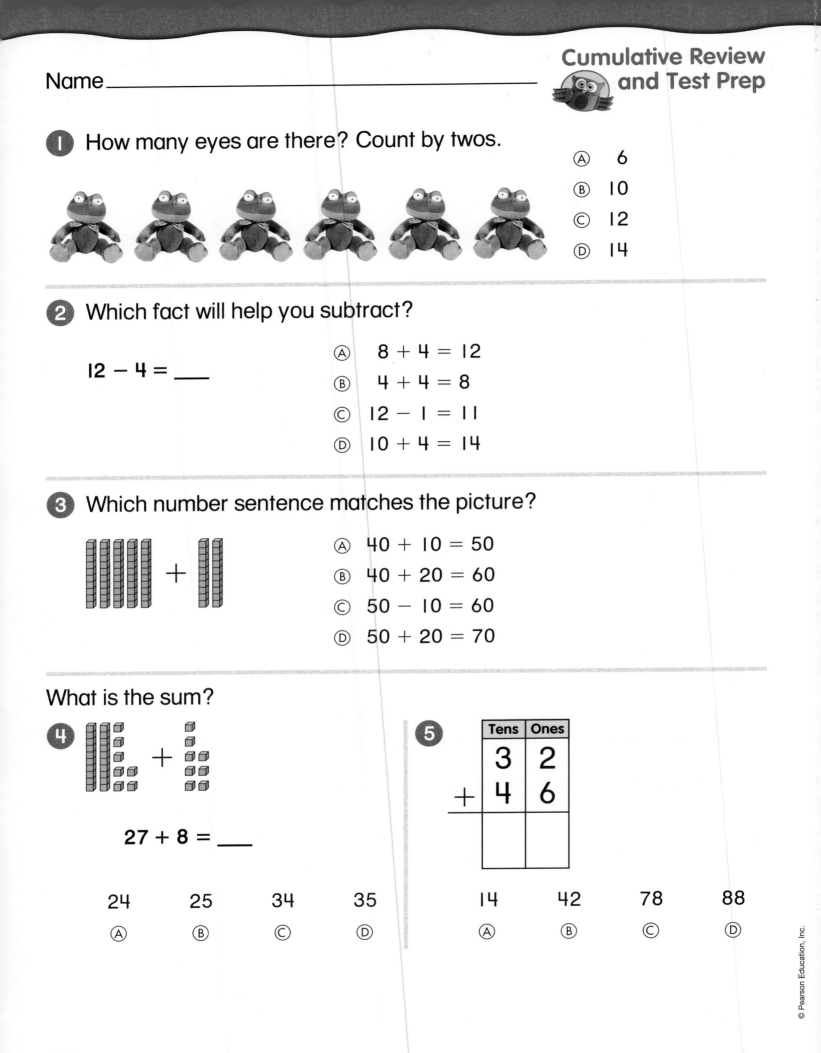

Ⓐ   6
Ⓑ   10
Ⓒ   12
Ⓓ   14

2 Which fact will help you subtract?

12 − 4 = ___

Ⓐ   8 + 4 = 12
Ⓑ   4 + 4 = 8
Ⓒ   12 − 1 = 11
Ⓓ   10 + 4 = 14

3 Which number sentence matches the picture?

Ⓐ   40 + 10 = 50
Ⓑ   40 + 20 = 60
Ⓒ   50 − 10 = 60
Ⓓ   50 + 20 = 70

What is the sum?

4

27 + 8 = ___

24   25   34   35
Ⓐ   Ⓑ   Ⓒ   Ⓓ

5

Tens	Ones
3	2
+ 4	6

14   42   78   88
Ⓐ   Ⓑ   Ⓒ   Ⓓ

Adding and Subtracting Three-Digit Numbers

First add the ones. Then add the tens and then the hundreds.

Add

Hundreds	Tens	Ones
1	5	7
+ 4	2	1
5	7	8

First subtract the ones. Then subtract the tens and then the hundreds.

Subtract

Hundreds	Tens	Ones
6	3	9
− 2	2	8
4	1	1

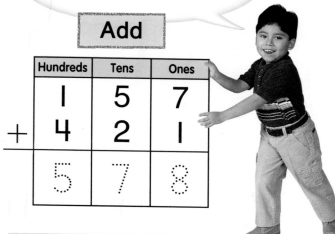

Add. Use models if you like.

1

Hundreds	Tens	Ones
2	1	0
+ 7	5	9

Hundreds	Tens	Ones
6	3	8
+ 3	4	1

Hundreds	Tens	Ones
5	6	2
+ 4	2	7

Subtract. Use models if you like.

2

Hundreds	Tens	Ones
7	7	5
− 4	6	2

Hundreds	Tens	Ones
9	9	9
− 3	5	1

Hundreds	Tens	Ones
8	6	3
− 1	4	0

Home Connection Your child added and subtracted three-digit numbers without regrouping. **Home Activity** Ask your child to explain how he or she did the first problem in each exercise.

Name_____

Add and Subtract Using a Calculator

You can use a calculator to add and subtract.

Draw a path from **Start** to **Target**.
Use your calculator to help you.

1 Add.
Find the **Target Sum.**

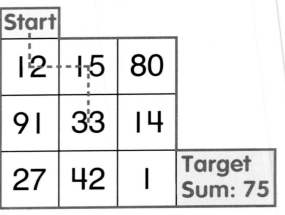

Start		
12	15	80
91	33	14
27	42	1

Target Sum: 75

2 Subtract.
Find the **Target Difference.**

Start		
92	58	76
25	37	11
14	10	9

Target Difference: 11

Add and subtract in Exercises 3 and 4.
Find the **Target** number.

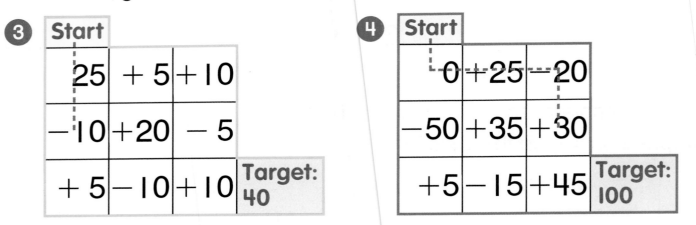

3

Start		
25	+ 5	+ 10
− 10	+ 20	− 5
+ 5	− 10	+ 10

Target: 40

4

Start		
0	+ 25	− 20
− 50	+ 35	+ 30
+ 5	− 15	+ 45

Target: 100

Think About It   Number Sense

In Exercise 2, how did you use a calculator to figure
out that you were close to the Target Difference?

Home Connection Your child used a calculator to add and
subtract two-digit numbers. **Home Activity** Ask your child to
explain how to find the sum of 23 and 48 on a calculator.

Name_____

Use Writing in Math

When you write an answer to a math question, your answer should be **short** but **complete.**

Test-Taking Strategies

Understand the Question

Get Information for the Answer

Plan How to Find the Answer

Make Smart Choices

Use Writing in Math

1 There were 43 cans in the recycling bin. Sharon put 20 more cans in the bin. How many cans are in the bin now?

Now there are 63 cans in the recycling bin.
_____

Here is how a boy named Tony solved this problem. He added the number of cans: 43 cans + 20 cans = 63 cans in all. Then he used words from the question to help him write his answer.

Which words did Tony use?
Raise your hand if you can find some of them.

Your Turn

Read the problem. Then write a **short** but **complete** answer to the question.

2 In May, Mr. Murphy's class collected 59 cans. Ms. Nelson's class collected 38 cans. How many more cans did Mr. Murphy's class collect?

_____

_____

Home Connection Your child prepared for standardized tests by writing a complete answer to a math question. **Home Activity** Have your child explain how he or she solved the problem in Exercise 2. Then ask your child which words from the question he or she used in the answer.

four hundred eighty-nine   **489**

Name _____

Discover Math in Your World

 Read Together

All Aboard!

Have you ever been on a train? It is fun to travel
by train. The first trains in the United States
were built many years ago. Today's trains can
go much faster than the first ones could.
Use subtraction to find out how much faster.

Tracking Train Speeds

1 The first trains could travel 20 miles in one hour.
Stagecoaches could travel only 7 miles in one hour.
How many more miles could the first trains travel
in one hour?

_____ miles

2 Today, most passenger trains in the United States
travel 79 miles in one hour. How many more miles
can they travel in one hour than the first trains?

_____ miles

3 The fastest trains in Japan and France can travel
186 miles in one hour. The fastest train in the United States
can travel 150 miles in one hour. How many more miles
can the trains in Japan and France travel in one hour?

_____ miles

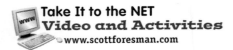 **Take It to the NET
Video and Activities**
www.scottforesman.com

 Home Connection Your child solved problems that compared the speeds
of different trains and a stagecoach. **Home Activity** Discuss the distance
20 miles in relation to your home and another location. Then ask your child
to tell you how many more miles a passenger train in the United States can
travel in one hour than a stagecoach could travel decades ago. *(143 miles)*

Chapter 12

Name_____

Write each number sentence.

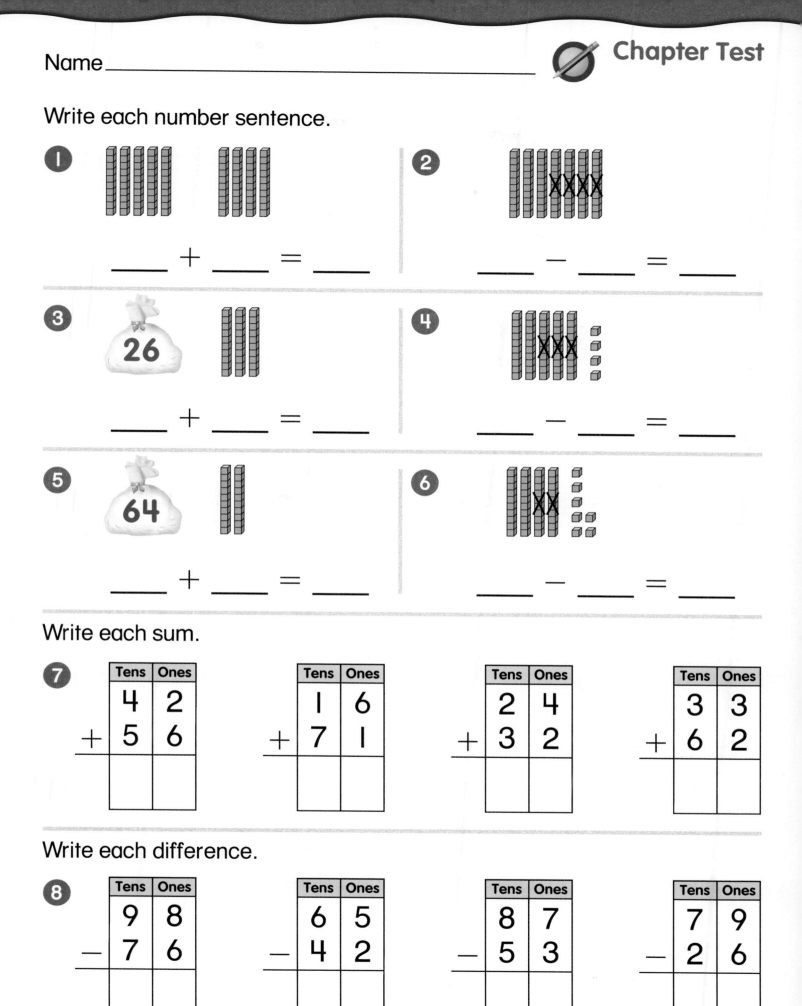

1
___ + ___ = ___

2
___ − ___ = ___

3 26
___ + ___ = ___

4
___ − ___ = ___

5 64
___ + ___ = ___

6
___ − ___ = ___

Write each sum.

7

Tens	Ones
4	2
+ 5	6

Tens	Ones
1	6
+ 7	1

Tens	Ones
2	4
+ 3	2

Tens	Ones
3	3
+ 6	2

Write each difference.

8

Tens	Ones
9	8
− 7	6

Tens	Ones
6	5
− 4	2

Tens	Ones
8	7
− 5	3

Tens	Ones
7	9
− 2	6

Use cubes and Workmat 4. Do you need to regroup?
Circle **yes** or **no.** Then write the sum.

Show.	Add.	Do you need to regroup?		Find the sum.
⑨ 55	8	yes	no	55 + 8 = ____
⑩ 34	5	yes	no	34 + 5 = ____
⑪ 47	6	yes	no	47 + 6 = ____

Use cubes and Workmat 4. Do you need to regroup?
Circle **yes** or **no.** Then write the difference.

Show.	Subtract.	Do you need to regroup?		Find the difference.
⑫ 52	8	yes	no	52 − 8 = ____
⑬ 29	7	yes	no	29 − 7 = ____
⑭ 35	9	yes	no	35 − 9 = ____

Circle **exact answer** or **estimate.**

⑮ Julio has 2 baskets of apples.
Each basket has 12 apples.
There are 20 children in his class.
Are there enough apples for all of the children?

Do we need an exact answer or an estimate?

exact answer   estimate

Subtract.

1

$$\begin{array}{r} 70 \\ -\ 20 \\ \hline \end{array}$$

40   50   60   70
Ⓐ   Ⓑ   Ⓒ   Ⓓ

2

$$\begin{array}{r} 83 \\ -\ 50 \\ \hline \end{array}$$

13   30   33   43
Ⓐ   Ⓑ   Ⓒ   Ⓓ

3 Which shape is divided into equal parts?

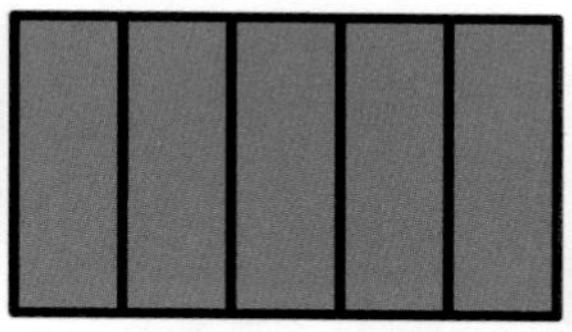

Ⓐ   Ⓑ   Ⓒ   Ⓓ

4 Which would you use to find how long the bug is?

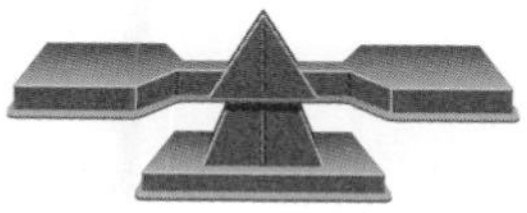

Ⓐ   Ⓑ   Ⓒ   Ⓓ

5 Which fact completes the fact family?

$$9 + 4 = 13$$
$$4 + 9 = 13$$
$$13 - 9 = 4$$
$$?$$

Ⓐ $13 - 4 = 9$
Ⓑ $13 - 7 = 6$
Ⓒ $4 + 5 = 9$
Ⓓ $9 - 4 = 5$

Add.

6

50	22	23	58	43
+ 30	+ 20	+ 65	+ 7	+ 7

Circle the shape that shows a flip of the first boot.

7

Add. Then use the addition fact to help you.

8

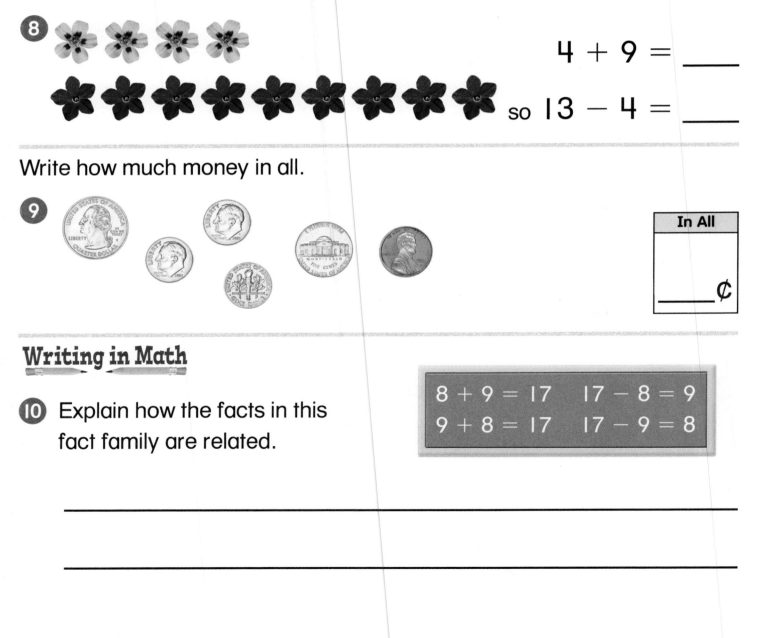

$4 + 9 = \underline{}$

so $13 - 4 = \underline{}$

Write how much money in all.

9

In All
$\underline{}$ ¢

Writing in Math

10 Explain how the facts in this fact family are related.

$8 + 9 = 17$	$17 - 8 = 9$
$9 + 8 = 17$	$17 - 9 = 8$

_____

_____

492B

Picture Glossary

add

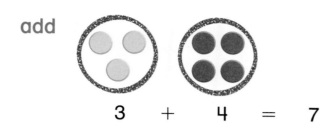

$$3 \quad + \quad 4 \quad = \quad 7$$

---

addition sentence

$$3 + 2 = 5$$

addends

---

after

5 comes **after** 4.

---

bar graph

Favorite Pets

| | 0 | 1 | 2 | 3 | 4 | 5 |

---

before

2 comes **before** 3.

---

between

3 comes **between** 2 and 4.

---

calendar

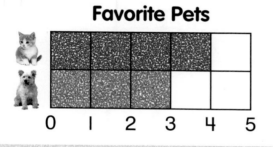

month
days
date
week

---

cent (¢)

A penny is 1 **cent** (1¢).

---

centimeter

CENTIMETERS

---

circle

---

cone

---

count back

$$8 - 2 = 6$$

---

count on

$$6 + 3 = 9$$

---

cube

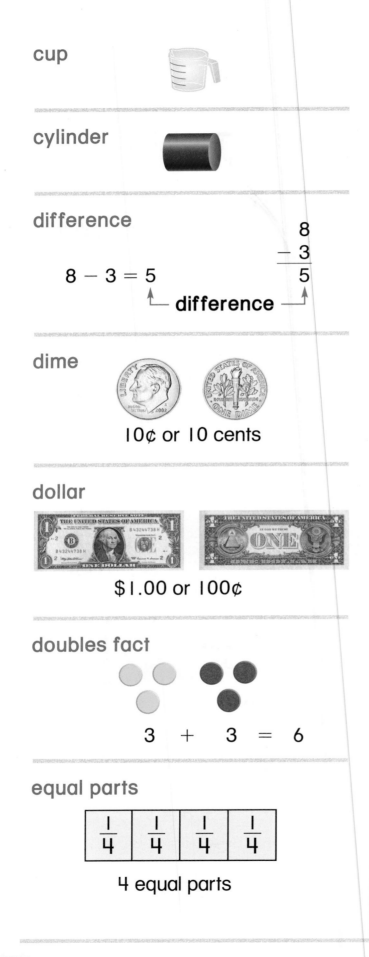

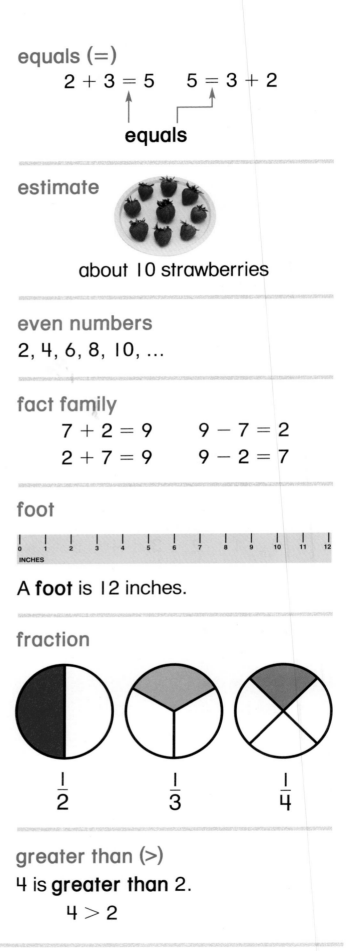

cup

cylinder

difference

$8 - 3 = 5$

$$\begin{array}{r} 8 \\ -\ 3 \\ \hline 5 \end{array}$$

difference

dime

10¢ or 10 cents

dollar

$1.00 or 100¢

doubles fact

$3\ +\ 3\ =\ 6$

equal parts

$$\begin{array}{|c|c|c|c|} \hline \frac{1}{4} & \frac{1}{4} & \frac{1}{4} & \frac{1}{4} \\ \hline \end{array}$$

4 equal parts

equals (=)

$2 + 3 = 5 \qquad 5 = 3 + 2$

equals

estimate

about 10 strawberries

even numbers

2, 4, 6, 8, 10, …

fact family

$7 + 2 = 9 \qquad 9 - 7 = 2$

$2 + 7 = 9 \qquad 9 - 2 = 7$

foot

A **foot** is 12 inches.

fraction

$\dfrac{1}{2}$ $\qquad$ $\dfrac{1}{3}$ $\qquad$ $\dfrac{1}{4}$

greater than (>)

4 is **greater than** 2.

$4 > 2$

half-dollar

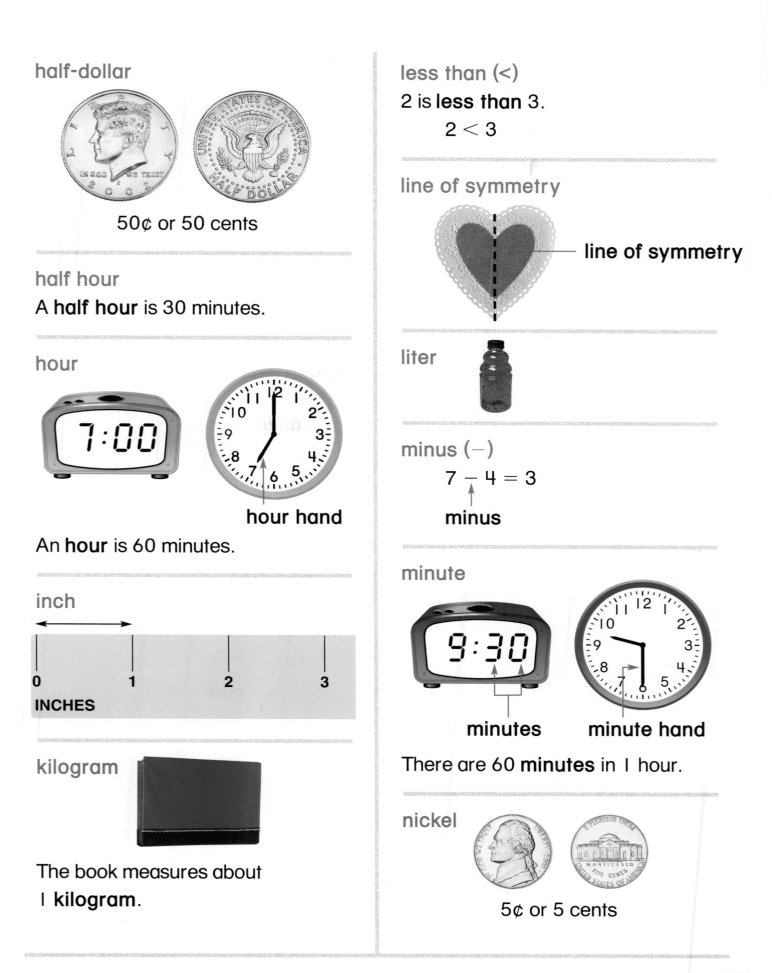

50¢ or 50 cents

half hour

A **half hour** is 30 minutes.

hour

7:00

hour hand

An **hour** is 60 minutes.

inch

0　1　2　3
INCHES

kilogram

The book measures about
1 **kilogram**.

less than (<)

2 is **less than** 3.

2 < 3

line of symmetry

line of symmetry

liter

minus (−)

7 − 4 = 3

minus

minute

9:30

minutes　　minute hand

There are 60 **minutes** in 1 hour.

nickel

5¢ or 5 cents

number line

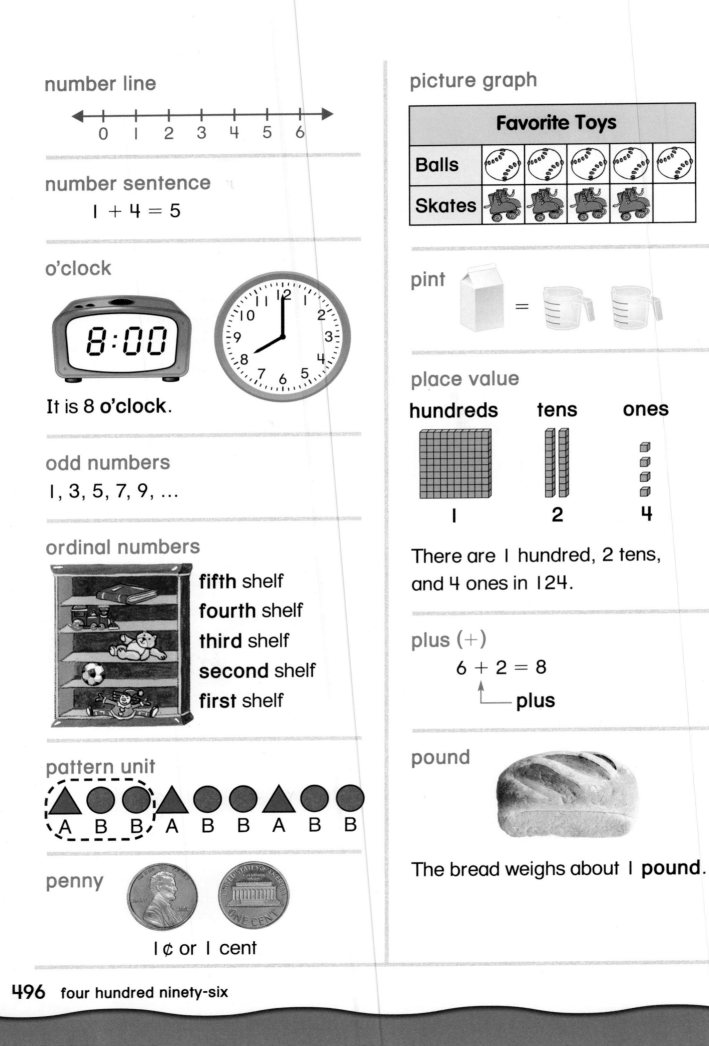

number sentence

$1 + 4 = 5$

o'clock

It is 8 **o'clock**.

odd numbers

1, 3, 5, 7, 9, ...

ordinal numbers

fifth shelf
fourth shelf
third shelf
second shelf
first shelf

pattern unit

A B B A B B A B B

penny

1¢ or 1 cent

picture graph

Favorite Toys					
Balls	⚾	⚾	⚾	⚾	⚾
Skates	🛼	🛼	🛼	🛼	

pint

place value

hundreds	tens	ones
1	2	4

There are 1 hundred, 2 tens, and 4 ones in 124.

plus (+)

$6 + 2 = 8$

plus

pound

The bread weighs about 1 **pound**.

probability

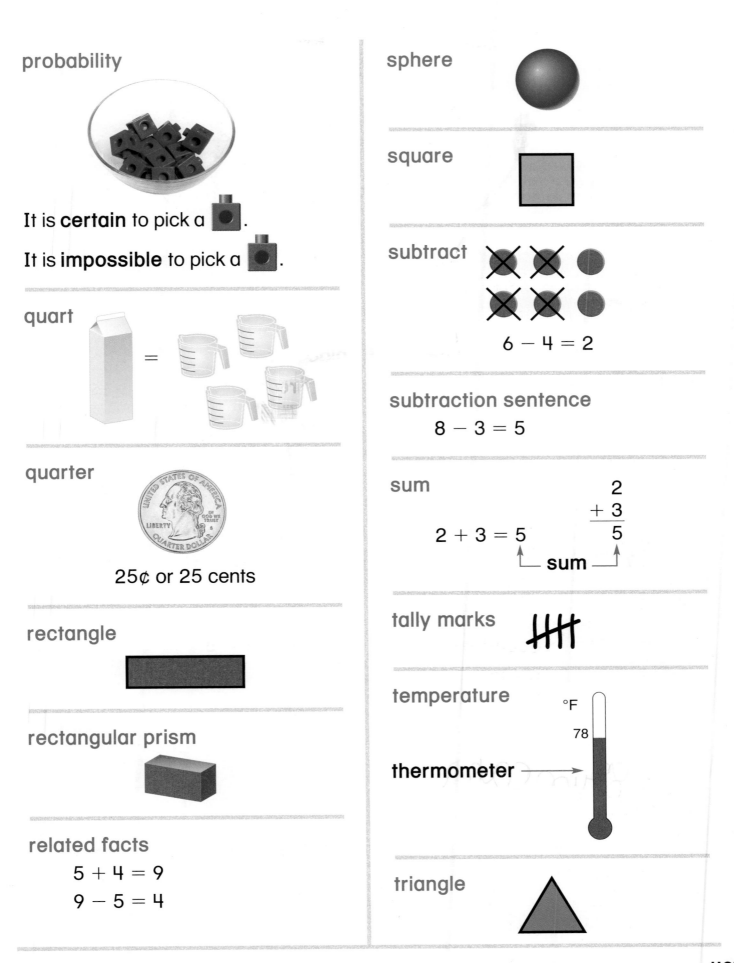

It is **certain** to pick a ■.

It is **impossible** to pick a ■.

quart

=

quarter

25¢ or 25 cents

rectangle

rectangular prism

related facts

5 + 4 = 9

9 − 5 = 4

sphere

square

subtract

6 − 4 = 2

subtraction sentence

8 − 3 = 5

sum

2 + 3 = 5

2
+ 3
5

sum

tally marks

temperature

°F

78

thermometer

triangle

Credits

Cover: Jose Pardo

Text: Dorling Kindersley (DK) is an international publishing company specializing in the creation of high-quality reference content for books, CD-ROMs, online materials, and video. The hallmark of content is its unique combination of educational value and strong visual style. This combination allows DK to deliver appealing, accessible, and engaging educational content that delights children, parents, and teachers around the world. Scott Foresman is delighted to have been able to use selected extracts of DK content within this Scott Foresman Math program.

33–34: *Flip-Flap* by Sandra Jenkins. Copyright ©1995 by Dorling Kindersley Limited; 79–80: *Bugs! Bugs! Bugs!* by Jennifer Dussling. Copyright ©1998 by Dorling Kindersley Limited; 113–114: *Rabbit* by Mark Evans. Text copyright ©1992 by Mark Evans. Foreword copyright ©1992 by Roger Caras. Copyright ©1992 by Dorling Kindersley Limited; 145–146: *Puppies* by Carey Scott. Copyright ©1997 by Dorling Kindersley Limited; 193–194: *My Very First Colors, Shapes, Sizes, and Opposites Book* by Angela Wilkes. Copyright ©1993 by Dorling Kindersley Limited; 229–230: *Egg* by Robert Burton, photographed by Jane Burton and Kim Taylor. Copyright ©1994 by Dorling Kindersley Limited; 269–270: *My First Math Book* by David and Wendy Clemson. Copyright ©1994 by Dorling Kindersley Limited; 319–320: *My First Number Book* by Marie Heinst. Copyright ©1992, 1999 by Dorling Kindersley Limited; 353–354: *Counting Book* photographed by Dave King. Copyright ©1998 by Dorling Kindersley Limited; 405–406: *Children's Quick & Easy Cookbook* by Angela Wilkes. Text copyright ©1997 by Angela Wilkes. Copyright ©1997 by Dorling Kindersley Limited; 447–448: *A Day at Greenhill Farm* by Sue Nicholson. Copyright ©1998 by Dorling Kindersley Limited; 483–484: *Kitten* by Mark Evans. Text copyright ©1992 by Mark Evans. Foreword copyright ©1992 by Roger Caras. Copyright ©1992 by Dorling Kindersley Limited.

Illustrations:

R2 **Carly Castillon**
R3, R4 **Marisol Sarrazin**
1A, 1B, 1C, 1D, 1E, 1F, 2, 6, 11, 14, 16, 18, 21, 22, 25, 26, 28, 30, 35, 37 **Carly Castillon**
2A, 2B, 2C, 2D, 2E, 2F, 43, 44, 47, 48, 52, 63, 69, 70, 75, 76, 77, 342, 382 **Kathi Ember**
3A, 3B, 3C, 3D, 3E, 3F, 89, 90, 92, 93, 95, 97, 98, 101, 105, 106, 107, 108, 109, 111,

117 **John Patience**
4A, 4B, 4C, 4D, 4E, 4F, 80, 123, 124, 125, 126, 139, 140, 141, 142, 429, 430 **Karen Stormer Brooks**
4, 10, 12, 393, 394 **Janet Skiles**
5A, 5B, 5C, 5D, 5E, 5F, 155, 156, 157, 158, 166, 167, 168, 170, 171, 172, 173, 183, 184, 185, 189, 190 **Will Terry**
6A, 6B, 6C, 6D, 6E, 6F, 203, 204, 207, 208, 211, 212, 213, 217, 224, 226, 227, 228 **Jason Wolff**
7A, 7B, 7C, 7D, 7E, 7F, 240, 242, 251, 265, 266, 273 **Amy Vangsgard**
7, 8, 9, 32 **Remy Simard**
8A, 8B, 8C, 8D, 8E, 8F, 279, 280, 283, 284, 287, 288, 297, 300, 313, 323, 324 **Cameron Eagle**
9A, 9B, 9C, 9D, 9F, 329, 330, 333, 335, 336, 337, 338, 345, 357 **Laura Ovresat**
10A, 10B, 10C, 10D, 10E, 10F, 363, 364, 369, 370, 372, 377, 378, 395, 398, 403 **Bridget Starr Taylor**
11A, 11B, 11C, 11D, 11E, 11F, 415, 416, 417, 419, 420, 421, 425, 428, 427, 431, 432, 437, 440, 443, 444, 452 **Diane Greenseid**
12A, 12B, 12C, 12D, 12E, 12F, 461, 462, 463, 464, 471, 472, 473, 475, 476, 477, **Jackie Snider**
19, 20, 102, 109, 110, 116, 180, 197, 418 **Rose Mary Berlin**
45, 46, 61, 62, 65, 66, 88, 215, 216, 217, 219, 220, 231, 232, 238, 238B, 328A **Suwin Chan**
50, 57, 58, 59, 60, 82 **Jane Maday**
71, 72, 73, 218 **Paul Sharp**
94 **Terry Taylor**
103, 104 **Claudine Gevry**
108, 223, 224, 285, 286, 293, 309, 310, 311, 312, 321, 327, 328, 414A, 492B **Mike Dammer**
117, 349, 350, 456 **Rusty Fletcher**
122, 367, 368, 413 **Chi Chung**
127, 128, 130, 135, 153, 295, 296, 305 **Maryn Roos**
188, 191 **Ginna Magee**
213, 214 **George Ulrich**
244, 272, 278, 437, 438, 449 **Reggie Holladay**
257, 258, 395, 396, 399 **Margeaux Lucas**
257, 258, 408 **Eldon Doty**
259, 260 **Thomas Taylor**
261, 262 **John Sandford**
267, 268 **Linda Howard Bittner**
289, 290 **Nan Brooks**
301, 302, 305, 327 **Joe Stites**
315, 316, 317, 318, 321, 328, 400 **Donna Catanese**
326 **Carolyn Croll**
479, 480 **Jane Miles Smith**

©2005 edition R 15, R16 **Mike Dammer**
3, 8, 14, 22, 30 **Carly Castillon**
6 **Janet Skiles** 31 **Eldon Doty**

Photographs:

Every effort has been made to secure permission and provide appropriate credit for photographic material. The publisher deeply regrets any omission and pledges to correct errors called to its attention in subsequent editions. Unless otherwise acknowledged, all photographs are the property of Scott Foresman, a division of Pearson Education.

Photo locators denoted as follows: Top (T), Center (C), Bottom (B), Left (L), Right (R), Background (Bkgd)

1, 4 (BCL), 36 (TL, BR), 49 (T), 60, 67 (BR), 88A, 88B, 89, 102 (T), 116, 136, 143 (B), 144 (TC, BC, B), 154A, 154B, 157, 162 (All Other), 164, 176 (L), 187 (TL, TR, CR, BL), 202, 236 (CL), 238A, 271, 291 (T), 322, 328B, 339, 340 (BL, TR), 341, 366, 373, 374 (C), 376 (T, B), 384, 386, 387, 388 (TR), 391 (CR), 392 (CL, TR), 397, 398 (T, CC, CL, BL), 399 (TL, CL, CR), 408, 412 (TR), 414B (TL, TR), 431, 439 (TT, TB, CLT, CLB, BLT, BLB), 440, 450, 456 (T, C), 470, 472, 486, 492A, 492, 493 (TL), 496 (BR) **Hemera Technologies** 4 (TL, TR, BL, BC, BR), 10, 18, 36 (BC), 49 (CL), 51, 59 (R), 67 (TL, TR, CL, CR, BL), 68, 81, 87, 99, 100 (T, C), 101 (B), 102 (B), 111, 112 (BC), 115, 121, 133, 136, 144 (T), 154, 175, 187 (CL, BR), 276, 372, 374 (BL, BR), 375 (BL), 376 (C, BL, BR), 390, 391 (CL, BL), 392 (BL, CR, BR), 399 (BL, BCL, BCR, BR), 414B (BR), 434, 439 (CRT, BRT, BRB), 446 (B, T), 456 (BL, BR), 468 (T), 492B, 493 (BL) **Getty Images** 4 (TC, BCR), 33 (TL, CL), 34, 56, 79, 80 (TL, TR), 86, 100 (B), 113, 114, 142, 143 (T), 145, 146, 152, 193, 194, 221, 229, 230, 236 (TL), 269, 270, 319, 320, 353, 354, 388 (CRT), 405, 406, 439 (CRB), 445 (B), 446 (C), 447, 448, 483, 484 **©Dorling Kindersley** 33 (BR) **Philip Dowell**/**©Dorling Kindersley** **Artville** 36 (TR), 49 (CR, BL, BR), 59 (L), 375 (CL) **©Comstock Inc.** 73 (L, R), 101 (T), 112 (TC), 162 (CTR), 254, 340 (TC), 398 (TC), 80 (CR) **Brian Kenney** 222 **©John Lamb**/**Getty Images** 375 (TL, B), 381, 385 **Corbis** 412 (TC) **Digital Stock** 445 (T) **Tracy Morgan**/**©Dorling Kindersley** WM1, WM3 **Getty Images** 347 (TR), 357 (TL, CL, BL, BC) **Golden Dollar Obverse. 1999 United States Mint. All rights reserved. Used with permission**/**United States Mint.**
©2005 edition R1 **Getty Images, Brand X Pictures** R2 **Getty Images, Brand X Pictures** R5 **Getty Images** R7 **Getty Images** R8 **Getty Images** 1 **Hemera Technologies** 14 **Getty Images, Rubberball Productions** 27 **Rubberball Productions** 33,34 **©Dorling Kindersley** 36 **Getty Images**